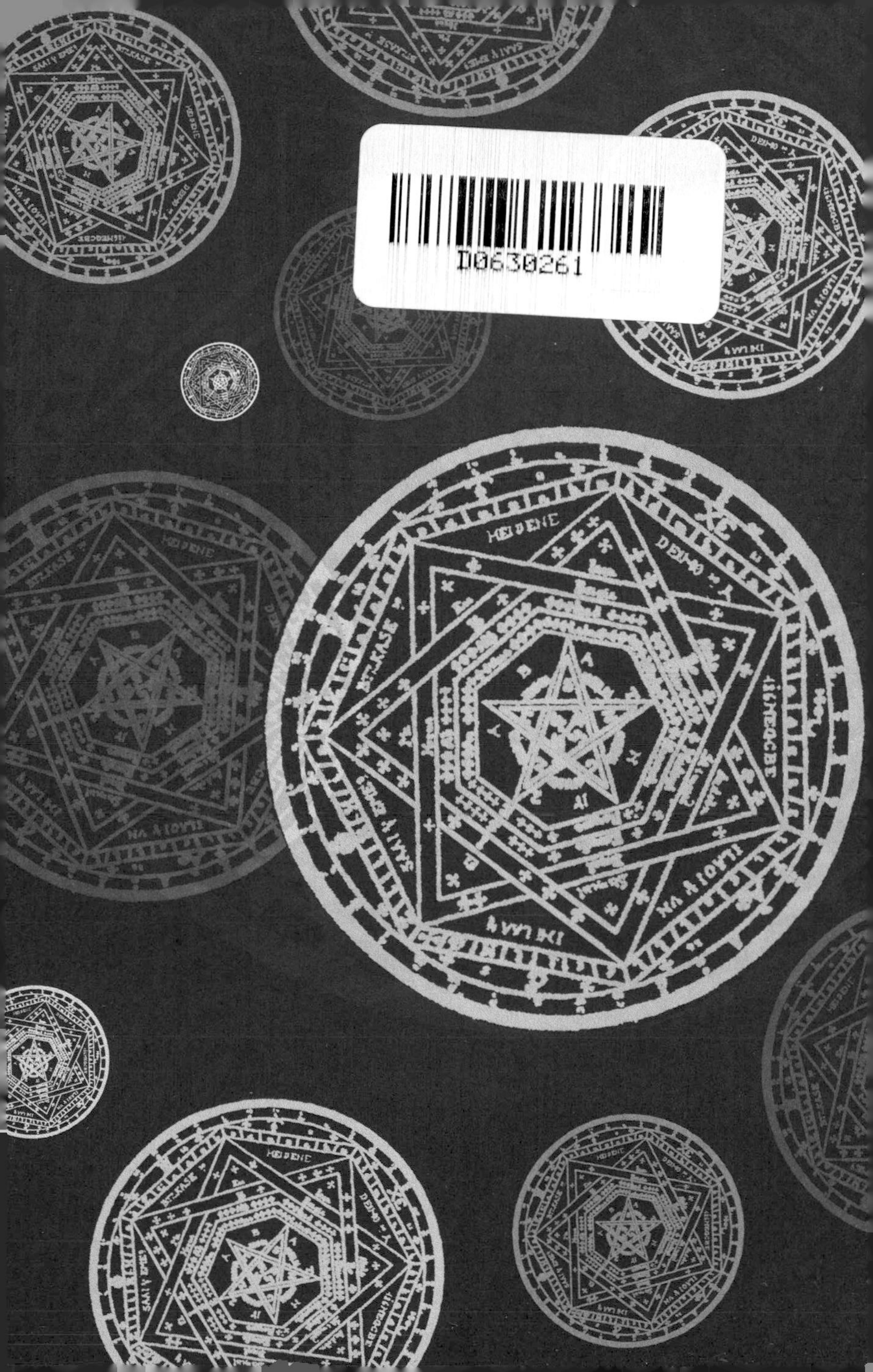

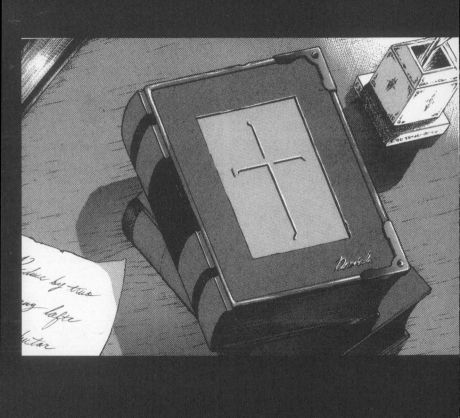

VOLUME 10

STORY AND ART BY
WOO

HAMBURG // LONDON // LOS ANGELES // TOKYO

Rebirth Vol. 10
Created by WOO

Translation - Jennifer Hahm
English Adaptation - Bryce P. Coleman
Copy Editor - Troy Lewter
Retouch and Lettering - Louis Csontos
Production Artist - James Lee
Cover Layout - Patrick Hook

Editor - Bryce P. Coleman
Digital Imaging Manager - Chris Buford
Pre-Press Manager - Antonio DePietro
Production Managers - Jennifer Miller and Mutsumi Miyazaki
Art Director - Matt Alford
Managing Editor - Jill Freshney
VP of Production - Ron Klamert
President and C.O.O. - John Parker
Publisher and C.E.O. - Stuart Levy

A 🔘 **TOKYOPOP** Manga

TOKYOPOP Inc.
5900 Wilshire Blvd. Suite 2000
Los Angeles, CA 90036

E-mail: info@TOKYOPOP.com
Come visit us online at www.TOKYOPOP.com

ISBN: 1-59182-528-8

First TOKYOPOP printing: October 2004
10 9 8 7 6 5 4 3 2 1
Printed in the USA

Story Thus Far

The mid-seventeenth century — Eastern Europe:
Once the scourge of all humankind, Deshwitat L. Rudbich
has at last found that which he thought he would never
have again — friendship. This unlikely fellowship consists
of Kalutika Maybus, now a Captain in the Church's Sacred
Knights Brigade. Then there is the boisterous Rett Butler,
whose prowess on the battlefield nearly rivals that of
the vampire himself. But for Deshwitat, the most cherished
is the young maiden Lilith Servino, the girl who, years
before, had been the only person to ever treat the caged
boy-vampire with kindness. For the first time in decades,
Deshwitat may truly be happy. But it is to be the calm before
the storm...
Even now, unseen forces are at work to shape the future
of Kalutika for some terrible apocalyptic purpose. To that
end, the power mad Cardinal Josimov has sent his minions
to seek out and destroy the one man who may stand in
the way of the Verkadh cult's insane plans...the vampire
Deshwitat.

DESHWITAT — THE VAMPIRE

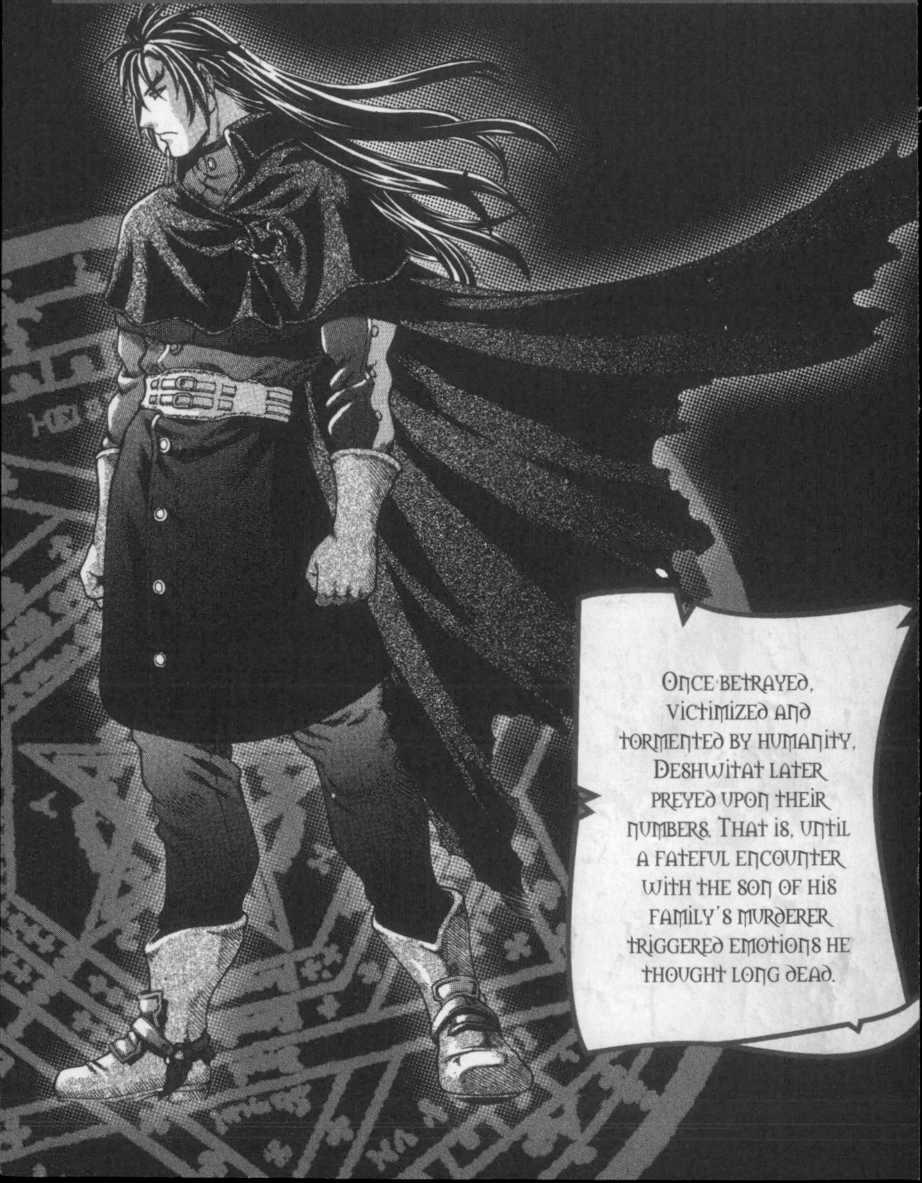
Once betrayed, victimized and tormented by humanity, Deshwitat later preyed upon their numbers. That is, until a fateful encounter with the son of his family's murderer triggered emotions he thought long dead.

KALUTIKA—THE SOLDIER

Born into a life of privilege, Kalutika Maybus II strived to meet the expectations of his domineering father. But there may be darker secrets in Kalutika's past that even he could have never predicted.

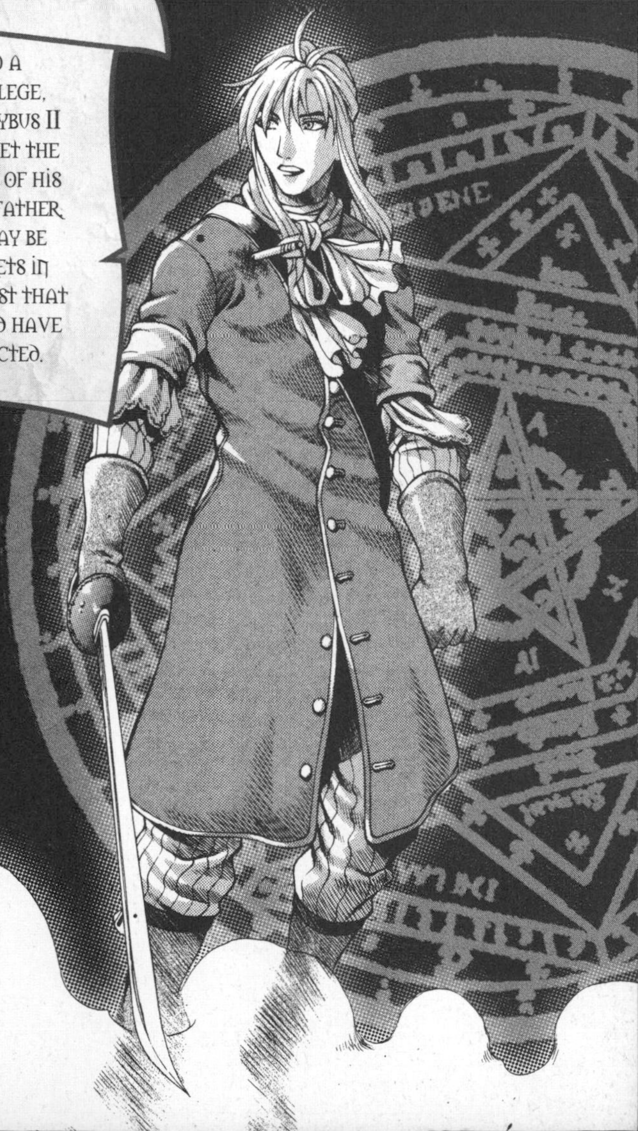

RETT — THE HELLRAISER

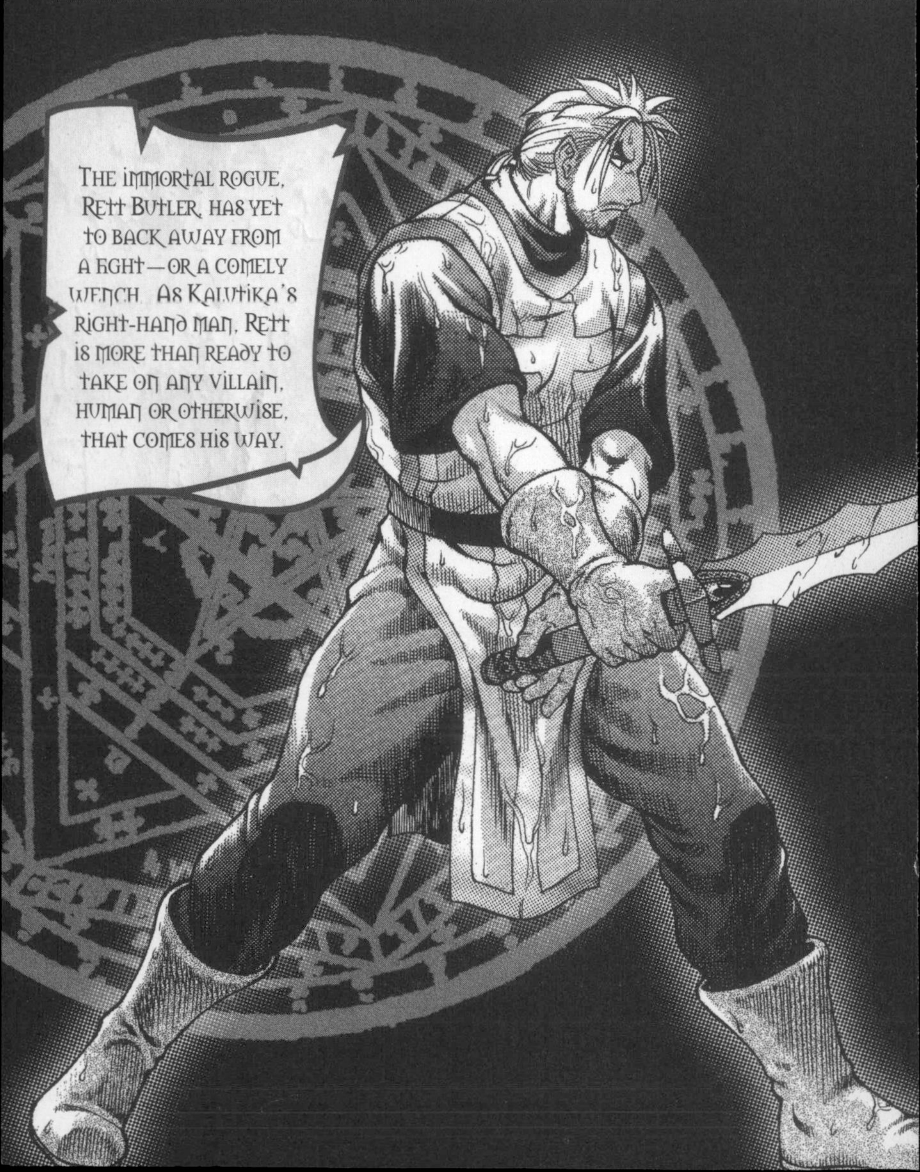
THE IMMORTAL ROGUE, RETT BUTLER, HAS YET TO BACK AWAY FROM A FIGHT — OR A COMELY WENCH. AS KALUTIKA'S RIGHT-HAND MAN, RETT IS MORE THAN READY TO TAKE ON ANY VILLAIN, HUMAN OR OTHERWISE, THAT COMES HIS WAY.

LILITH — THE MAIDEN

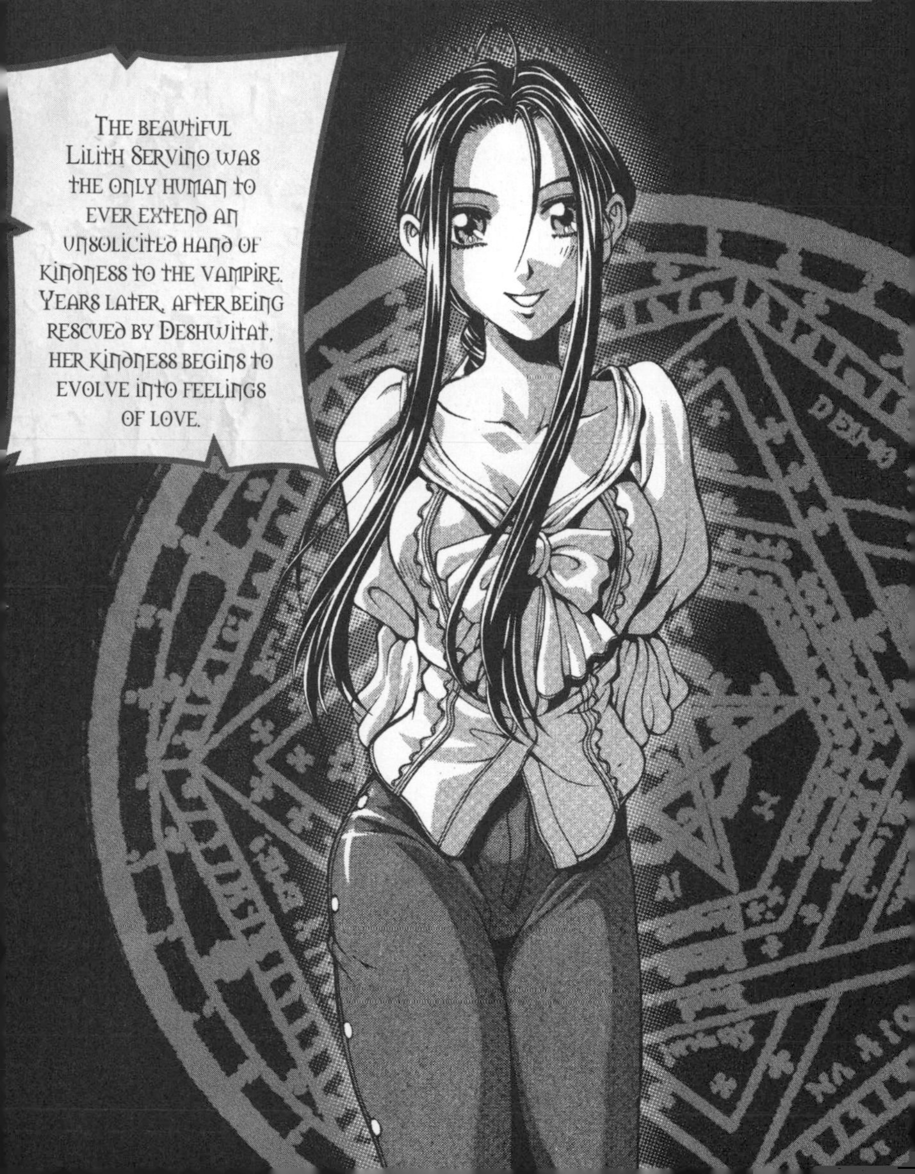
THE BEAUTIFUL LILITH SERVINO WAS THE ONLY HUMAN TO EVER EXTEND AN UNSOLICITED HAND OF KINDNESS TO THE VAMPIRE. YEARS LATER, AFTER BEING RESCUED BY DESHWITAT, HER KINDNESS BEGINS TO EVOLVE INTO FEELINGS OF LOVE.

DANUBE—THE SISTER

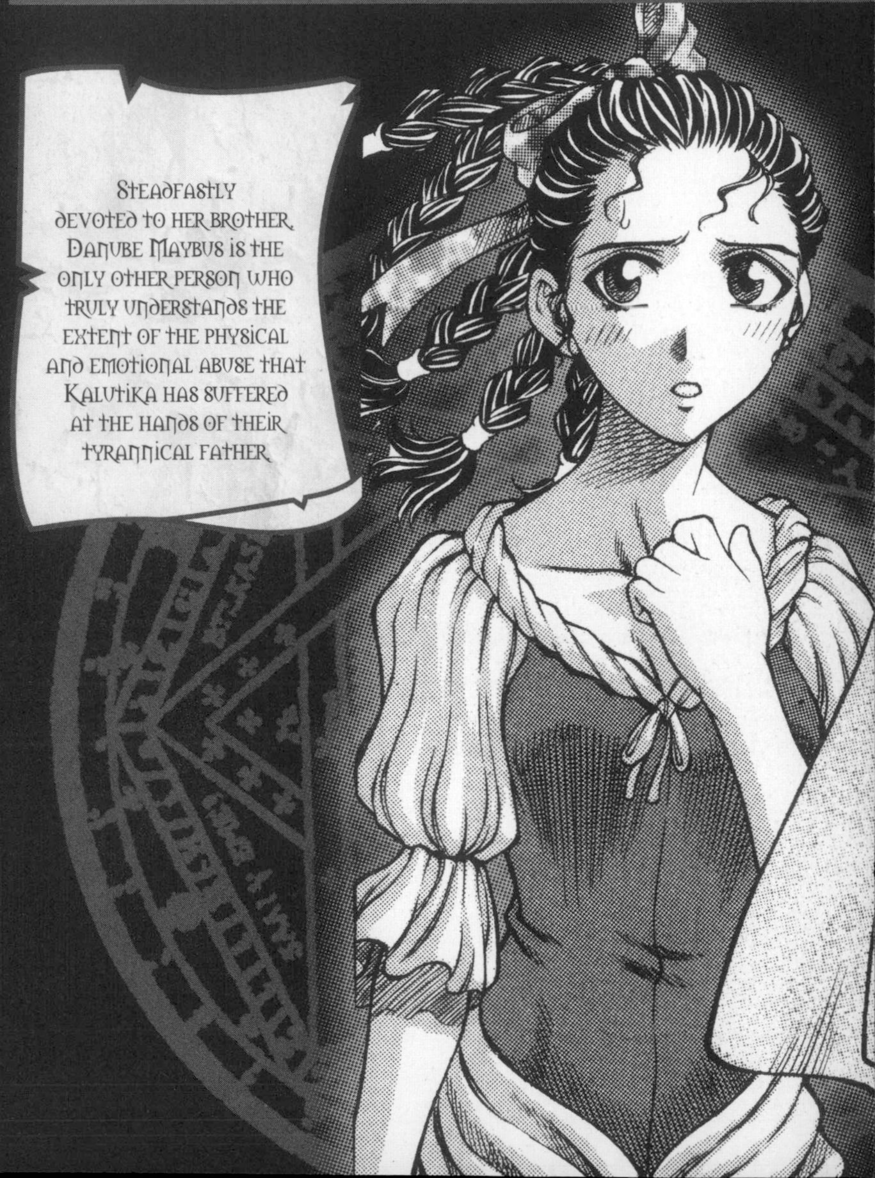
STEADFASTLY DEVOTED TO HER BROTHER, DANUBE MAYBUS IS THE ONLY OTHER PERSON WHO TRULY UNDERSTANDS THE EXTENT OF THE PHYSICAL AND EMOTIONAL ABUSE THAT KALUTIKA HAS SUFFERED AT THE HANDS OF THEIR TYRANNICAL FATHER.

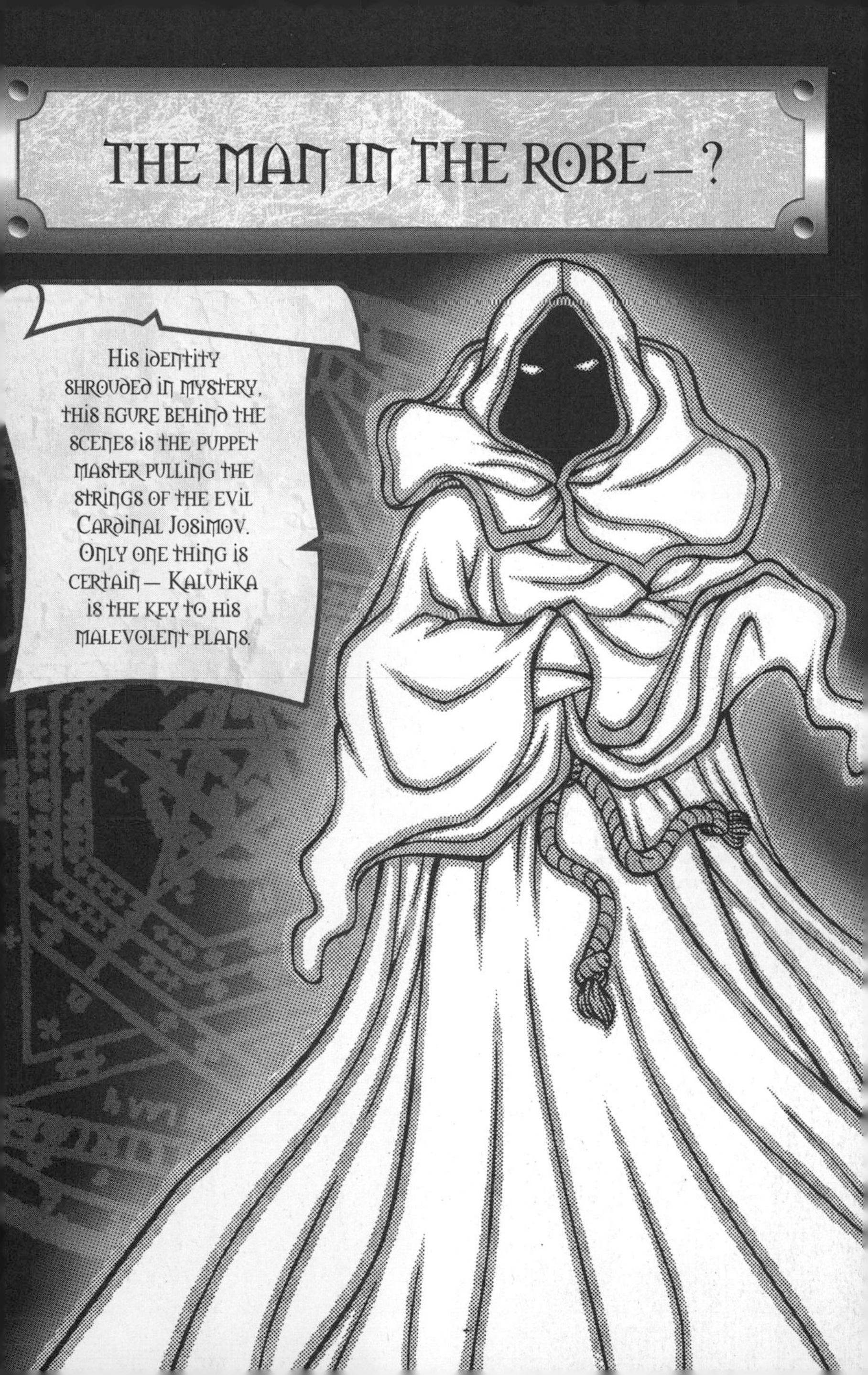
THE MAN IN THE ROBE—?
His identity shrouded in mystery, this figure behind the scenes is the puppet master pulling the strings of the evil Cardinal Josimov. Only one thing is certain — Kalutika is the key to his malevolent plans.

REBÍRTH

Vol 10

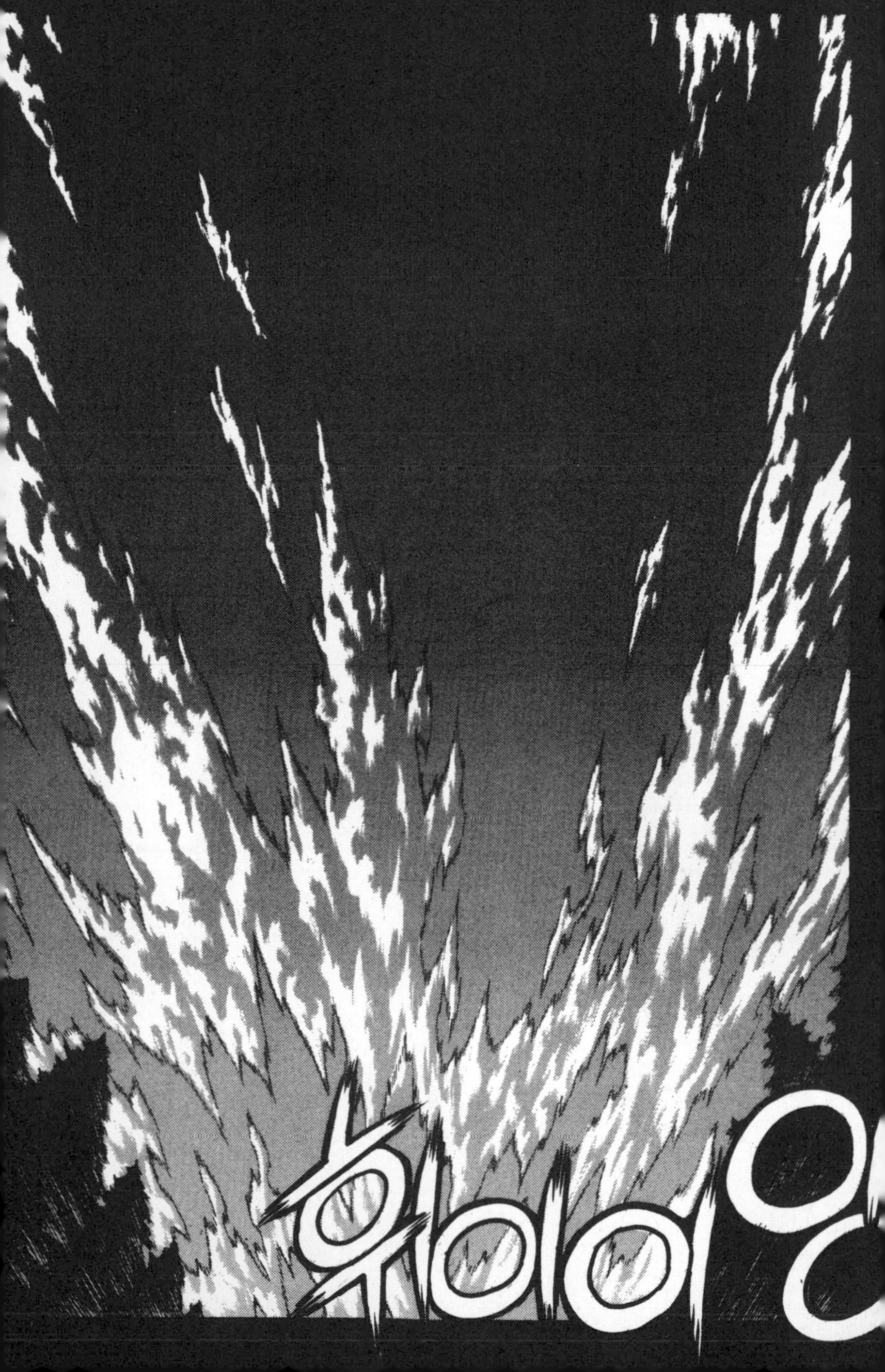

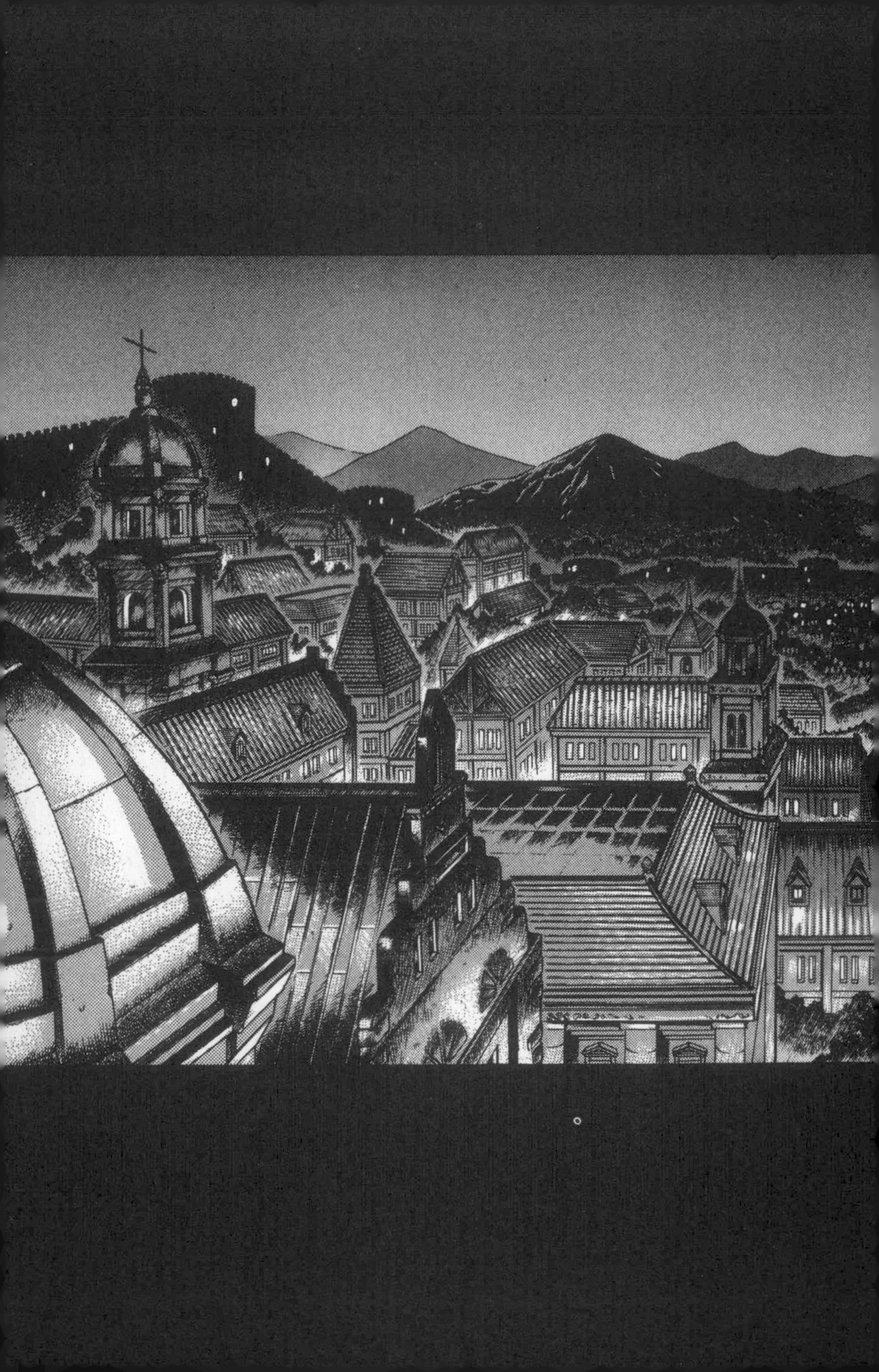

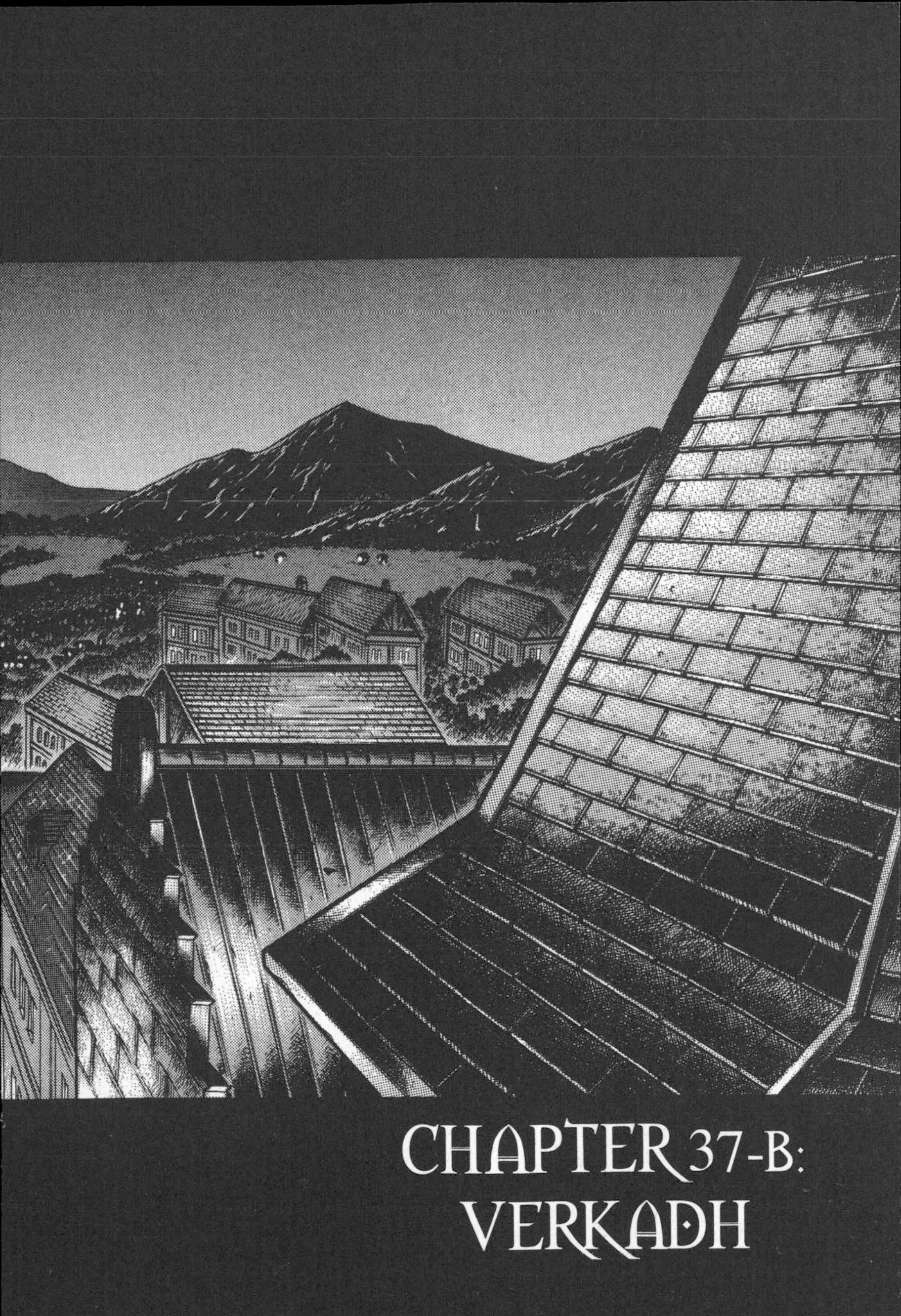

CHAPTER 37-B: VERKADH

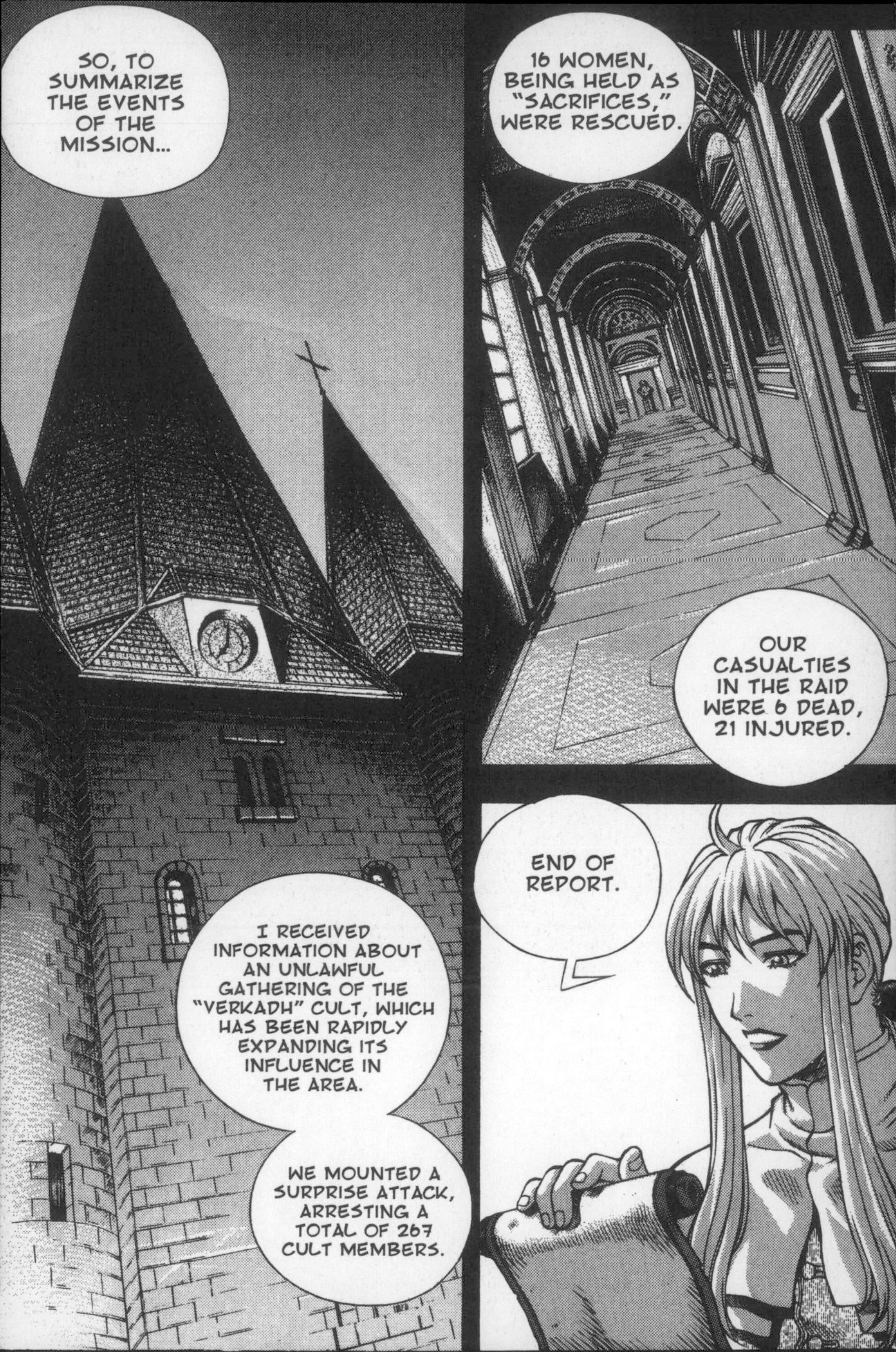
SO, TO SUMMARIZE THE EVENTS OF THE MISSION...
I RECEIVED INFORMATION ABOUT AN UNLAWFUL GATHERING OF THE "VERKADH" CULT, WHICH HAS BEEN RAPIDLY EXPANDING ITS INFLUENCE IN THE AREA.
WE MOUNTED A SURPRISE ATTACK, ARRESTING A TOTAL OF 267 CULT MEMBERS.
16 WOMEN, BEING HELD AS "SACRIFICES," WERE RESCUED.
OUR CASUALTIES IN THE RAID WERE 6 DEAD, 21 INJURED.
END OF REPORT.

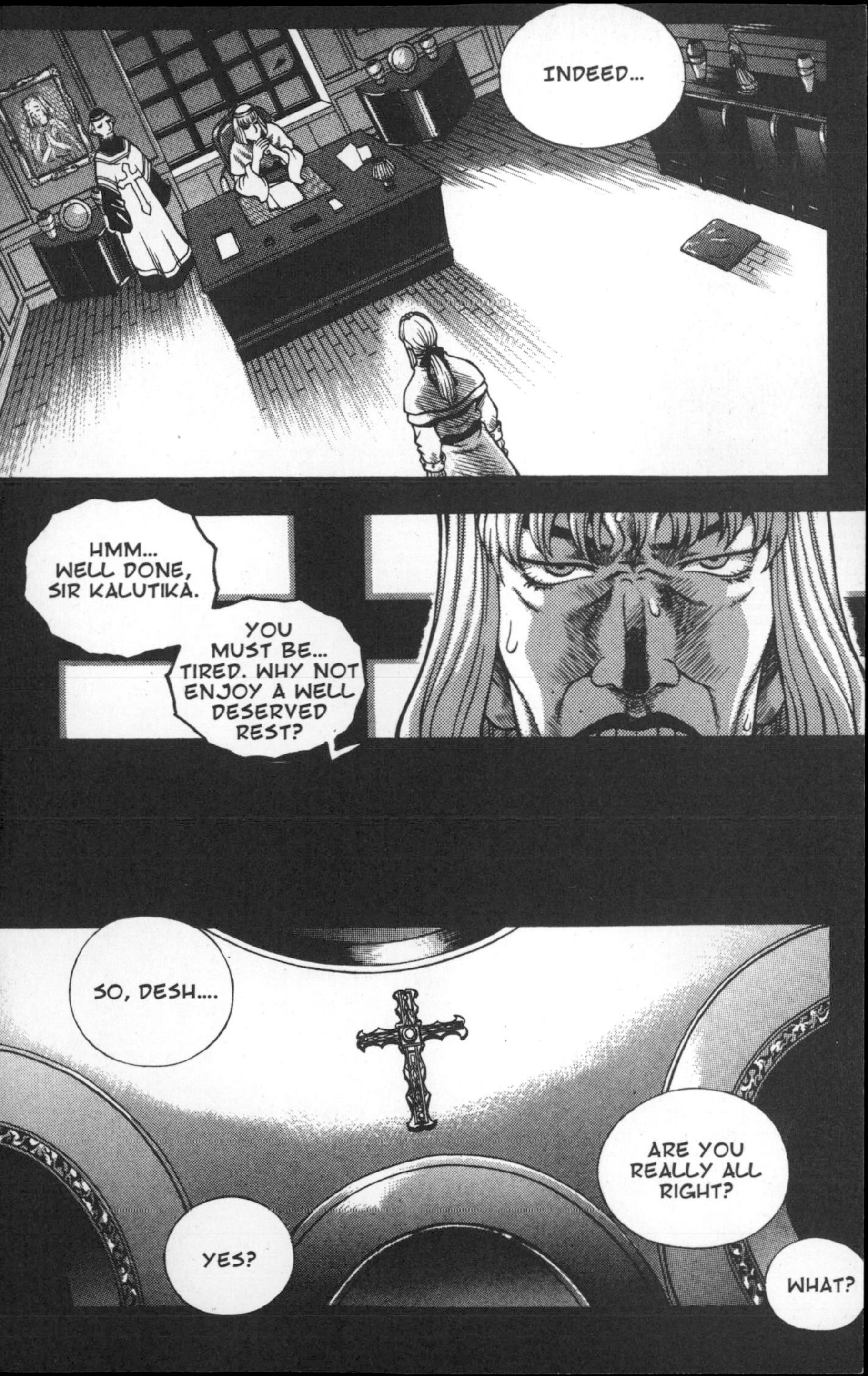
INDEED...
HMM... WELL DONE, SIR KALUTIKA.
YOU MUST BE... TIRED. WHY NOT ENJOY A WELL DESERVED REST?
SO, DESH....
ARE YOU REALLY ALL RIGHT?
YES?
WHAT?

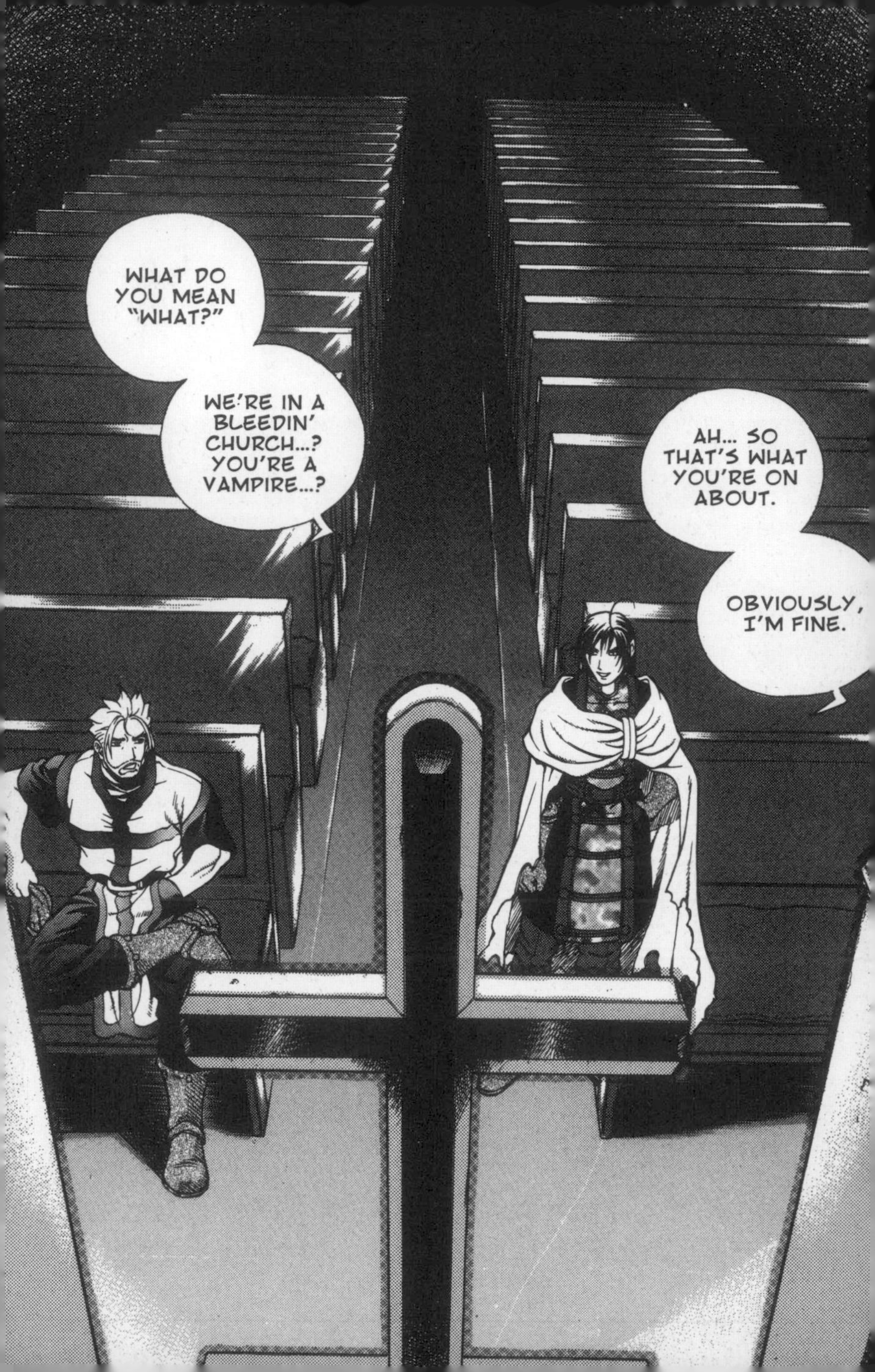
WHAT DO YOU MEAN "WHAT?"
WE'RE IN A BLEEDIN' CHURCH...? YOU'RE A VAMPIRE...?
AH... SO THAT'S WHAT YOU'RE ON ABOUT.
OBVIOUSLY, I'M FINE.

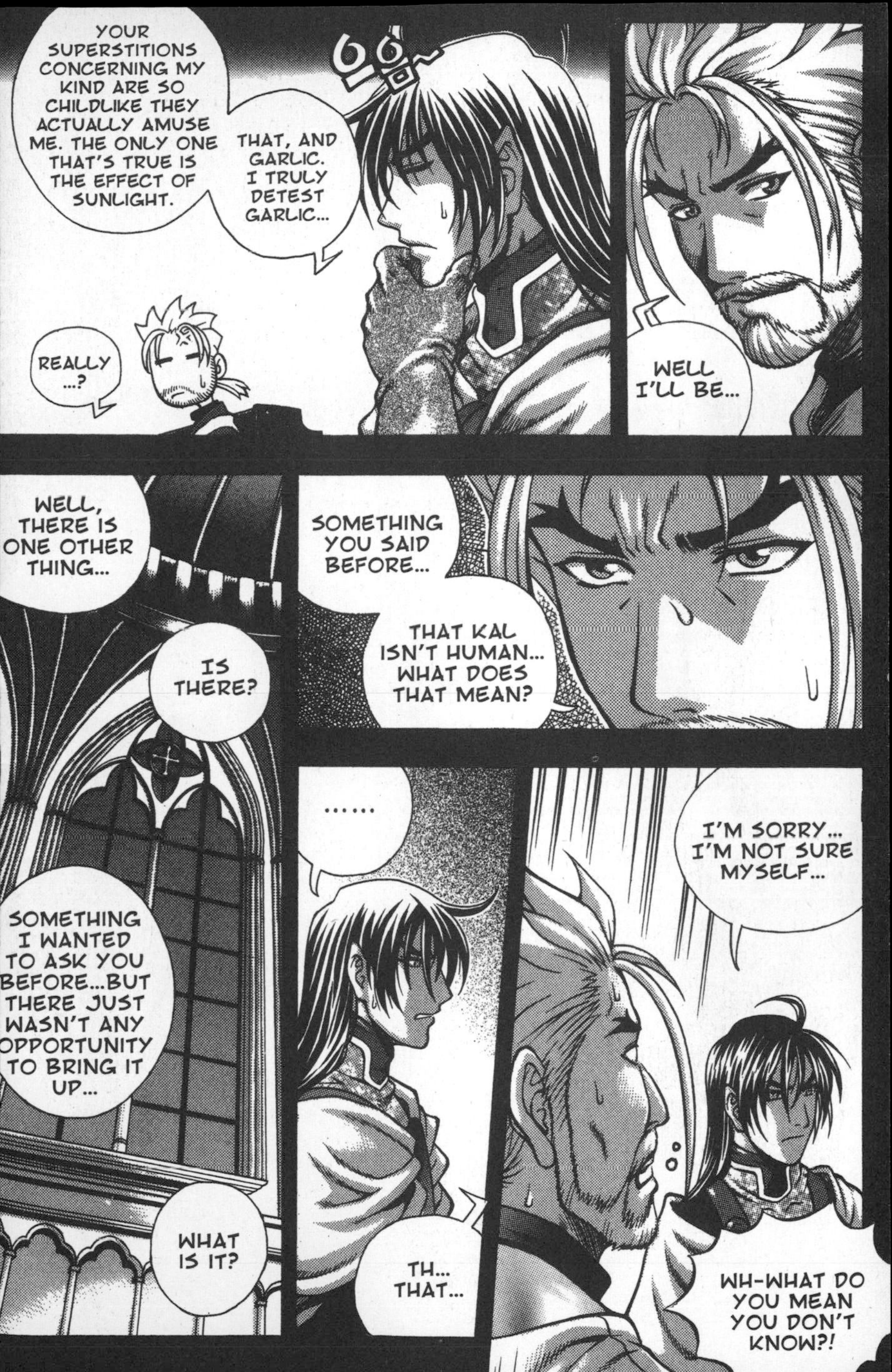

YOUR SUPERSTITIONS CONCERNING MY KIND ARE SO CHILDLIKE THEY ACTUALLY AMUSE ME. THE ONLY ONE THAT'S TRUE IS THE EFFECT OF SUNLIGHT.
THAT, AND GARLIC. I TRULY DETEST GARLIC...
REALLY ...?
WELL I'LL BE...
WELL, THERE IS ONE OTHER THING...
IS THERE?
SOMETHING I WANTED TO ASK YOU BEFORE...BUT THERE JUST WASN'T ANY OPPORTUNITY TO BRING IT UP...
WHAT IS IT?
SOMETHING YOU SAID BEFORE...
THAT KAL ISN'T HUMAN... WHAT DOES THAT MEAN?
......
TH... THAT...
I'M SORRY... I'M NOT SURE MYSELF...
WH-WHAT DO YOU MEAN YOU DON'T KNOW?!

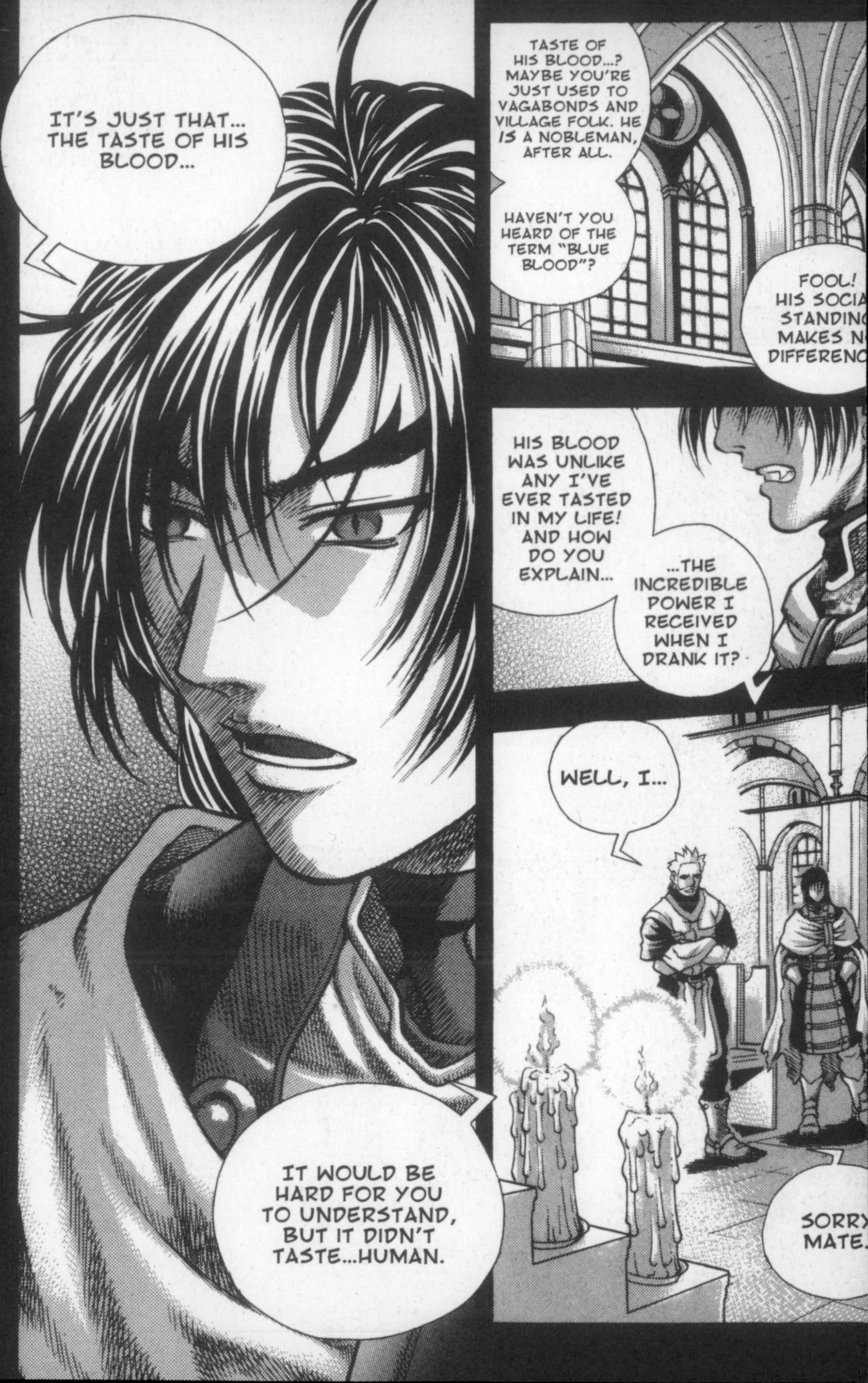
IT'S JUST THAT... THE TASTE OF HIS BLOOD...
IT WOULD BE HARD FOR YOU TO UNDERSTAND, BUT IT DIDN'T TASTE...HUMAN.
TASTE OF HIS BLOOD...? MAYBE YOU'RE JUST USED TO VAGABONDS AND VILLAGE FOLK. HE IS A NOBLEMAN, AFTER ALL.
HAVEN'T YOU HEARD OF THE TERM "BLUE BLOOD"?
FOOL! HIS SOCIA STANDIN MAKES N DIFFERENC
HIS BLOOD WAS UNLIKE ANY I'VE EVER TASTED IN MY LIFE! AND HOW DO YOU EXPLAIN...
...THE INCREDIBLE POWER I RECEIVED WHEN I DRANK IT?
WELL, I...
SORR MATE.

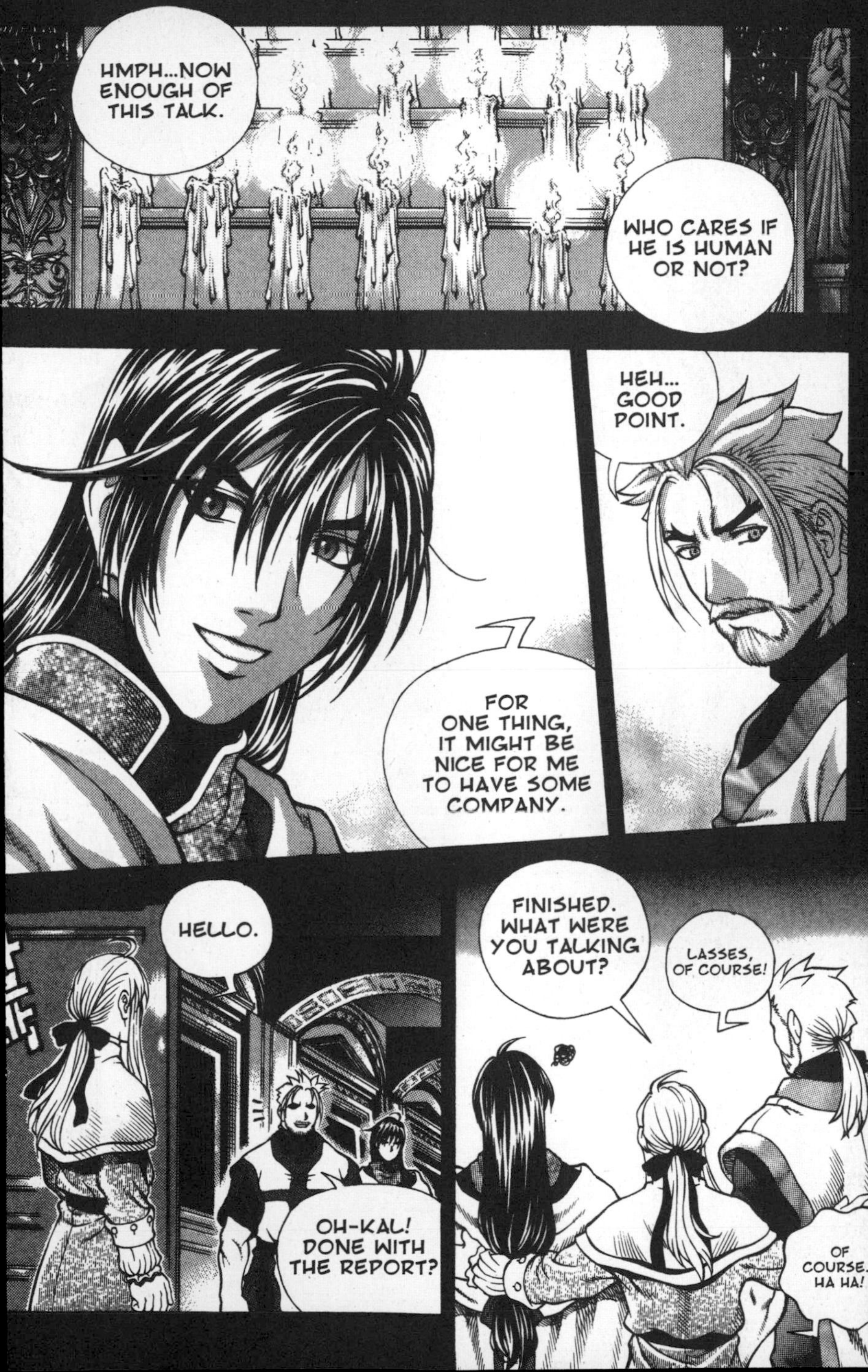
HMPH...NOW ENOUGH OF THIS TALK.
WHO CARES IF HE IS HUMAN OR NOT?
FOR ONE THING, IT MIGHT BE NICE FOR ME TO HAVE SOME COMPANY.
HEH... GOOD POINT.
HELLO.
OH-KAL! DONE WITH THE REPORT?
FINISHED. WHAT WERE YOU TALKING ABOUT?
LASSES, OF COURSE!
OF COURSE. HA HA!

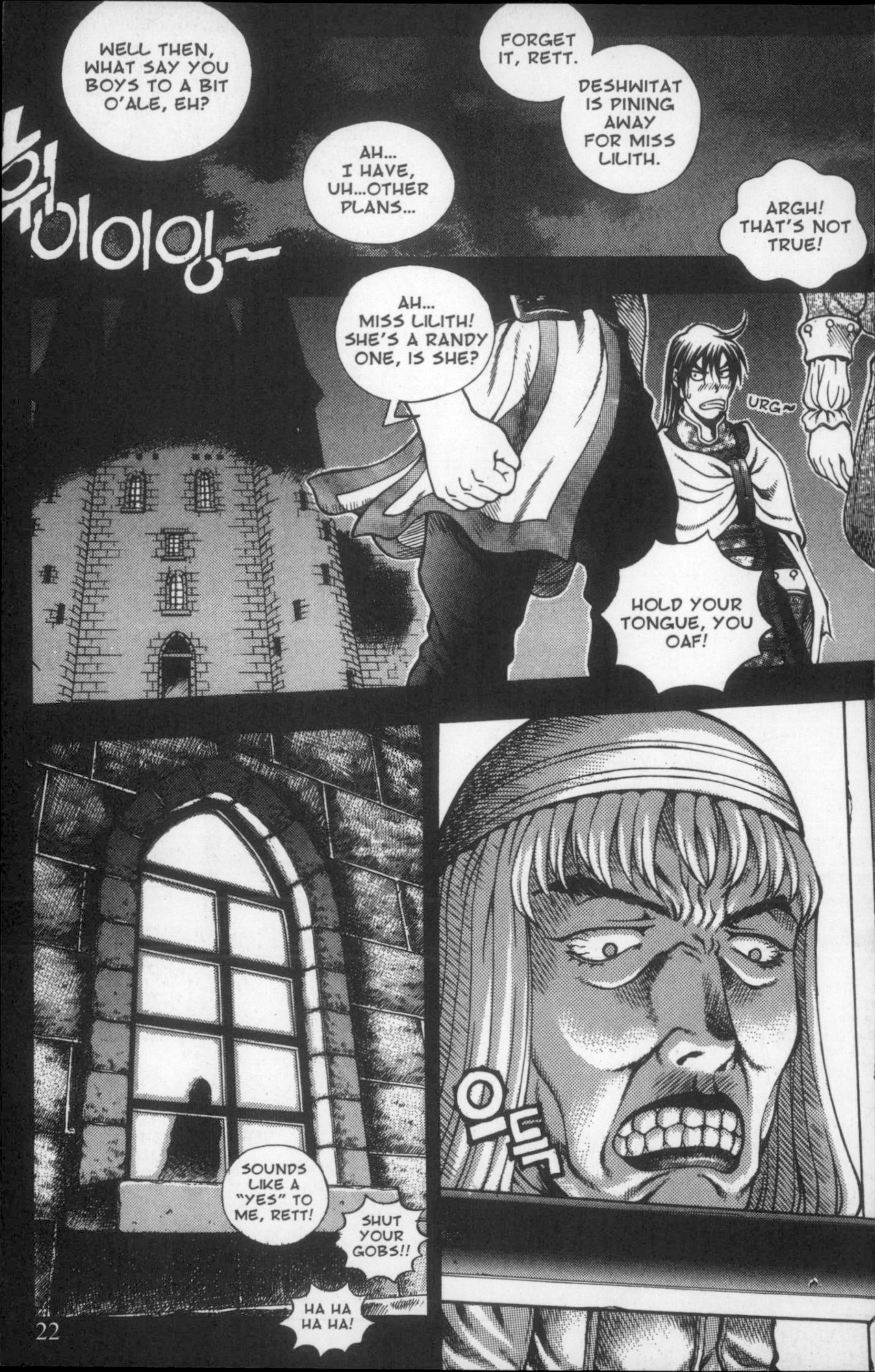

WELL THEN, WHAT SAY YOU BOYS TO A BIT O'ALE, EH?
AH... I HAVE, UH...OTHER PLANS...
FORGET IT, RETT.
DESHWITAT IS PINING AWAY FOR MISS LILITH.
ARGH! THAT'S NOT TRUE!
AH... MISS LILITH! SHE'S A RANDY ONE, IS SHE?
URG~
HOLD YOUR TONGUE, YOU OAF!
SOUNDS LIKE A "YES" TO ME, RETT!
SHUT YOUR GOBS!!
HA HA HA HA!

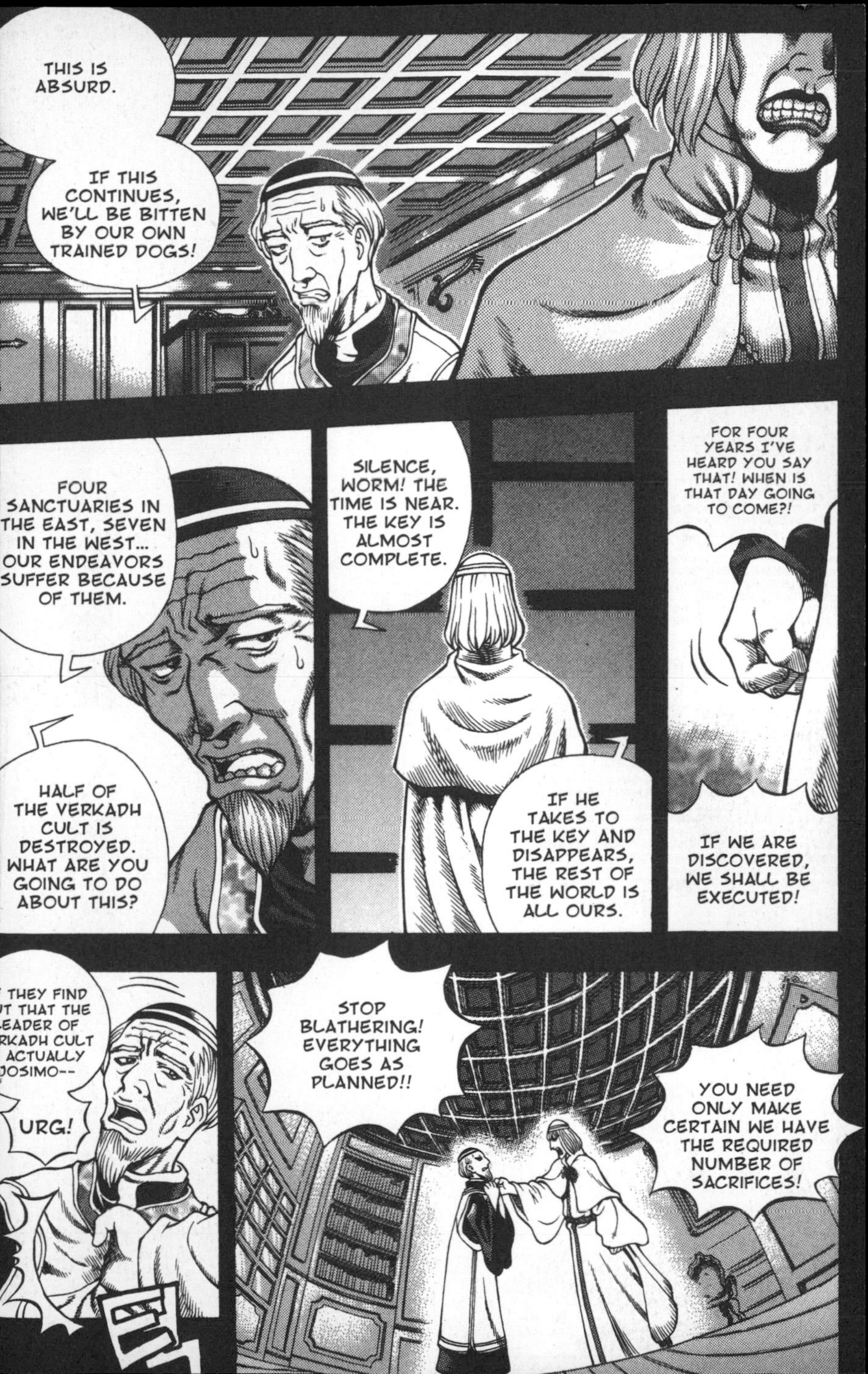
THIS IS ABSURD.
IF THIS CONTINUES, WE'LL BE BITTEN BY OUR OWN TRAINED DOGS!
FOUR SANCTUARIES IN THE EAST, SEVEN IN THE WEST... OUR ENDEAVORS SUFFER BECAUSE OF THEM.
HALF OF THE VERKADH CULT IS DESTROYED. WHAT ARE YOU GOING TO DO ABOUT THIS?
SILENCE, WORM! THE TIME IS NEAR. THE KEY IS ALMOST COMPLETE.
IF HE TAKES TO THE KEY AND DISAPPEARS, THE REST OF THE WORLD IS ALL OURS.
FOR FOUR YEARS I'VE HEARD YOU SAY THAT! WHEN IS THAT DAY GOING TO COME?!
IF WE ARE DISCOVERED, WE SHALL BE EXECUTED!
URG!
STOP BLATHERING! EVERYTHING GOES AS PLANNED!!
YOU NEED ONLY MAKE CERTAIN WE HAVE THE REQUIRED NUMBER OF SACRIFICES!

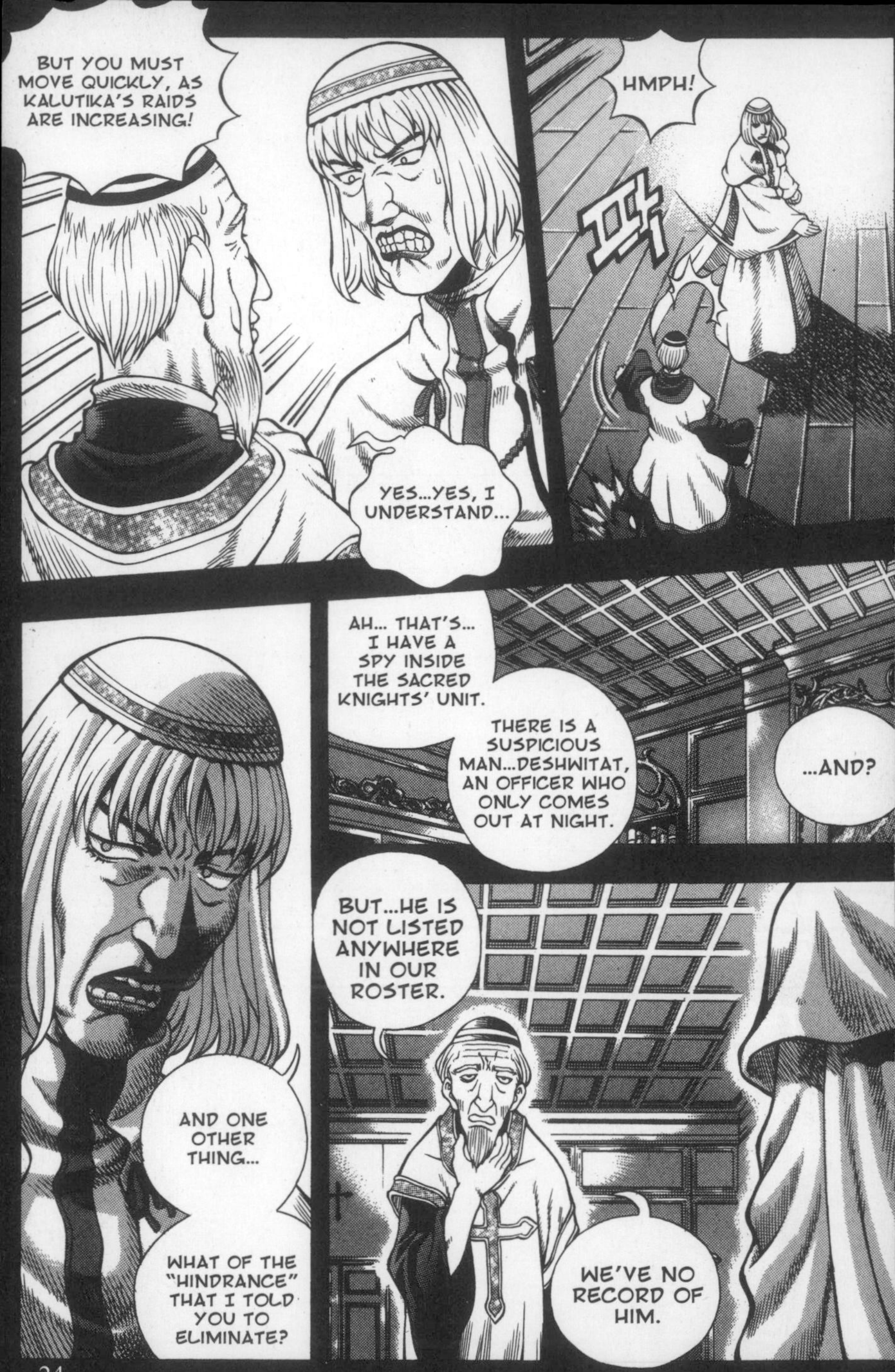
BUT YOU MUST MOVE QUICKLY, AS KALUTIKA'S RAIDS ARE INCREASING!
YES...YES, I UNDERSTAND...
HMPH!
AND ONE OTHER THING...
WHAT OF THE "HINDRANCE" THAT I TOLD YOU TO ELIMINATE?
AH... THAT'S... I HAVE A SPY INSIDE THE SACRED KNIGHTS' UNIT.
THERE IS A SUSPICIOUS MAN...DESHWITAT, AN OFFICER WHO ONLY COMES OUT AT NIGHT.
...AND?
BUT...HE IS NOT LISTED ANYWHERE IN OUR ROSTER.
WE'VE NO RECORD OF HIM.

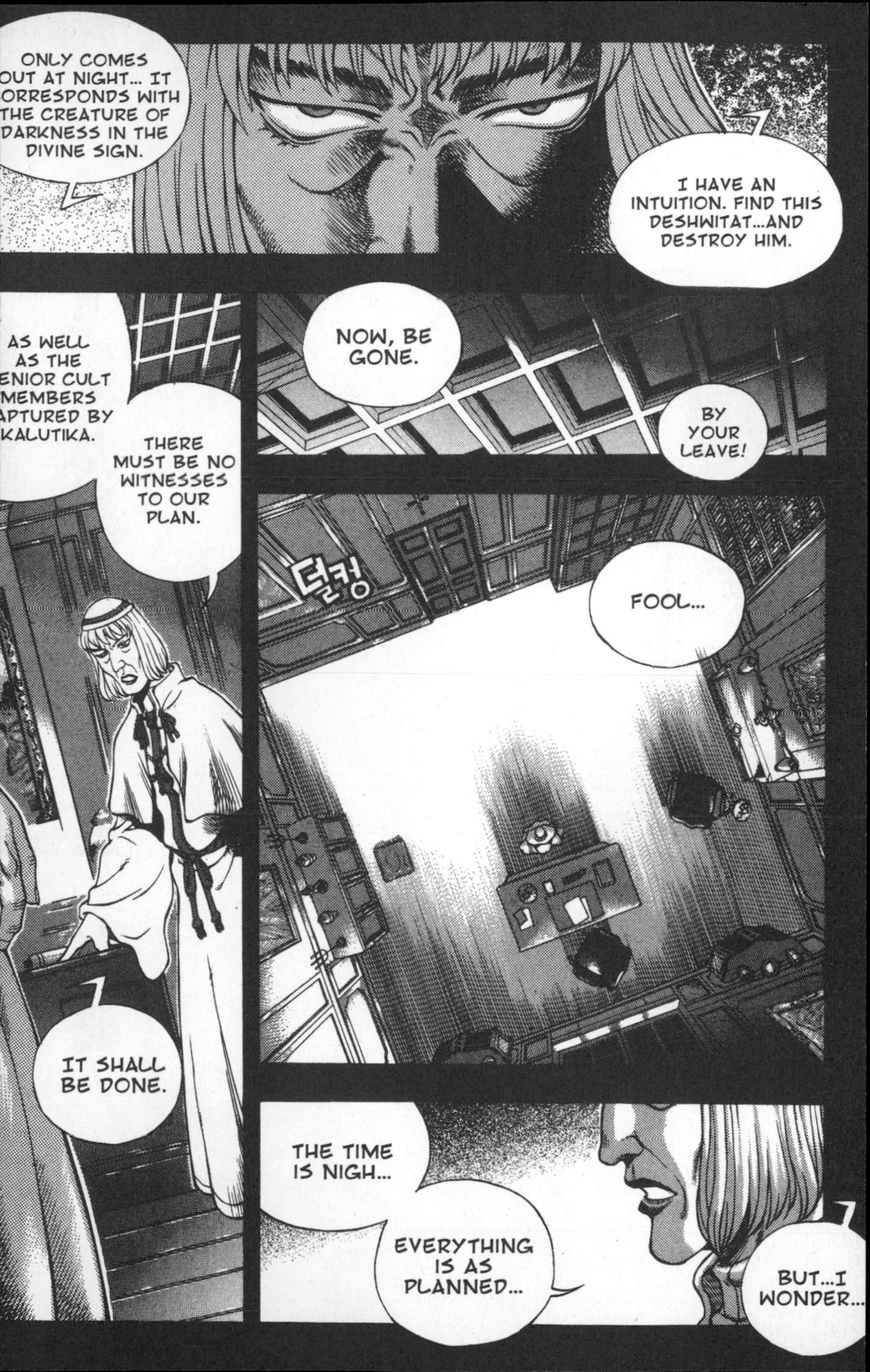
ONLY COMES OUT AT NIGHT... IT ORRESPONDS WITH THE CREATURE OF DARKNESS IN THE DIVINE SIGN.
I HAVE AN INTUITION. FIND THIS DESHWITAT...AND DESTROY HIM.
AS WELL AS THE ENIOR CULT MEMBERS APTURED BY KALUTIKA.
THERE MUST BE NO WITNESSES TO OUR PLAN.
IT SHALL BE DONE.
NOW, BE GONE.
BY YOUR LEAVE!
덜컹
FOOL...
THE TIME IS NIGH...
EVERYTHING IS AS PLANNED...
BUT...I WONDER...

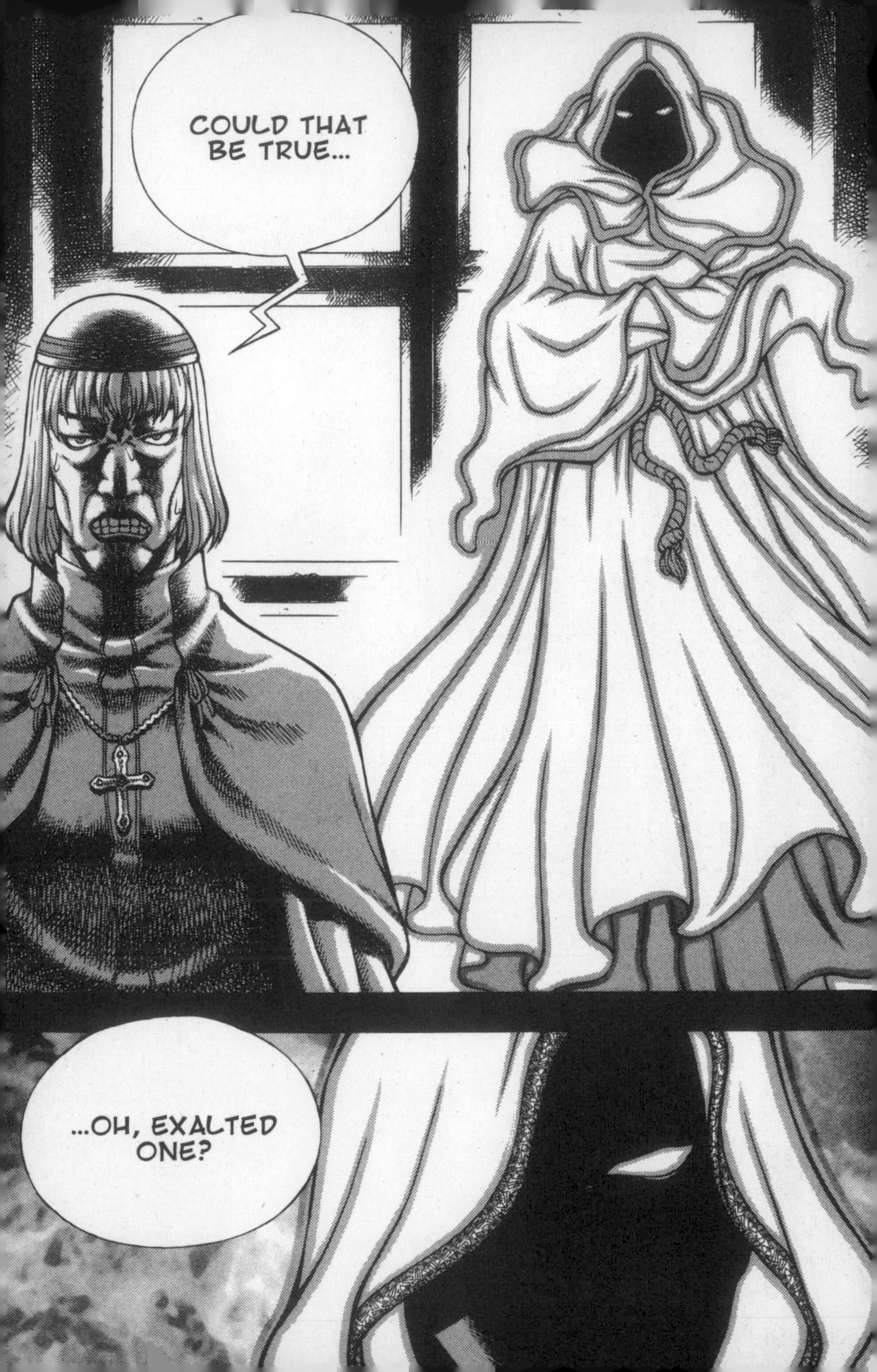
COULD THAT BE TRUE...
...OH, EXALTED ONE?

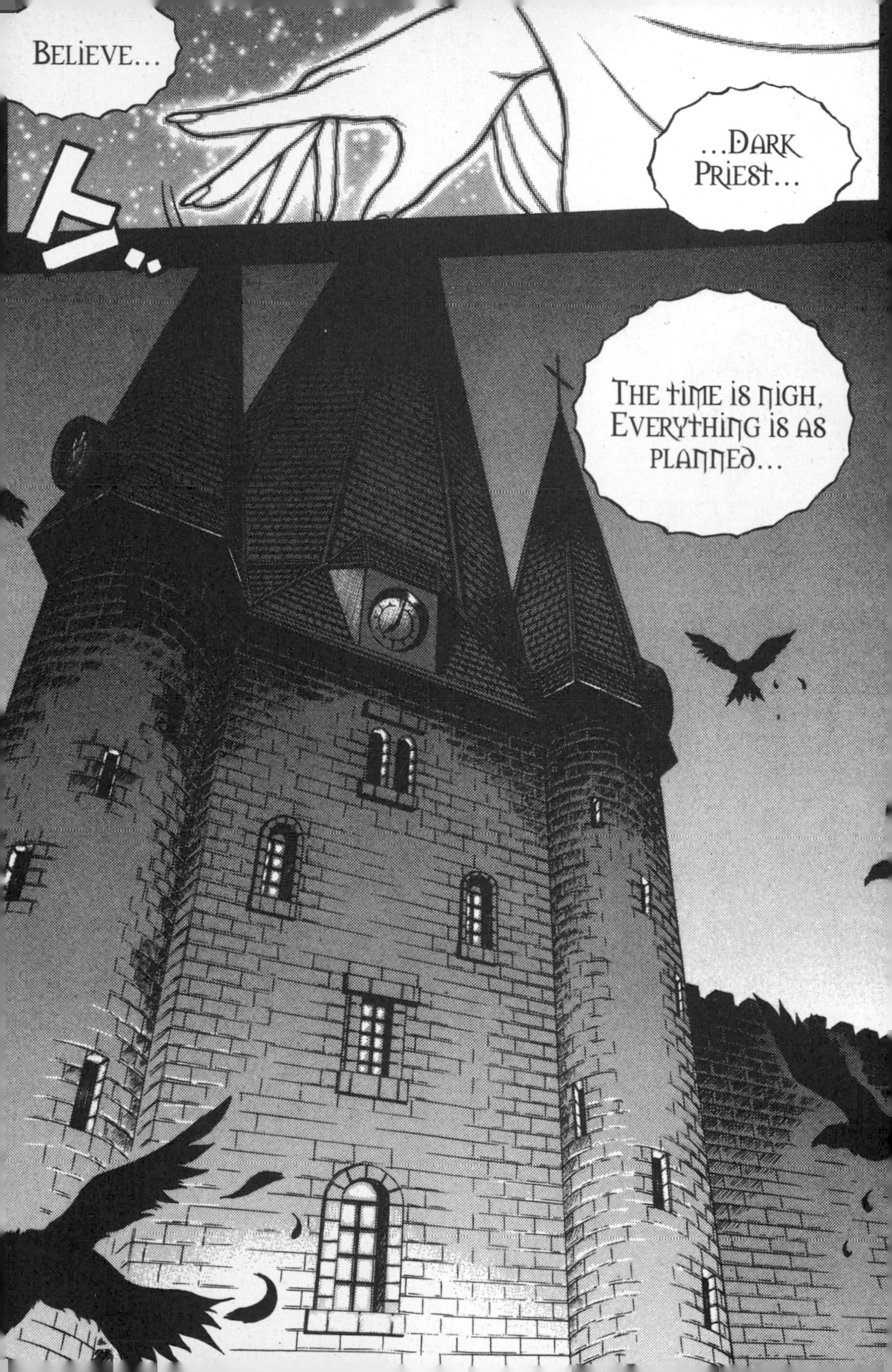
BELIEVE…
…DARK PRIEST…
THE TIME IS NIGH, EVERYTHING IS AS PLANNED…

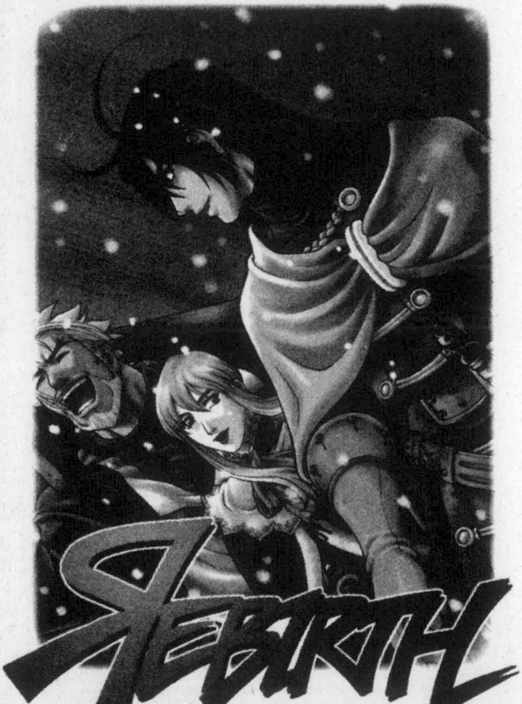
REBIRTH

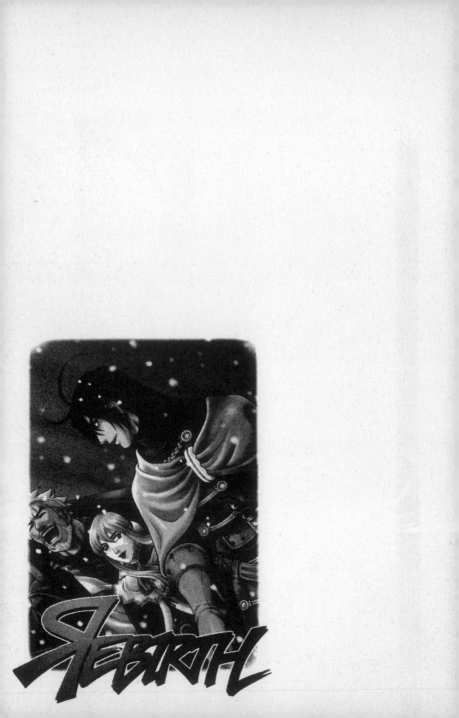

CHAPTER 38:
RINGS OF ALL SPIRITS

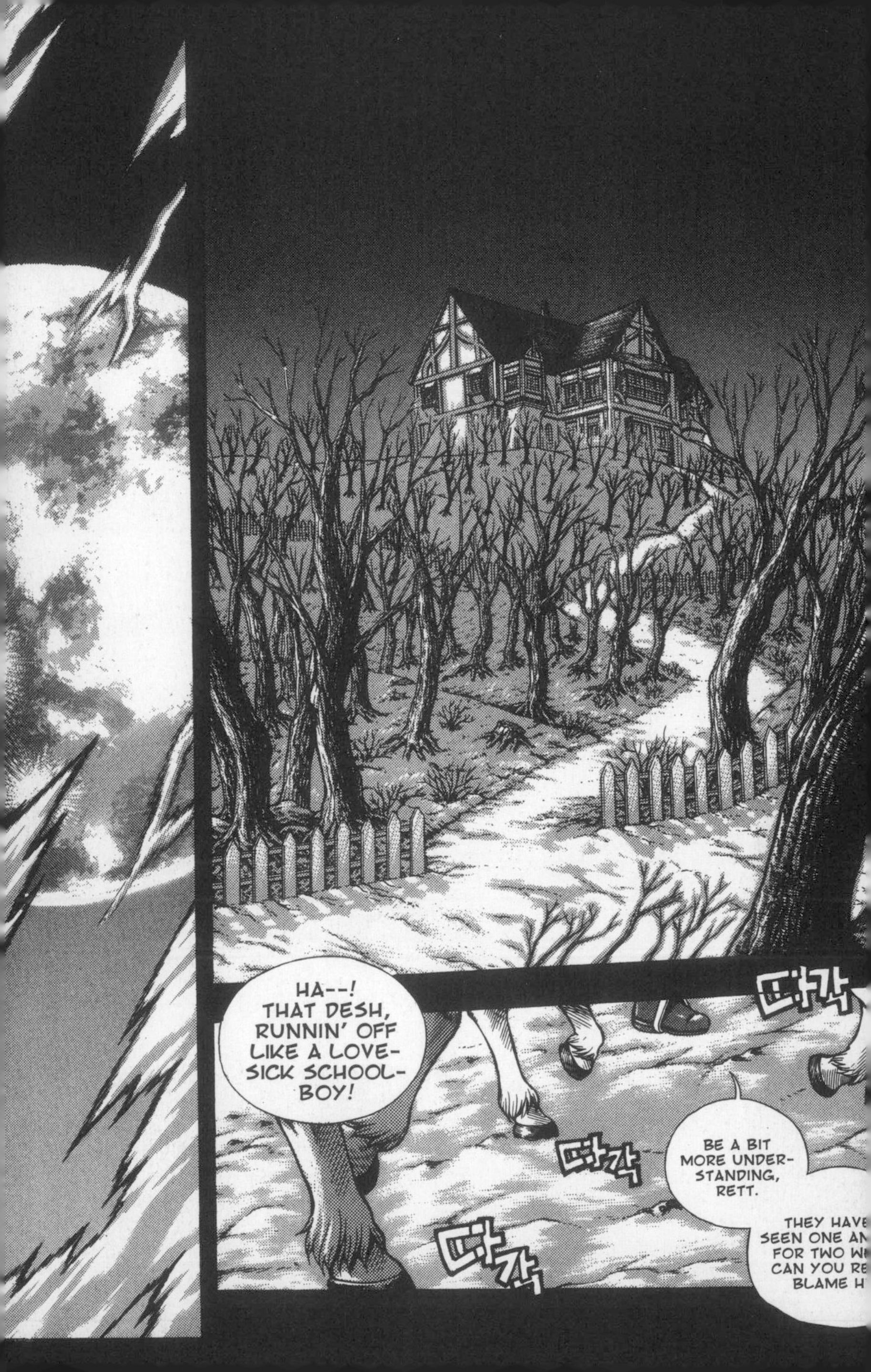
HA--! THAT DESH, RUNNIN' OFF LIKE A LOVE-SICK SCHOOL-BOY!
따각
따각
BE A BIT MORE UNDER-STANDING, RETT.
따각
THEY HAVE SEEN ONE AN FOR TWO W CAN YOU RE BLAME H

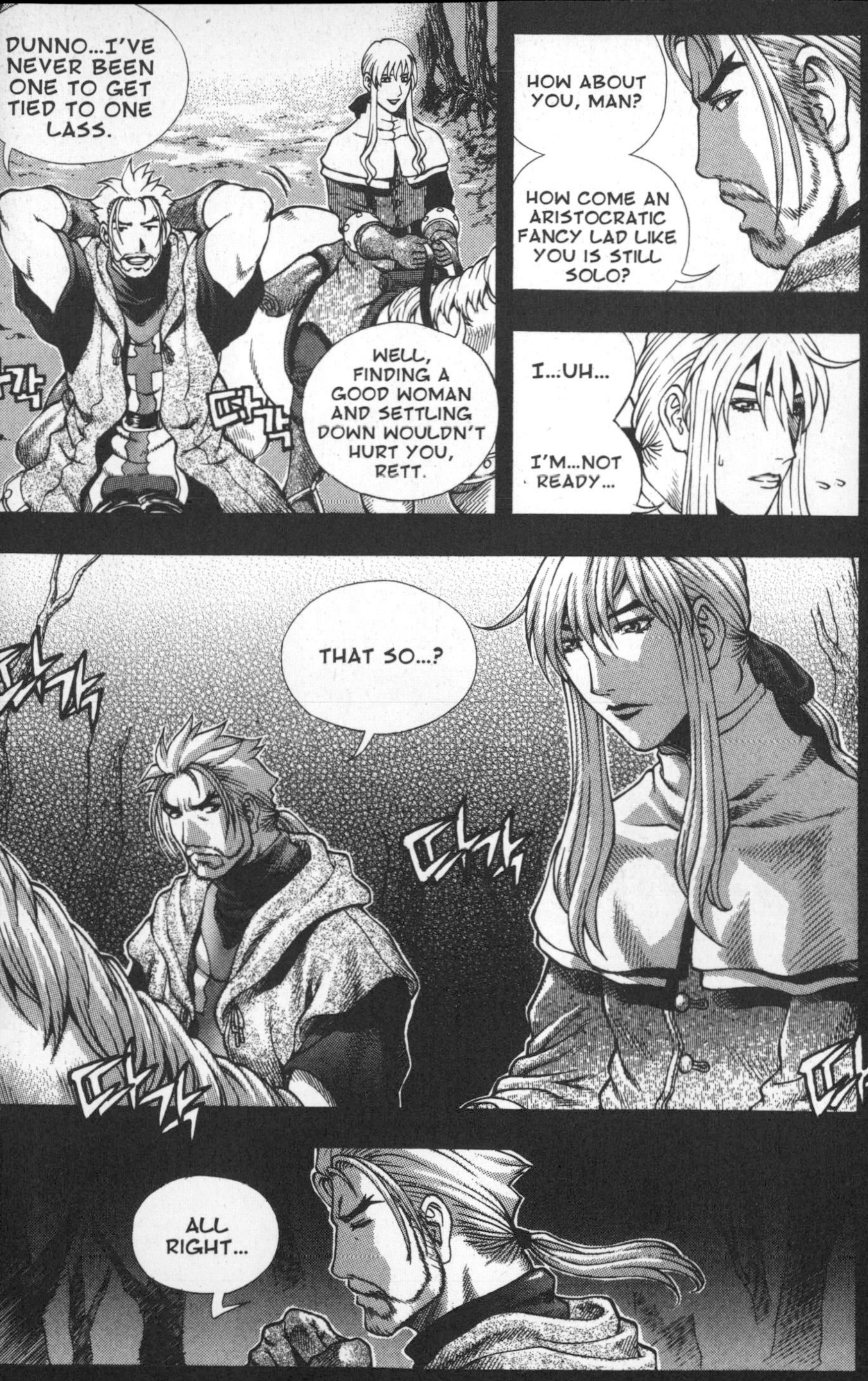
DUNNO...I'VE NEVER BEEN ONE TO GET TIED TO ONE LASS.
WELL, FINDING A GOOD WOMAN AND SETTLING DOWN WOULDN'T HURT YOU, RETT.
HOW ABOUT YOU, MAN?
HOW COME AN ARISTOCRATIC FANCY LAD LIKE YOU IS STILL SOLO?
I...UH...
I'M...NOT READY...
THAT SO...?
ALL RIGHT...

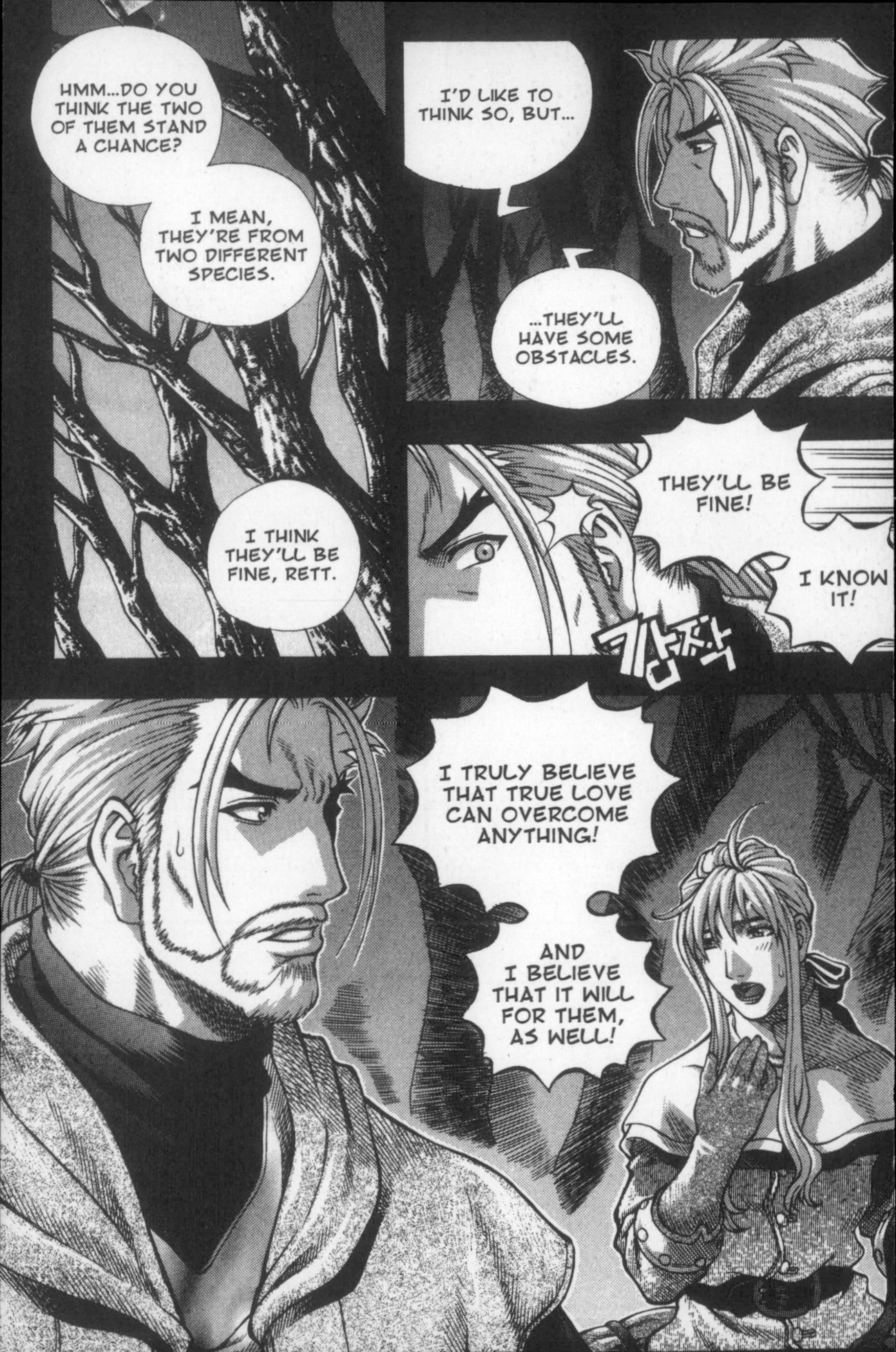
HMM...DO YOU THINK THE TWO OF THEM STAND A CHANCE?
I MEAN, THEY'RE FROM TWO DIFFERENT SPECIES.
I THINK THEY'LL BE FINE, RETT.
I'D LIKE TO THINK SO, BUT...
...THEY'LL HAVE SOME OBSTACLES.
THEY'LL BE FINE!
I KNOW IT!
I TRULY BELIEVE THAT TRUE LOVE CAN OVERCOME ANYTHING!
AND I BELIEVE THAT IT WILL FOR THEM, AS WELL!

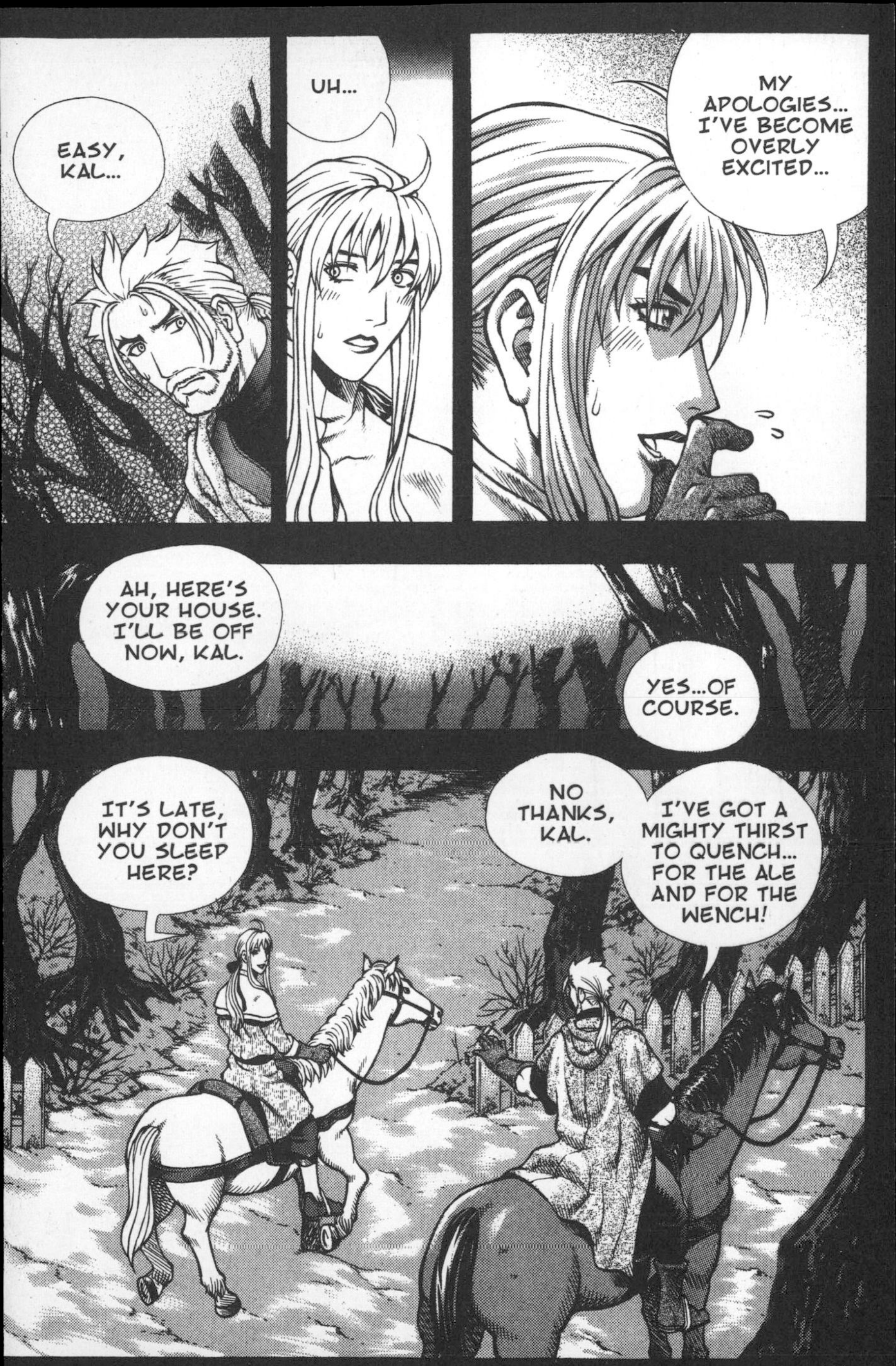
EASY, KAL...
UH...
MY APOLOGIES... I'VE BECOME OVERLY EXCITED...
AH, HERE'S YOUR HOUSE. I'LL BE OFF NOW, KAL.
YES...OF COURSE.
IT'S LATE, WHY DON'T YOU SLEEP HERE?
NO THANKS, KAL.
I'VE GOT A MIGHTY THIRST TO QUENCH... FOR THE ALE AND FOR THE WENCH!

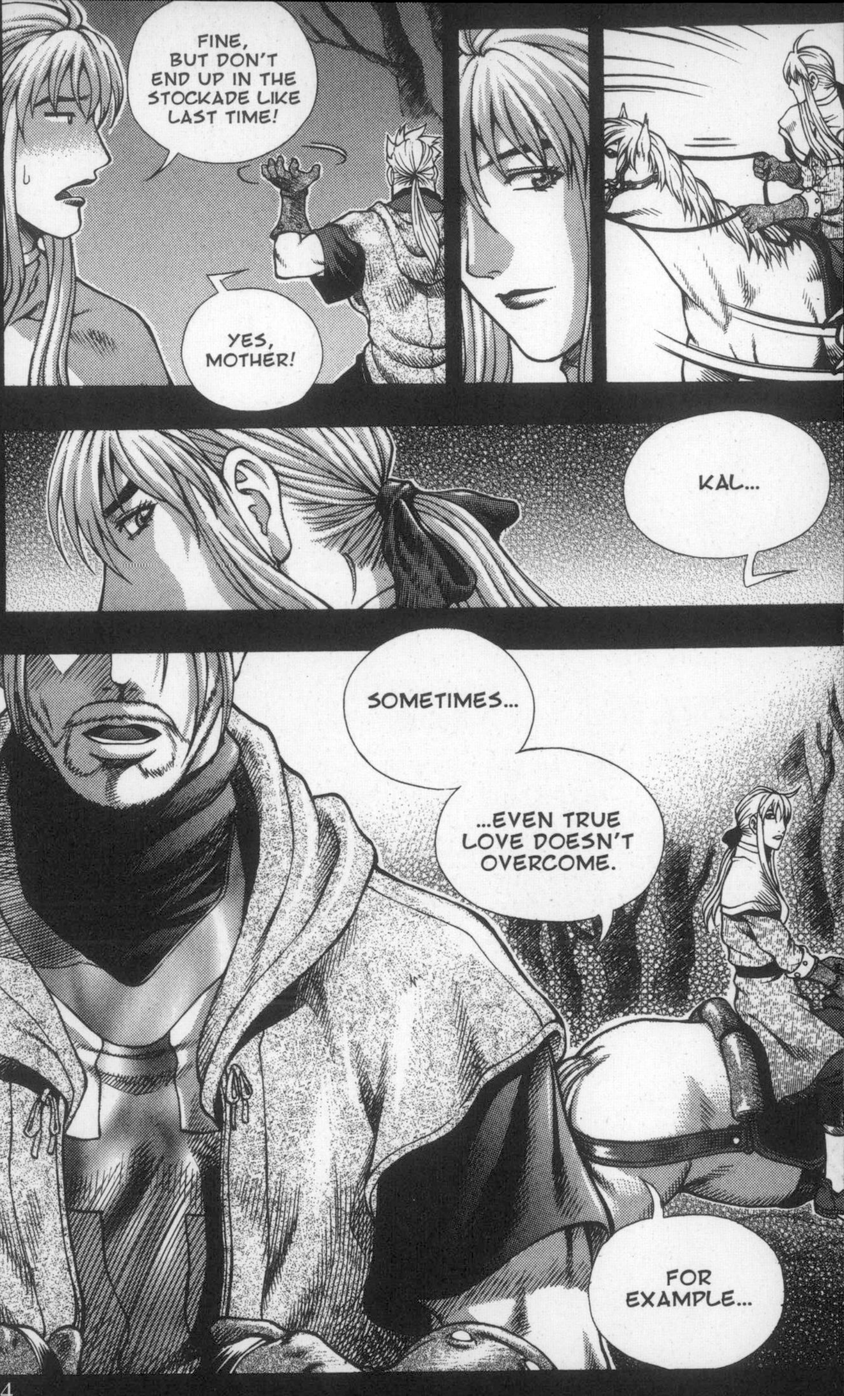
FINE, BUT DON'T END UP IN THE STOCKADE LIKE LAST TIME!
YES, MOTHER!
KAL...
SOMETIMES...
...EVEN TRUE LOVE DOESN'T OVERCOME.
FOR EXAMPLE...

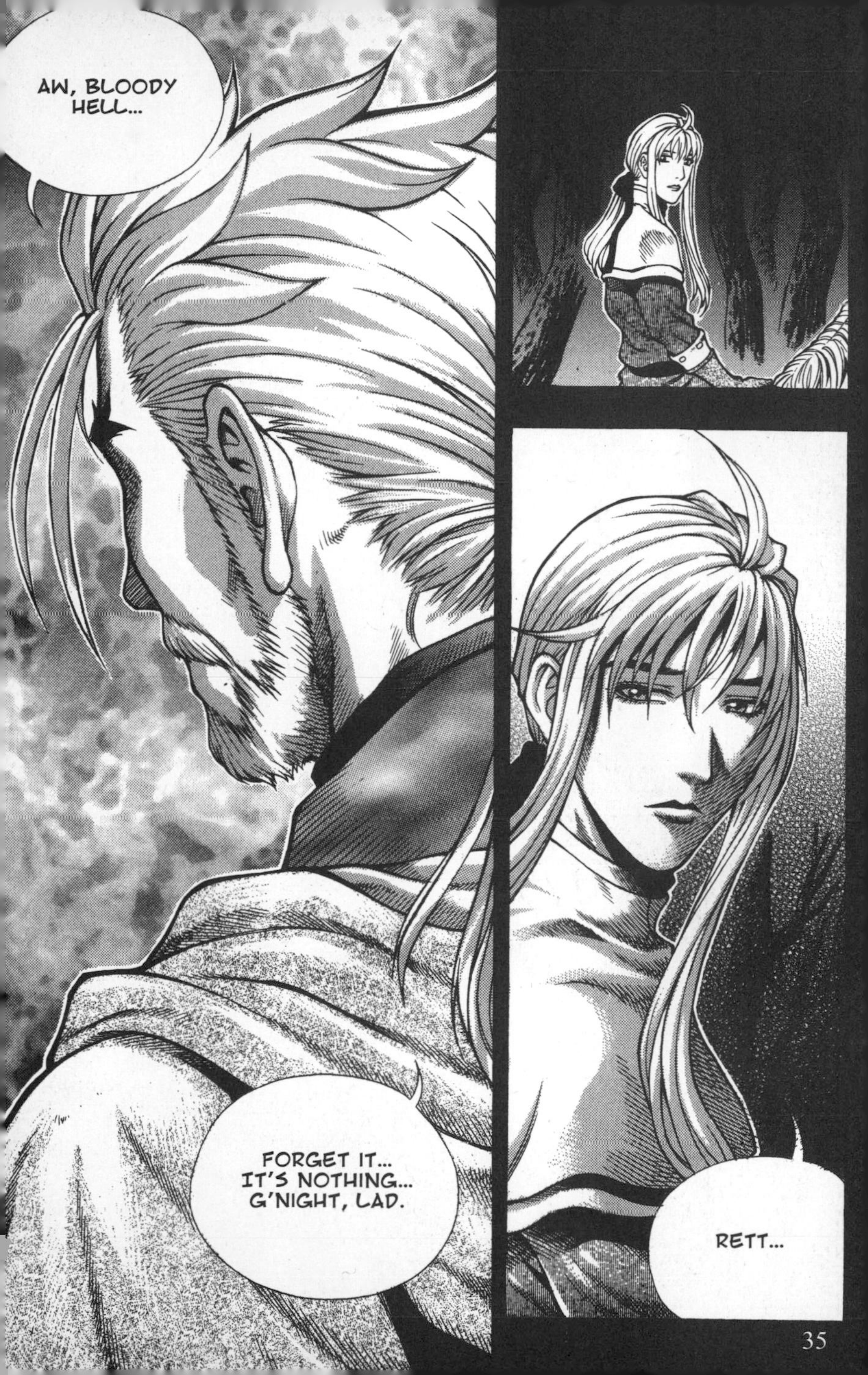
AW, BLOODY HELL...
FORGET IT... IT'S NOTHING... G'NIGHT, LAD.
RETT...

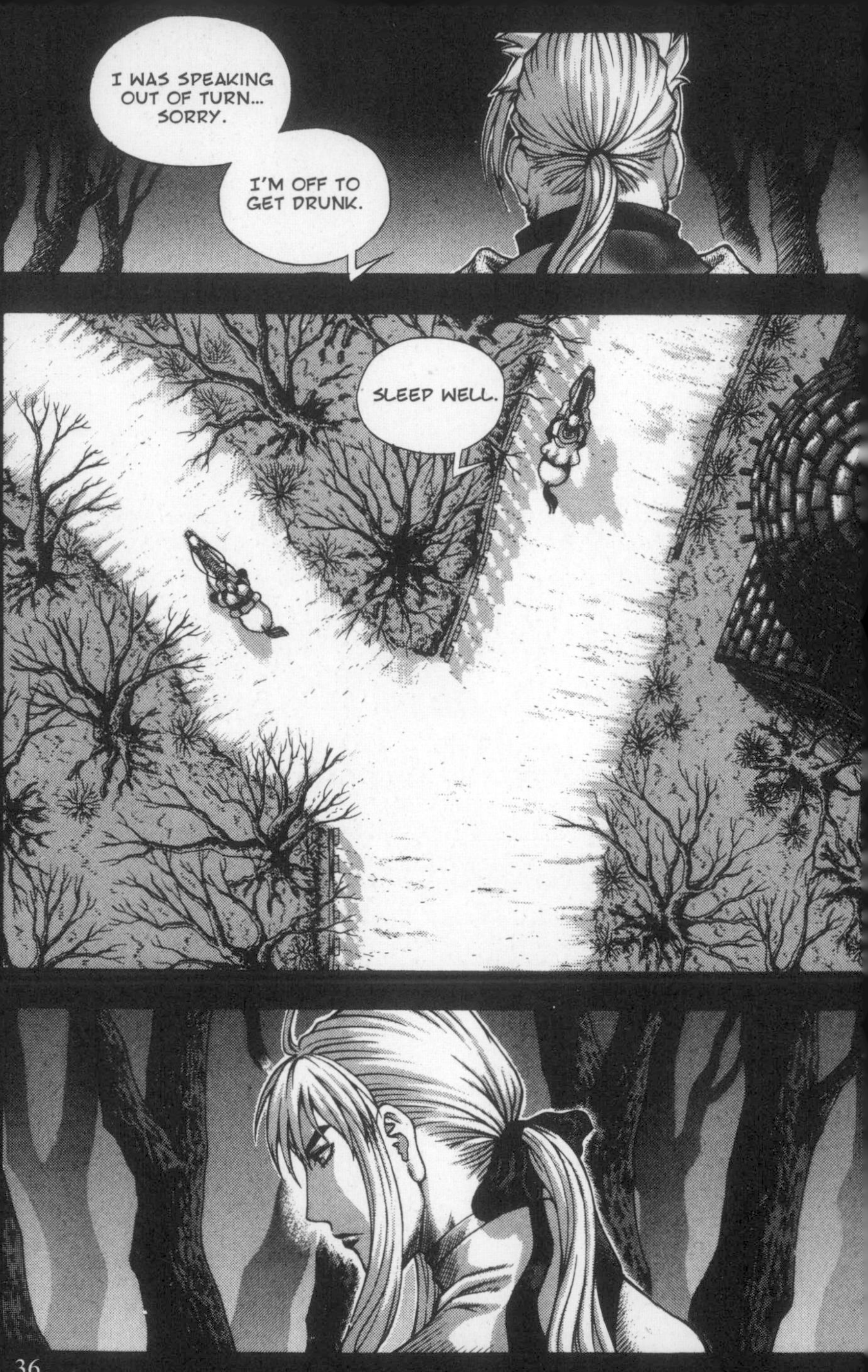
I WAS SPEAKING OUT OF TURN... SORRY.
I'M OFF TO GET DRUNK.
SLEEP WELL.

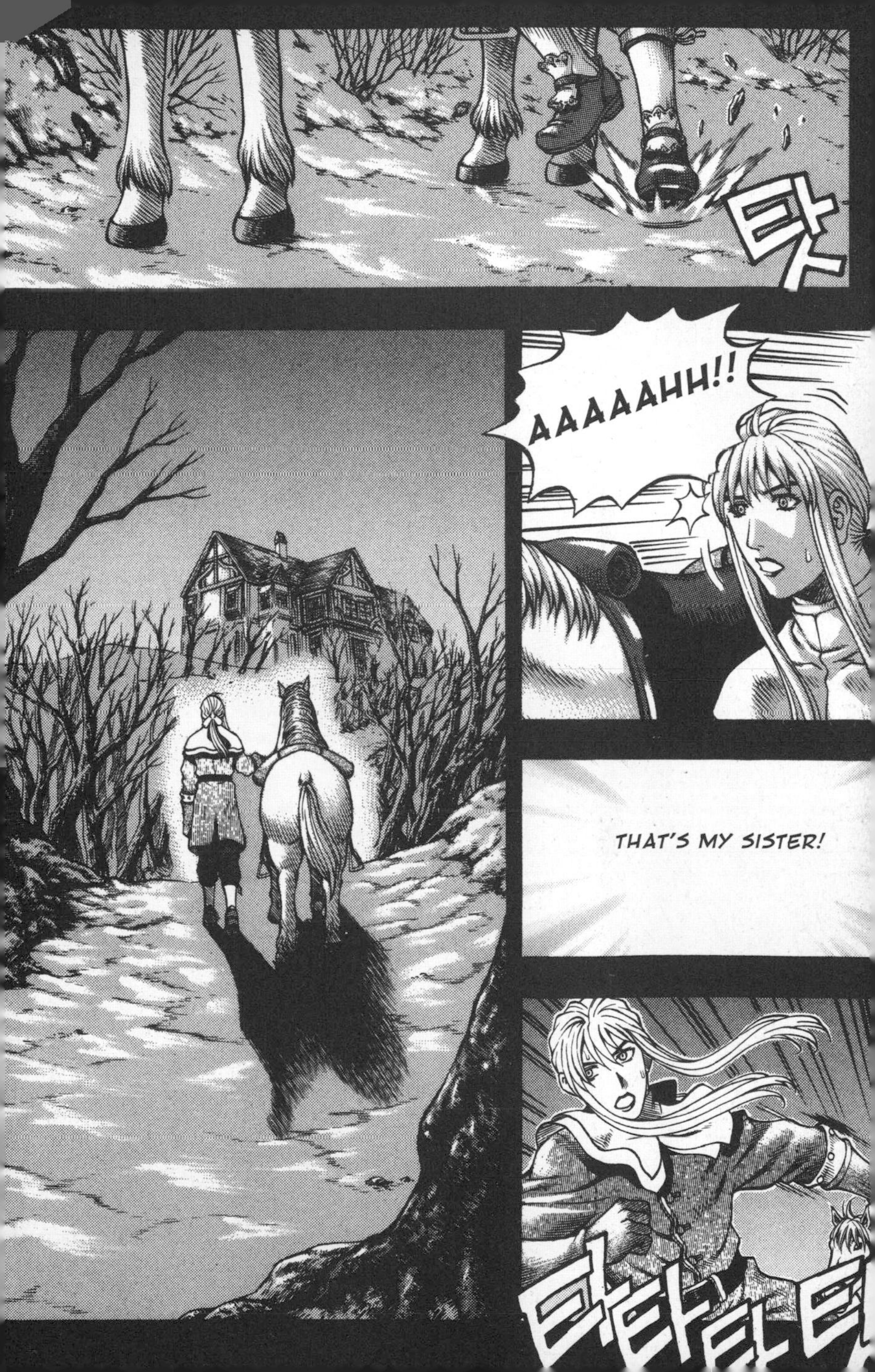
탁
AAAAAHH!!
THAT'S MY SISTER!

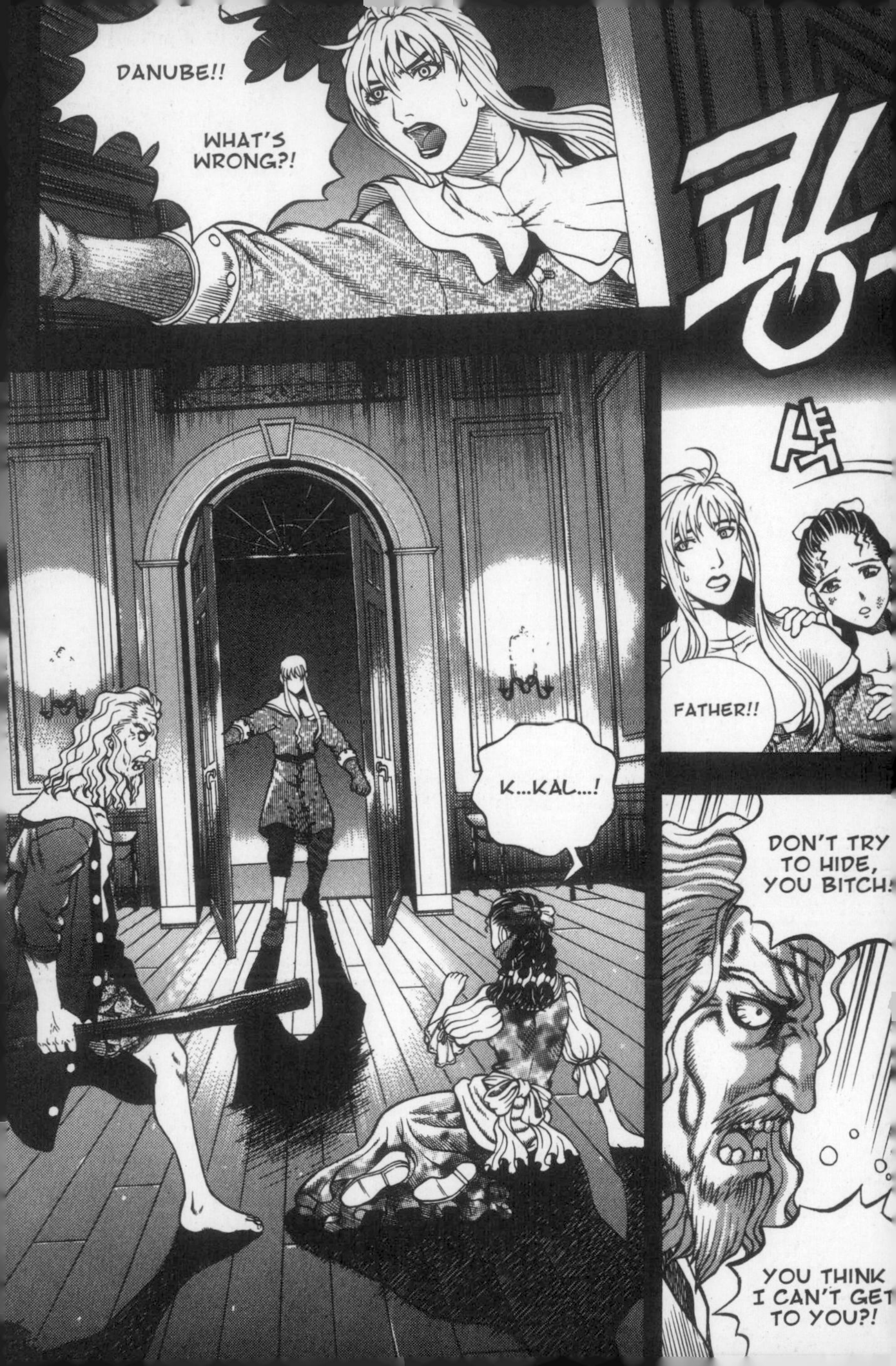
DANUBE!!
WHAT'S WRONG?!
쾅
K...KAL...!
슥
FATHER!!
DON'T TRY TO HIDE, YOU BITCH!
YOU THINK I CAN'T GET TO YOU?!

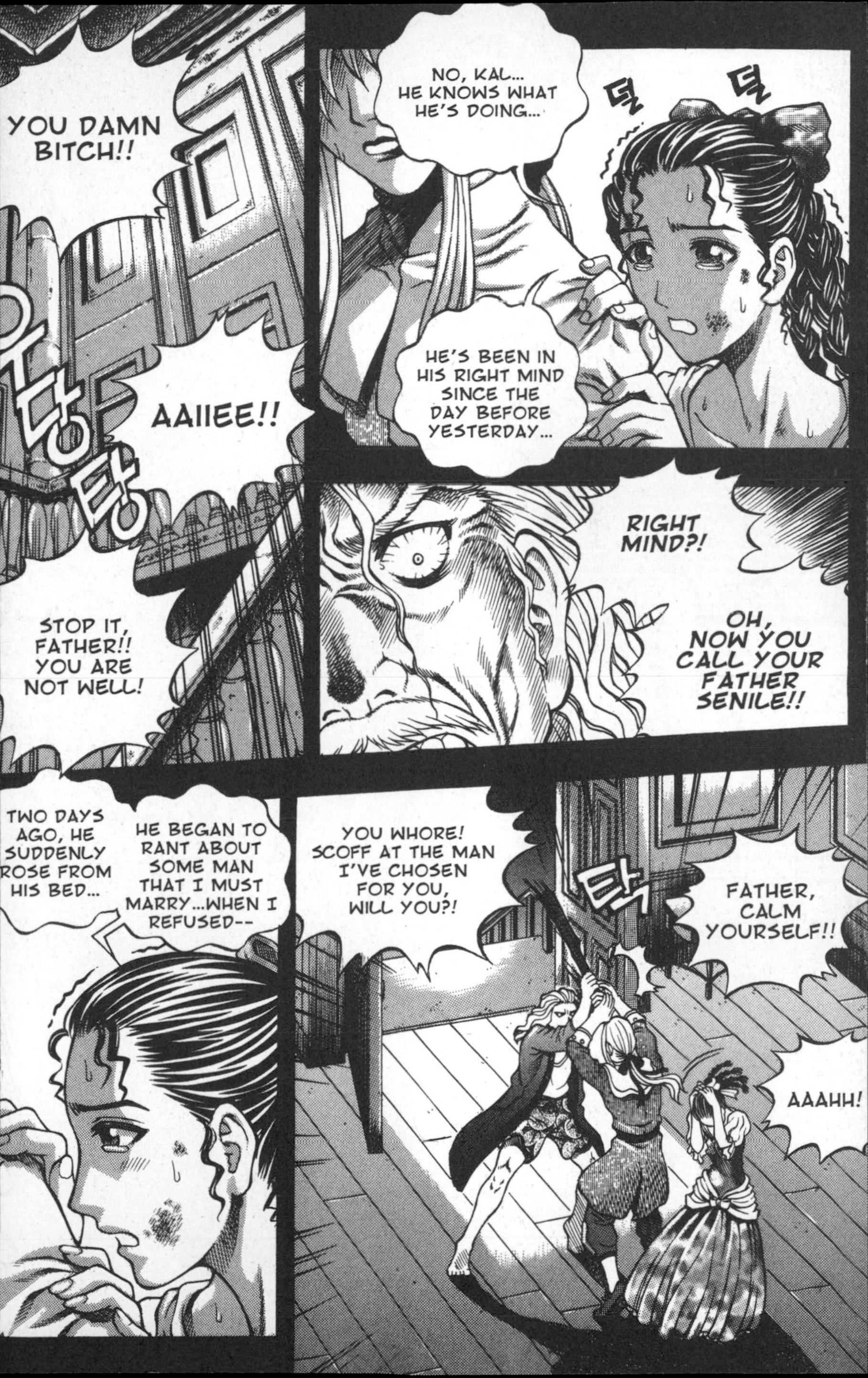
YOU DAMN BITCH!!
당탕
AAIIEE!!
STOP IT, FATHER!! YOU ARE NOT WELL!
NO, KAL... HE KNOWS WHAT HE'S DOING...
덜 덜
HE'S BEEN IN HIS RIGHT MIND SINCE THE DAY BEFORE YESTERDAY...
RIGHT MIND?!
OH, NOW YOU CALL YOUR FATHER SENILE!!
TWO DAYS AGO, HE SUDDENLY ROSE FROM HIS BED...
HE BEGAN TO RANT ABOUT SOME MAN THAT I MUST MARRY...WHEN I REFUSED--
YOU WHORE! SCOFF AT THE MAN I'VE CHOSEN FOR YOU, WILL YOU?!
탁
FATHER, CALM YOURSELF!!
AAAHH!

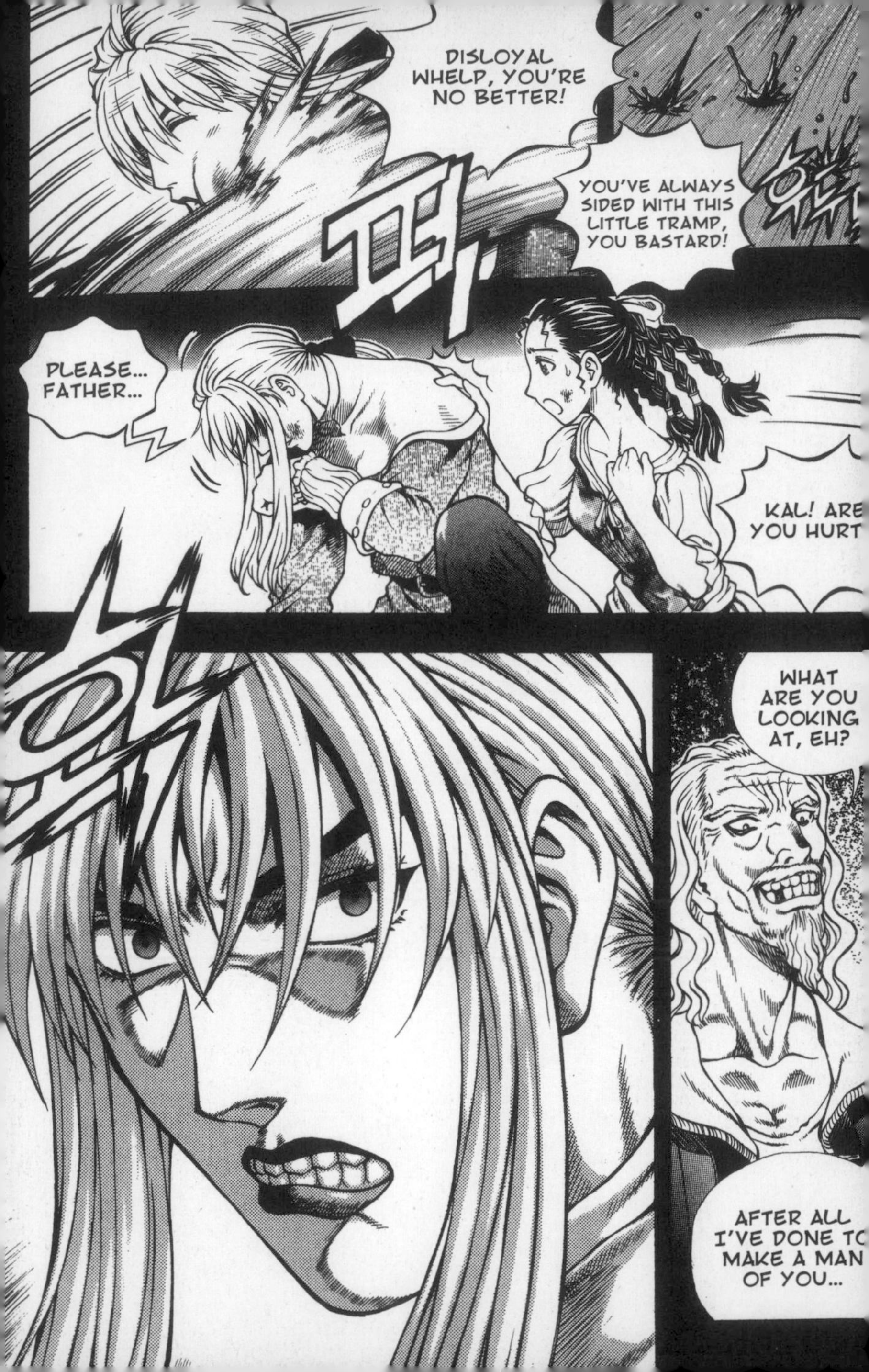
DISLOYAL WHELP, YOU'RE NO BETTER!
YOU'VE ALWAYS SIDED WITH THIS LITTLE TRAMP, YOU BASTARD!
PLEASE... FATHER...
KAL! ARE YOU HURT
WHAT ARE YOU LOOKING AT, EH?
AFTER ALL I'VE DONE TO MAKE A MAN OF YOU...

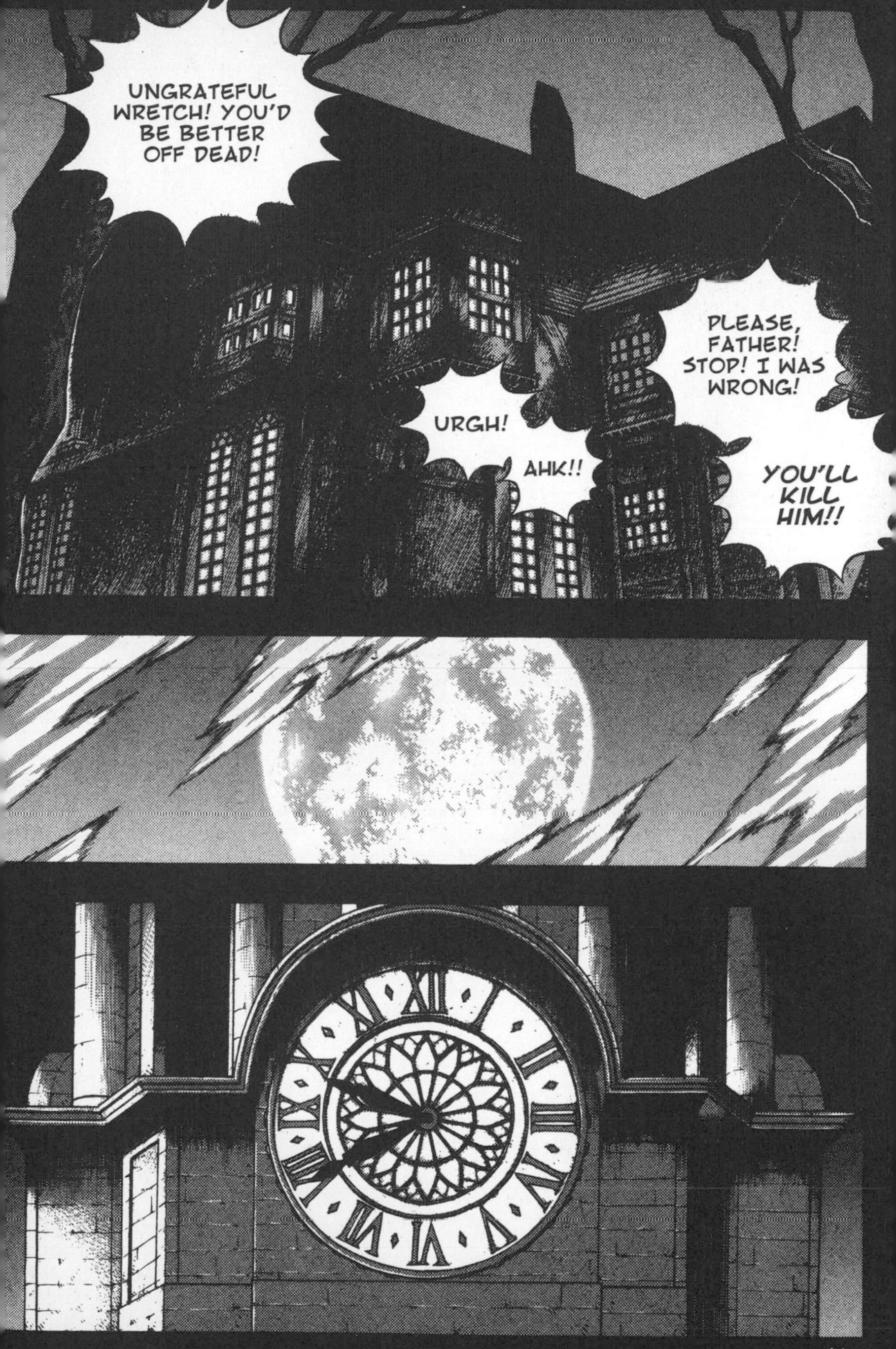
UNGRATEFUL WRETCH! YOU'D BE BETTER OFF DEAD!
URGH!
AHK!!
PLEASE, FATHER! STOP! I WAS WRONG!
YOU'LL KILL HIM!!

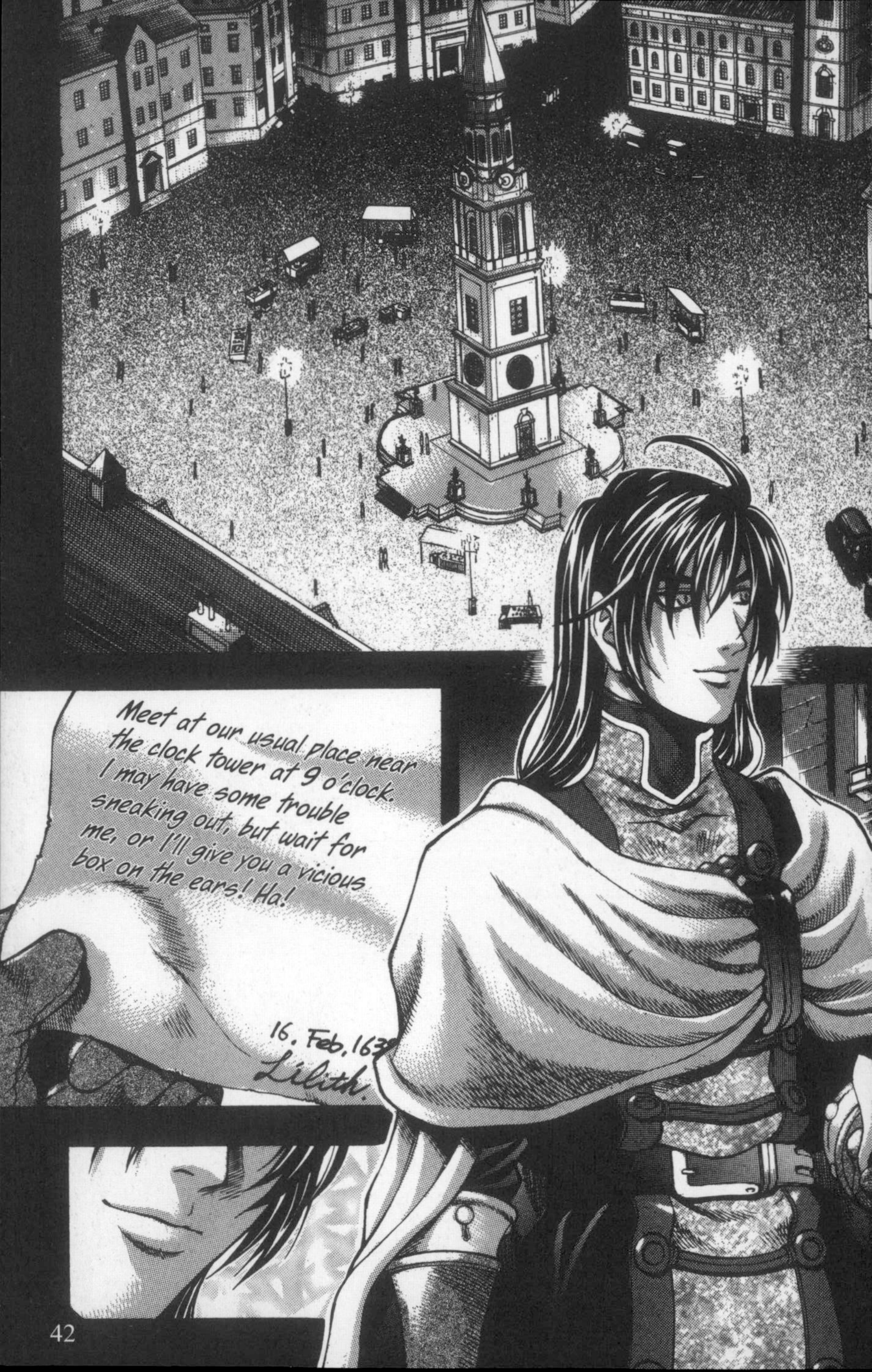
Meet at our usual place near the clock tower at 9 o'clock. I may have some trouble sneaking out, but wait for me, or I'll give you a vicious box on the ears! Ha!
16. Feb. 1639
Lilith.

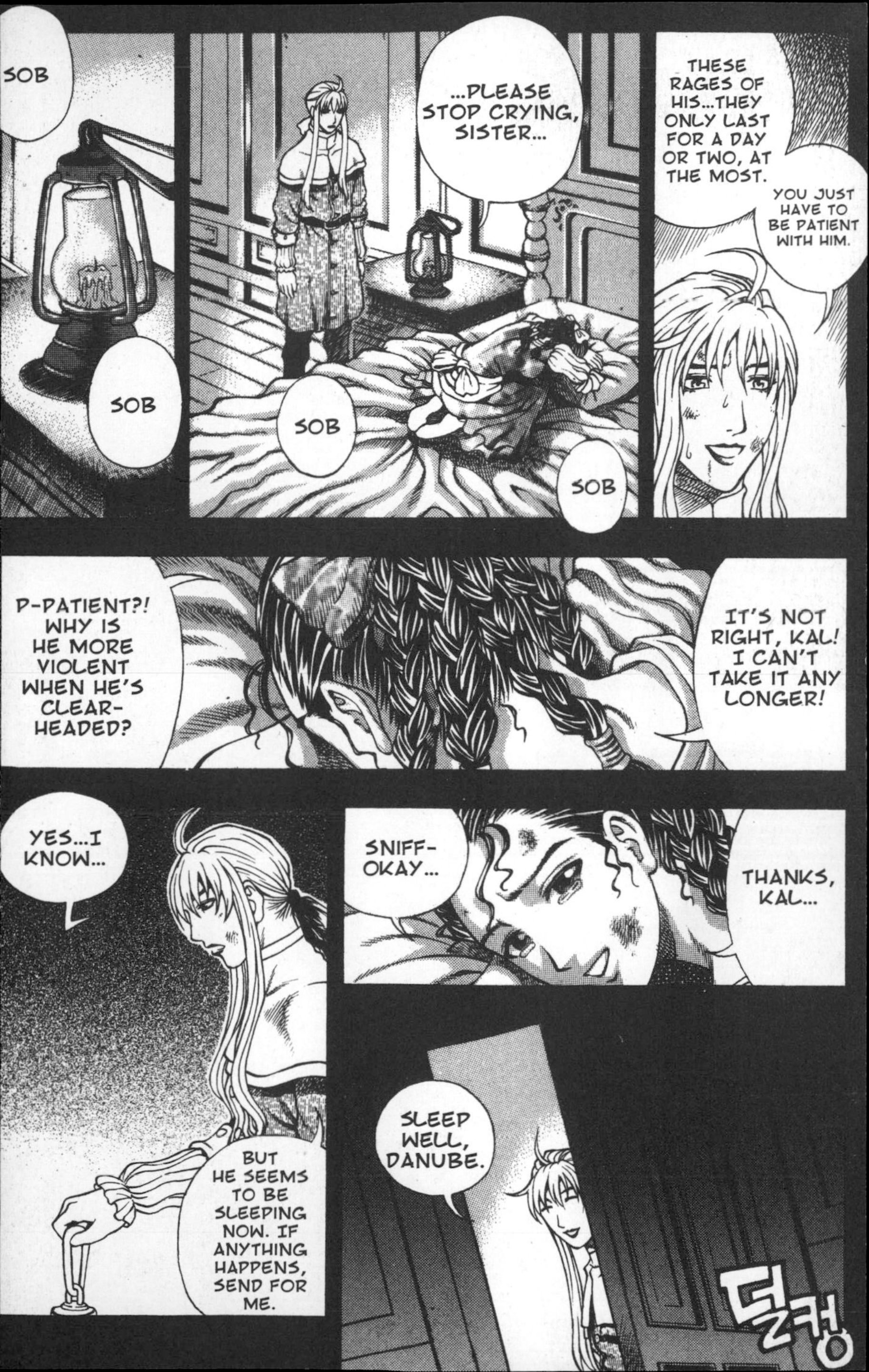
SOB
SOB
...PLEASE STOP CRYING, SISTER...
SOB
SOB
THESE RAGES OF HIS...THEY ONLY LAST FOR A DAY OR TWO, AT THE MOST.
YOU JUST HAVE TO BE PATIENT WITH HIM.
P-PATIENT?! WHY IS HE MORE VIOLENT WHEN HE'S CLEAR-HEADED?
IT'S NOT RIGHT, KAL! I CAN'T TAKE IT ANY LONGER!
YES...I KNOW...
BUT HE SEEMS TO BE SLEEPING NOW. IF ANYTHING HAPPENS, SEND FOR ME.
SNIFF-OKAY...
THANKS, KAL...
SLEEP WELL, DANUBE.
덜컹

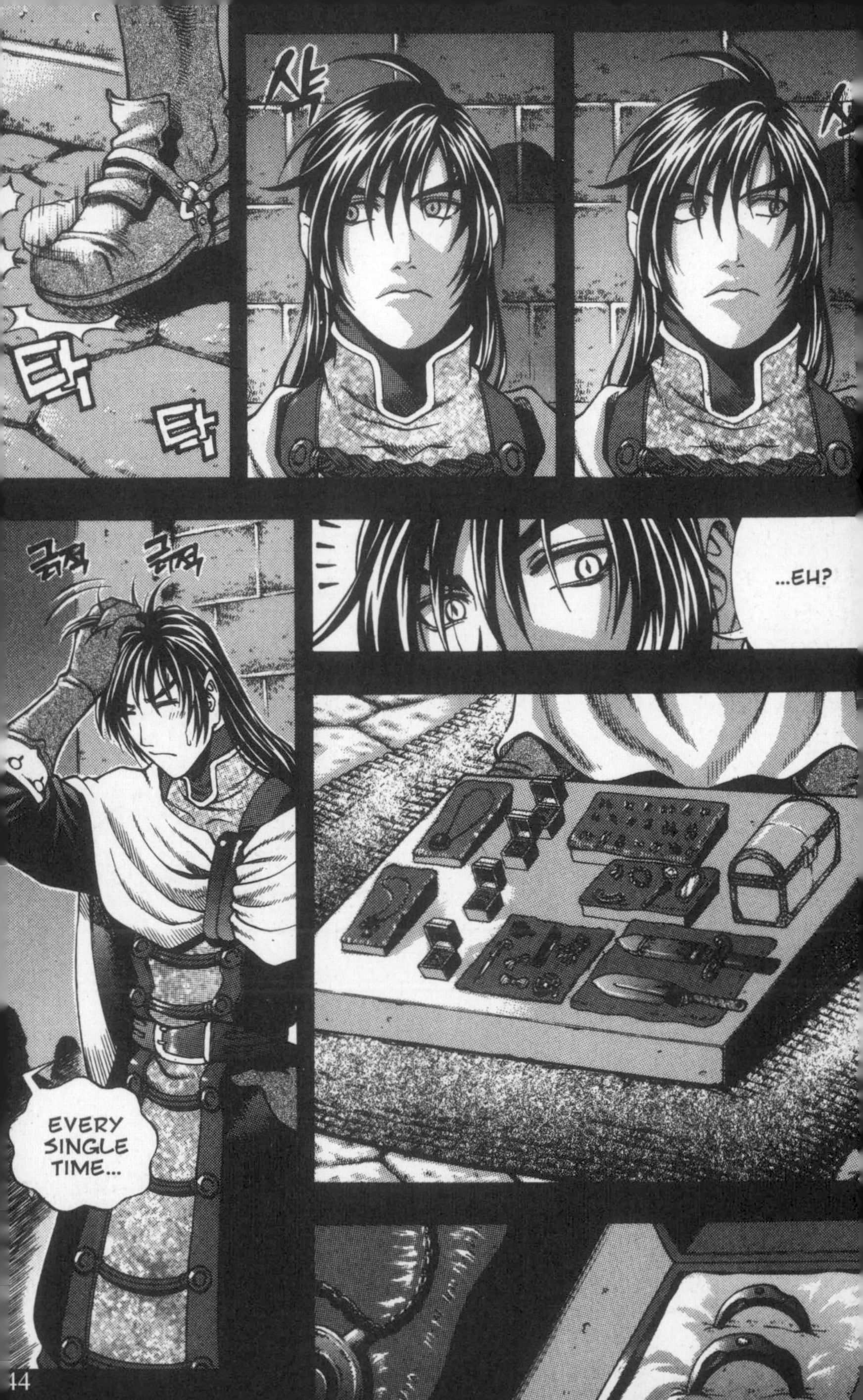

탁
탁
샥
긁적 긁적
EVERY SINGLE TIME...
...EH?

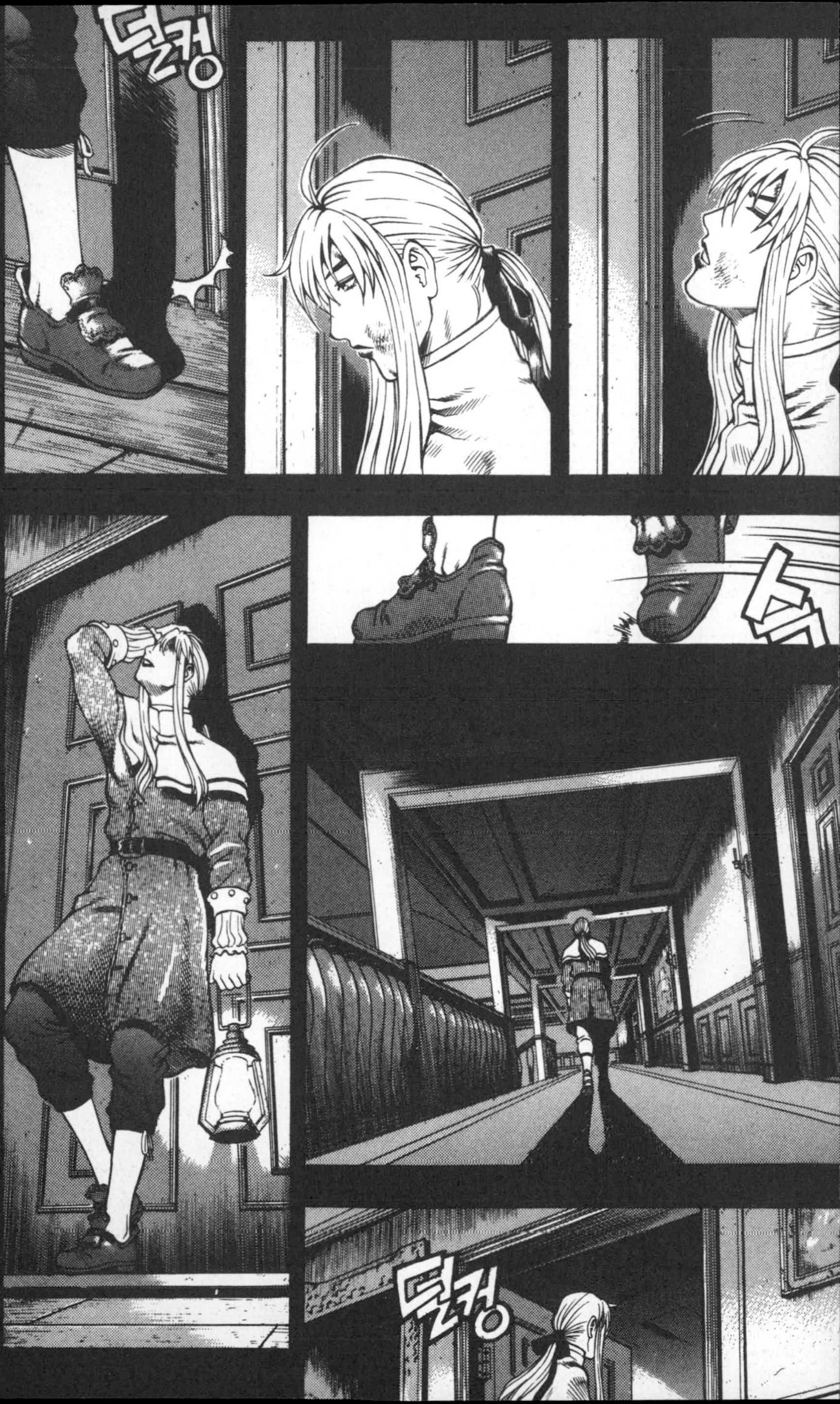
덜컹
슥
덜컹

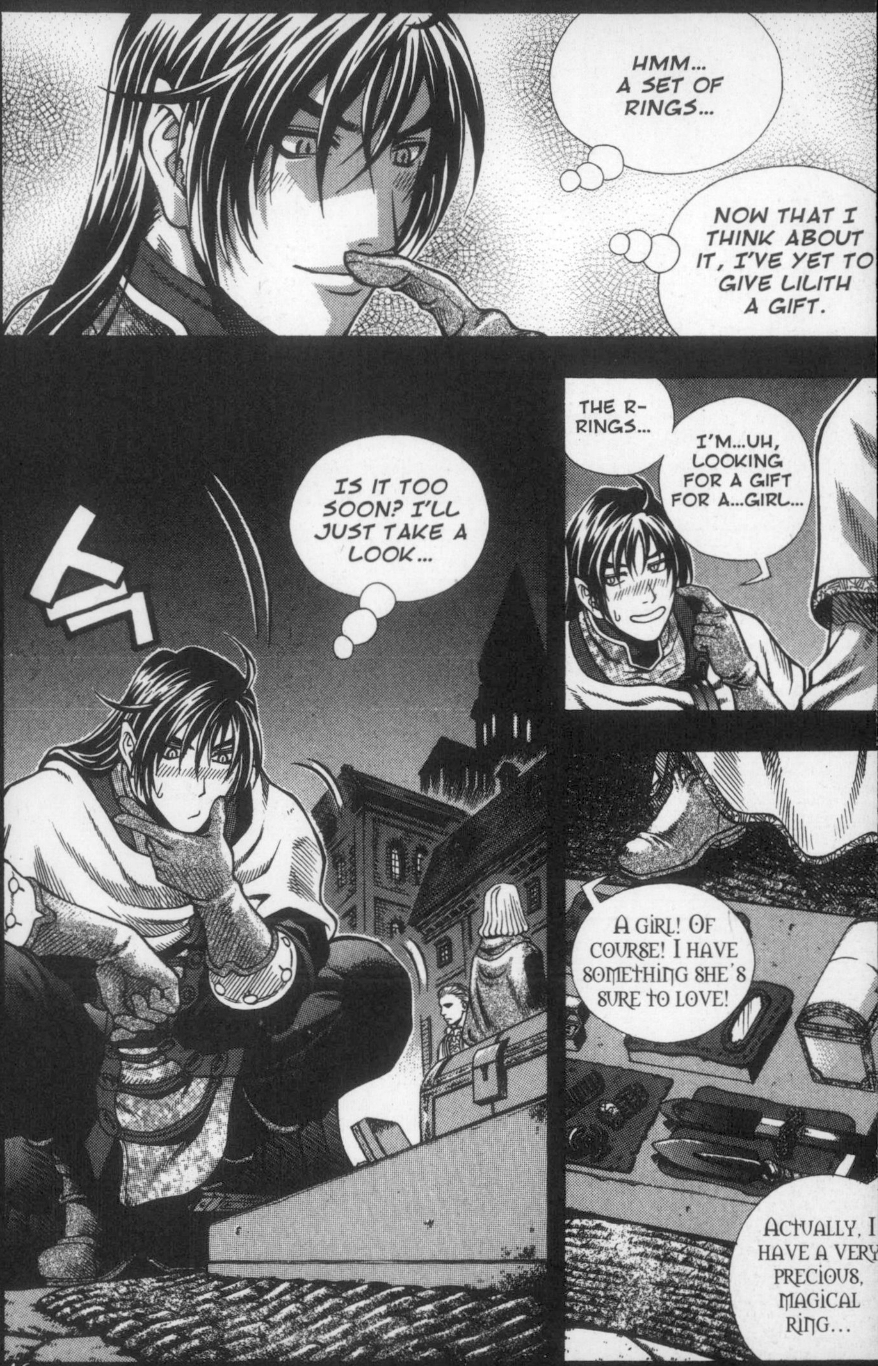
HMM... A SET OF RINGS...
NOW THAT I THINK ABOUT IT, I'VE YET TO GIVE LILITH A GIFT.
IS IT TOO SOON? I'LL JUST TAKE A LOOK...
THE R-RINGS...
I'M...UH, LOOKING FOR A GIFT FOR A...GIRL...
A GIRL! OF COURSE! I HAVE SOMETHING SHE'S SURE TO LOVE!
ACTUALLY, I HAVE A VERY PRECIOUS, MAGICAL RING...

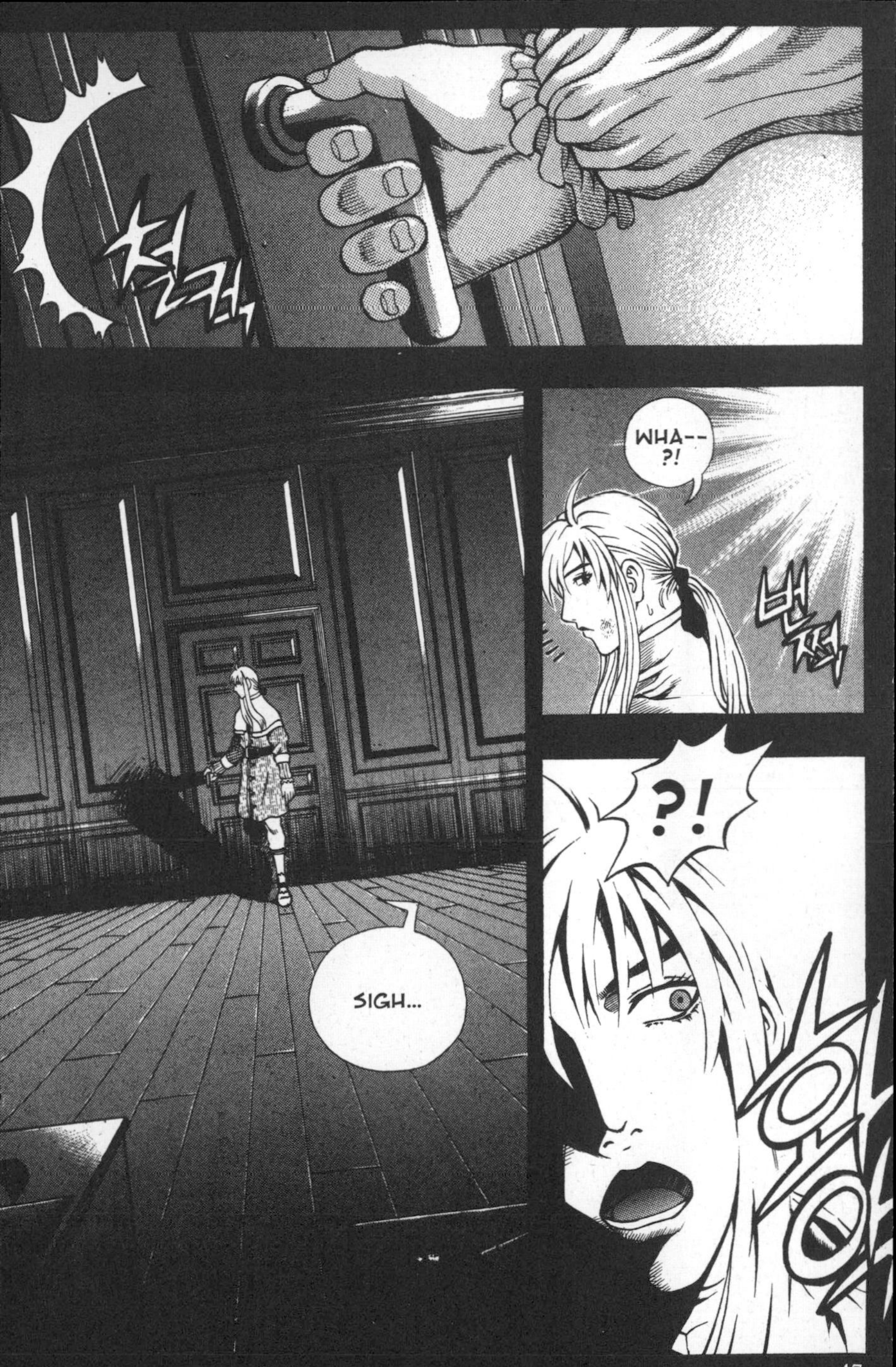
SIGH...
WHA-- ?!
?!

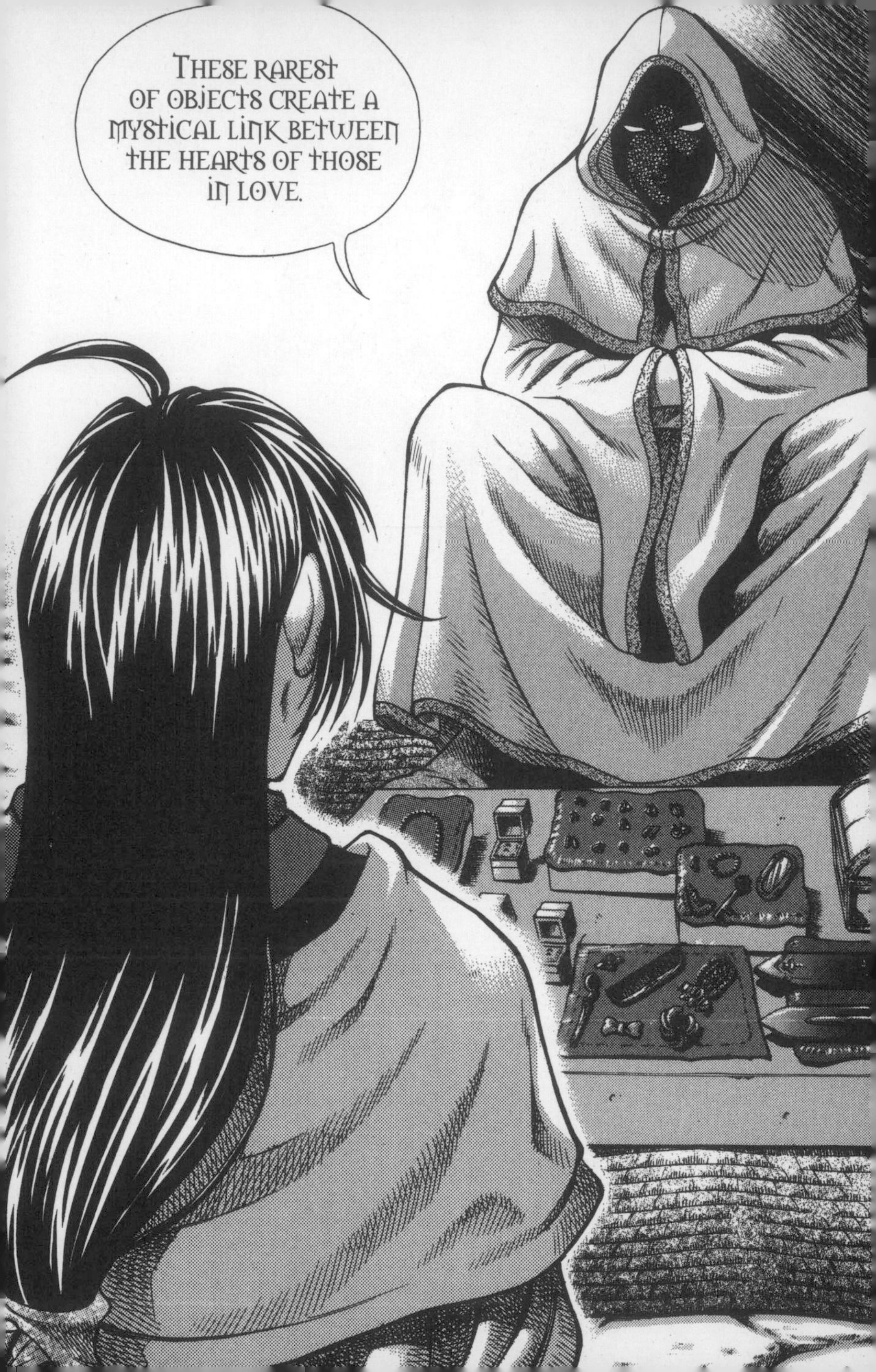
THESE RARESt OF OBJECtS CREAtE A MYStICAL LINK BEtWEEN tHE HEARtS OF tHOSE IN LOVE.

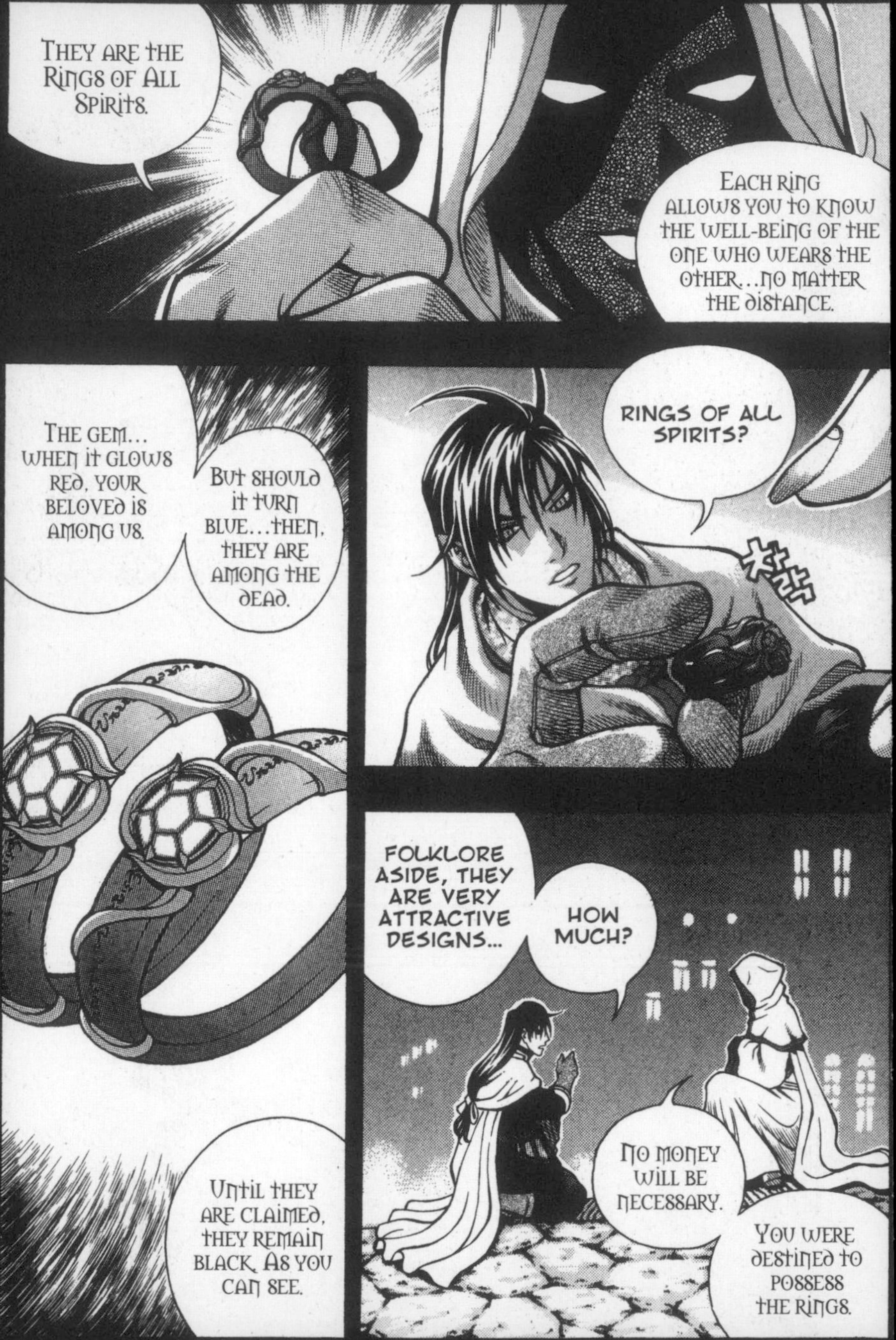
THEY ARE THE RINGS OF ALL SPIRITS.
EACH RING ALLOWS YOU TO KNOW THE WELL-BEING OF THE ONE WHO WEARS THE OTHER...NO MATTER THE DISTANCE.
THE GEM... WHEN IT GLOWS RED, YOUR BELOVED IS AMONG US.
BUT SHOULD IT TURN BLUE...THEN, THEY ARE AMONG THE DEAD.
UNTIL THEY ARE CLAIMED, THEY REMAIN BLACK. AS YOU CAN SEE.
RINGS OF ALL SPIRITS?
FOLKLORE ASIDE, THEY ARE VERY ATTRACTIVE DESIGNS...
HOW MUCH?
NO MONEY WILL BE NECESSARY.
YOU WERE DESTINED TO POSSESS THE RINGS.

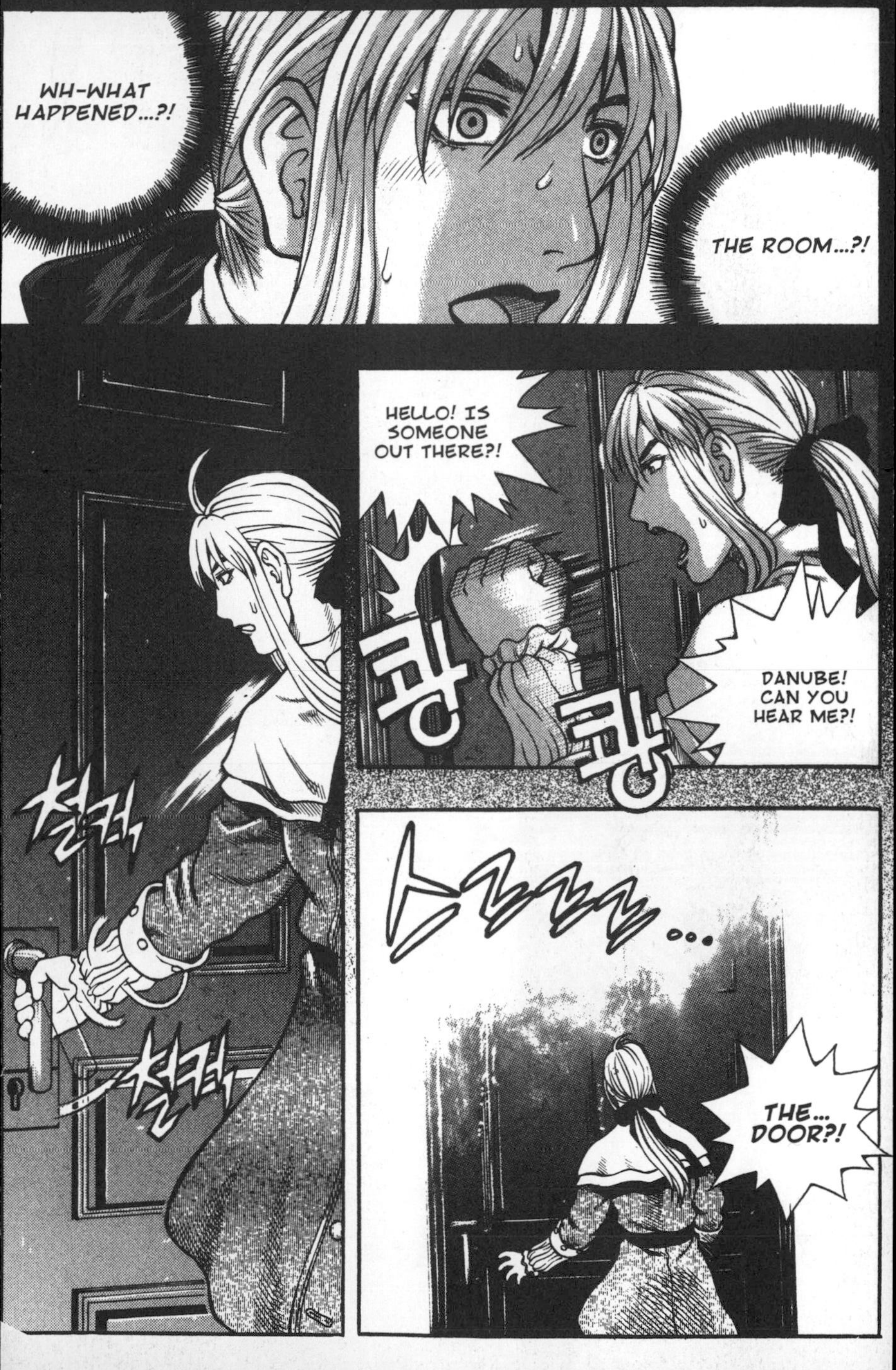
WH-WHAT HAPPENED...?!
THE ROOM...?!
철컥
철컥
HELLO! IS SOMEONE OUT THERE?!
쾅
쾅
DANUBE! CAN YOU HEAR ME?!
스르르르...
THE... DOOR?!

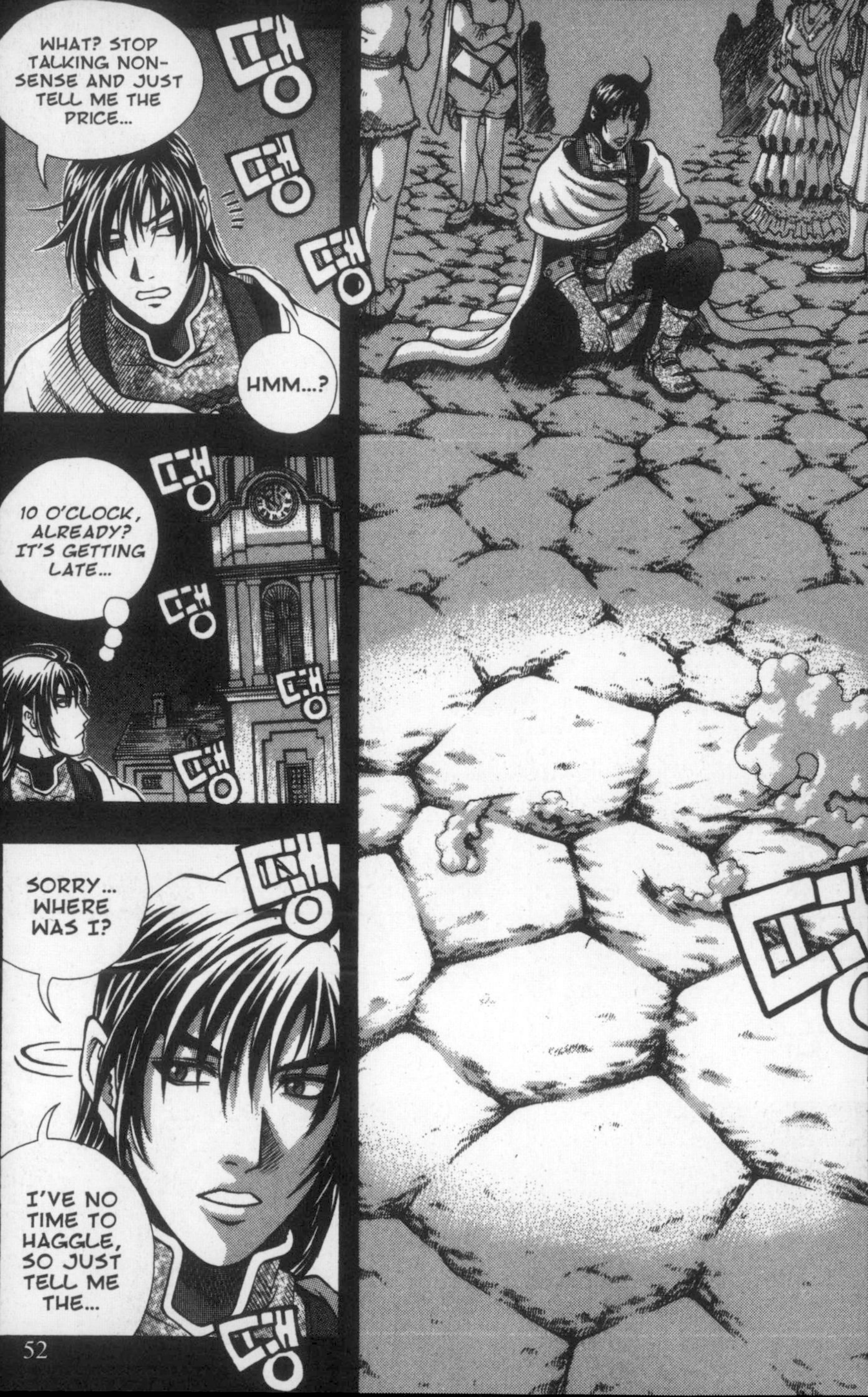
WHAT? STOP TALKING NON-SENSE AND JUST TELL ME THE PRICE...
HMM...?
10 O'CLOCK, ALREADY? IT'S GETTING LATE...
SORRY... WHERE WAS I?
I'VE NO TIME TO HAGGLE, SO JUST TELL ME THE...

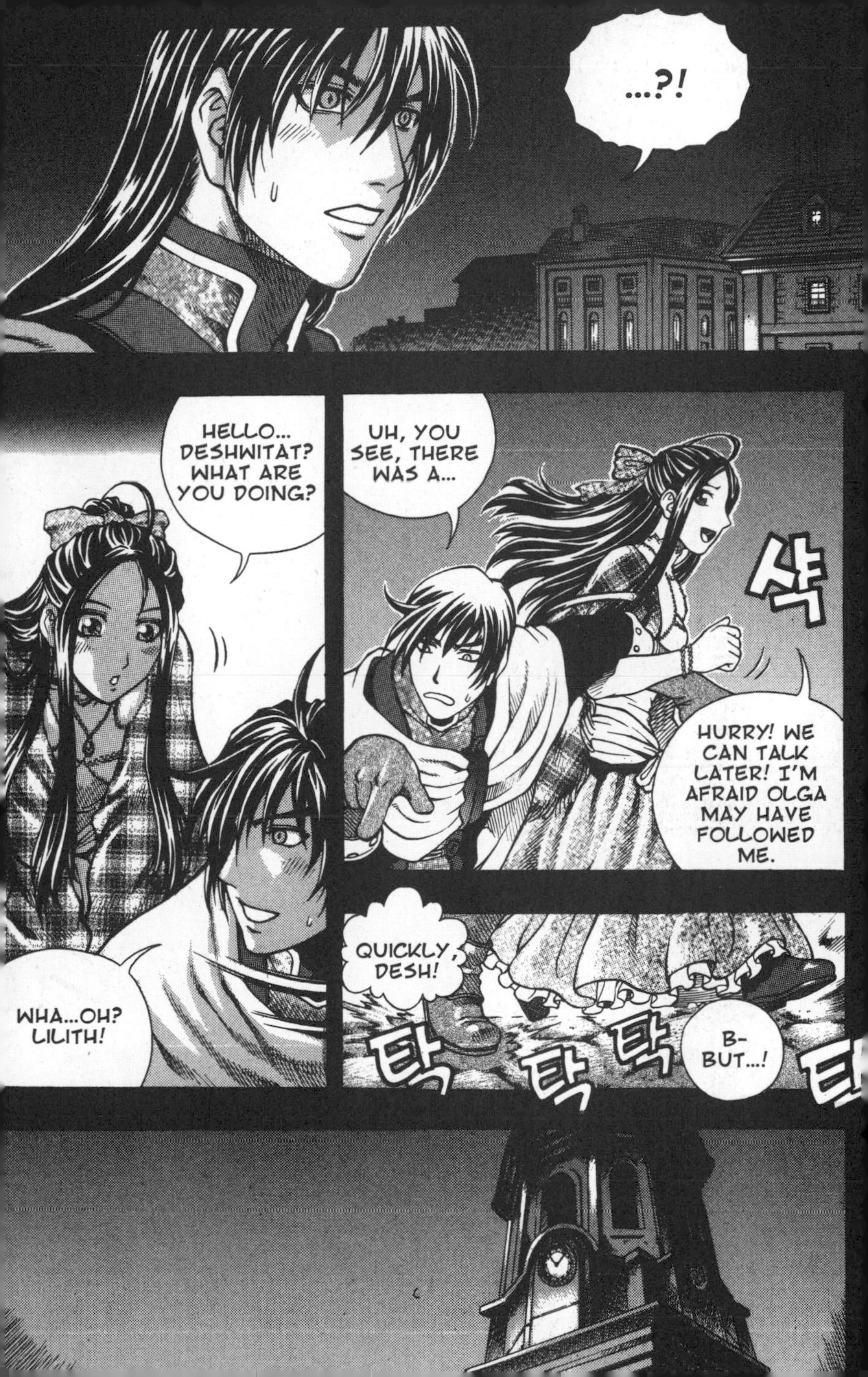
...?!
HELLO... DESHWITAT? WHAT ARE YOU DOING?
WHA...OH? LILITH!
UH, YOU SEE, THERE WAS A...
샥
HURRY! WE CAN TALK LATER! I'M AFRAID OLGA MAY HAVE FOLLOWED ME.
QUICKLY, DESH!
탁 탁 탁
B- BUT...!

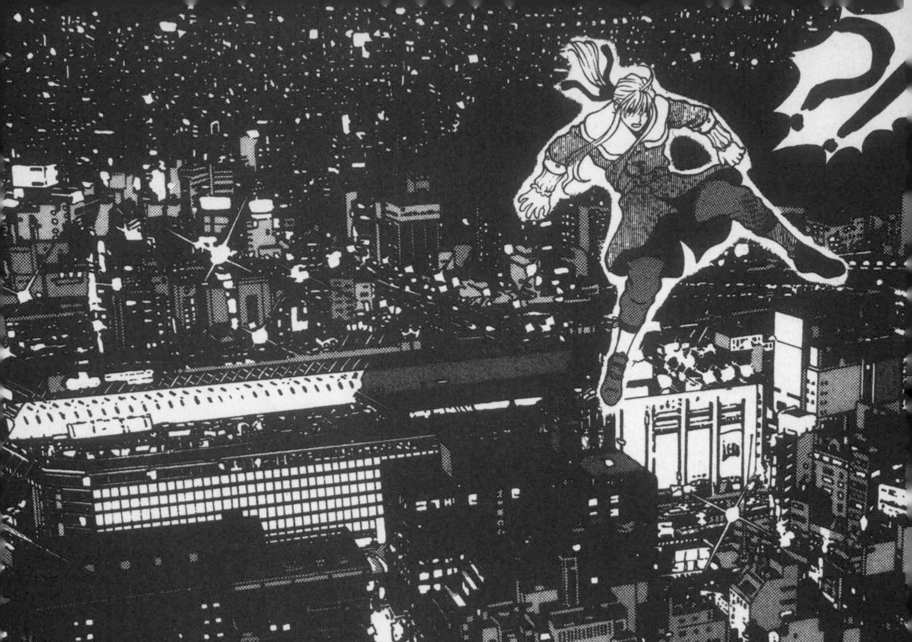
?!

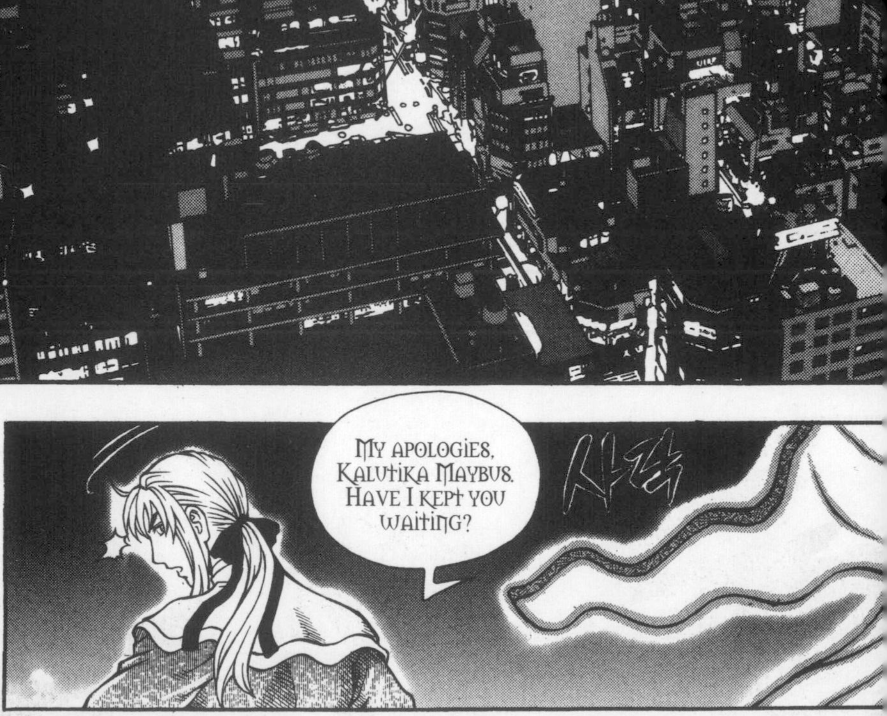
MY APOLOGIES, KALUTIKA MAYBUS. HAVE I KEPT YOU WAITING?

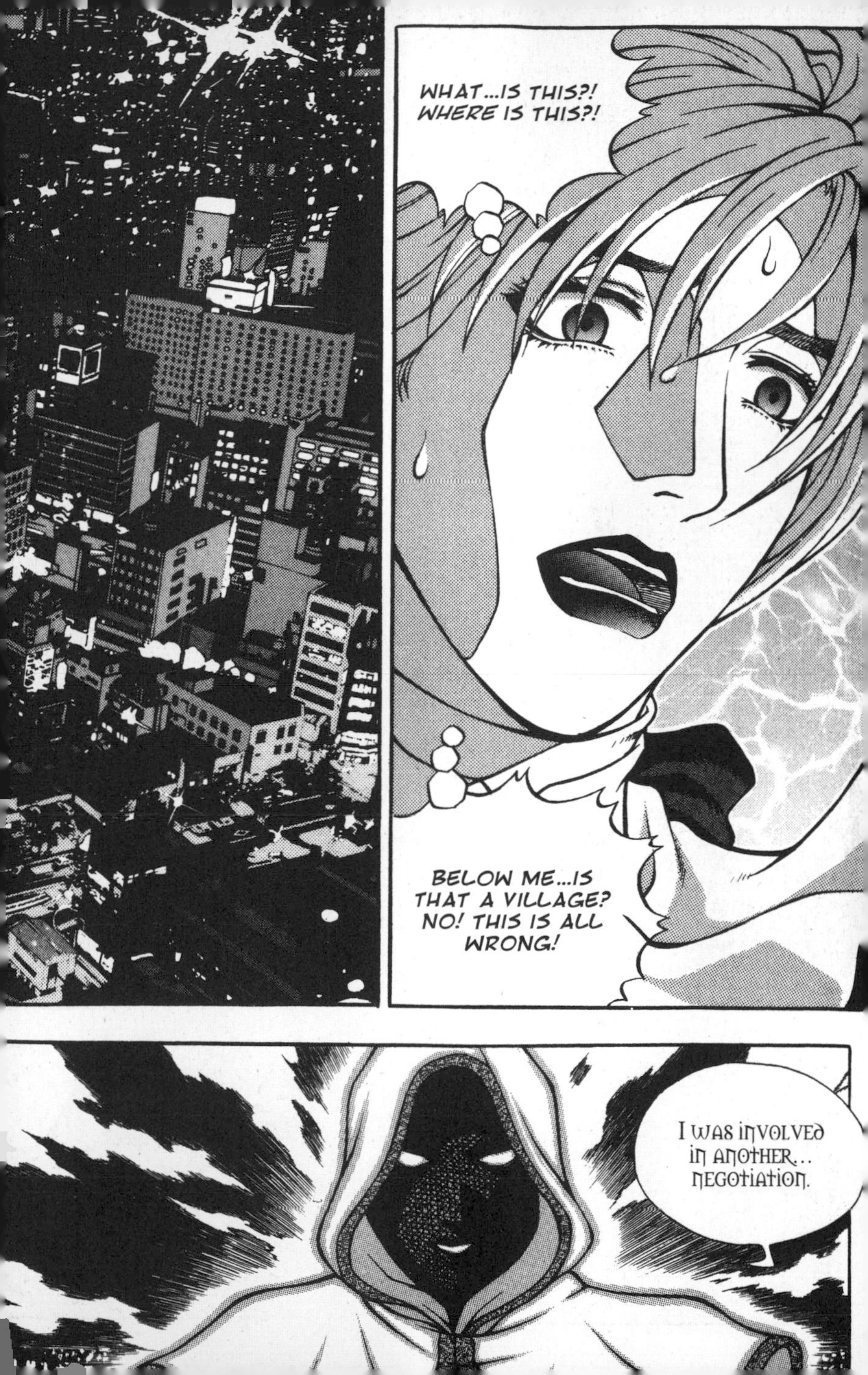
WHAT...IS THIS?! WHERE IS THIS?!
BELOW ME...IS THAT A VILLAGE? NO! THIS IS ALL WRONG!
I WAS INVOLVED IN ANOTHER... NEGOTIATION.

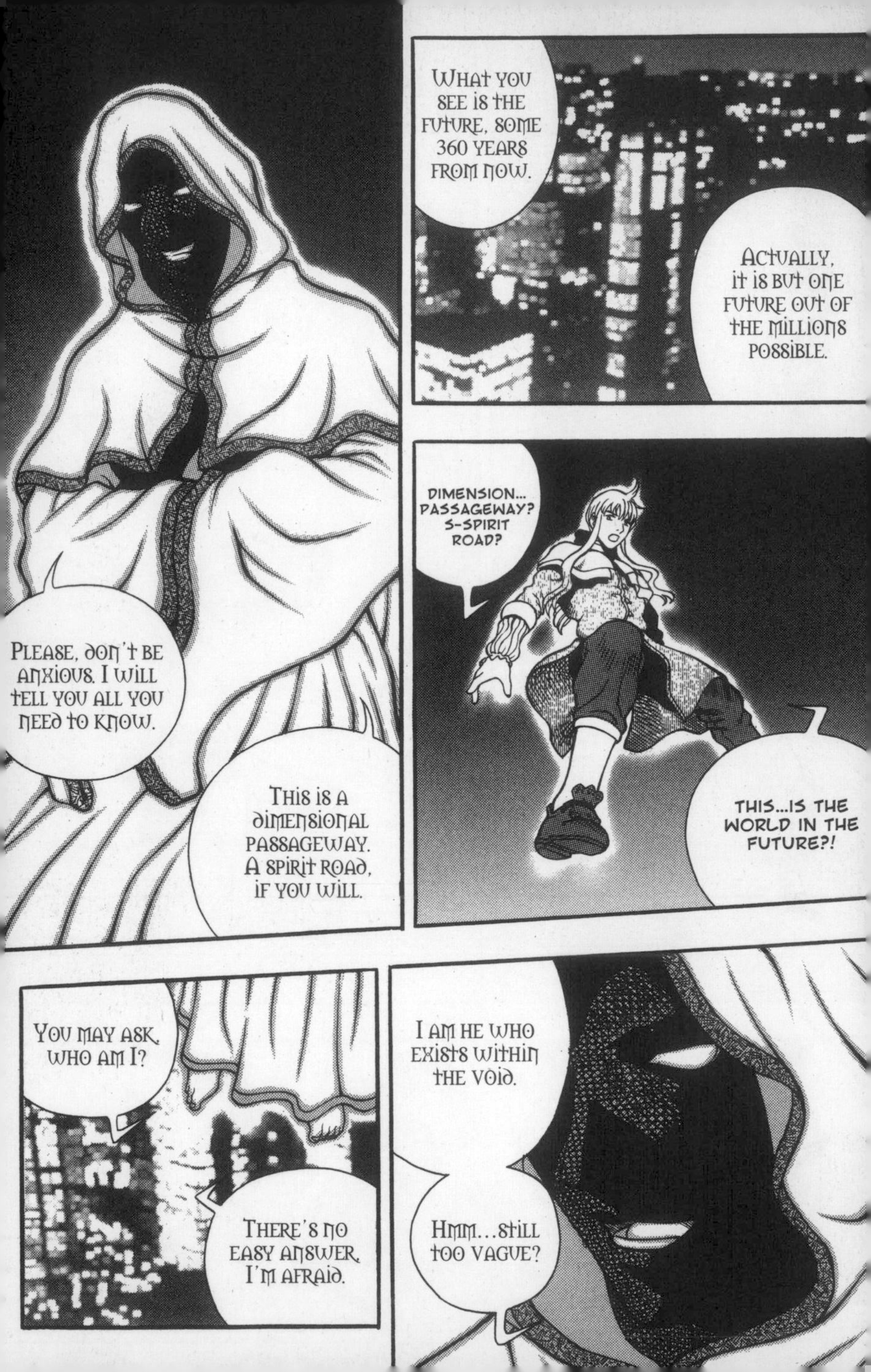
PLEASE, DON'T BE ANXIOUS. I WILL TELL YOU ALL YOU NEED TO KNOW.
THIS IS A DIMENSIONAL PASSAGEWAY. A SPIRIT ROAD, IF YOU WILL.
WHAT YOU SEE IS THE FUTURE, SOME 360 YEARS FROM NOW.
ACTUALLY, IT IS BUT ONE FUTURE OUT OF THE MILLIONS POSSIBLE.
DIMENSION... PASSAGEWAY? S-SPIRIT ROAD?
THIS...IS THE WORLD IN THE FUTURE?!
YOU MAY ASK, WHO AM I?
THERE'S NO EASY ANSWER, I'M AFRAID.
I AM HE WHO EXISTS WITHIN THE VOID.
HMM...STILL TOO VAGUE?

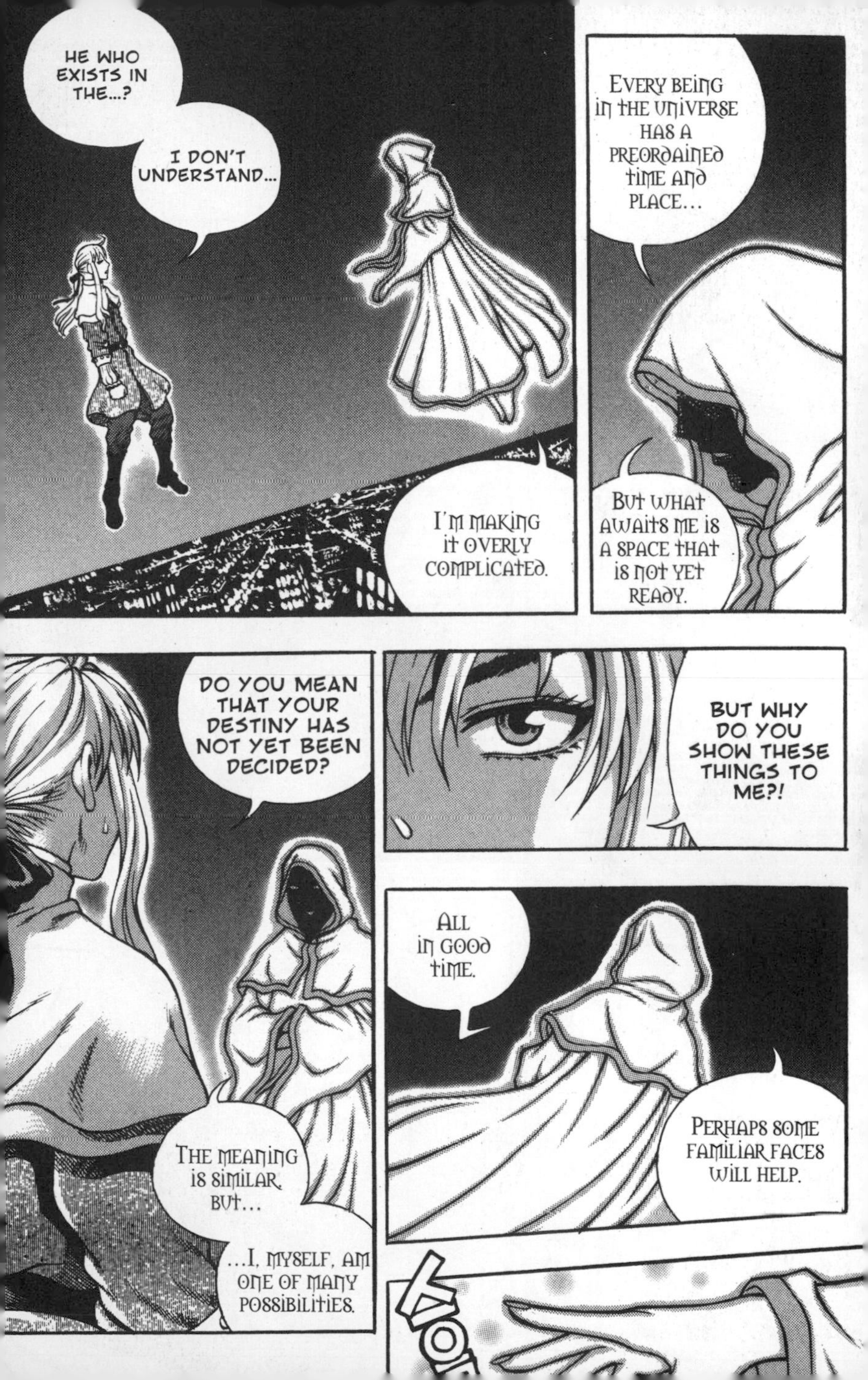
HE WHO EXISTS IN THE...?
I DON'T UNDERSTAND...
I'M MAKING IT OVERLY COMPLICATED.
EVERY BEING IN THE UNIVERSE HAS A PREORDAINED TIME AND PLACE...
BUT WHAT AWAITS ME IS A SPACE THAT IS NOT YET READY.
DO YOU MEAN THAT YOUR DESTINY HAS NOT YET BEEN DECIDED?
THE MEANING IS SIMILAR, BUT...
...I, MYSELF, AM ONE OF MANY POSSIBILITIES.
BUT WHY DO YOU SHOW THESE THINGS TO ME?!
ALL IN GOOD TIME.
PERHAPS SOME FAMILIAR FACES WILL HELP.

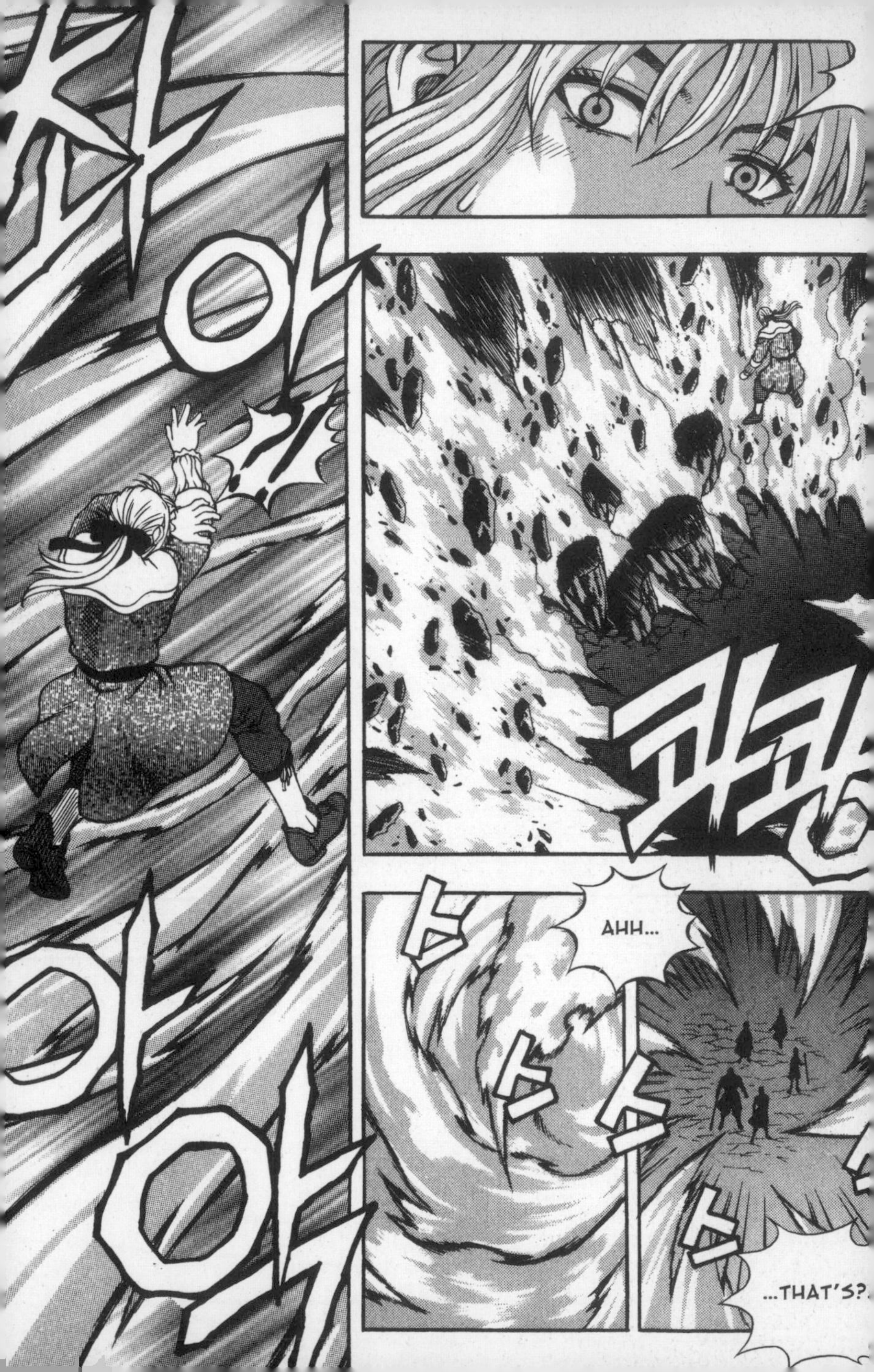
AHH...
...THAT'S?..

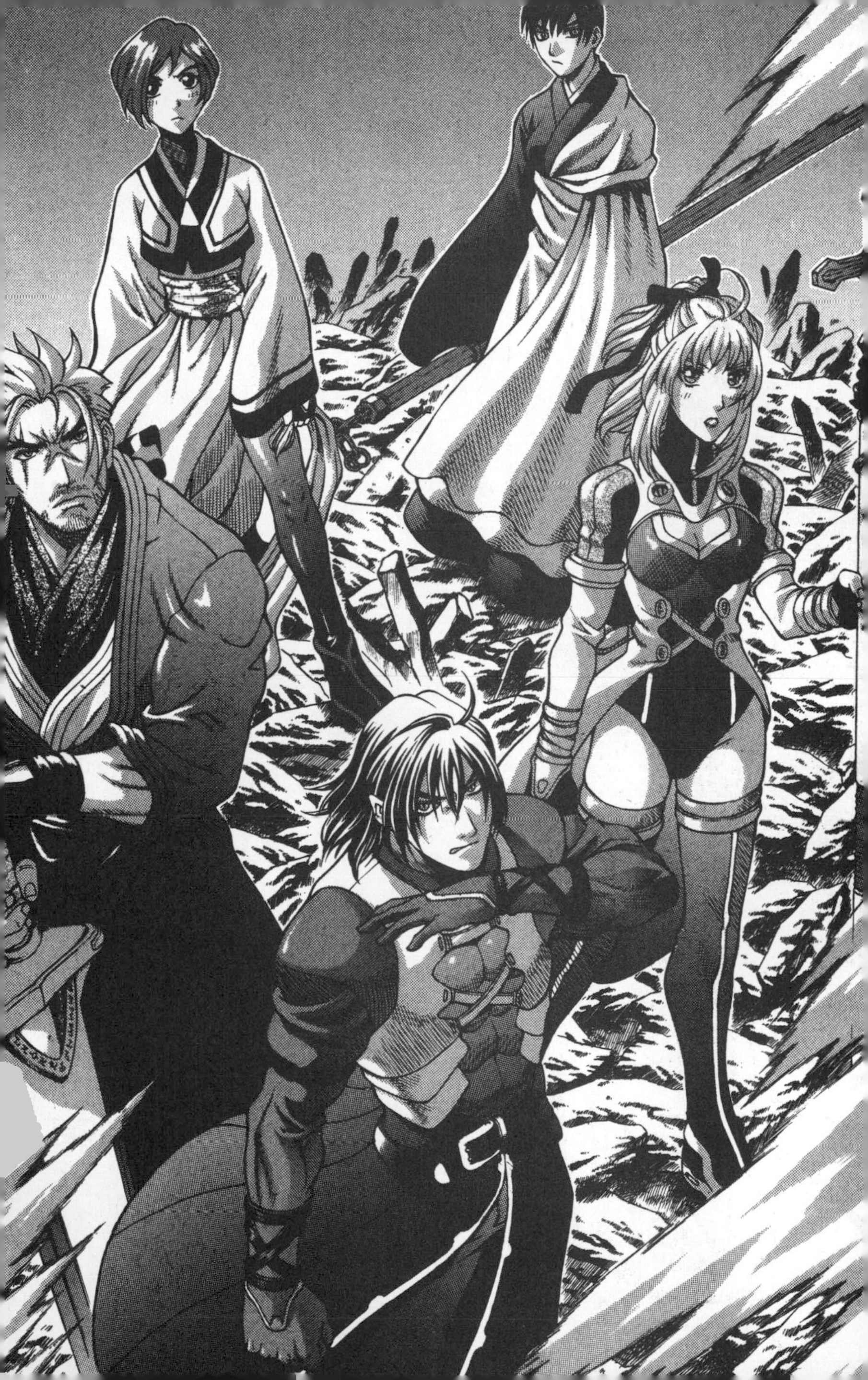

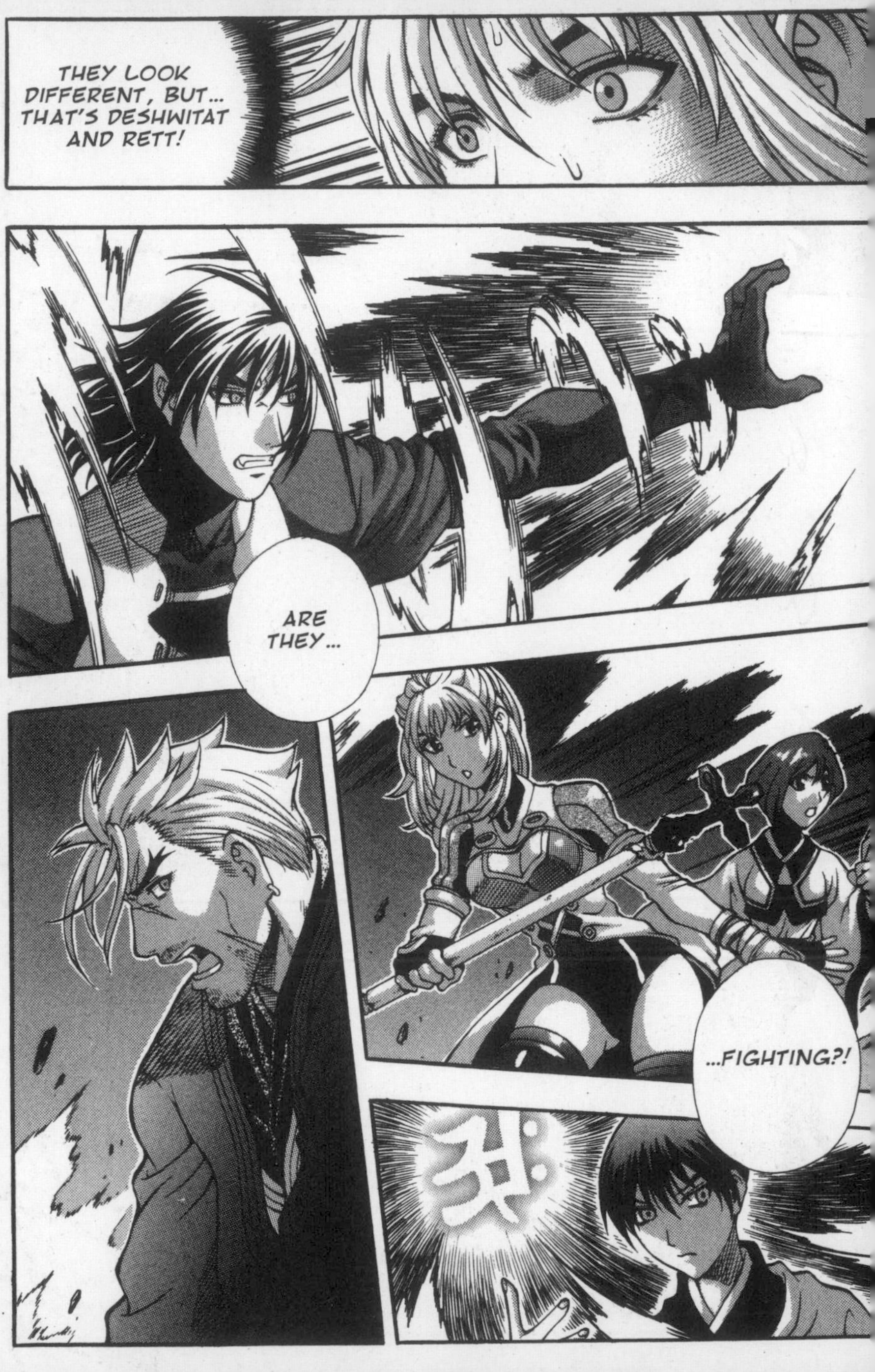
THEY LOOK DIFFERENT, BUT... THAT'S DESHWITAT AND RETT!
ARE THEY...
...FIGHTING?!

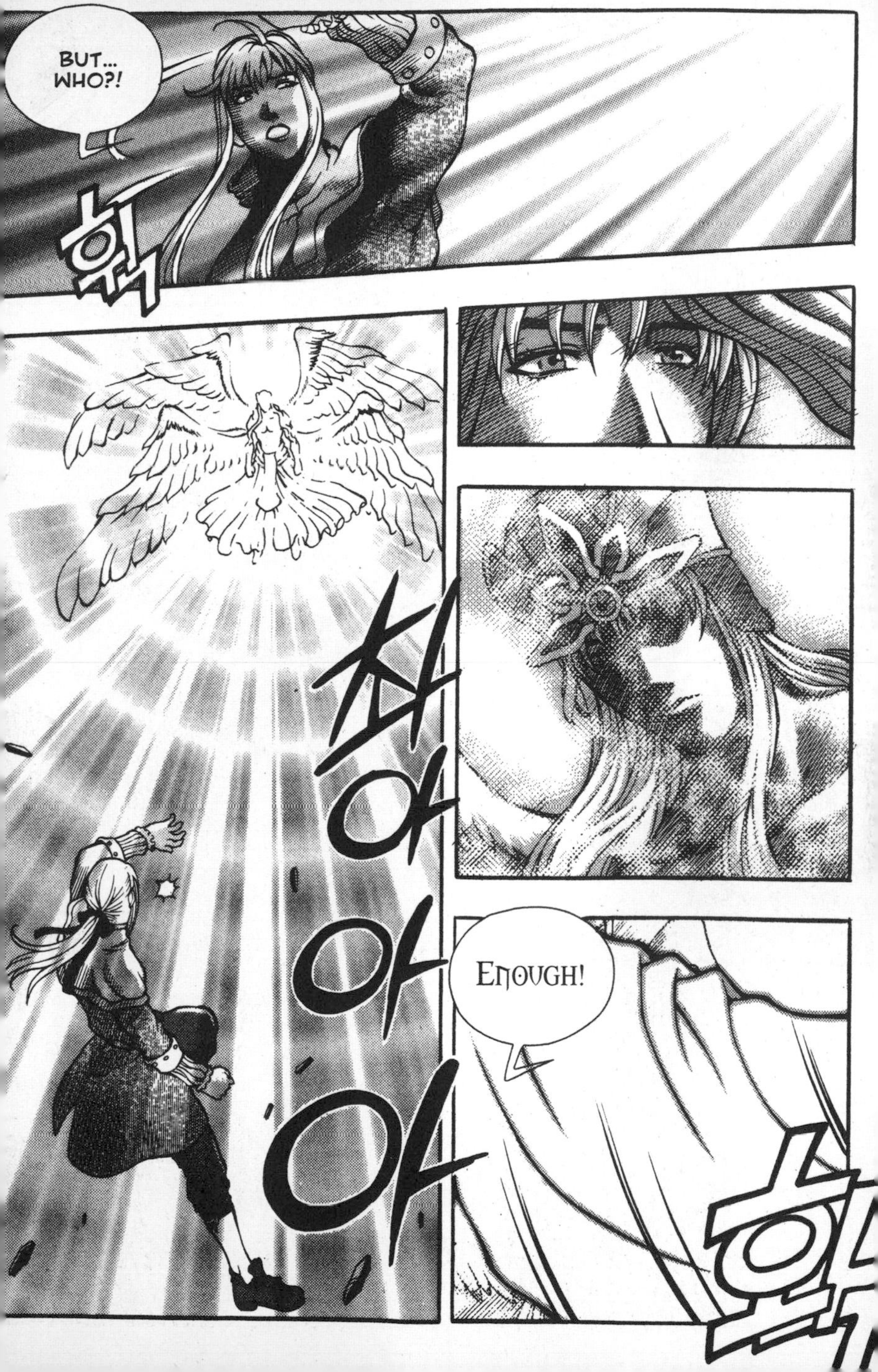

BUT... WHO?!
ENOUGH!

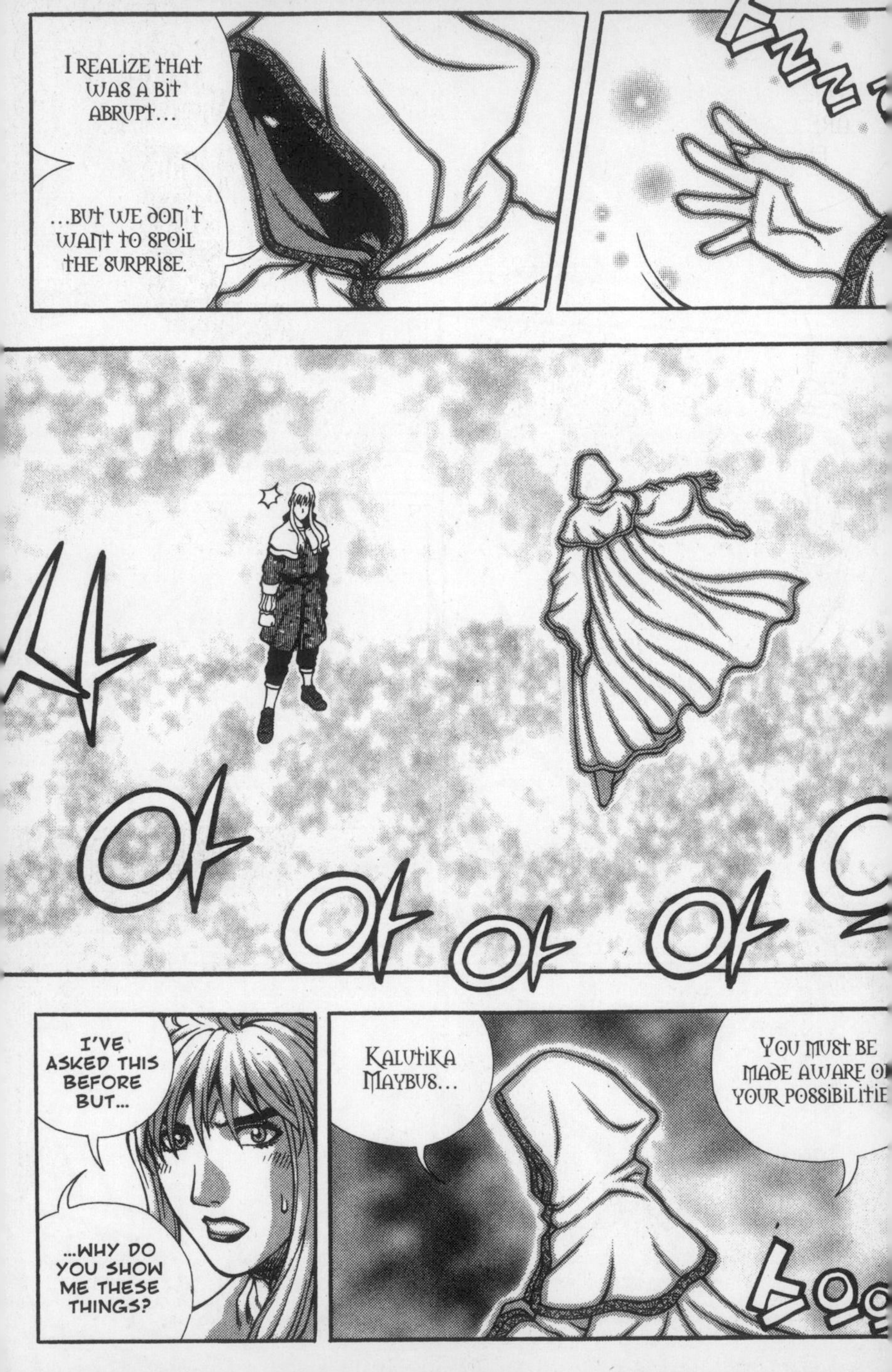
I REALIZE THAT WAS A BIT ABRUPT...
...BUT WE DON'T WANT TO SPOIL THE SURPRISE.
I'VE ASKED THIS BEFORE BUT...
...WHY DO YOU SHOW ME THESE THINGS?
KALUTIKA MAYBUS...
YOU MUST BE MADE AWARE O YOUR POSSIBILITIE

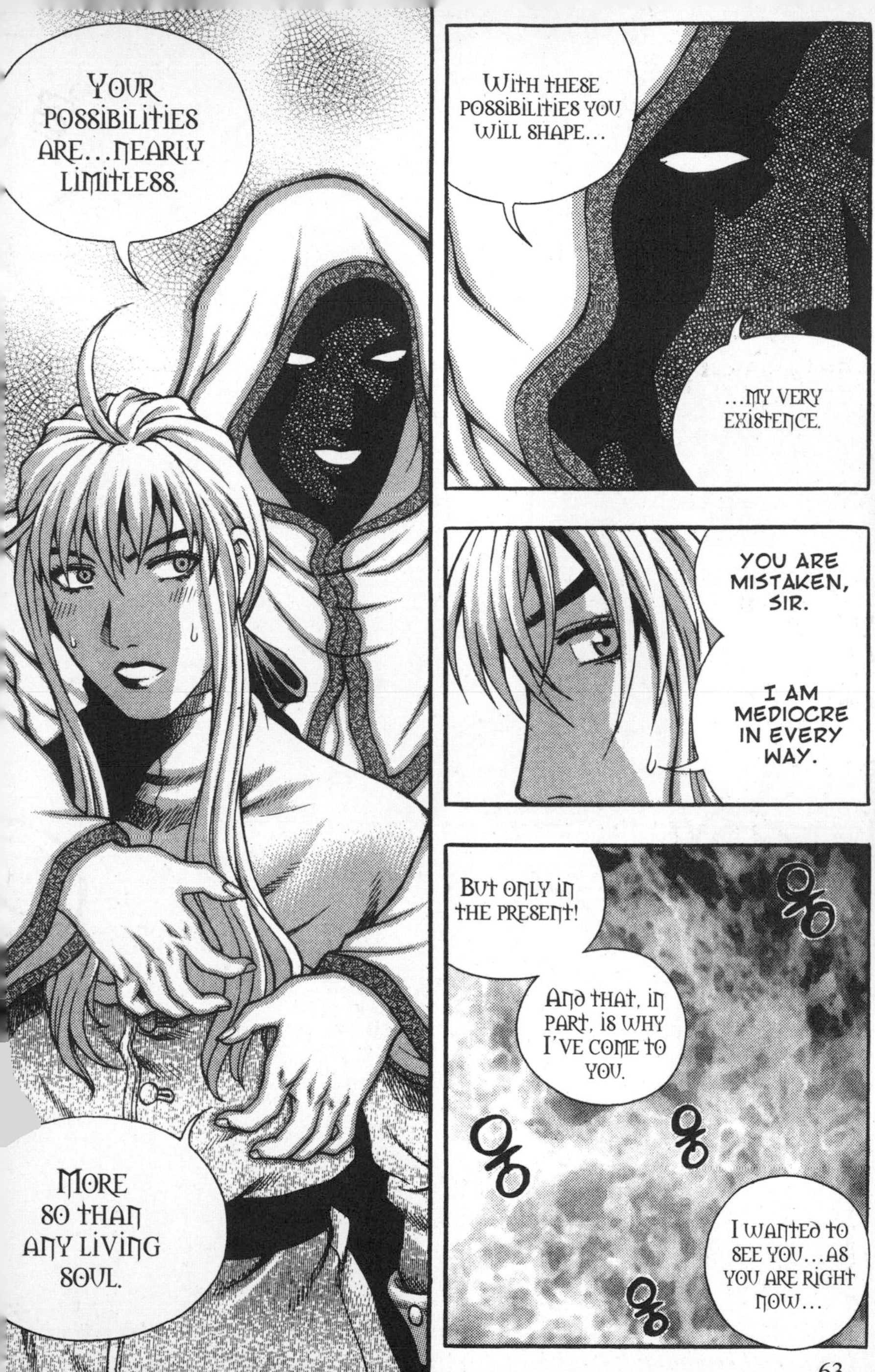
Your possibilities are…nearly limitless.
More so than any living soul.
With these possibilities you will shape…
…my very existence.
You are mistaken, sir.
I am mediocre in every way.
But only in the present!
And that, in part, is why I've come to you.
I wanted to see you…as you are right now…

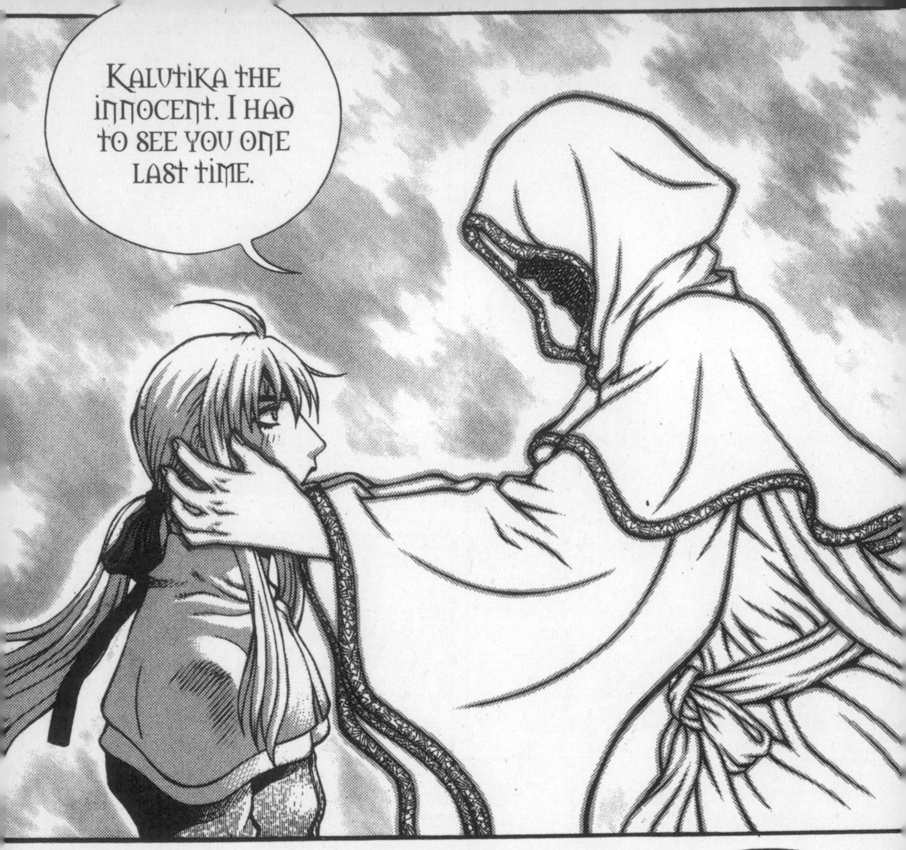
KALUTIKA THE INNOCENT. I HAD TO SEE YOU ONE LAST TIME.

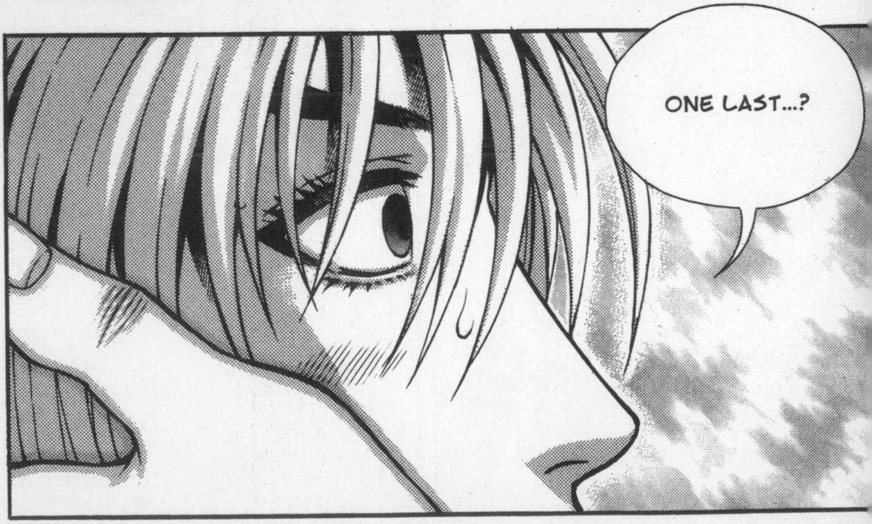
ONE LAST...?

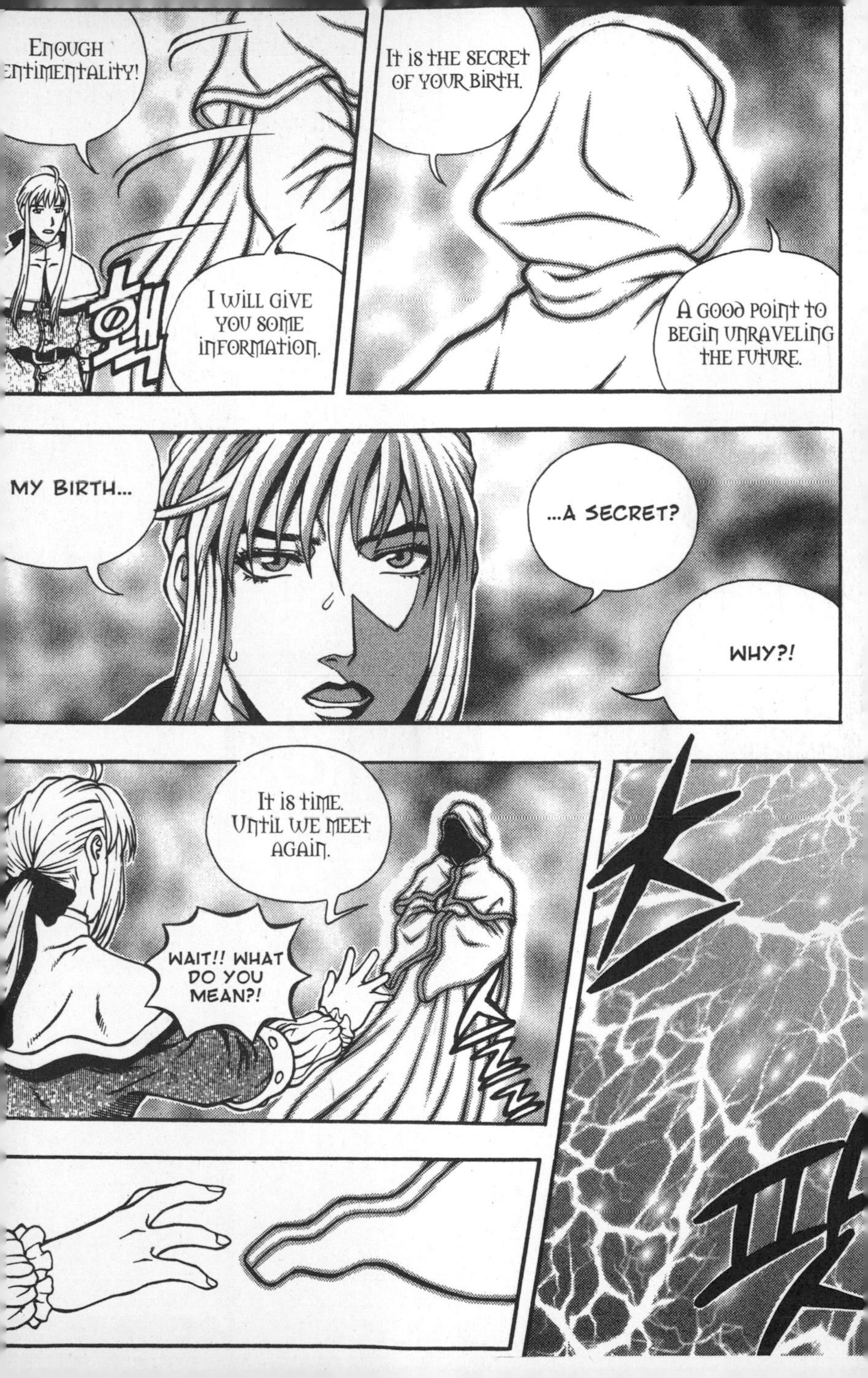
Enough entimentality!
I will give you some information.
It is the secret of your birth.
A good point to begin unraveling the future.
MY BIRTH...
...A SECRET?
WHY?!
It is time. Until we meet again.
WAIT!! WHAT DO YOU MEAN?!

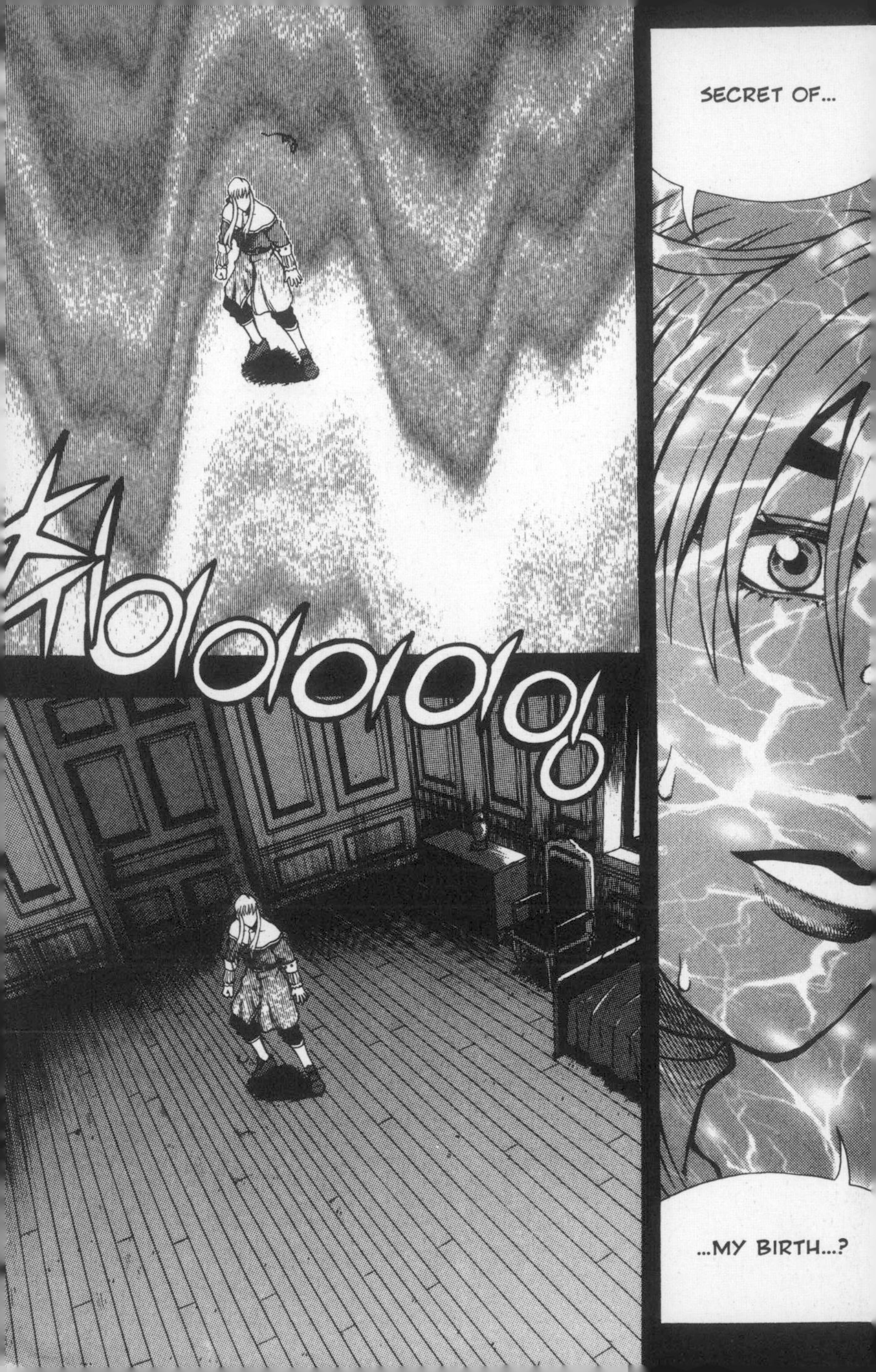
SECRET OF...
...MY BIRTH...?

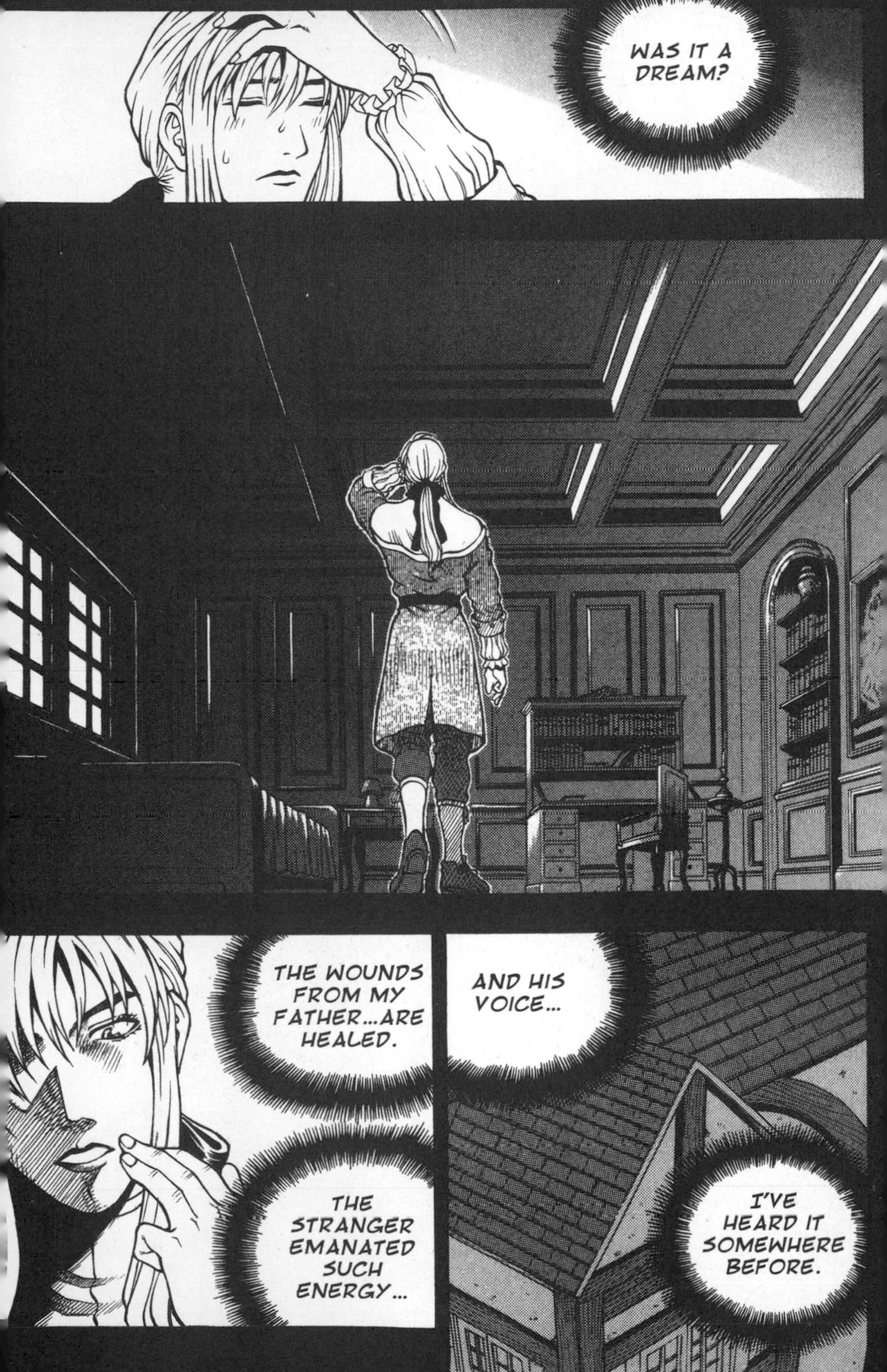
WAS IT A DREAM?
THE WOUNDS FROM MY FATHER...ARE HEALED.
THE STRANGER EMANATED SUCH ENERGY...
AND HIS VOICE...
I'VE HEARD IT SOMEWHERE BEFORE.

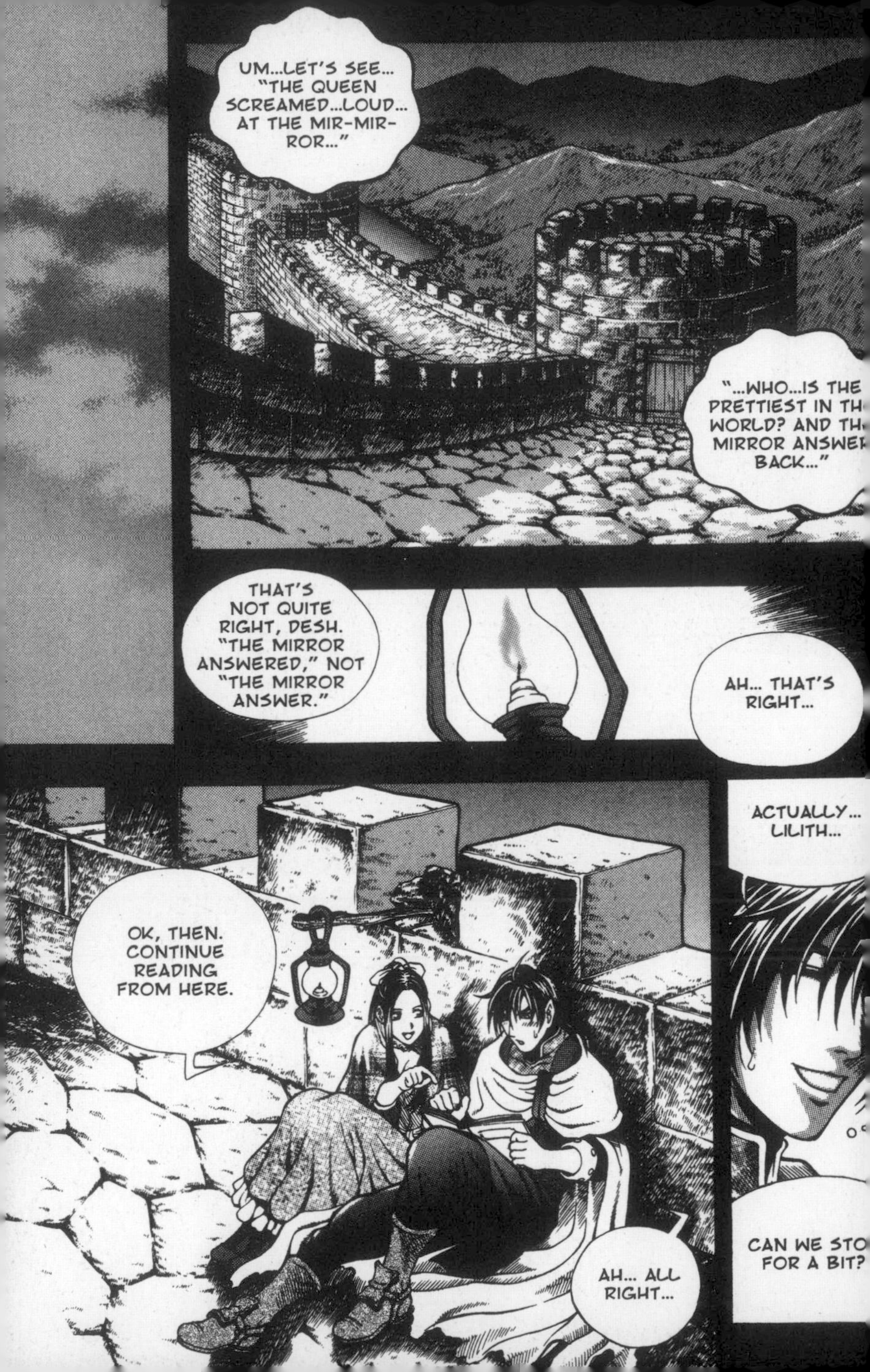
UM...LET'S SEE... "THE QUEEN SCREAMED...LOUD... AT THE MIR-MIRROR..."
"...WHO...IS THE PRETTIEST IN TH WORLD? AND TH MIRROR ANSWE BACK..."
THAT'S NOT QUITE RIGHT, DESH. "THE MIRROR ANSWERED," NOT "THE MIRROR ANSWER."
AH... THAT'S RIGHT...
OK, THEN. CONTINUE READING FROM HERE.
AH... ALL RIGHT...
ACTUALLY... LILITH...
CAN WE STO FOR A BIT?

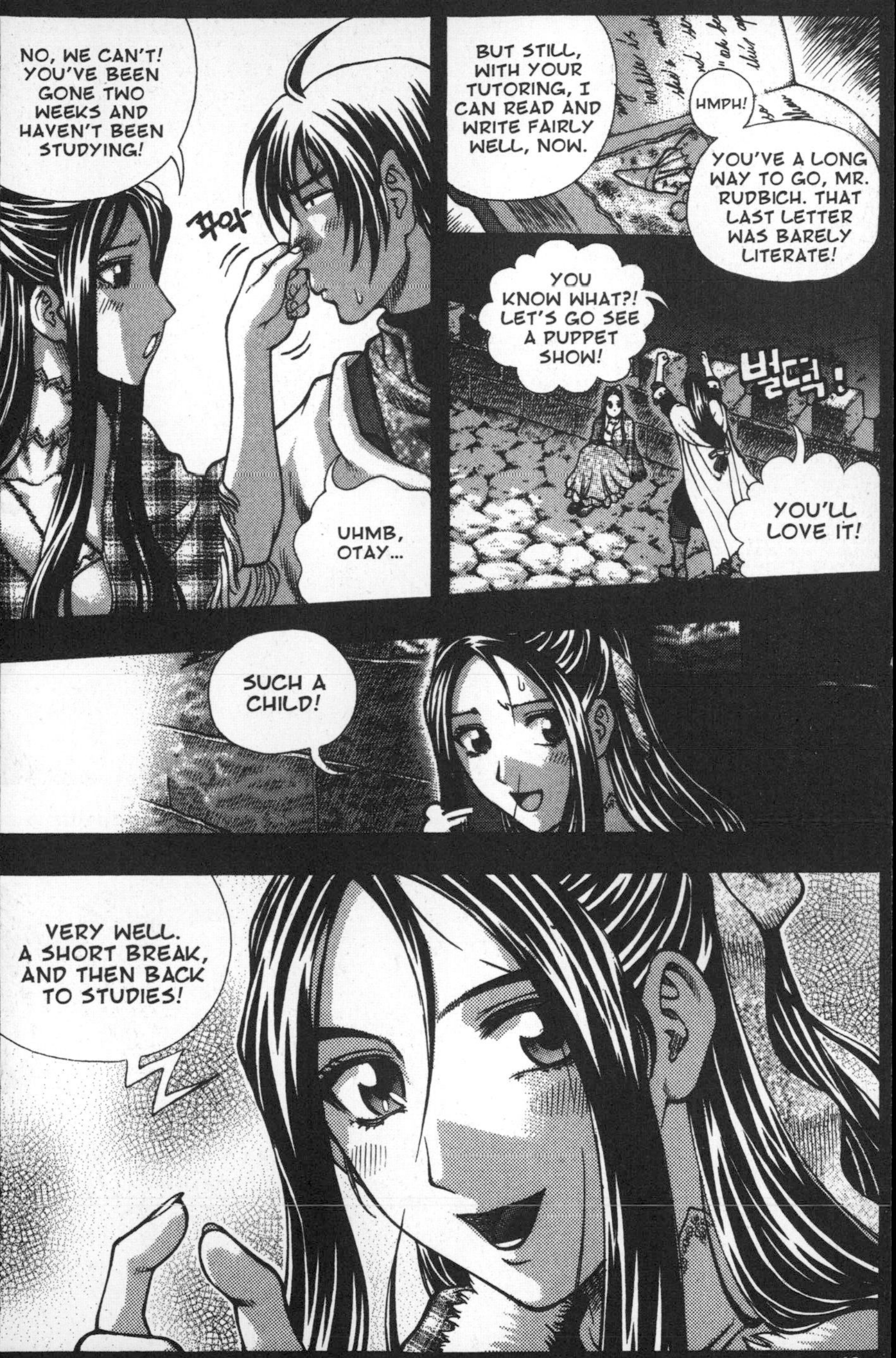
NO, WE CAN'T! YOU'VE BEEN GONE TWO WEEKS AND HAVEN'T BEEN STUDYING!
UHMB, OTAY...
BUT STILL, WITH YOUR TUTORING, I CAN READ AND WRITE FAIRLY WELL, NOW.
HMPH!
YOU'VE A LONG WAY TO GO, MR. RUDBICH. THAT LAST LETTER WAS BARELY LITERATE!
YOU KNOW WHAT?! LET'S GO SEE A PUPPET SHOW!
벌떡!
YOU'LL LOVE IT!
SUCH A CHILD!
VERY WELL. A SHORT BREAK, AND THEN BACK TO STUDIES!

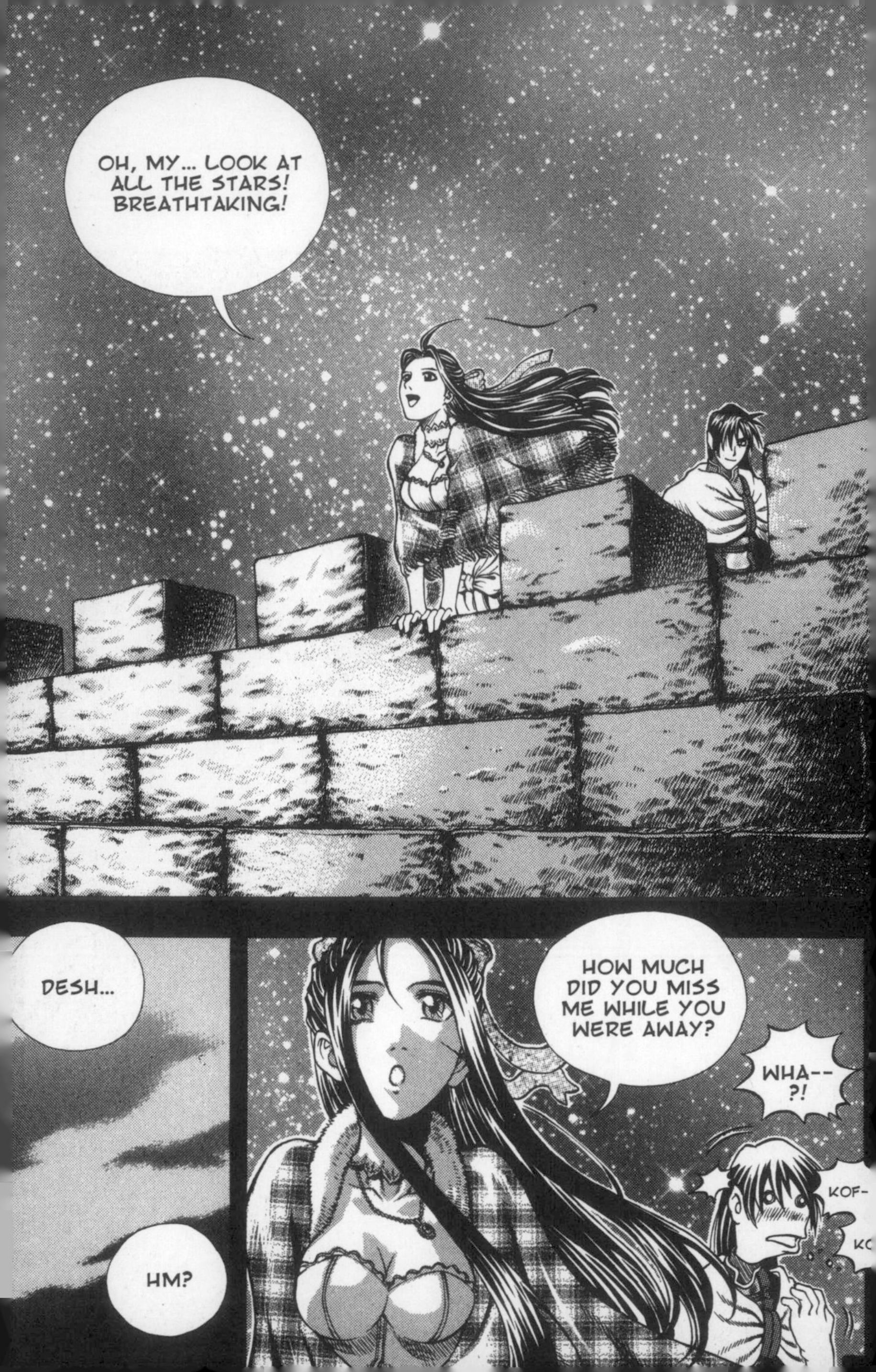

OH, MY... LOOK AT ALL THE STARS! BREATHTAKING!
DESH...
HM?
HOW MUCH DID YOU MISS ME WHILE YOU WERE AWAY?
WHA-- ?!
KOF-

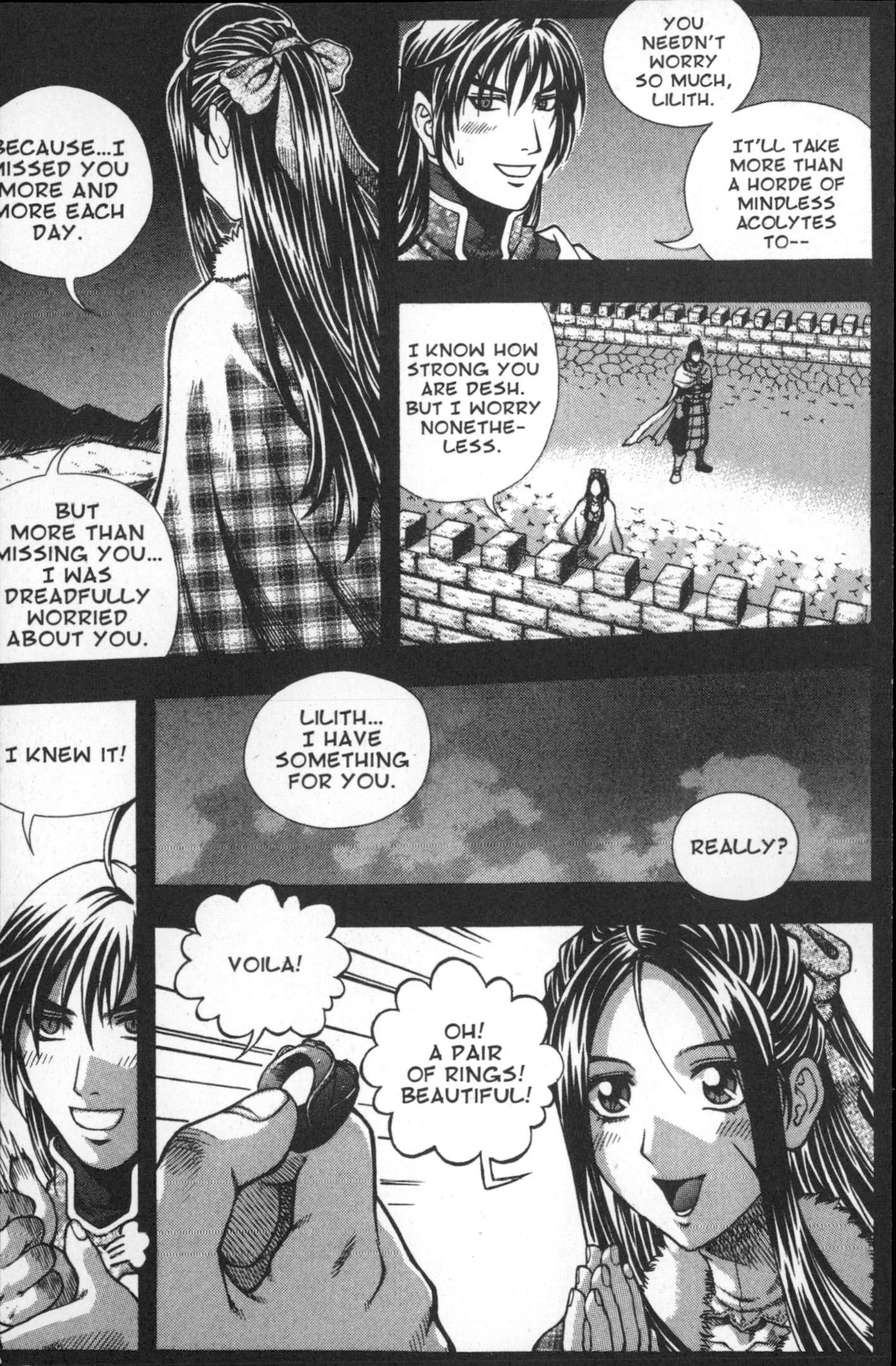
BECAUSE...I MISSED YOU MORE AND MORE EACH DAY.
BUT MORE THAN MISSING YOU... I WAS DREADFULLY WORRIED ABOUT YOU.
YOU NEEDN'T WORRY SO MUCH, LILITH.
IT'LL TAKE MORE THAN A HORDE OF MINDLESS ACOLYTES TO--
I KNOW HOW STRONG YOU ARE DESH. BUT I WORRY NONETHE-LESS.
I KNEW IT!
LILITH... I HAVE SOMETHING FOR YOU.
REALLY?
VOILA!
OH! A PAIR OF RINGS! BEAUTIFUL!

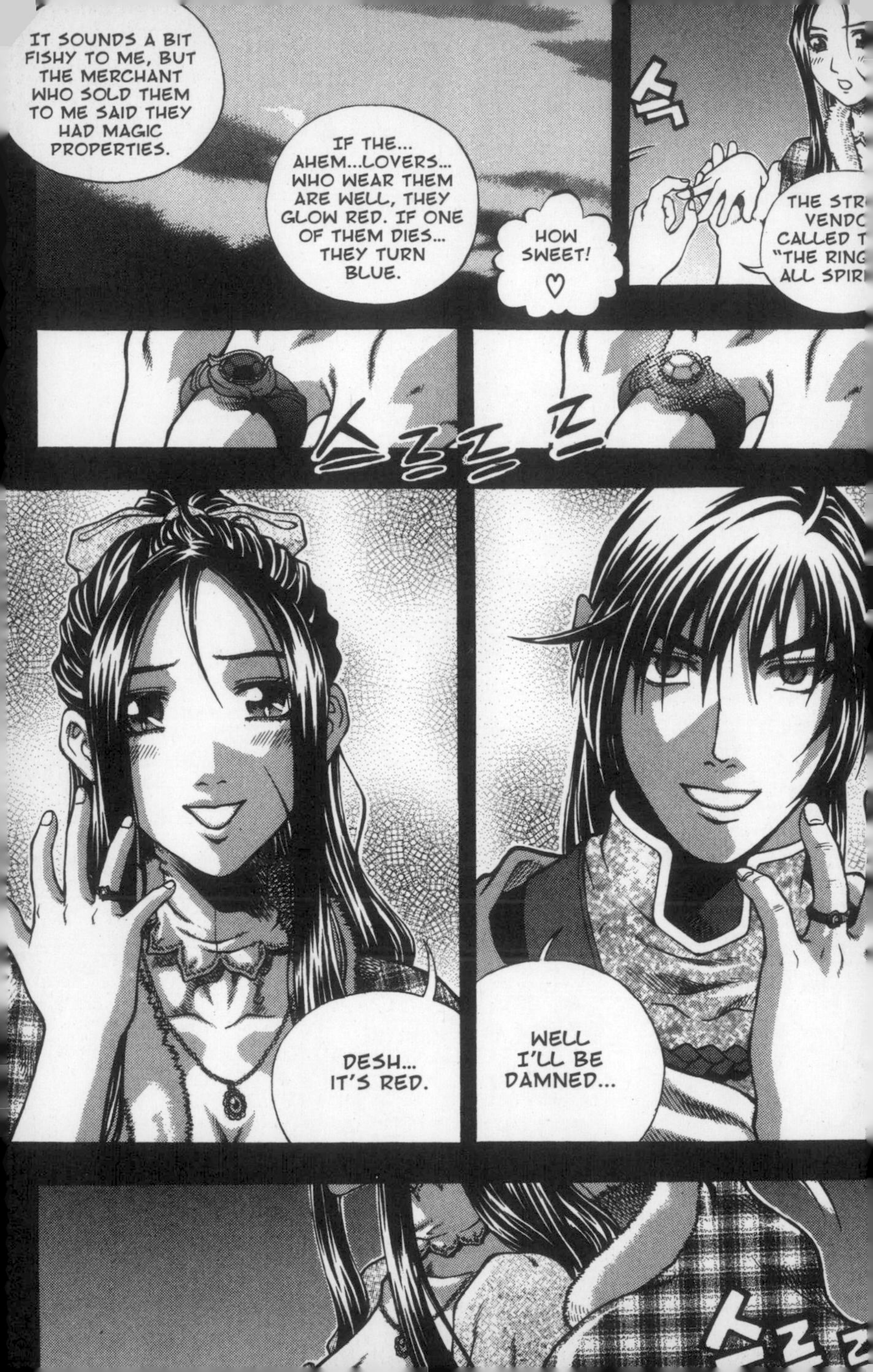

IT SOUNDS A BIT FISHY TO ME, BUT THE MERCHANT WHO SOLD THEM TO ME SAID THEY HAD MAGIC PROPERTIES.
IF THE... AHEM...LOVERS... WHO WEAR THEM ARE WELL, THEY GLOW RED. IF ONE OF THEM DIES... THEY TURN BLUE.
HOW SWEET! ♡
THE STR
VENDO
CALLED T
"THE RING
ALL SPIR
DESH... IT'S RED.
WELL I'LL BE DAMNED...

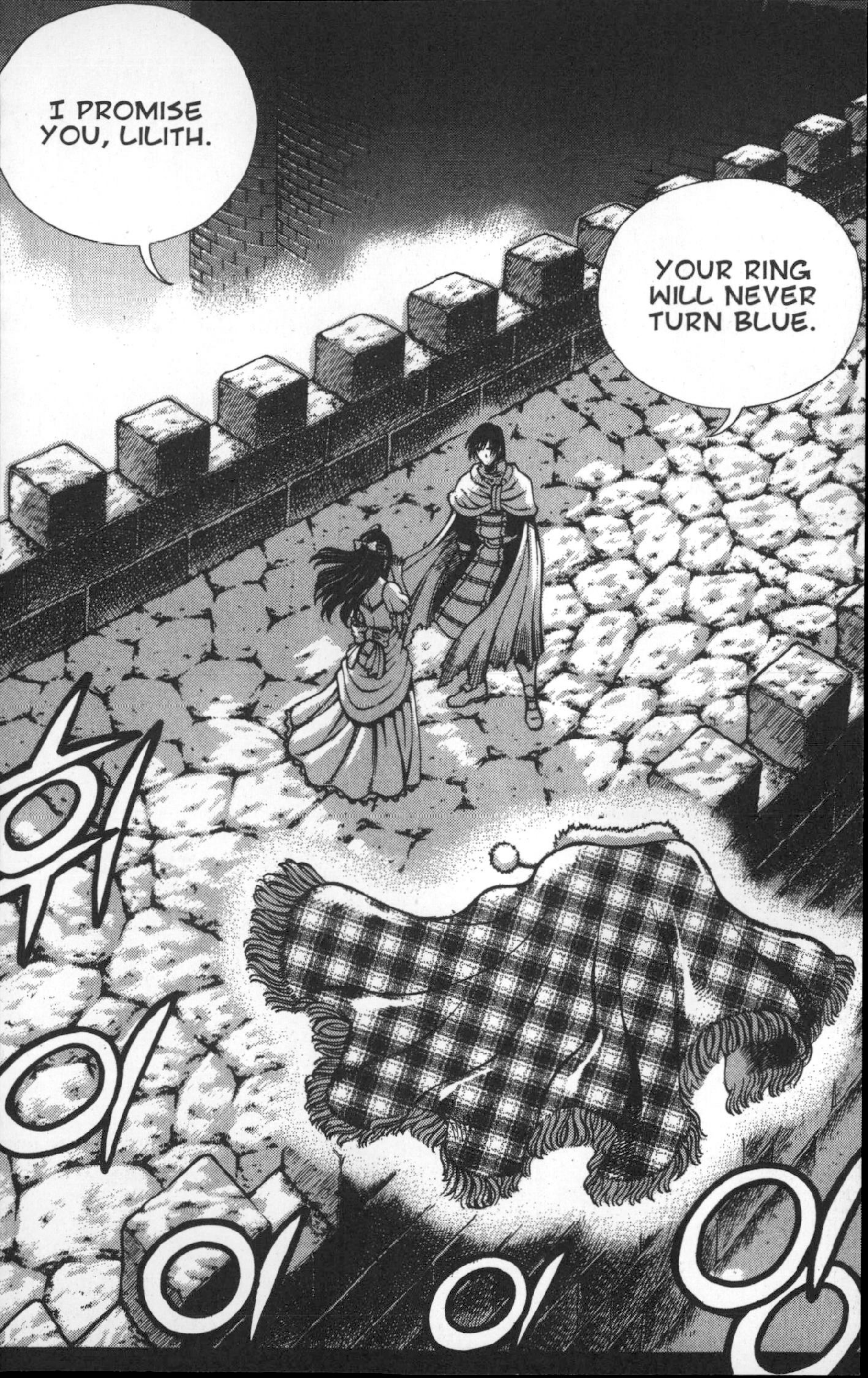
I PROMISE YOU, LILITH.
YOUR RING WILL NEVER TURN BLUE.

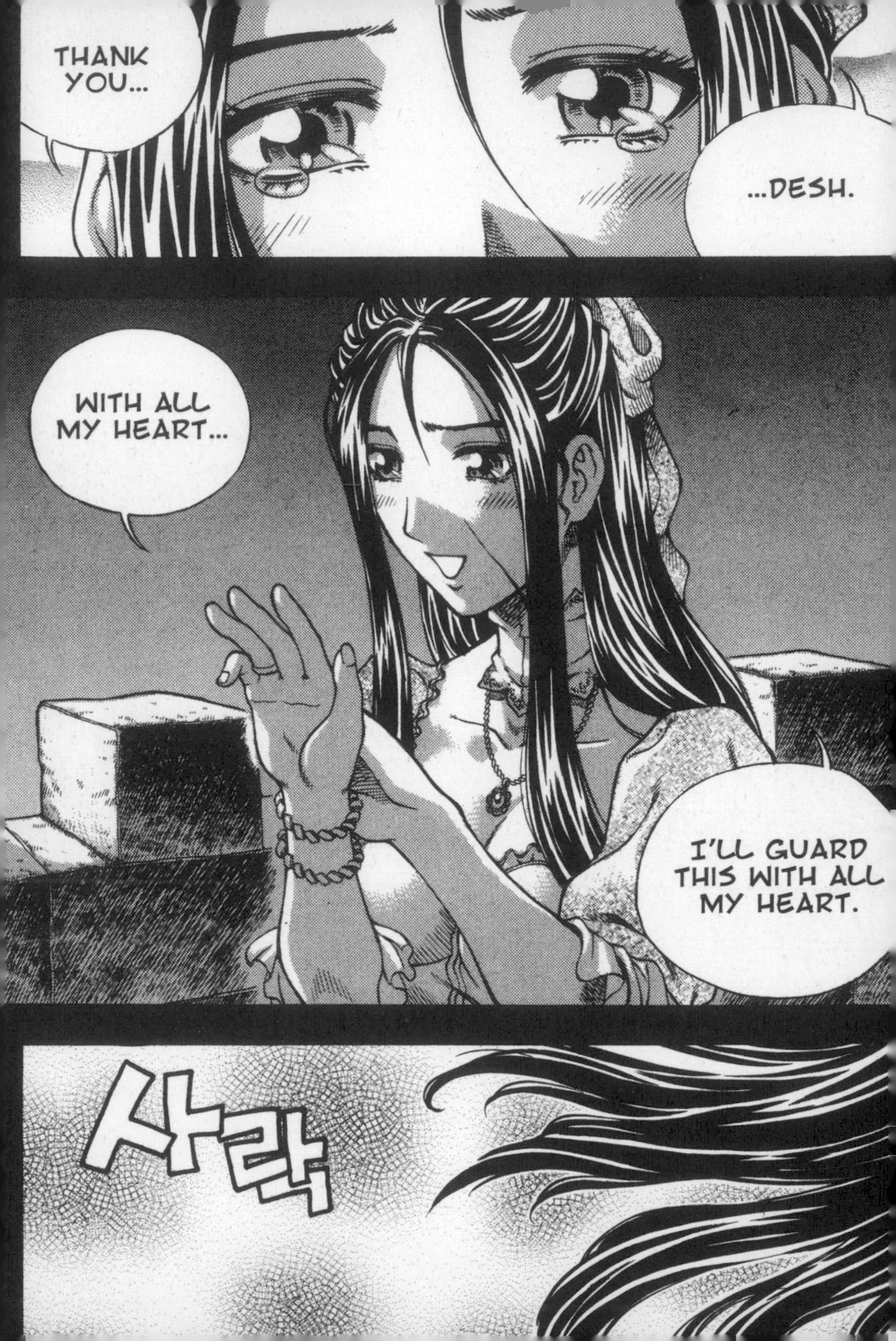
THANK YOU...
...DESH.
WITH ALL MY HEART...
I'LL GUARD THIS WITH ALL MY HEART.
사락

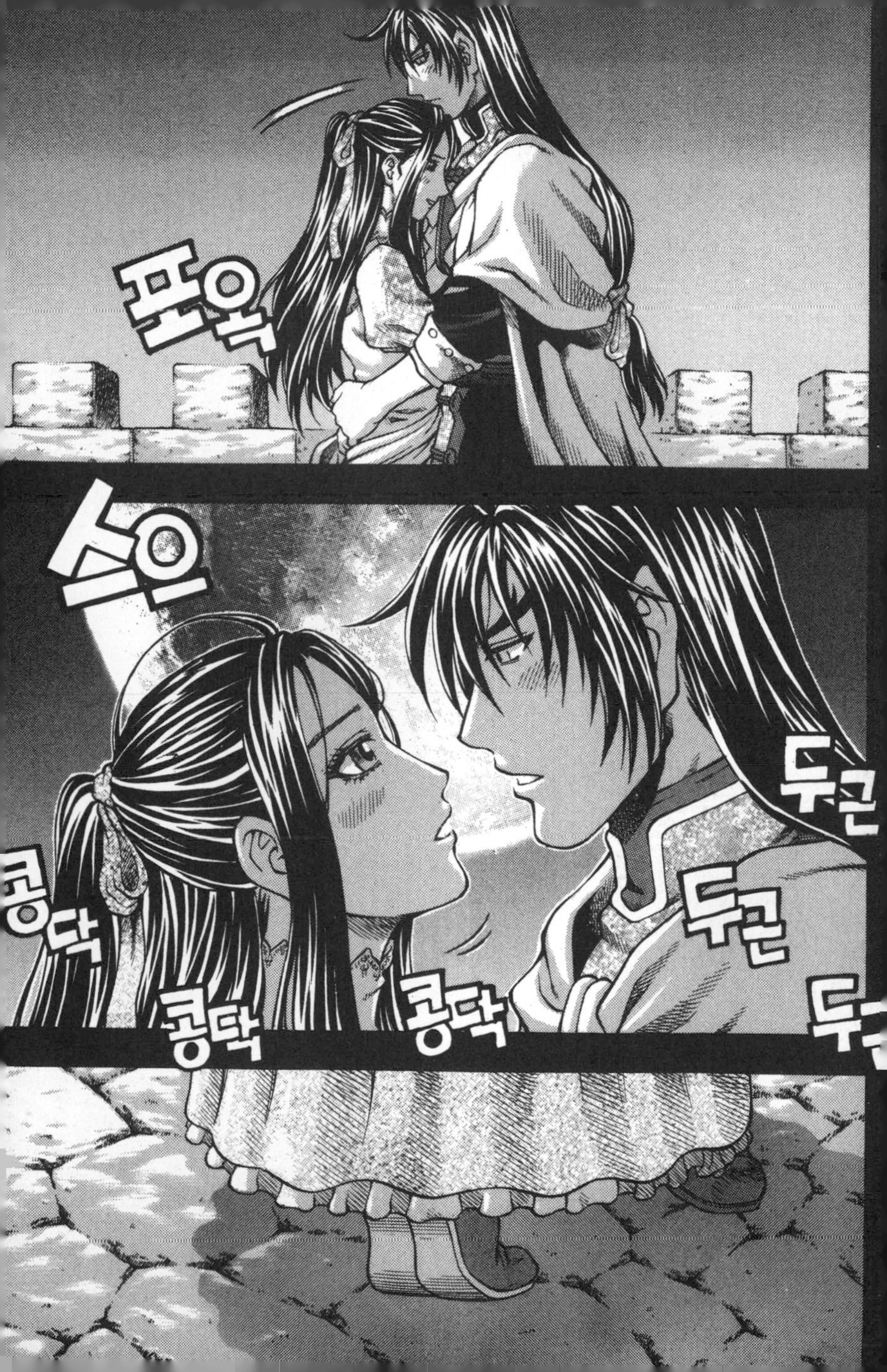
포옥
스윽
두근
콩닥
두근
콩닥
콩닥

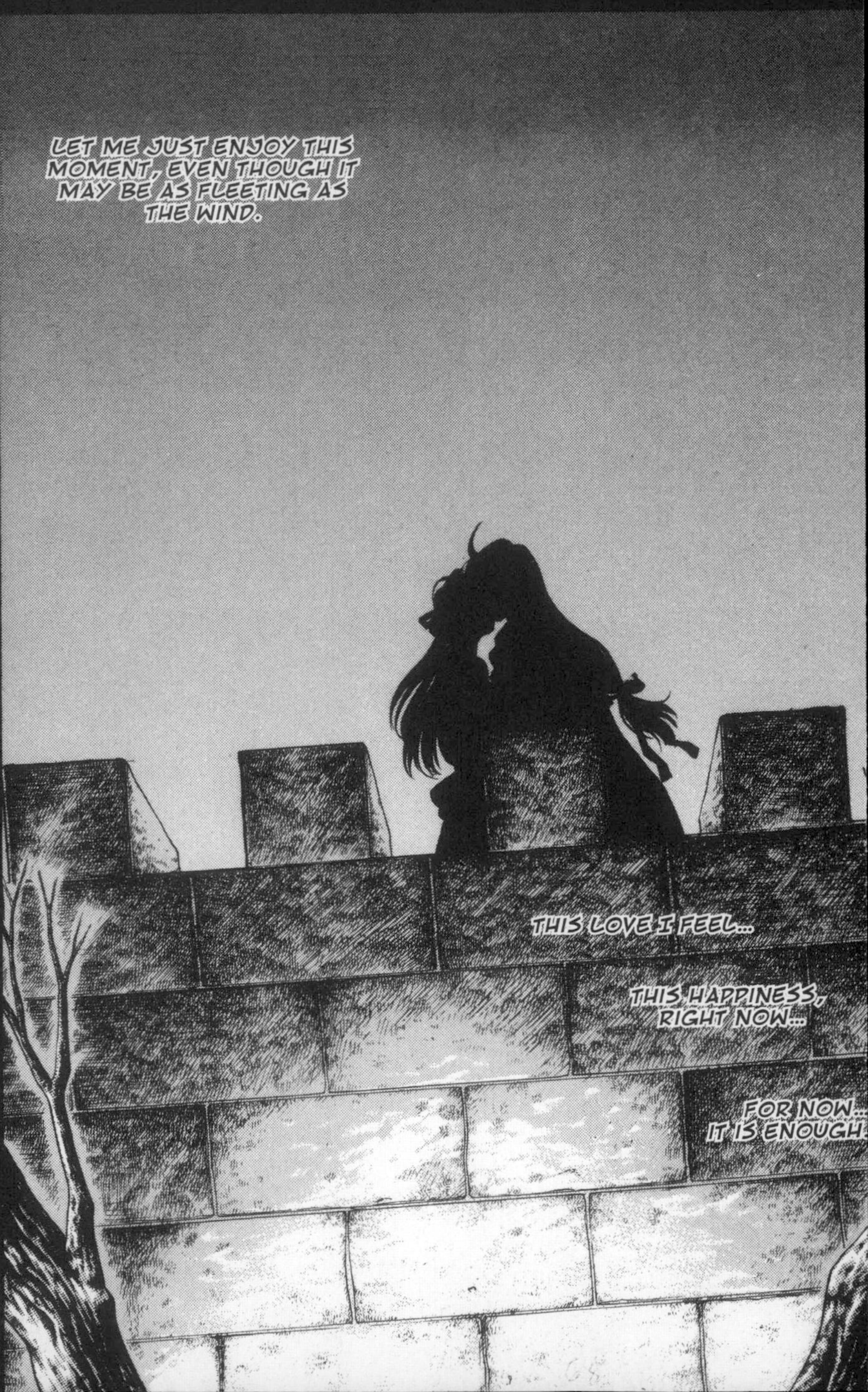
LET ME JUST ENJOY THIS MOMENT, EVEN THOUGH IT MAY BE AS FLEETING AS THE WIND.
THIS LOVE I FEEL...
THIS HAPPINESS, RIGHT NOW...
FOR NOW... IT IS ENOUGH.

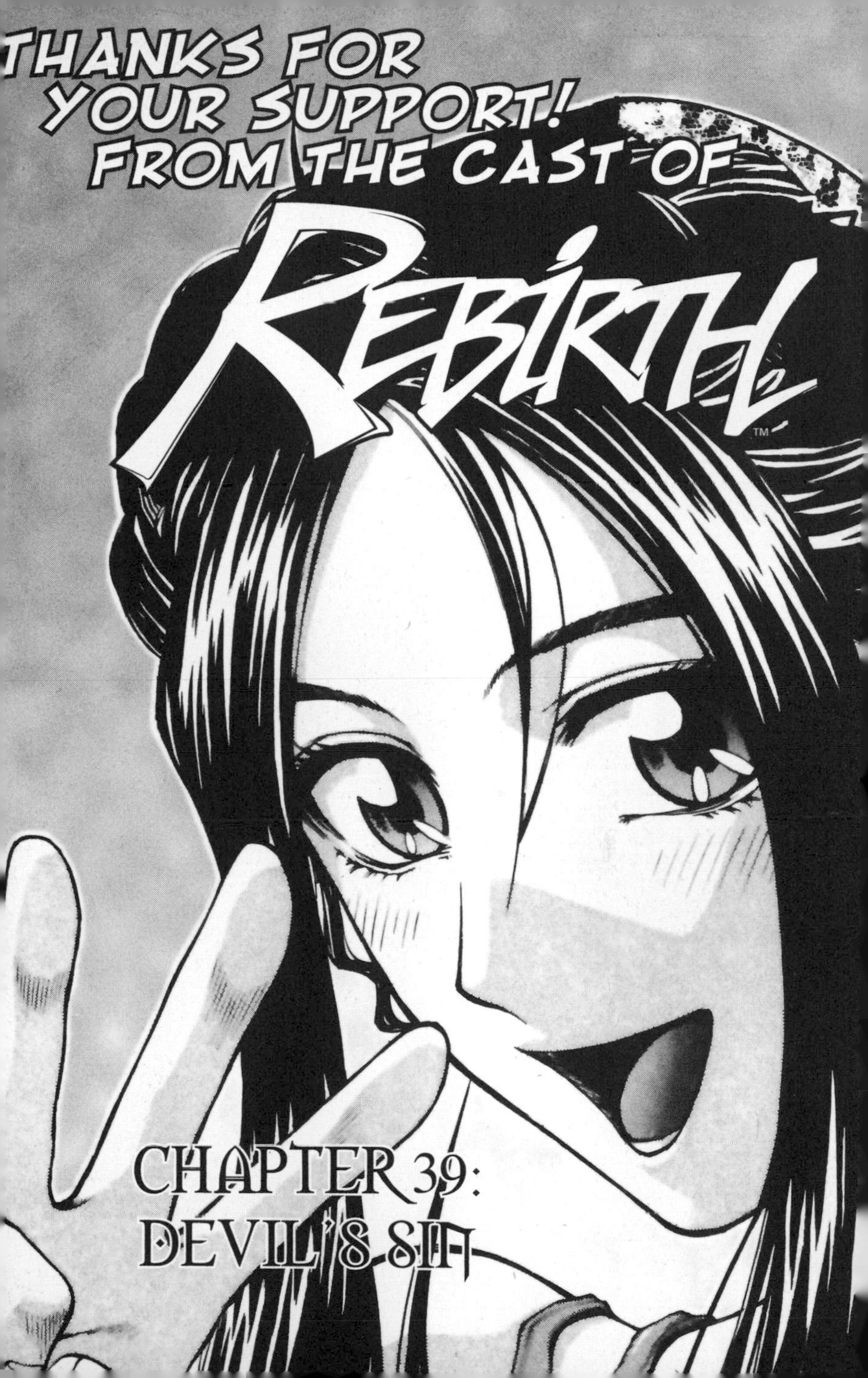
THANKS FOR YOUR SUPPORT! FROM THE CAST OF
REBIRTH™
CHAPTER 39:
DEVIL'S SIN

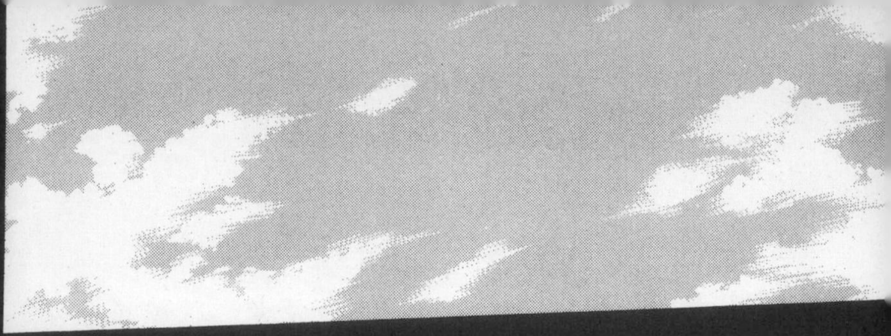
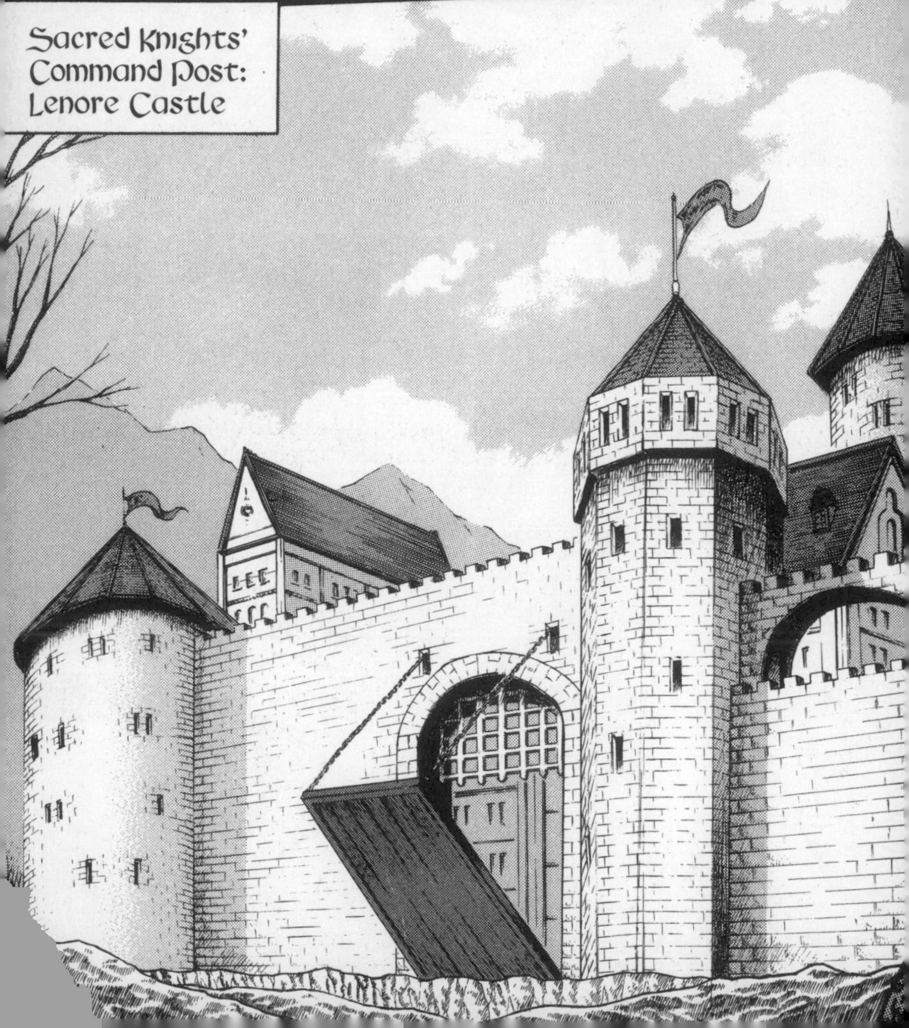
Sacred Knights' Command Post: Lenore Castle

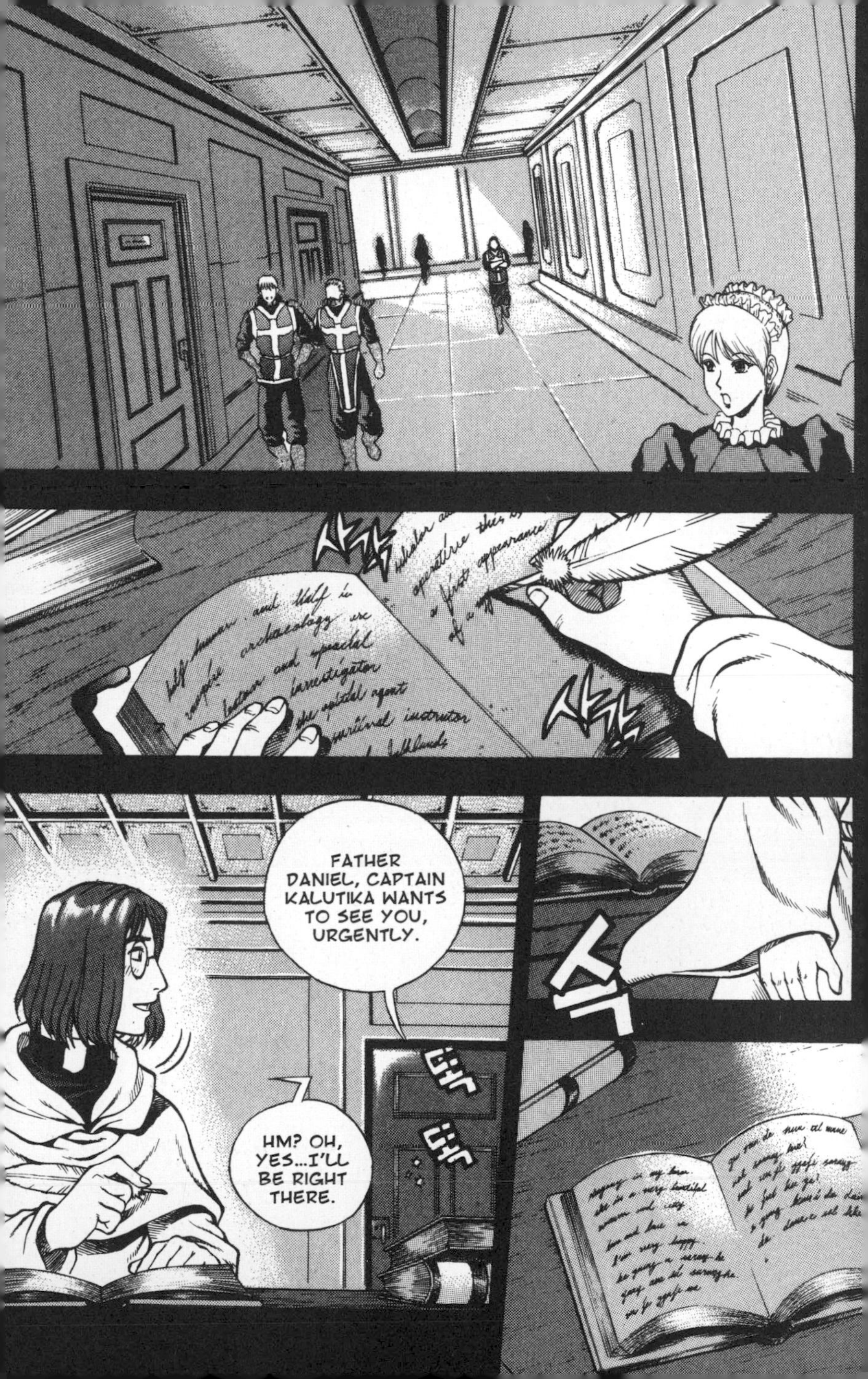
FATHER DANIEL, CAPTAIN KALUTIKA WANTS TO SEE YOU, URGENTLY.
HM? OH, YES...I'LL BE RIGHT THERE.

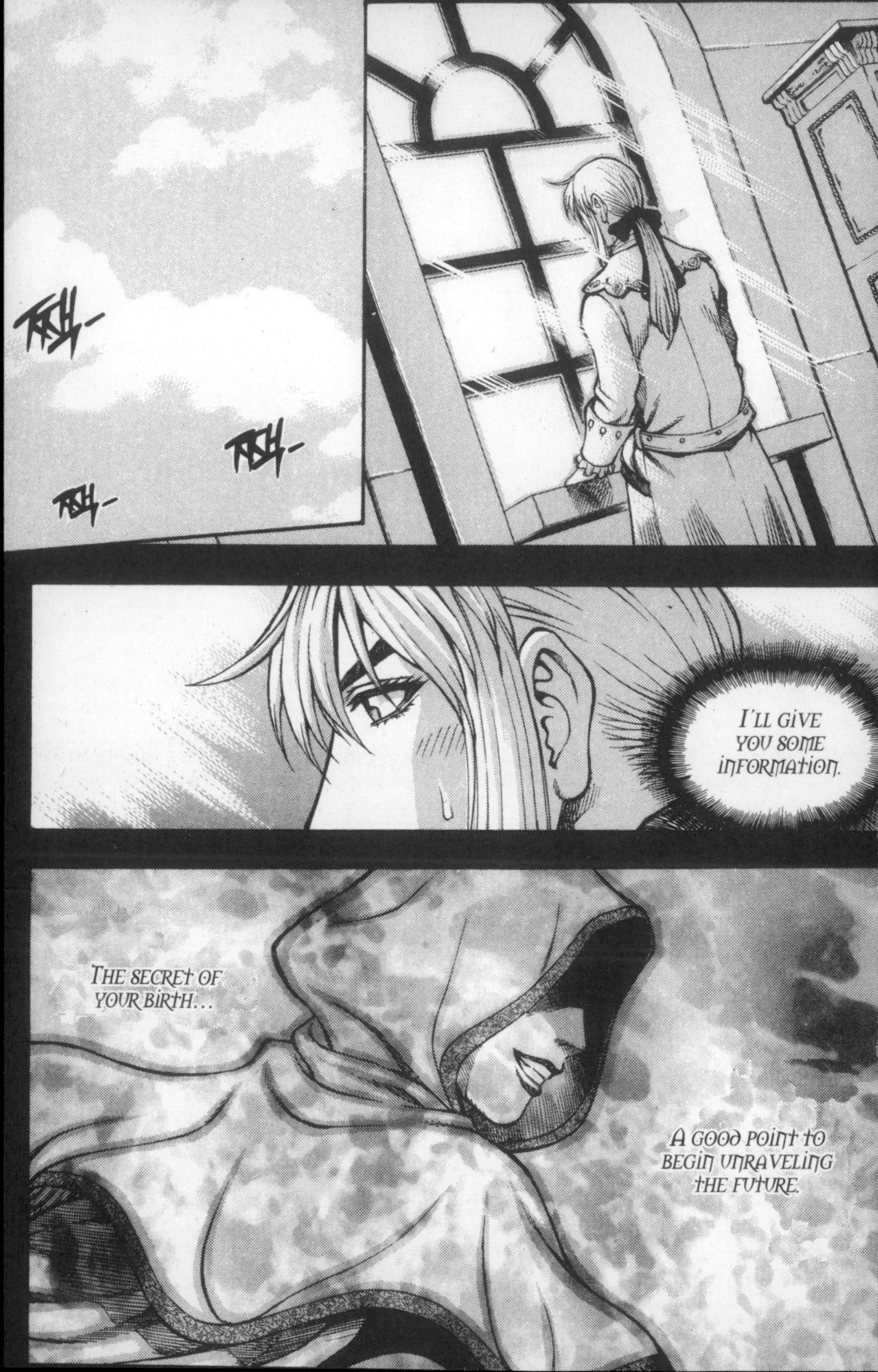
TASH-
TASH-
TASH-
I'LL GIVE YOU SOME INFORMATION.
THE SECRET OF YOUR BIRTH...
A GOOD POINT TO BEGIN UNRAVELING THE FUTURE.

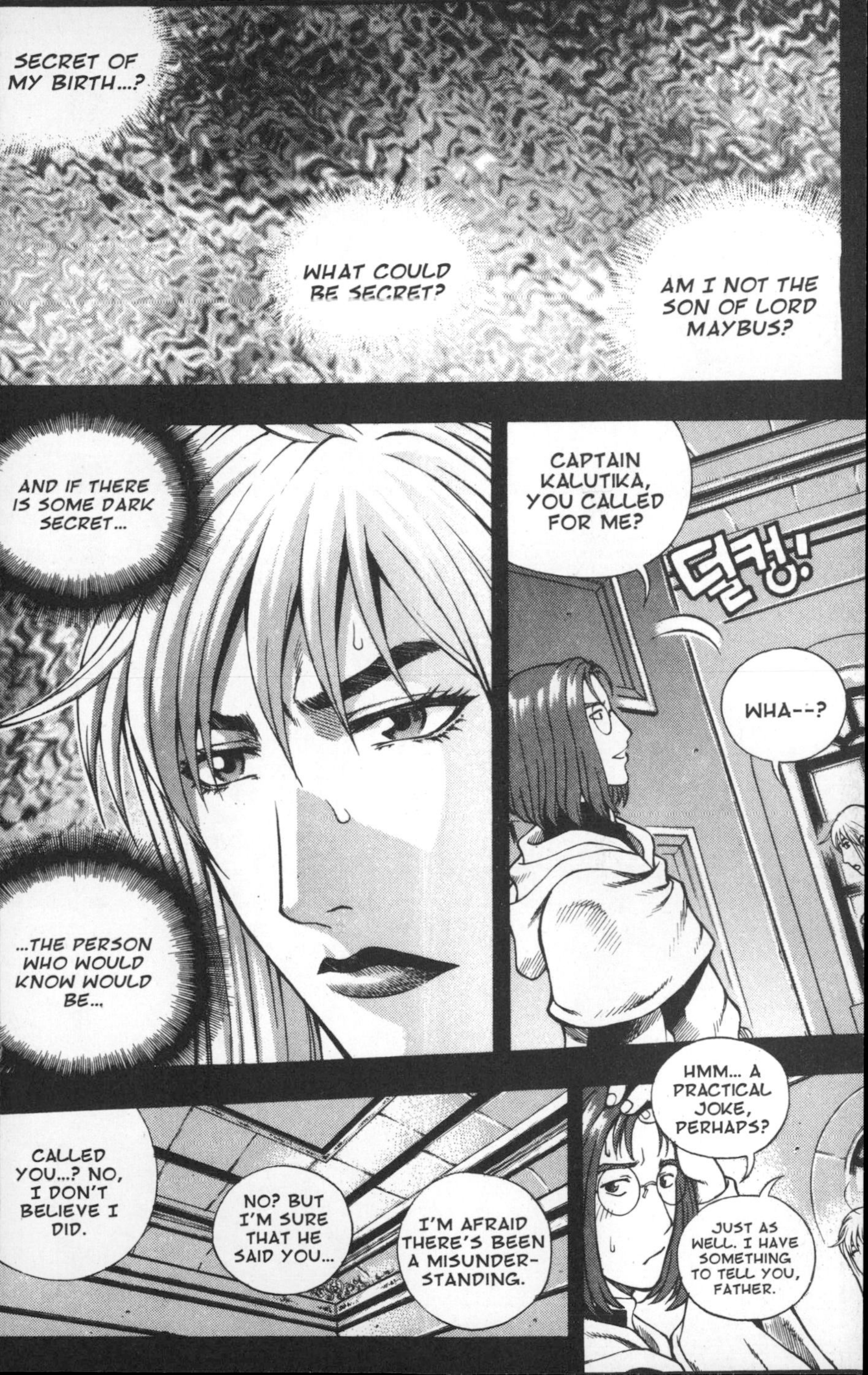
SECRET OF MY BIRTH...?
WHAT COULD BE SECRET?
AM I NOT THE SON OF LORD MAYBUS?
AND IF THERE IS SOME DARK SECRET...
...THE PERSON WHO WOULD KNOW WOULD BE...
CAPTAIN KALUTIKA, YOU CALLED FOR ME?
덜컹!
WHA--?
CALLED YOU...? NO, I DON'T BELIEVE I DID.
NO? BUT I'M SURE THAT HE SAID YOU...
I'M AFRAID THERE'S BEEN A MISUNDER-STANDING.
HMM... A PRACTICAL JOKE, PERHAPS?
JUST AS WELL. I HAVE SOMETHING TO TELL YOU, FATHER.

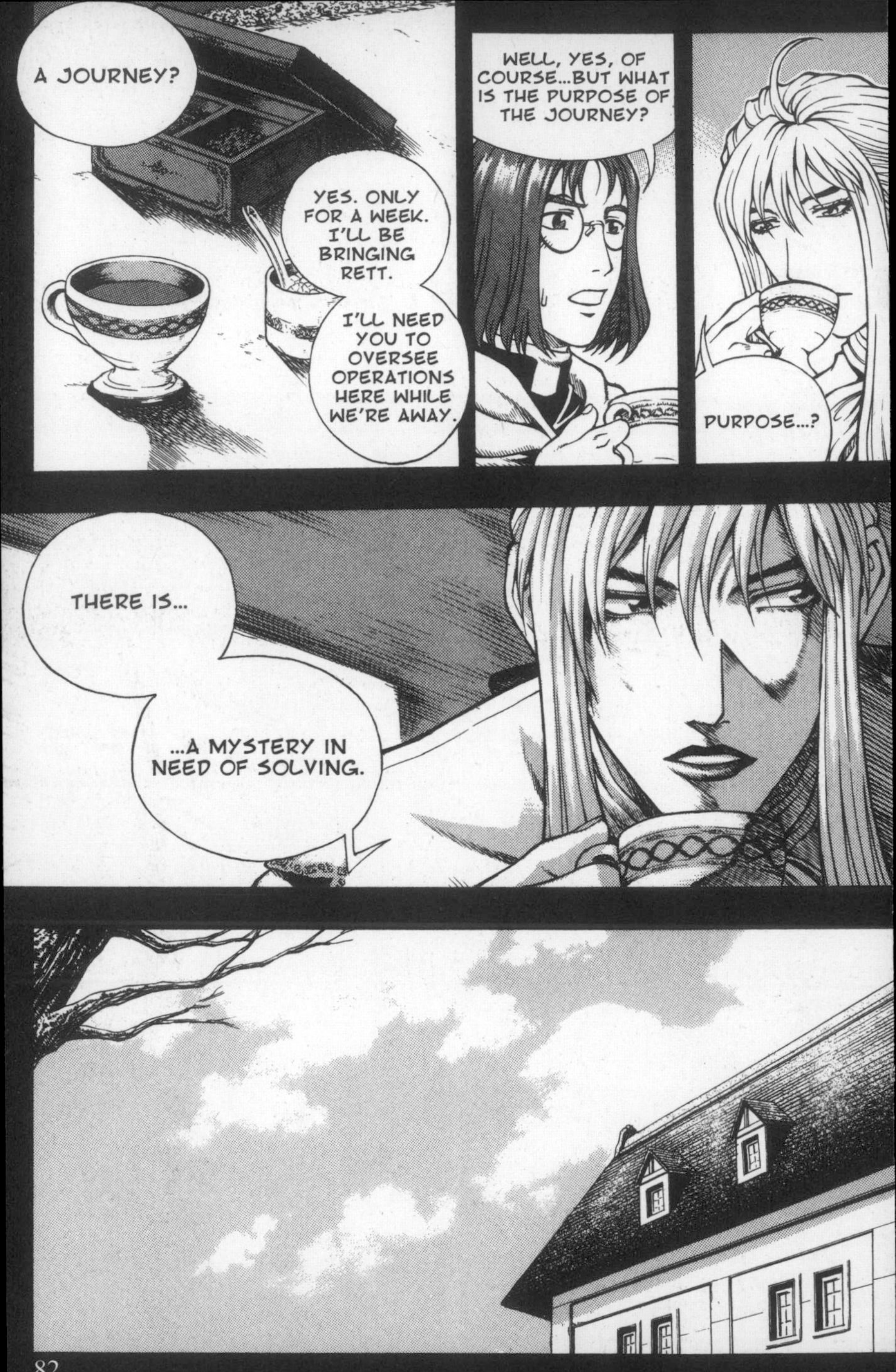
A JOURNEY?
YES. ONLY FOR A WEEK. I'LL BE BRINGING RETT.
I'LL NEED YOU TO OVERSEE OPERATIONS HERE WHILE WE'RE AWAY.
WELL, YES, OF COURSE...BUT WHAT IS THE PURPOSE OF THE JOURNEY?
PURPOSE...?
THERE IS...
...A MYSTERY IN NEED OF SOLVING.

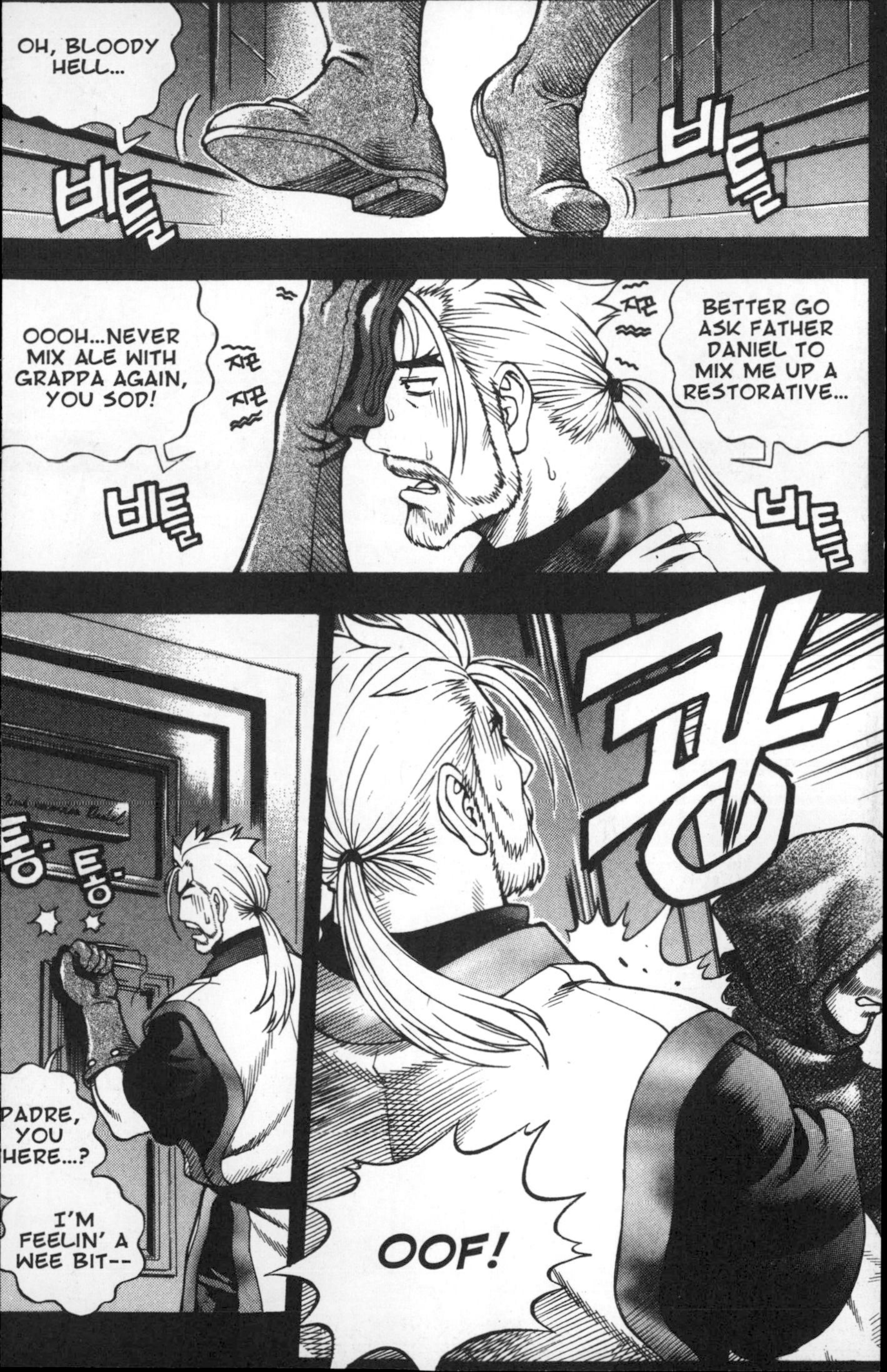
OH, BLOODY HELL...
비틀
비틀
OOOH...NEVER MIX ALE WITH GRAPPA AGAIN, YOU SOD!
비틀
BETTER GO ASK FATHER DANIEL TO MIX ME UP A RESTORATIVE...
비틀
PADRE, YOU HERE...?
I'M FEELIN' A WEE BIT--
쾅
OOF!

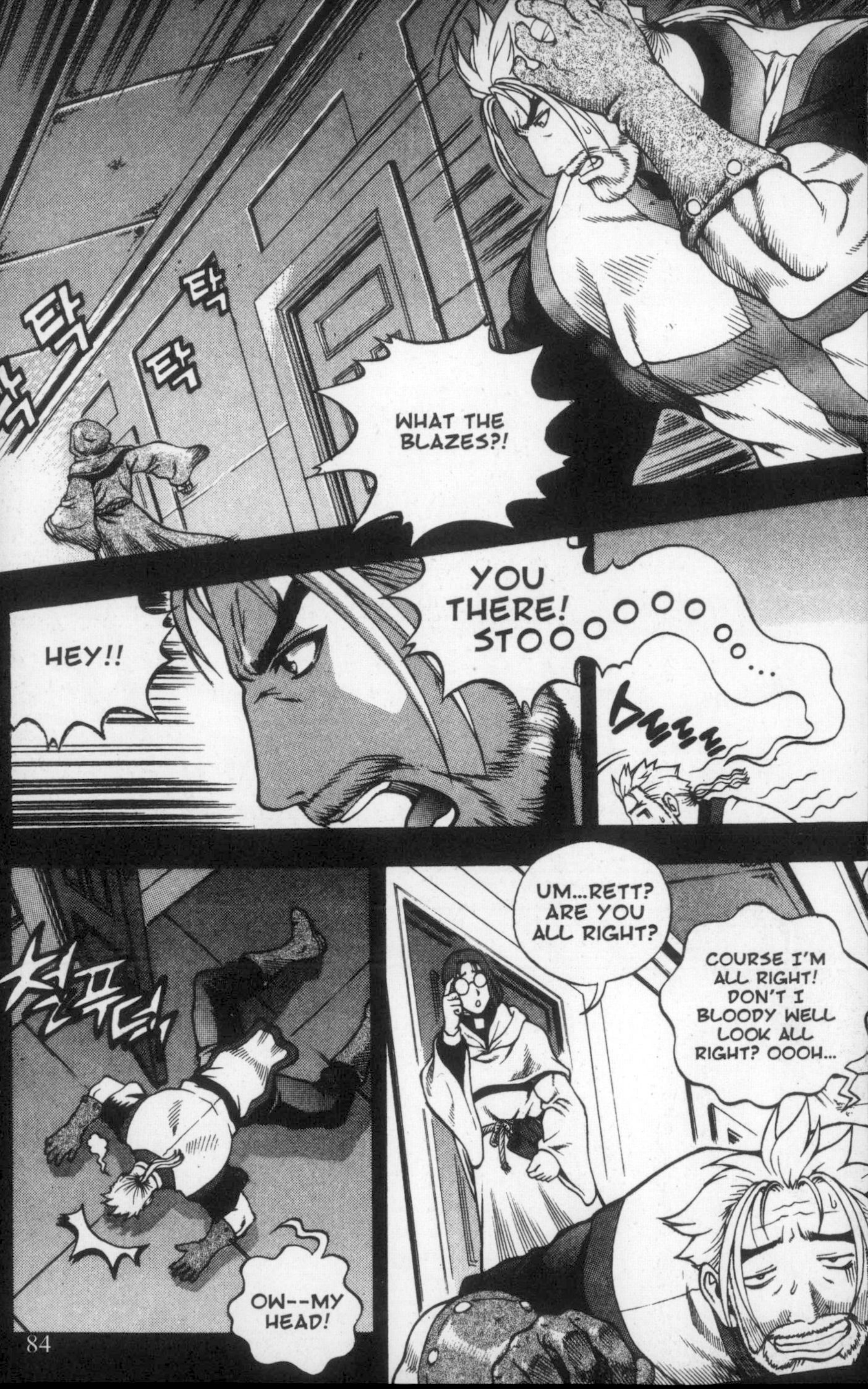
탁
탁
탁
WHAT THE BLAZES?!
HEY!!
YOU THERE! STOOOOOOOOO...
철푸덕
OW--MY HEAD!
UM...RETT? ARE YOU ALL RIGHT?
COURSE I'M ALL RIGHT! DON'T I BLOODY WELL LOOK ALL RIGHT? OOOH...

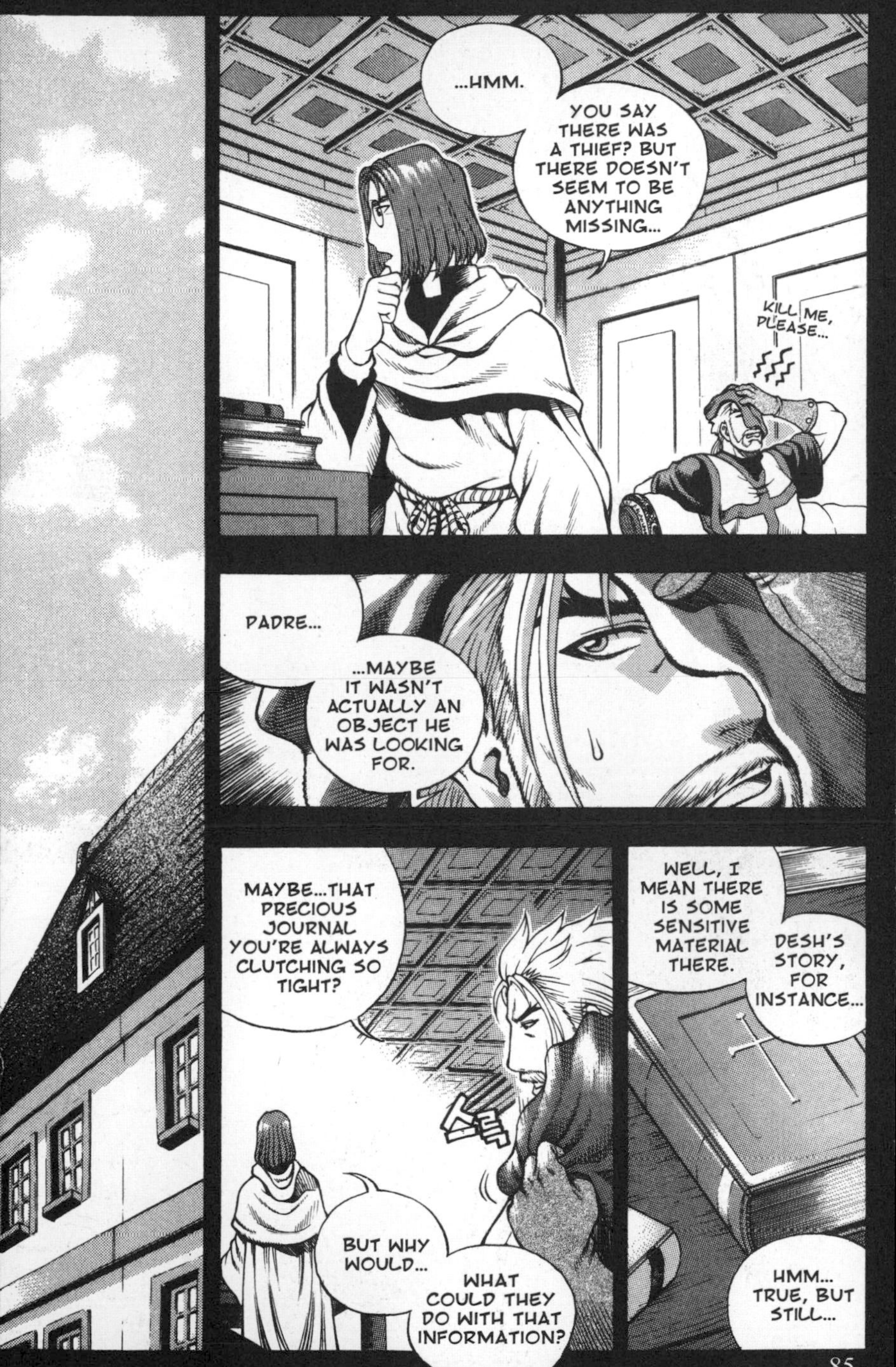
...HMM.
YOU SAY THERE WAS A THIEF? BUT THERE DOESN'T SEEM TO BE ANYTHING MISSING...
KILL ME, PLEASE...
PADRE...
...MAYBE IT WASN'T ACTUALLY AN OBJECT HE WAS LOOKING FOR.
MAYBE...THAT PRECIOUS JOURNAL YOU'RE ALWAYS CLUTCHING SO TIGHT?
BUT WHY WOULD...
WHAT COULD THEY DO WITH THAT INFORMATION?
WELL, I MEAN THERE IS SOME SENSITIVE MATERIAL THERE.
DESH'S STORY, FOR INSTANCE...
HMM... TRUE, BUT STILL...

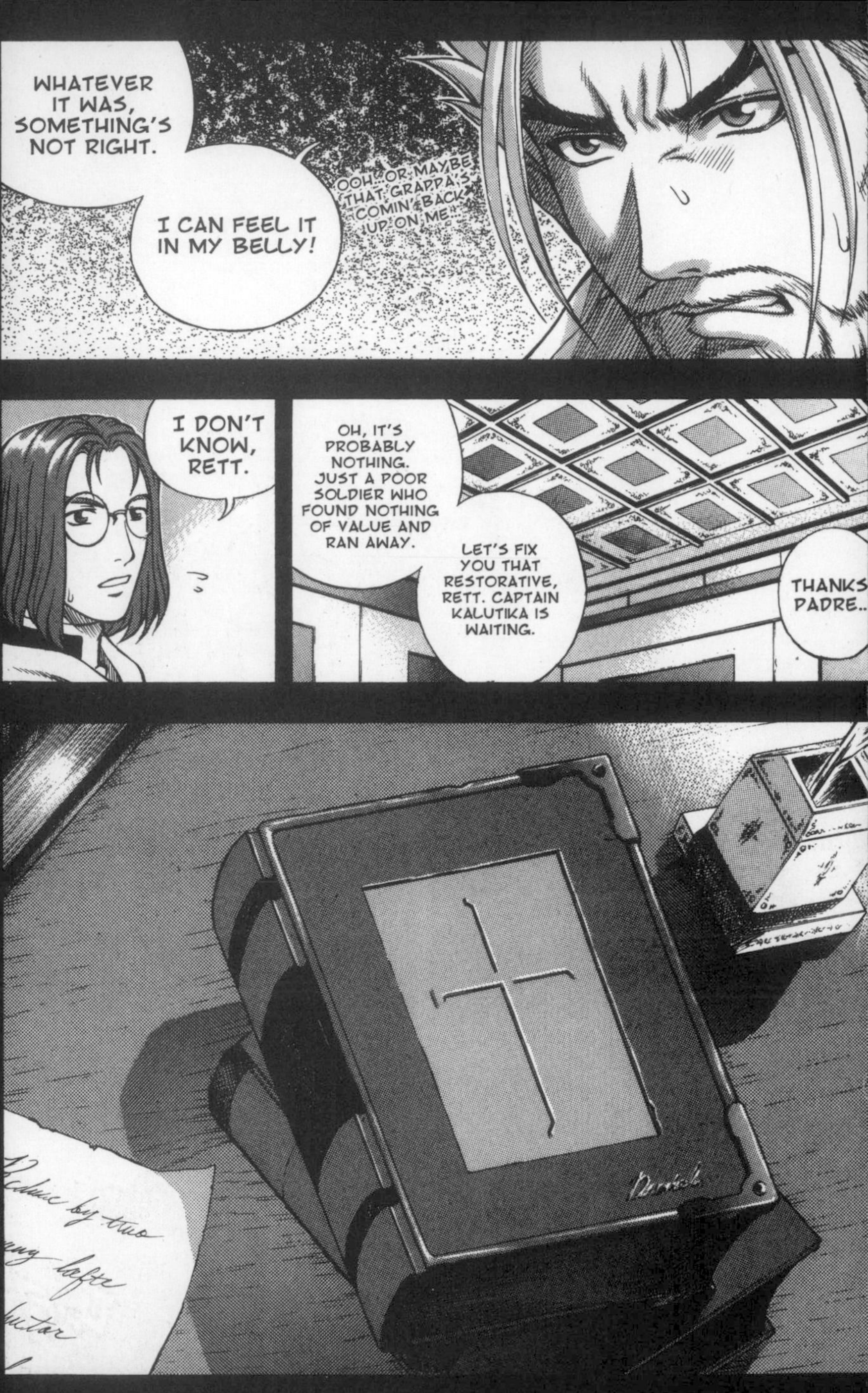
WHATEVER IT WAS, SOMETHING'S NOT RIGHT.
I CAN FEEL IT IN MY BELLY!
OOH... OR MAYBE THAT GRAPPA'S COMIN' BACK UP ON ME...
I DON'T KNOW, RETT.
OH, IT'S PROBABLY NOTHING. JUST A POOR SOLDIER WHO FOUND NOTHING OF VALUE AND RAN AWAY.
LET'S FIX YOU THAT RESTORATIVE, RETT. CAPTAIN KALUTIKA IS WAITING.
THANKS PADRE...

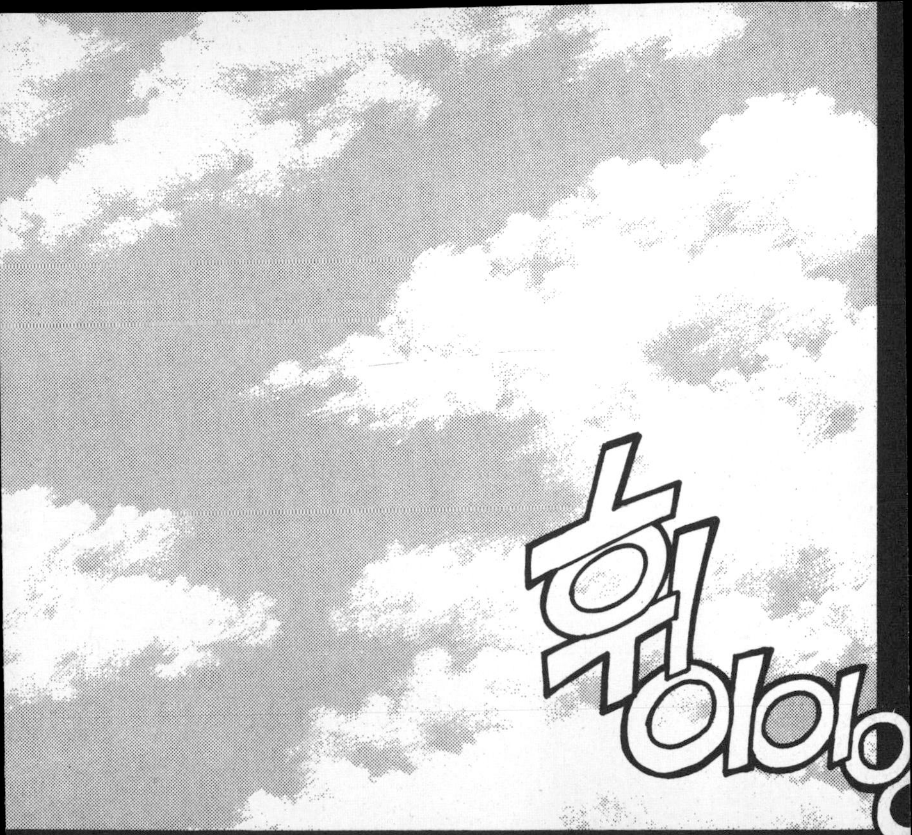
휘이이잉
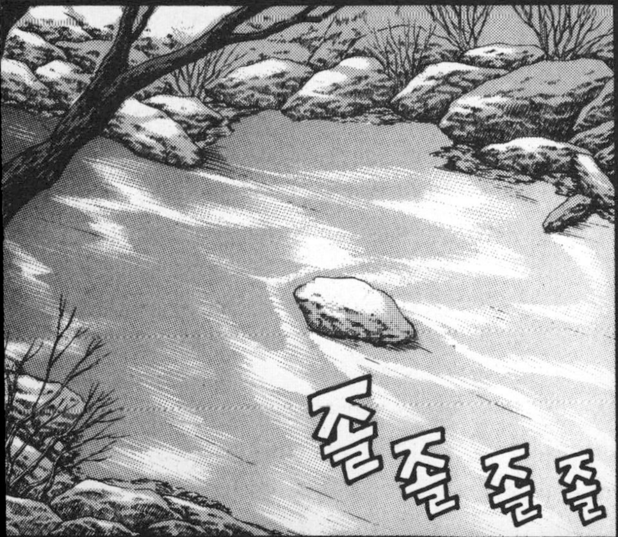
졸졸졸졸
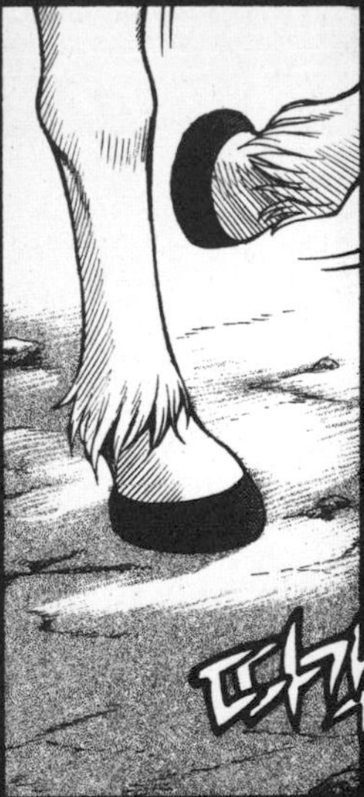
따각

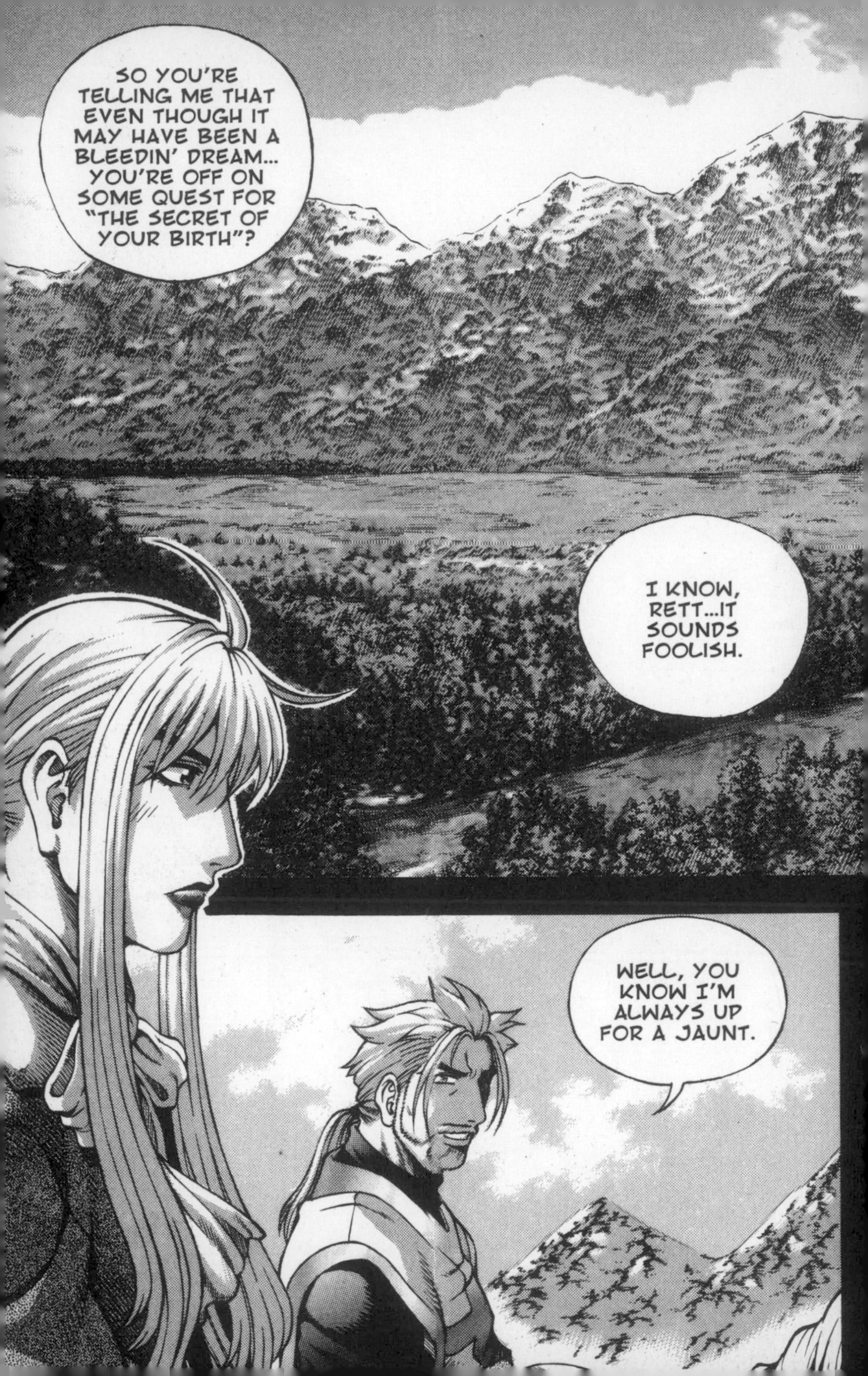
SO YOU'RE TELLING ME THAT EVEN THOUGH IT MAY HAVE BEEN A BLEEDIN' DREAM... YOU'RE OFF ON SOME QUEST FOR "THE SECRET OF YOUR BIRTH"?
I KNOW, RETT...IT SOUNDS FOOLISH.
WELL, YOU KNOW I'M ALWAYS UP FOR A JAUNT.

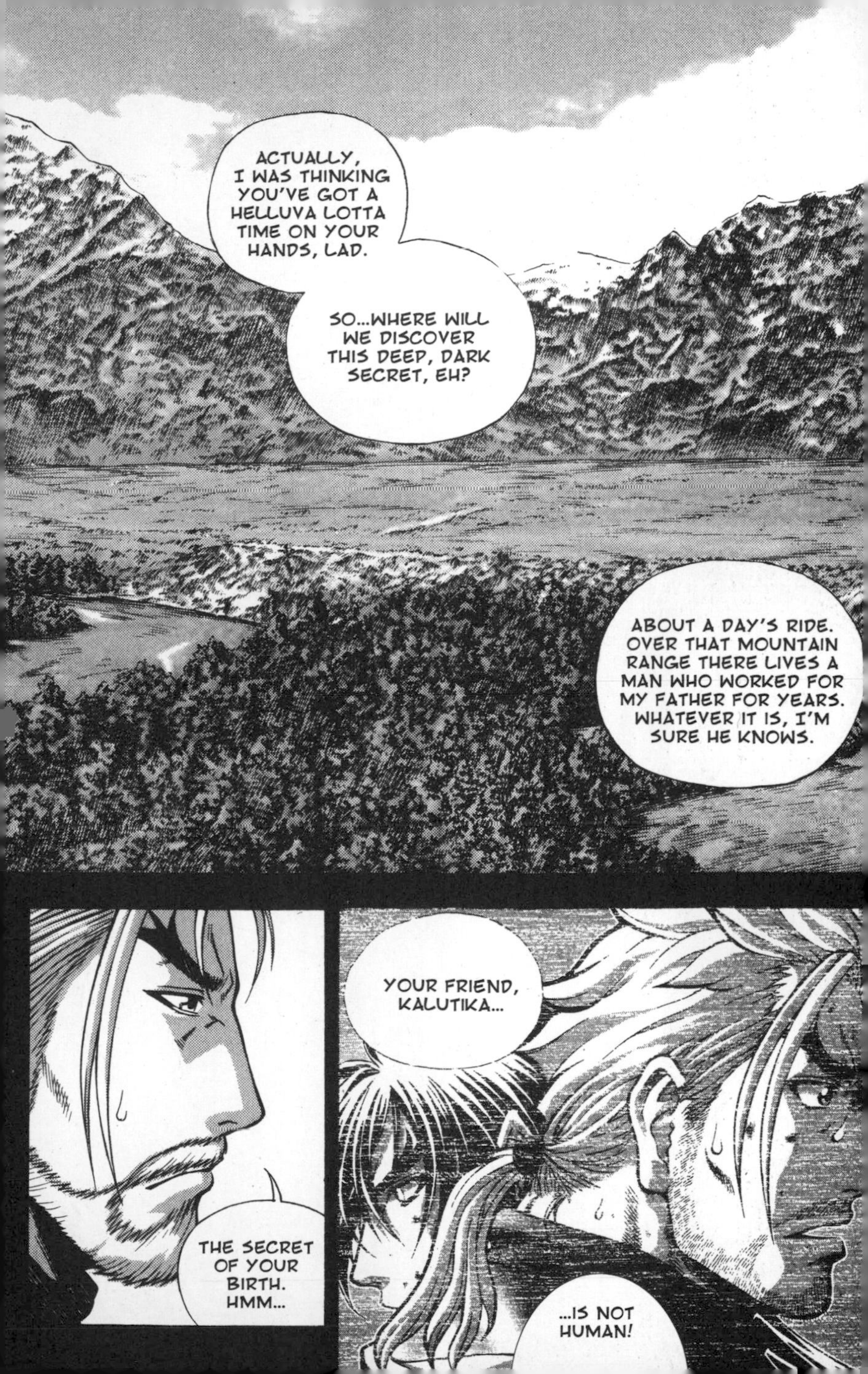
ACTUALLY, I WAS THINKING YOU'VE GOT A HELLUVA LOTTA TIME ON YOUR HANDS, LAD.
SO...WHERE WILL WE DISCOVER THIS DEEP, DARK SECRET, EH?
ABOUT A DAY'S RIDE. OVER THAT MOUNTAIN RANGE THERE LIVES A MAN WHO WORKED FOR MY FATHER FOR YEARS. WHATEVER IT IS, I'M SURE HE KNOWS.
THE SECRET OF YOUR BIRTH. HMM...
YOUR FRIEND, KALUTIKA...
...IS NOT HUMAN!

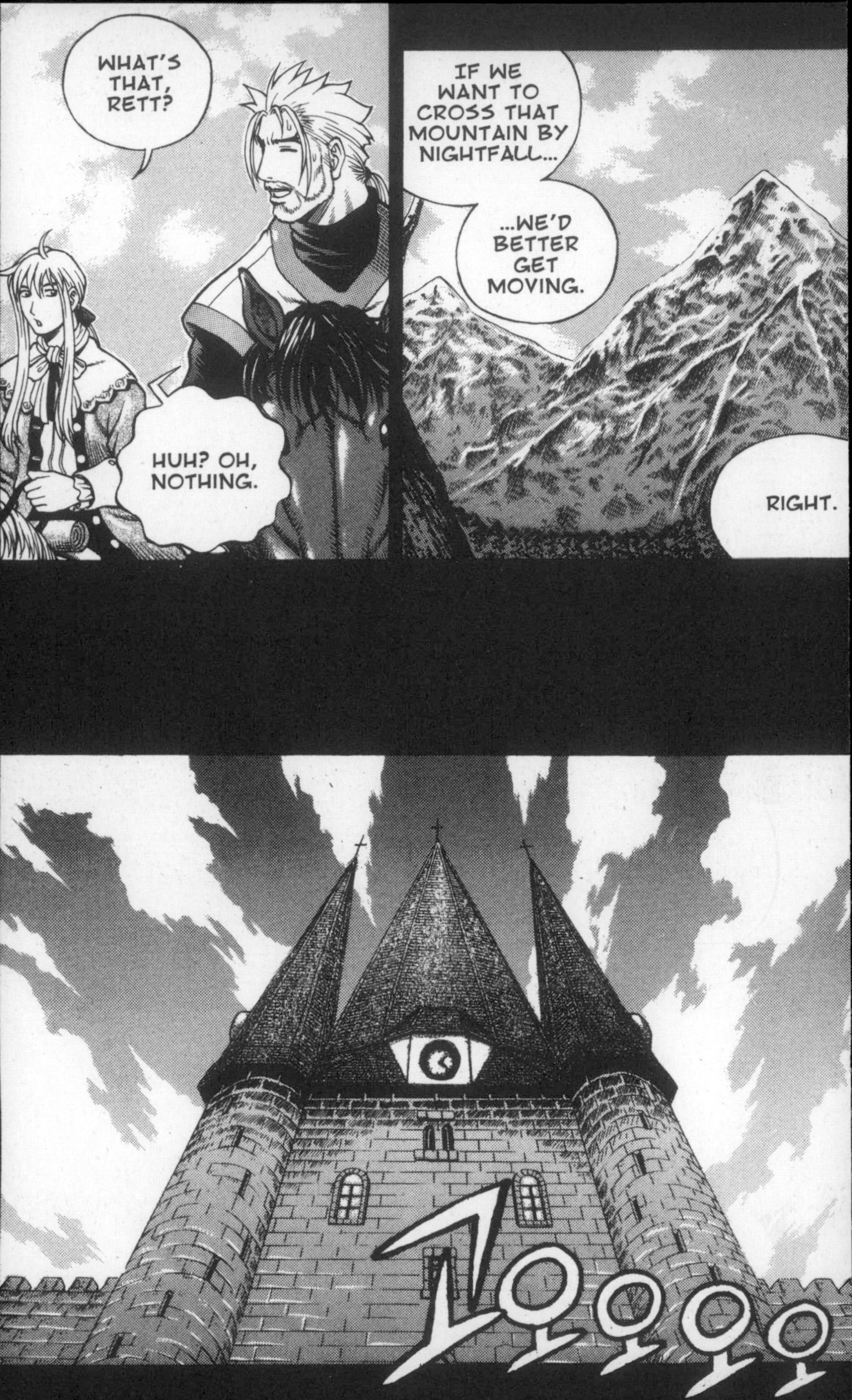
WHAT'S THAT, RETT?
HUH? OH, NOTHING.
IF WE WANT TO CROSS THAT MOUNTAIN BY NIGHTFALL...
...WE'D BETTER GET MOVING.
RIGHT.
ZOOOOO

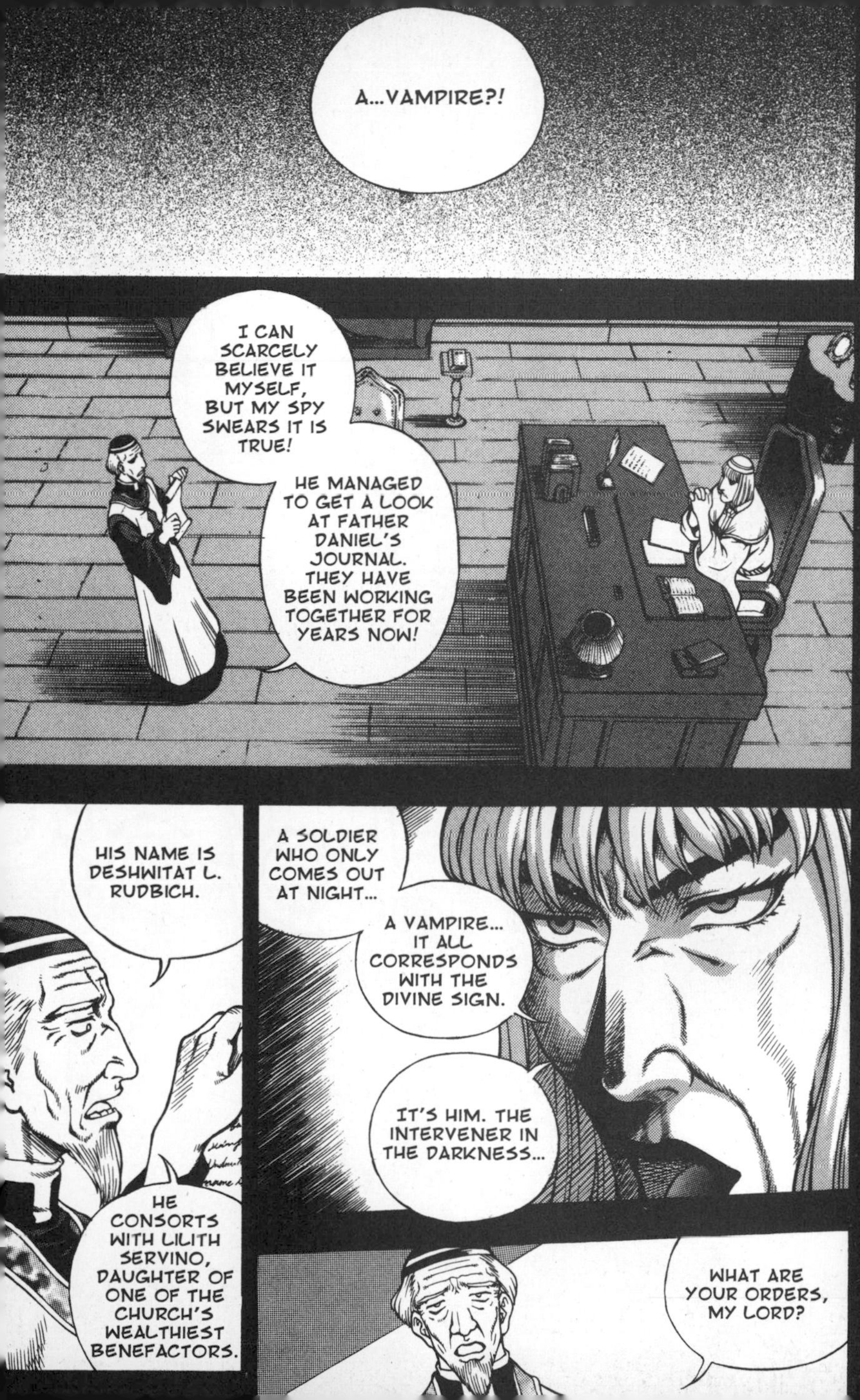
A...VAMPIRE?!
I CAN SCARCELY BELIEVE IT MYSELF, BUT MY SPY SWEARS IT IS TRUE!
HE MANAGED TO GET A LOOK AT FATHER DANIEL'S JOURNAL. THEY HAVE BEEN WORKING TOGETHER FOR YEARS NOW!
HIS NAME IS DESHWITAT L. RUDBICH.
HE CONSORTS WITH LILITH SERVINO, DAUGHTER OF ONE OF THE CHURCH'S WEALTHIEST BENEFACTORS.
A SOLDIER WHO ONLY COMES OUT AT NIGHT...
A VAMPIRE... IT ALL CORRESPONDS WITH THE DIVINE SIGN.
IT'S HIM. THE INTERVENER IN THE DARKNESS...
WHAT ARE YOUR ORDERS, MY LORD?

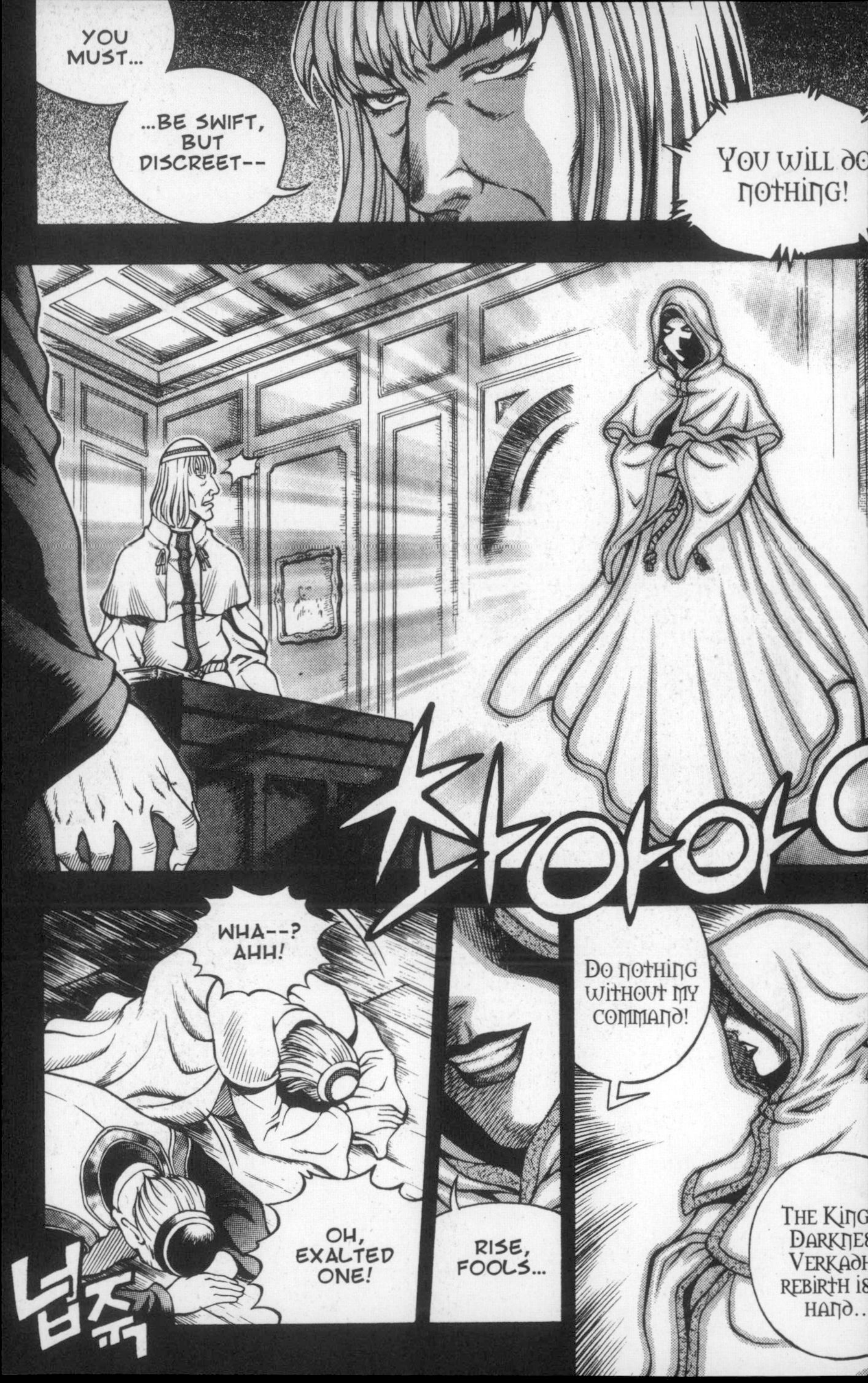
YOU MUST...
...BE SWIFT, BUT DISCREET--
YOU WILL DO NOTHING!
WHA--? AHH!
OH, EXALTED ONE!
넙죽
RISE, FOOLS...
DO NOTHING WITHOUT MY COMMAND!
THE KING
DARKNES
VERKADH
REBIRTH IS
HAND...

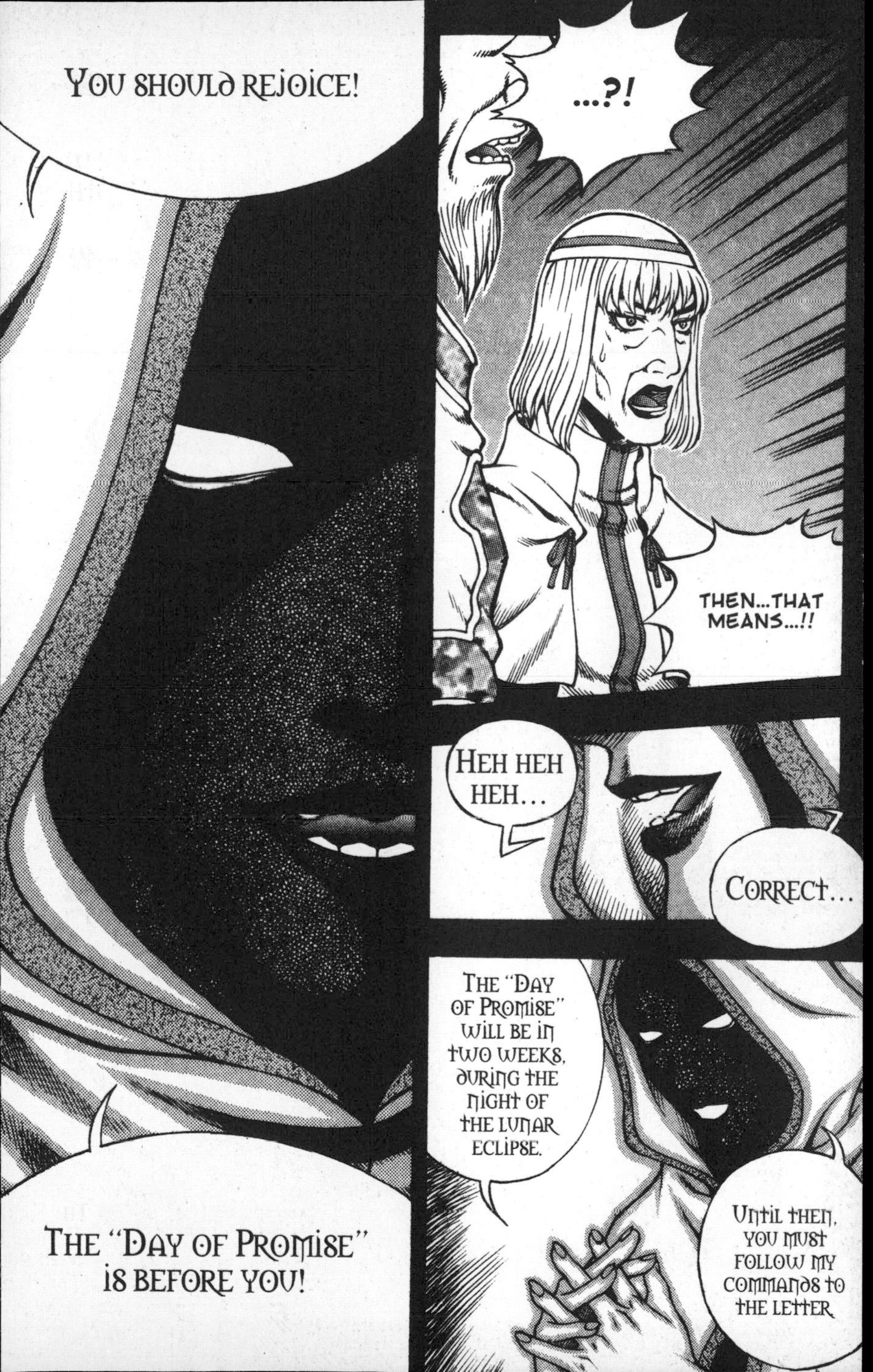
YOU SHOULD REJOICE!
THE "DAY OF PROMISE" IS BEFORE YOU!
...?!
THEN...THAT MEANS...!!
HEH HEH HEH...
CORRECT...
THE "DAY OF PROMISE" WILL BE IN TWO WEEKS, DURING THE NIGHT OF THE LUNAR ECLIPSE.
UNTIL THEN, YOU MUST FOLLOW MY COMMANDS TO THE LETTER

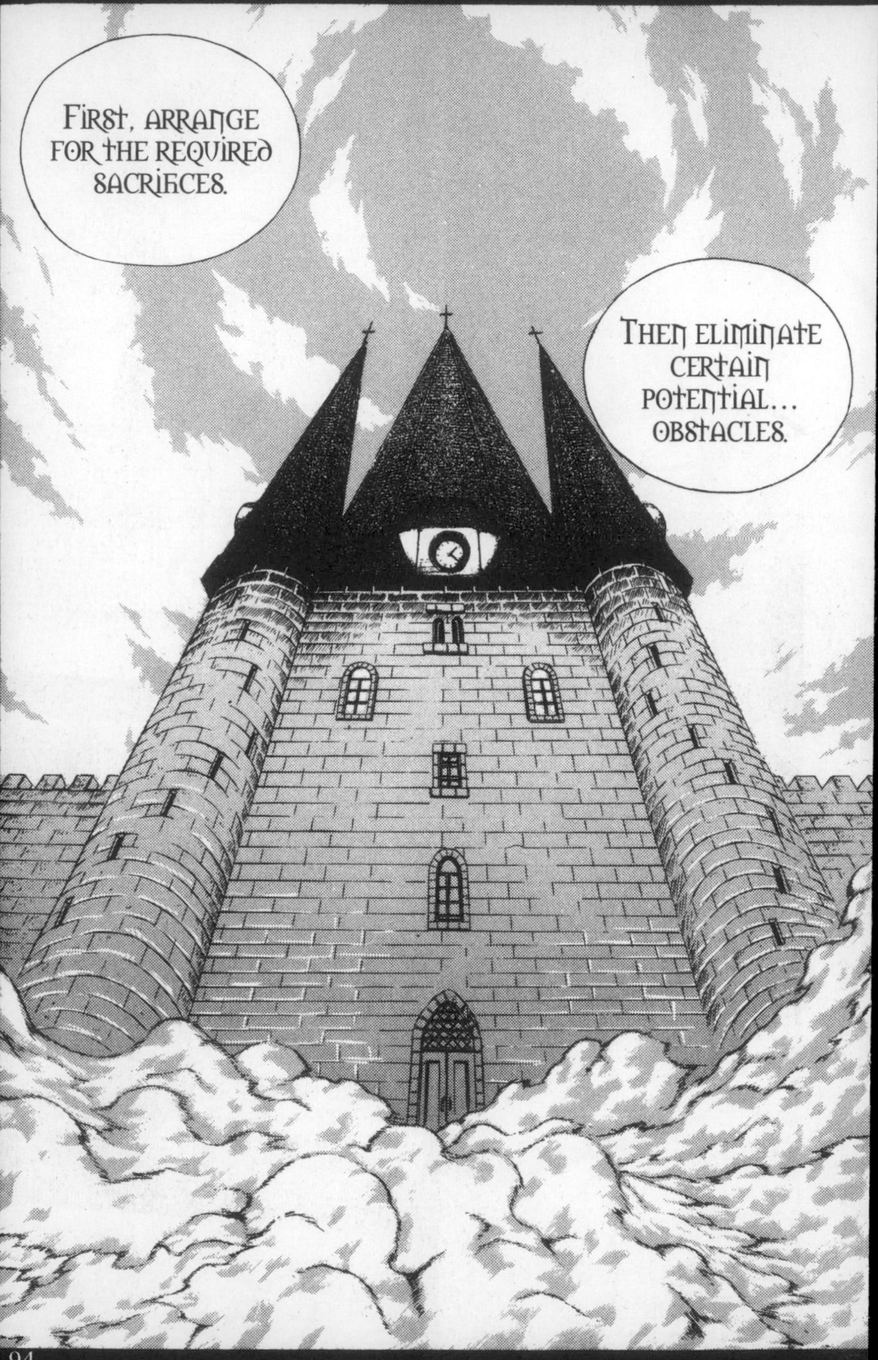
FIRST, ARRANGE FOR THE REQUIRED SACRIFICES.
THEN ELIMINATE CERTAIN POTENTIAL... OBSTACLES.

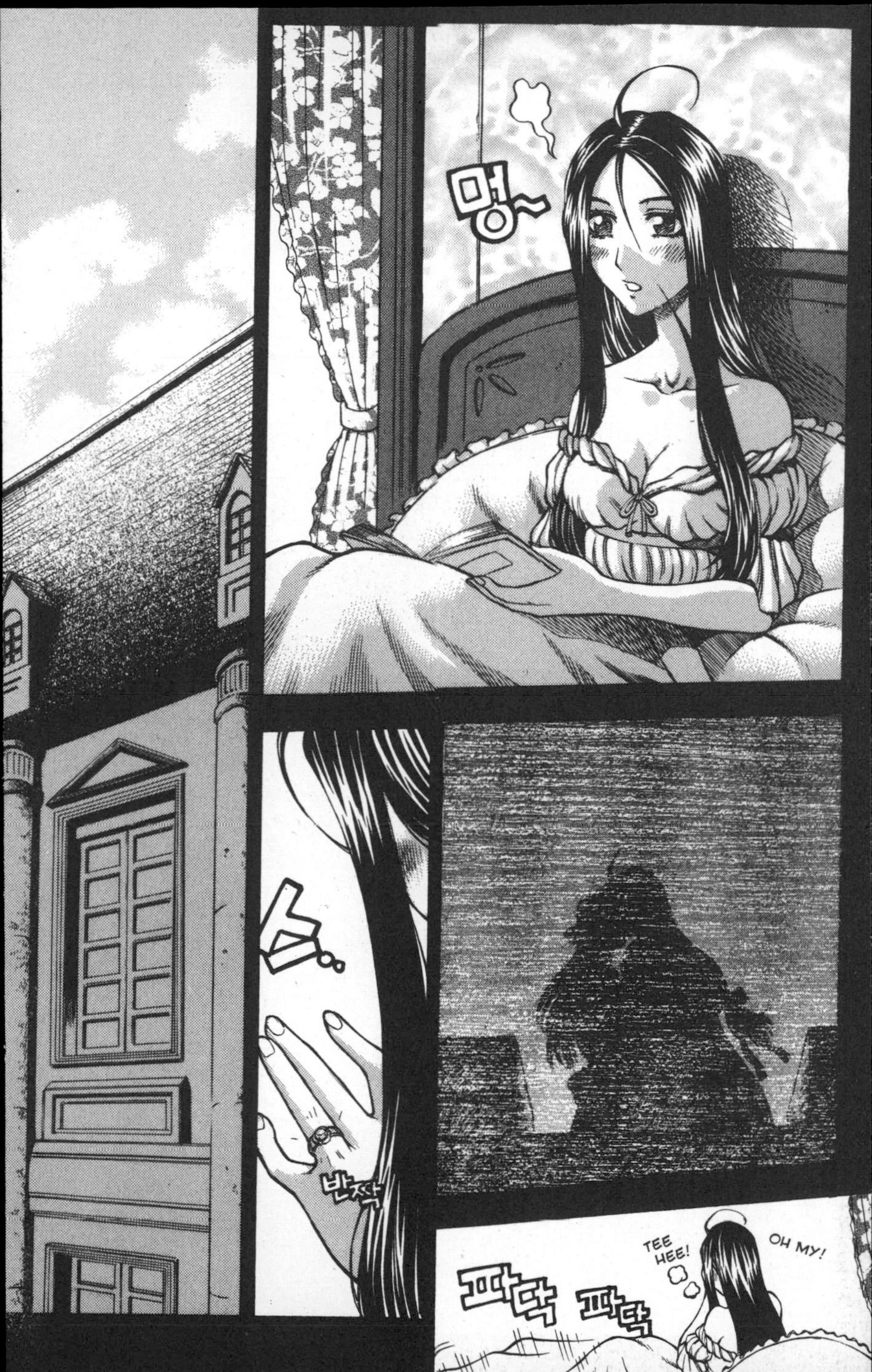
멍~
반짝
TEE HEE!
OH MY!
파닥 파닥

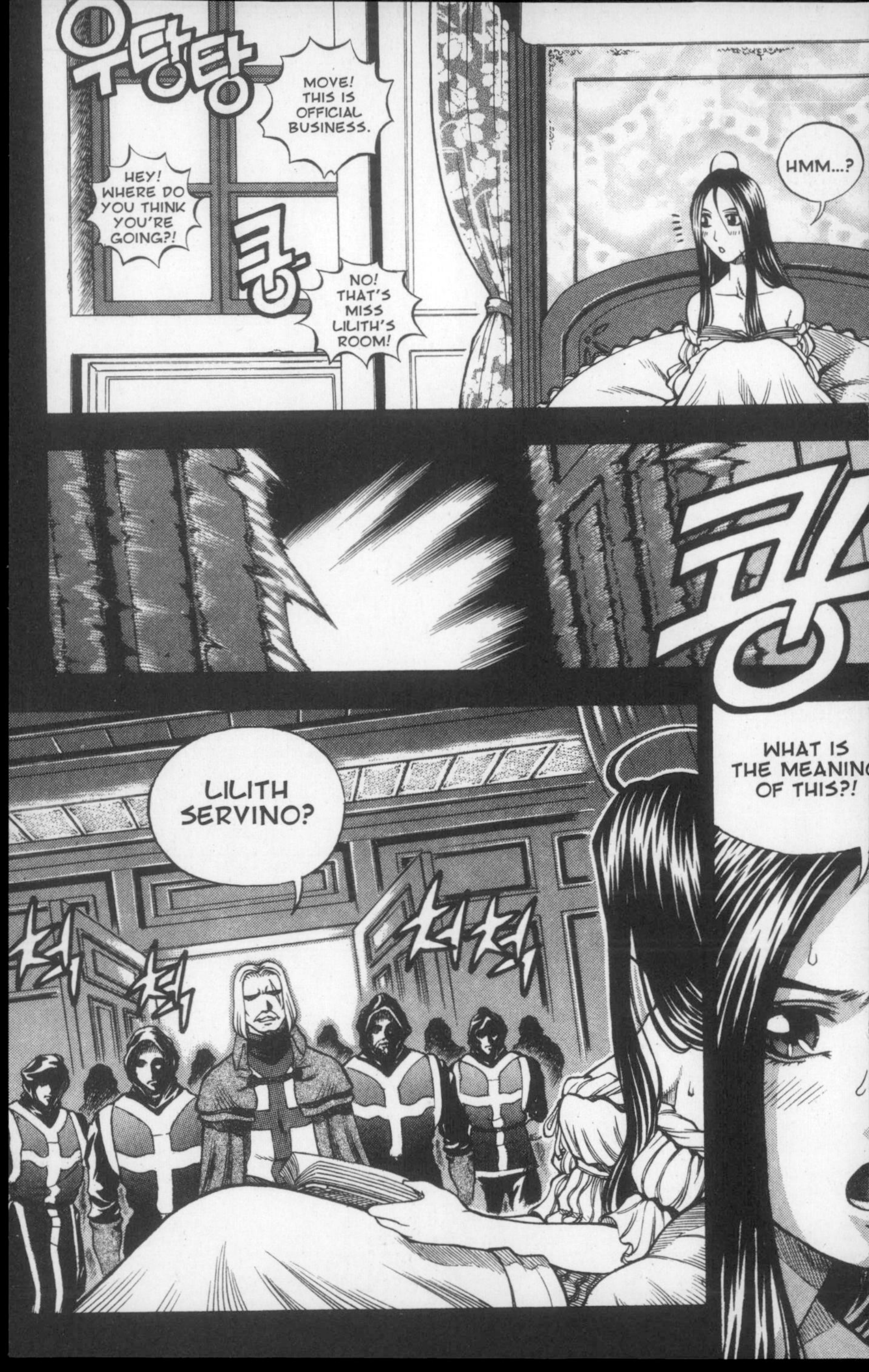
우당탕
MOVE! THIS IS OFFICIAL BUSINESS.
HEY! WHERE DO YOU THINK YOU'RE GOING?!
쿵
NO! THAT'S MISS LILITH'S ROOM!
HMM...?
쾅
LILITH SERVINO?
척 척
척 척 척
WHAT IS THE MEANIN
OF THIS?!

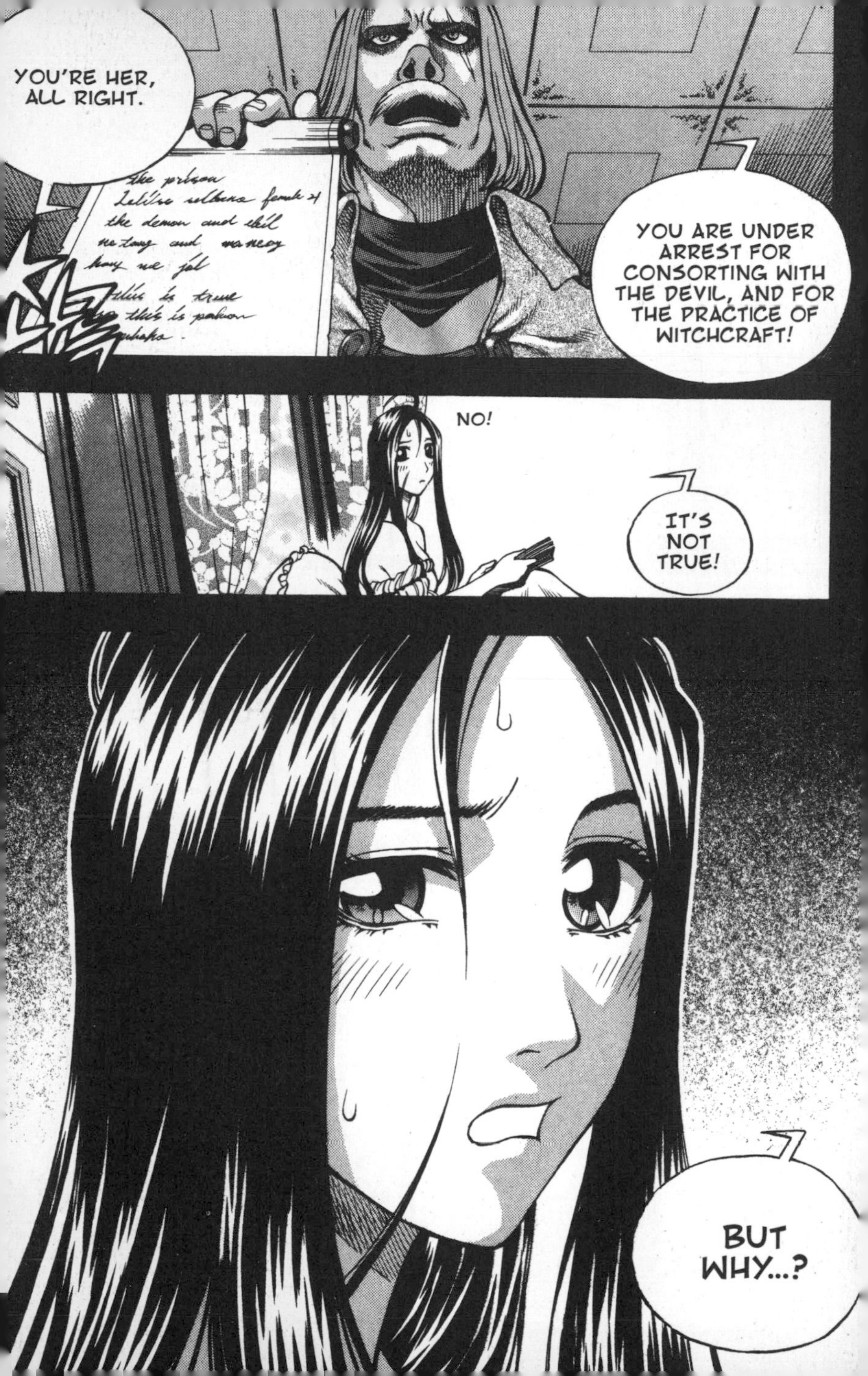
YOU'RE HER, ALL RIGHT.
YOU ARE UNDER ARREST FOR CONSORTING WITH THE DEVIL, AND FOR THE PRACTICE OF WITCHCRAFT!
NO!
IT'S NOT TRUE!
BUT WHY...?

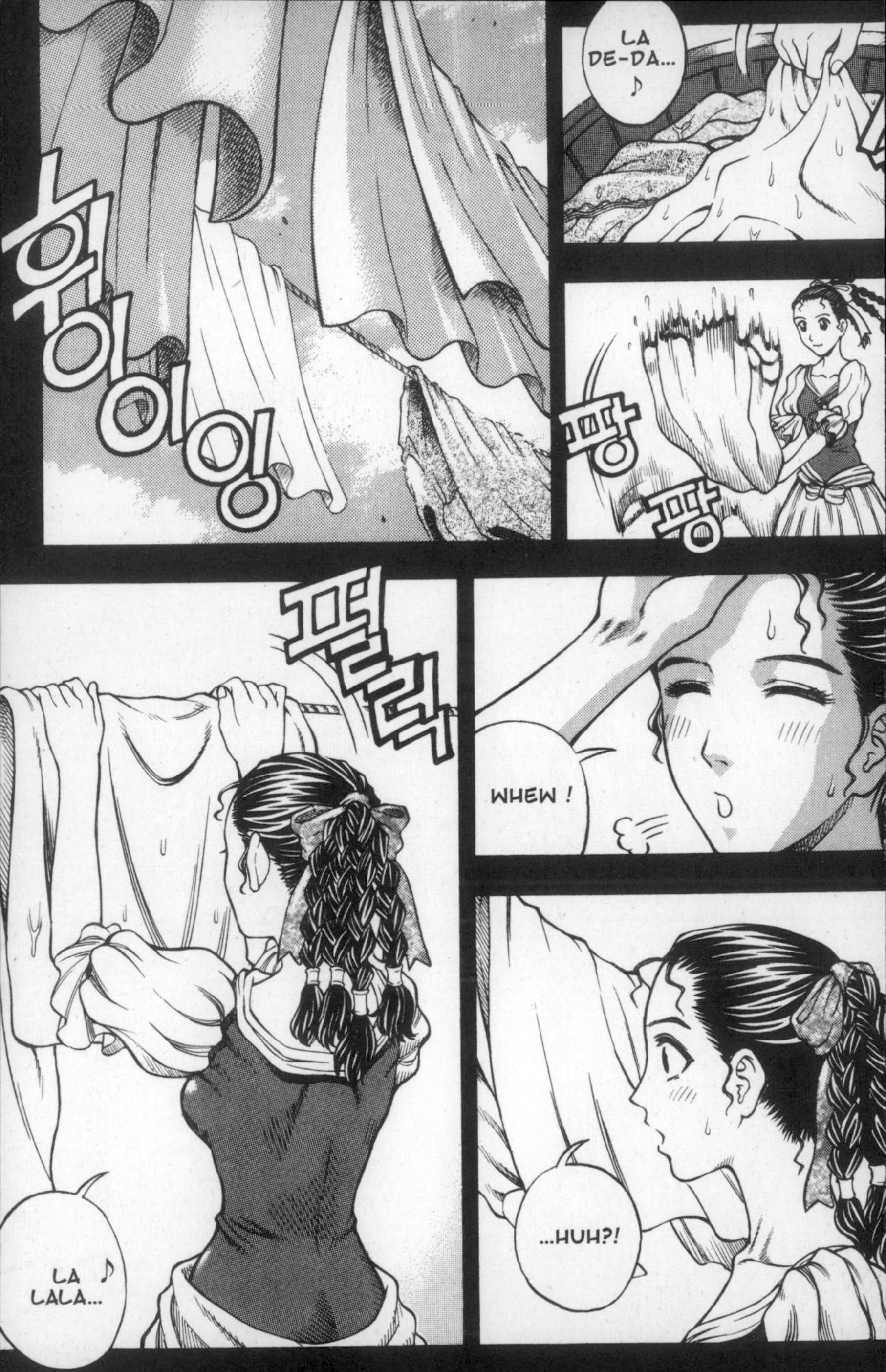
휘이이잉!
LA DE-DA... ♪
팡
팡
펄럭
LA LALA... ♪
WHEW !
...HUH?!

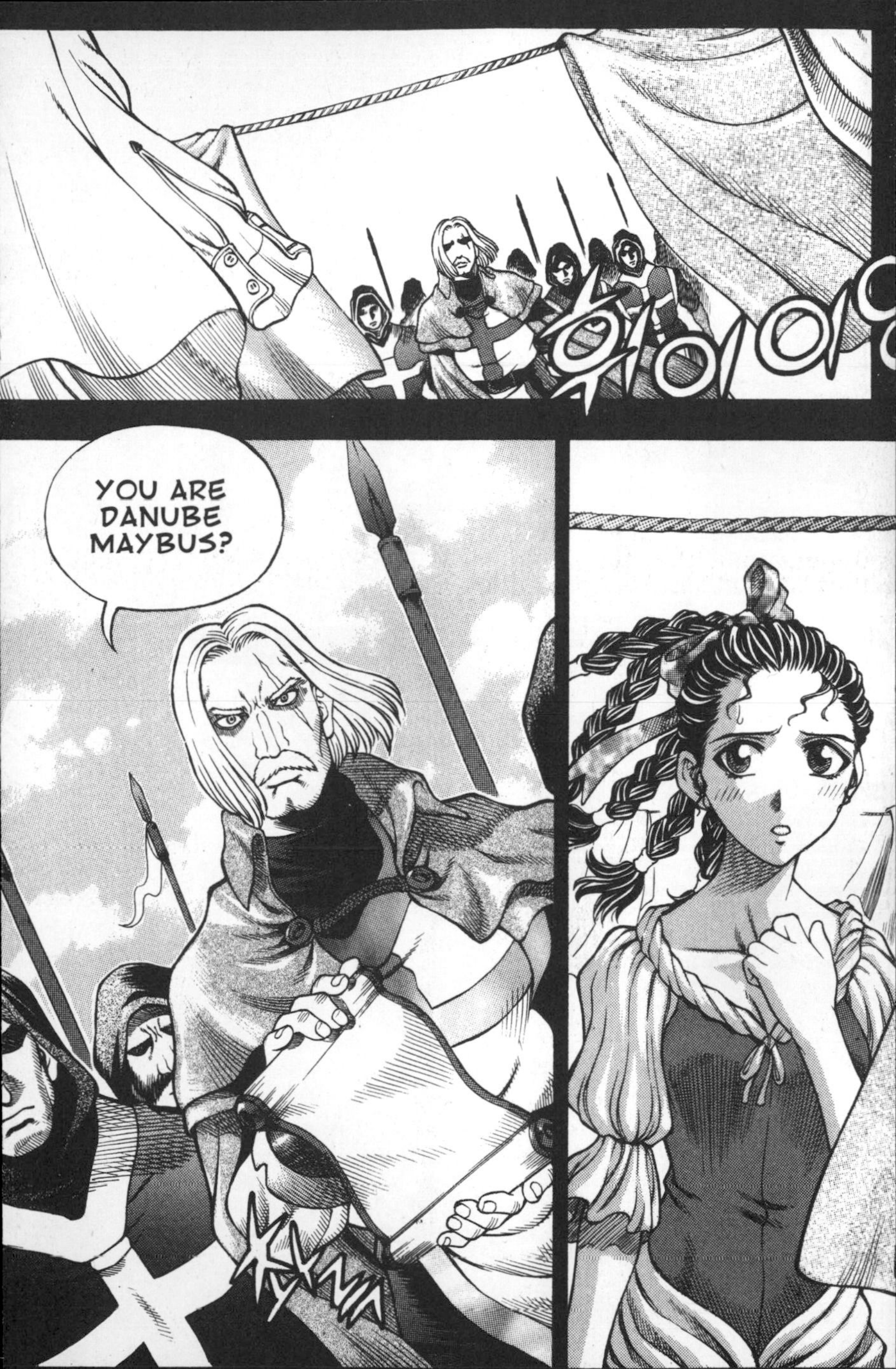
YOU ARE DANUBE MAYBUS?

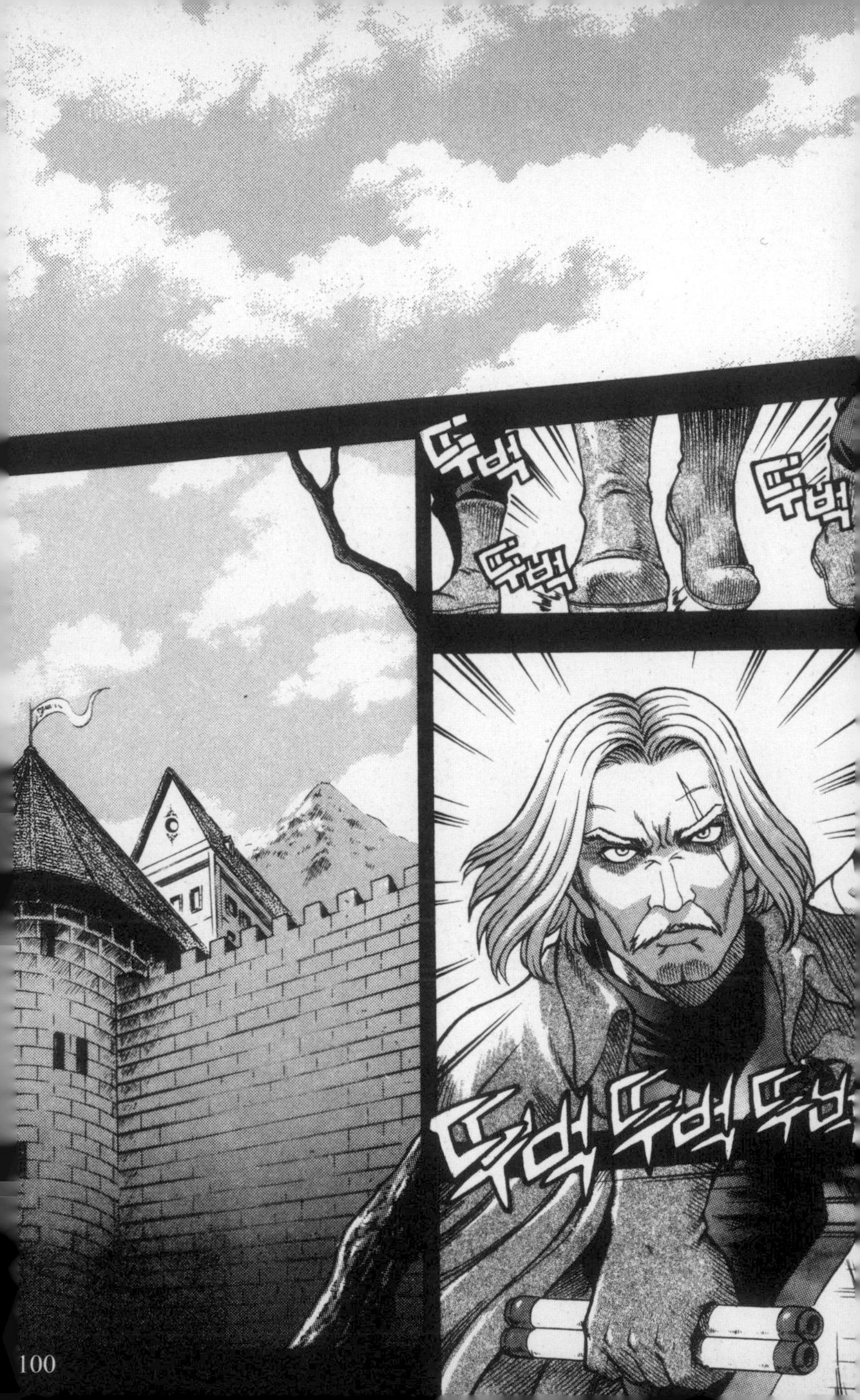

뚜벅
뚜벅
뚜벅
뚜벅 뚜벅

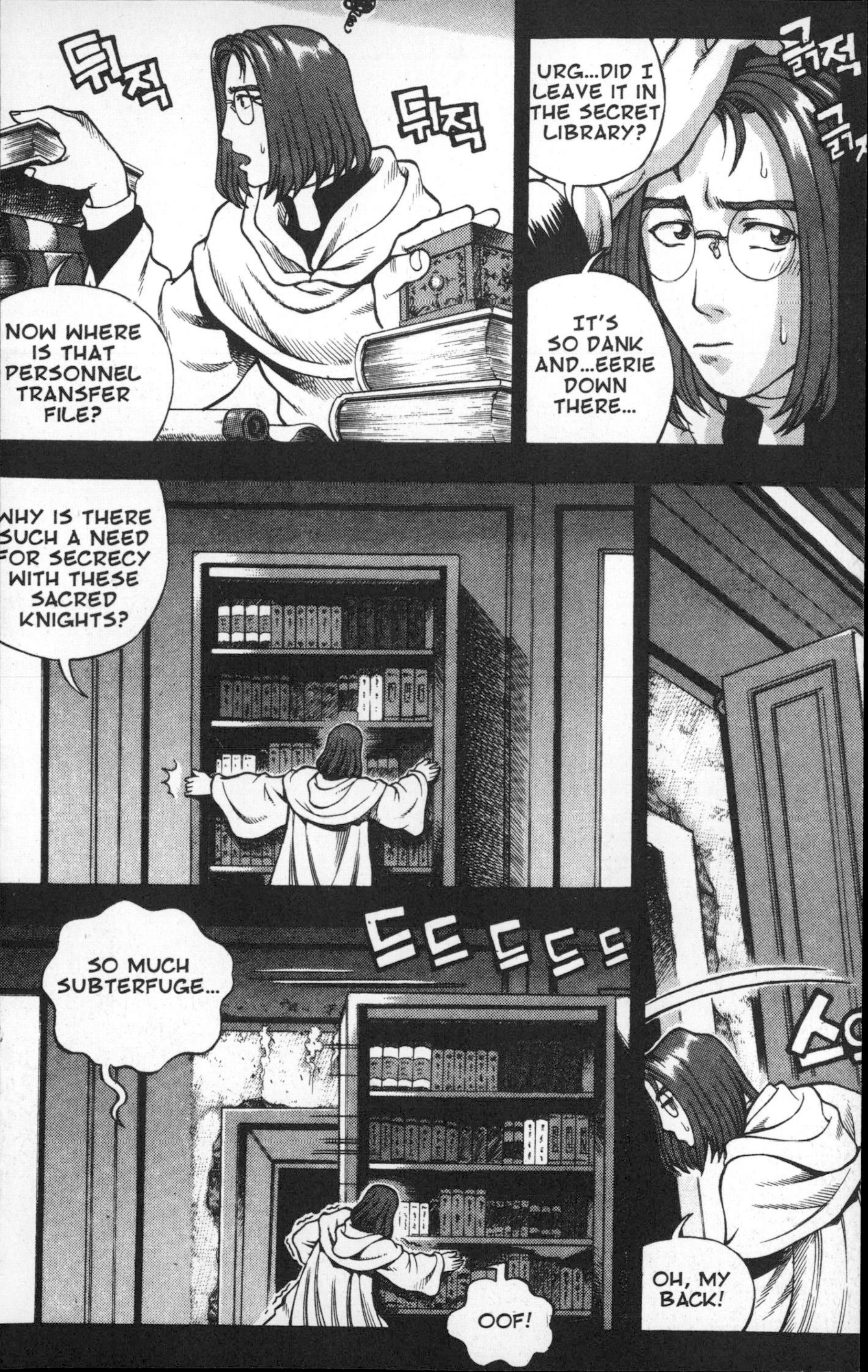

뒤적
뒤적
NOW WHERE IS THAT PERSONNEL TRANSFER FILE?
긁적
긁적
URG...DID I LEAVE IT IN THE SECRET LIBRARY?
IT'S SO DANK AND...EERIE DOWN THERE...
WHY IS THERE SUCH A NEED FOR SECRECY WITH THESE SACRED KNIGHTS?
SO MUCH SUBTERFUGE...
드드드드드
OOF!
OH, MY BACK!

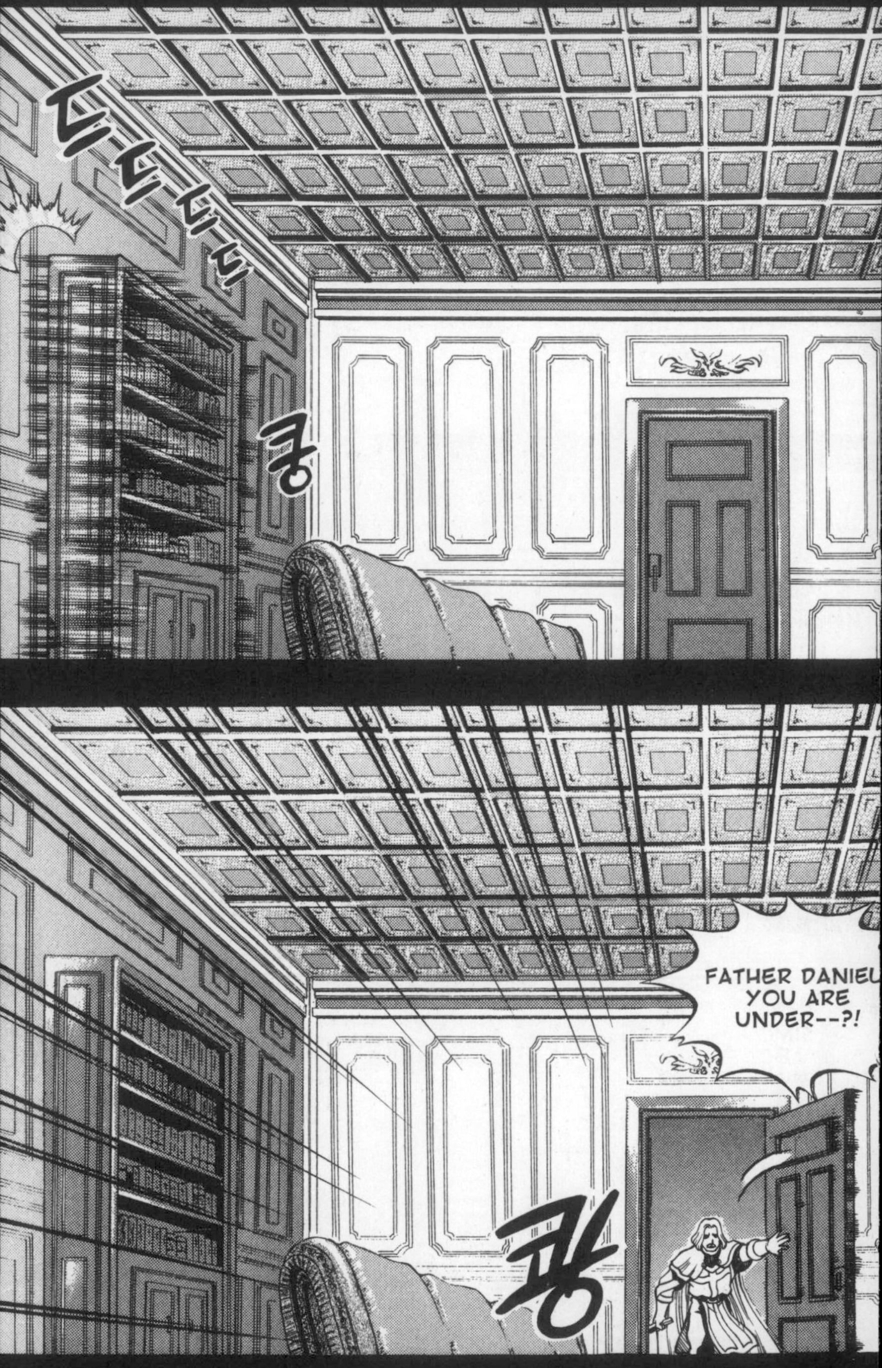
드드드드
쿵
FATHER DANIEL
YOU ARE
UNDER--?!
쾅

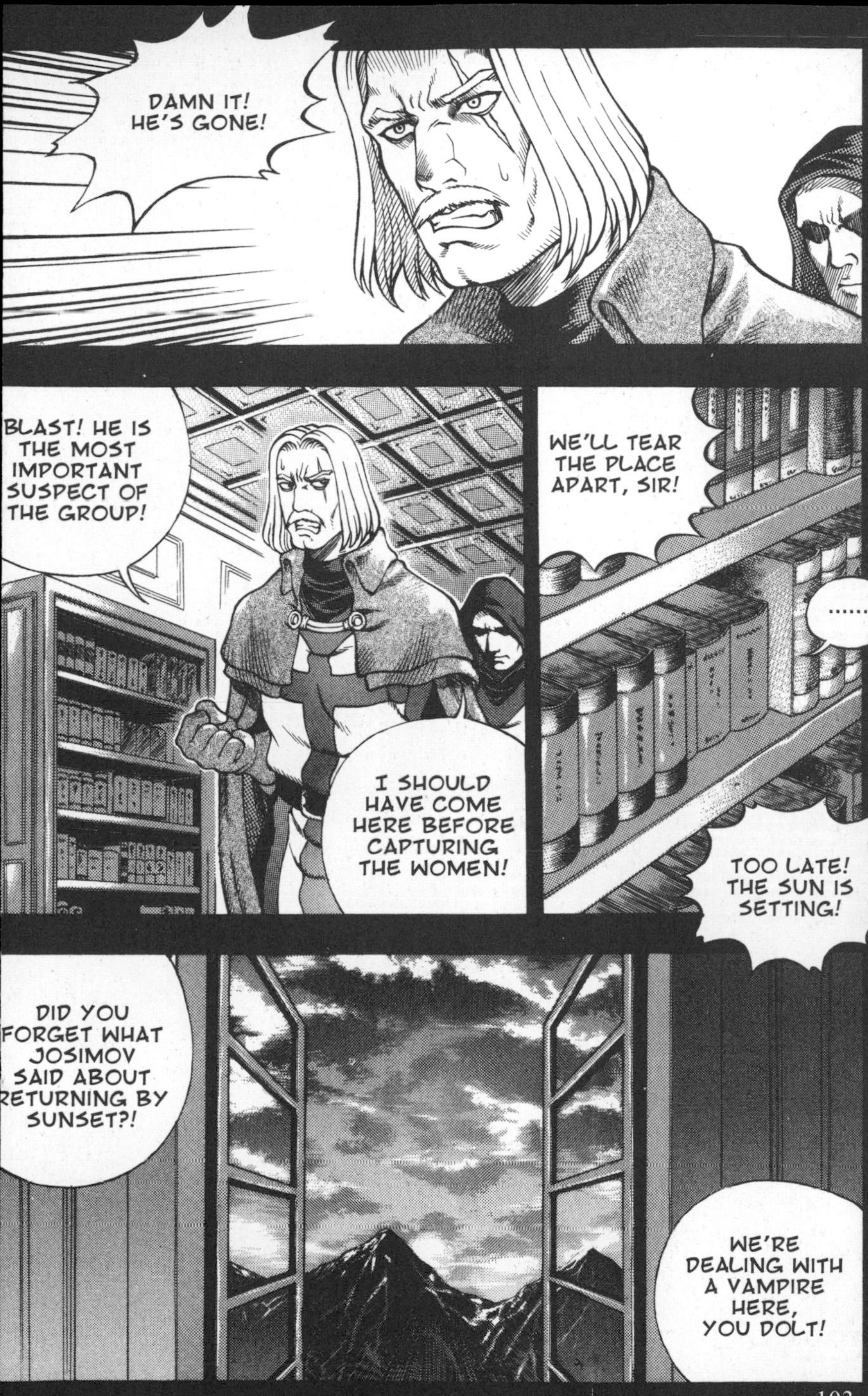
DAMN IT! HE'S GONE!
BLAST! HE IS THE MOST IMPORTANT SUSPECT OF THE GROUP!
I SHOULD HAVE COME HERE BEFORE CAPTURING THE WOMEN!
WE'LL TEAR THE PLACE APART, SIR!
......
TOO LATE! THE SUN IS SETTING!
DID YOU FORGET WHAT JOSIMOV SAID ABOUT RETURNING BY SUNSET?!
WE'RE DEALING WITH A VAMPIRE HERE, YOU DOLT!

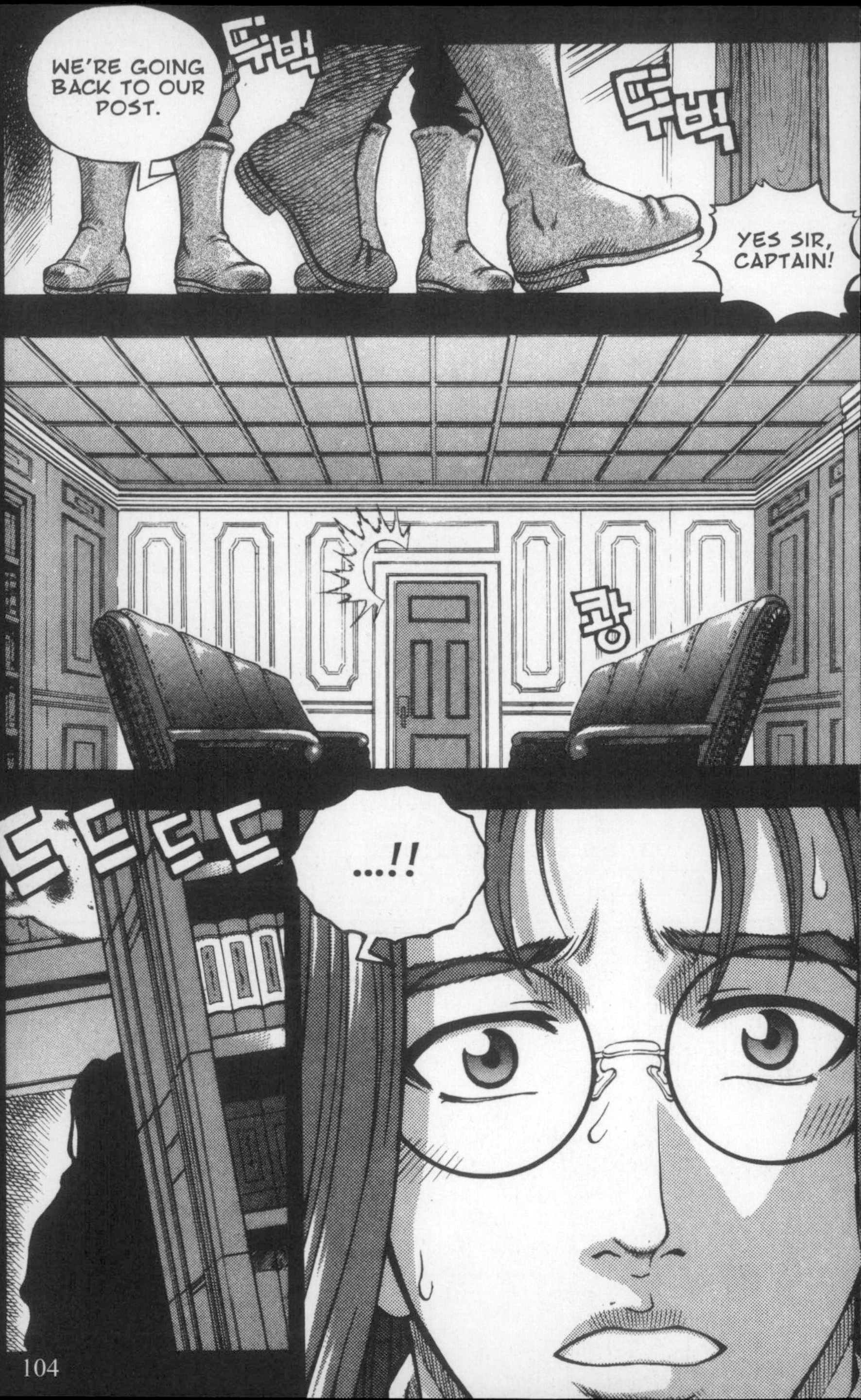
WE'RE GOING BACK TO OUR POST.
뚜벅
뚜벅
YES SIR, CAPTAIN!
광
드드드드
...!!

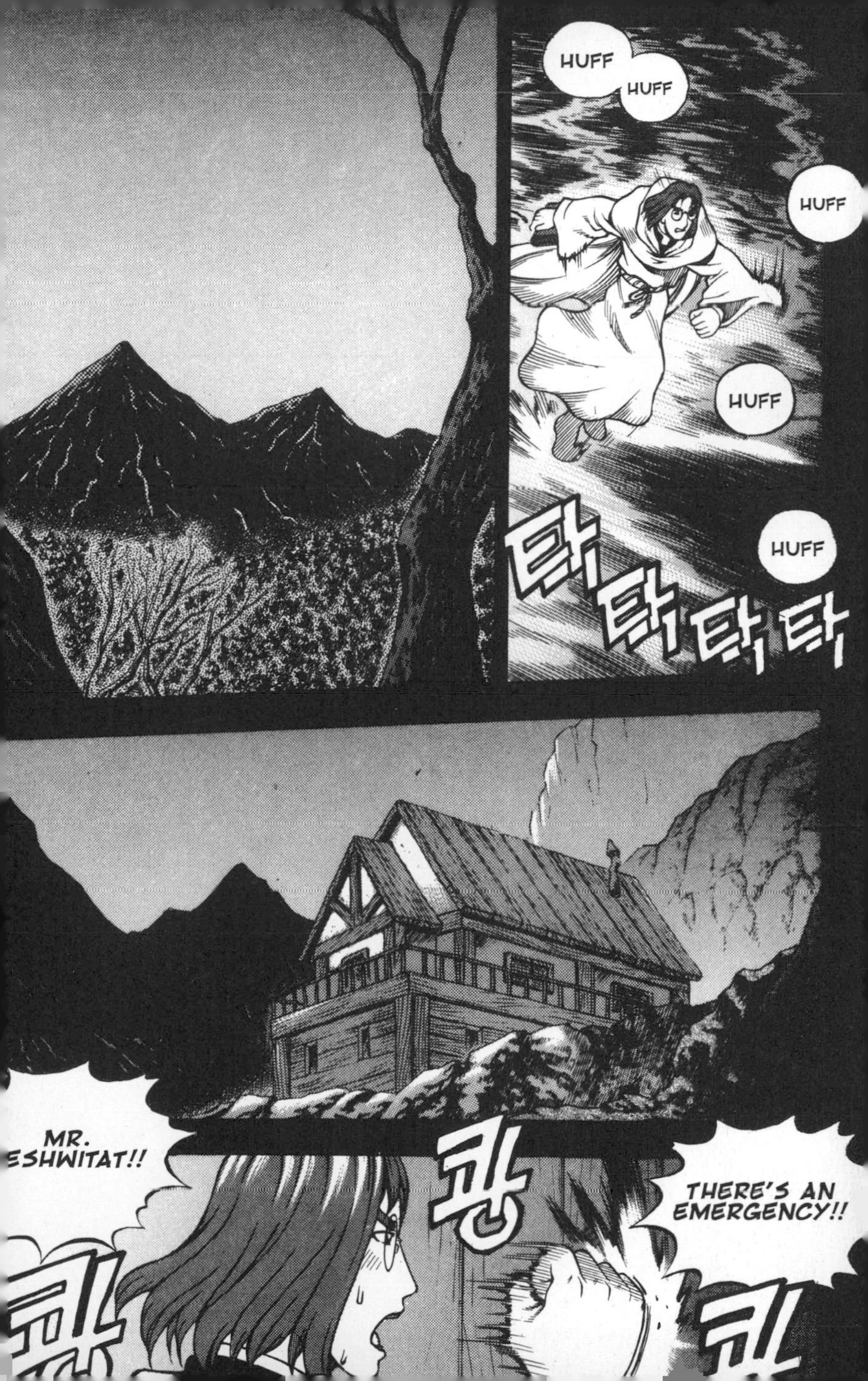
HUFF
HUFF
HUFF
HUFF
HUFF
타, 타, 타, 타,
MR. ESHWITAT!!
THERE'S AN EMERGENCY!!

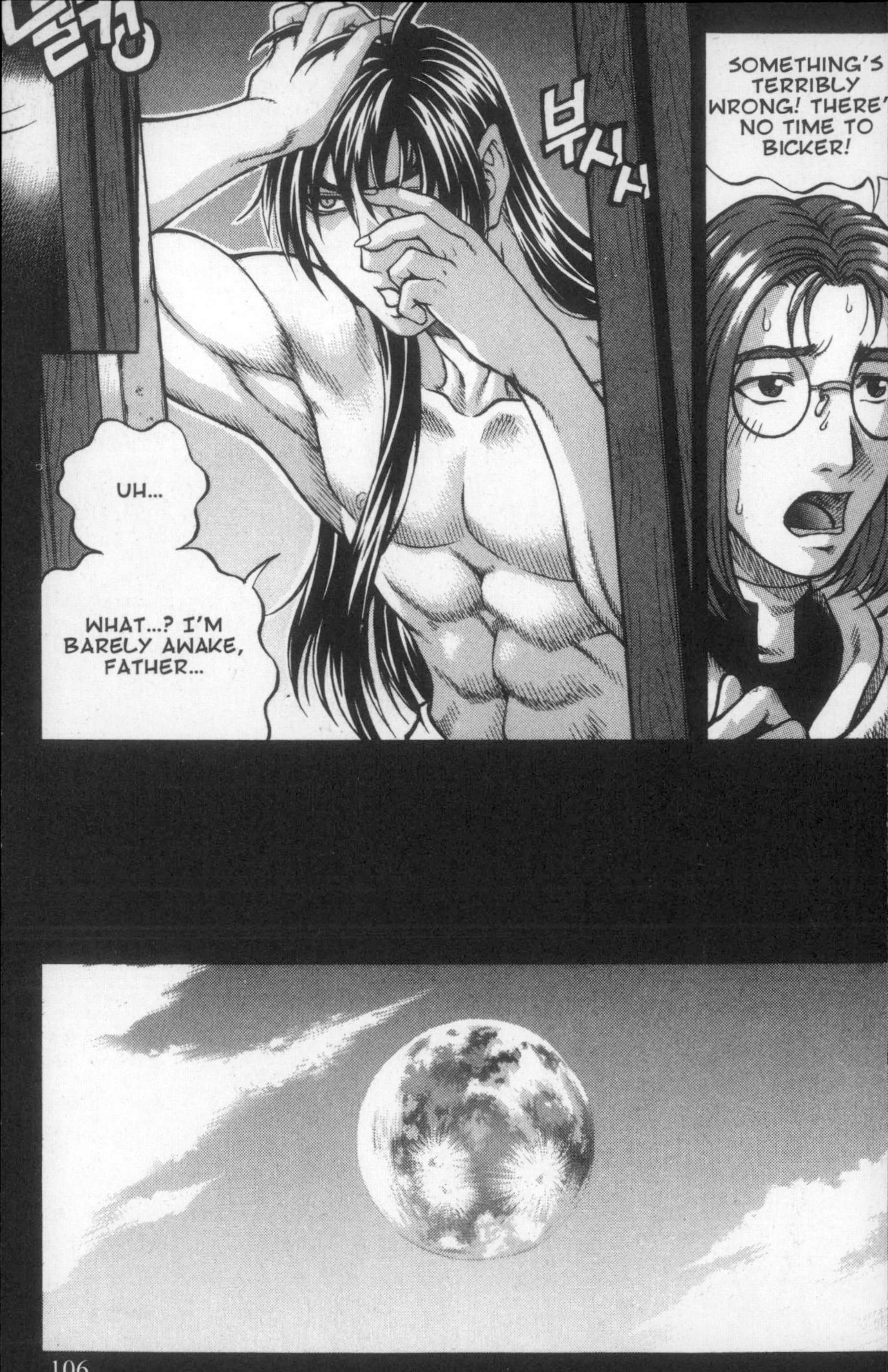
부시시
UH...
WHAT...? I'M BARELY AWAKE, FATHER...
SOMETHING'S TERRIBLY WRONG! THERE' NO TIME TO BICKER!

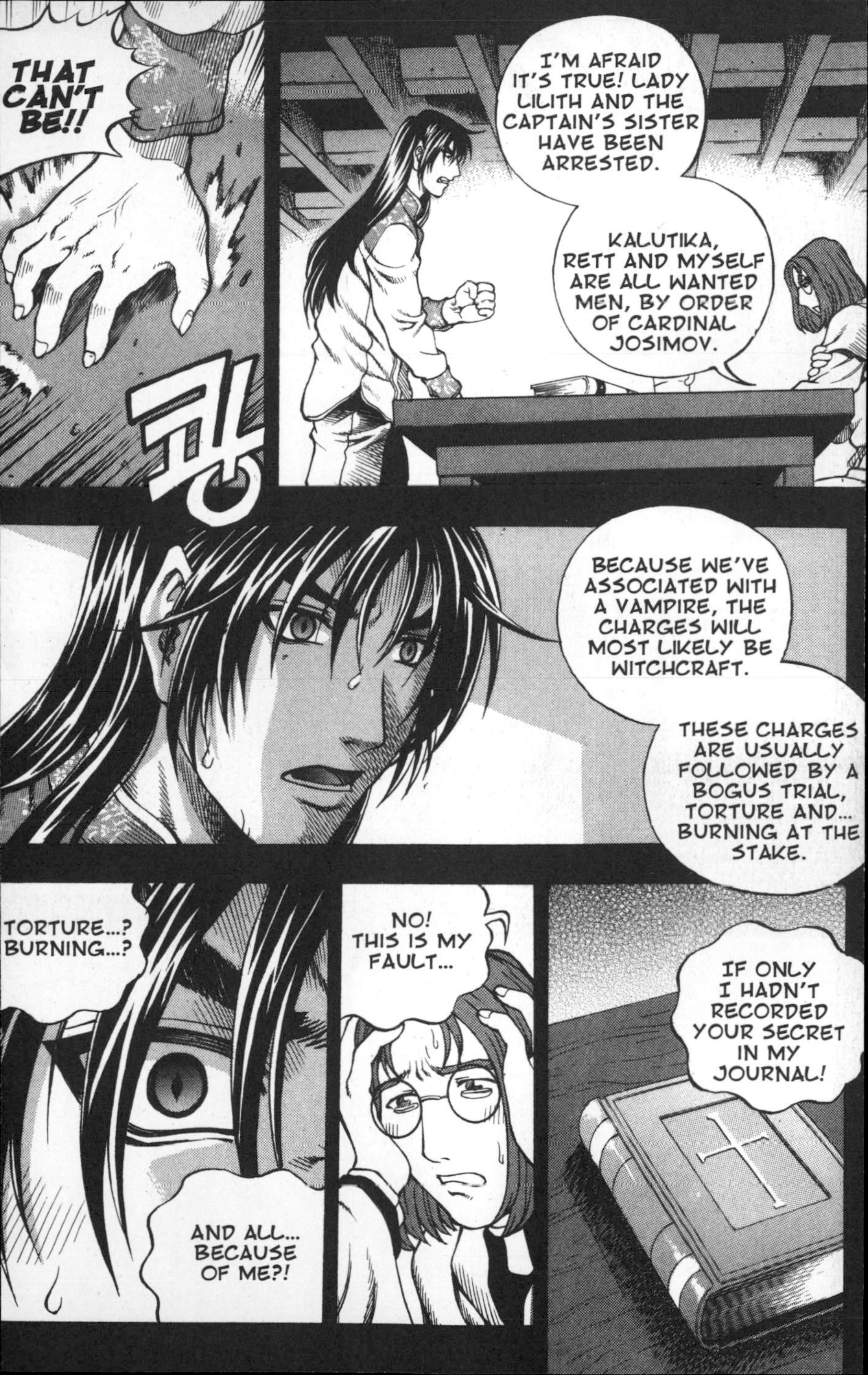
THAT CAN'T BE!!
쾅
I'M AFRAID IT'S TRUE! LADY LILITH AND THE CAPTAIN'S SISTER HAVE BEEN ARRESTED.
KALUTIKA, RETT AND MYSELF ARE ALL WANTED MEN, BY ORDER OF CARDINAL JOSIMOV.
BECAUSE WE'VE ASSOCIATED WITH A VAMPIRE, THE CHARGES WILL MOST LIKELY BE WITCHCRAFT.
THESE CHARGES ARE USUALLY FOLLOWED BY A BOGUS TRIAL, TORTURE AND... BURNING AT THE STAKE.
TORTURE...? BURNING...?
AND ALL... BECAUSE OF ME?!
NO! THIS IS MY FAULT...
IF ONLY I HADN'T RECORDED YOUR SECRET IN MY JOURNAL!

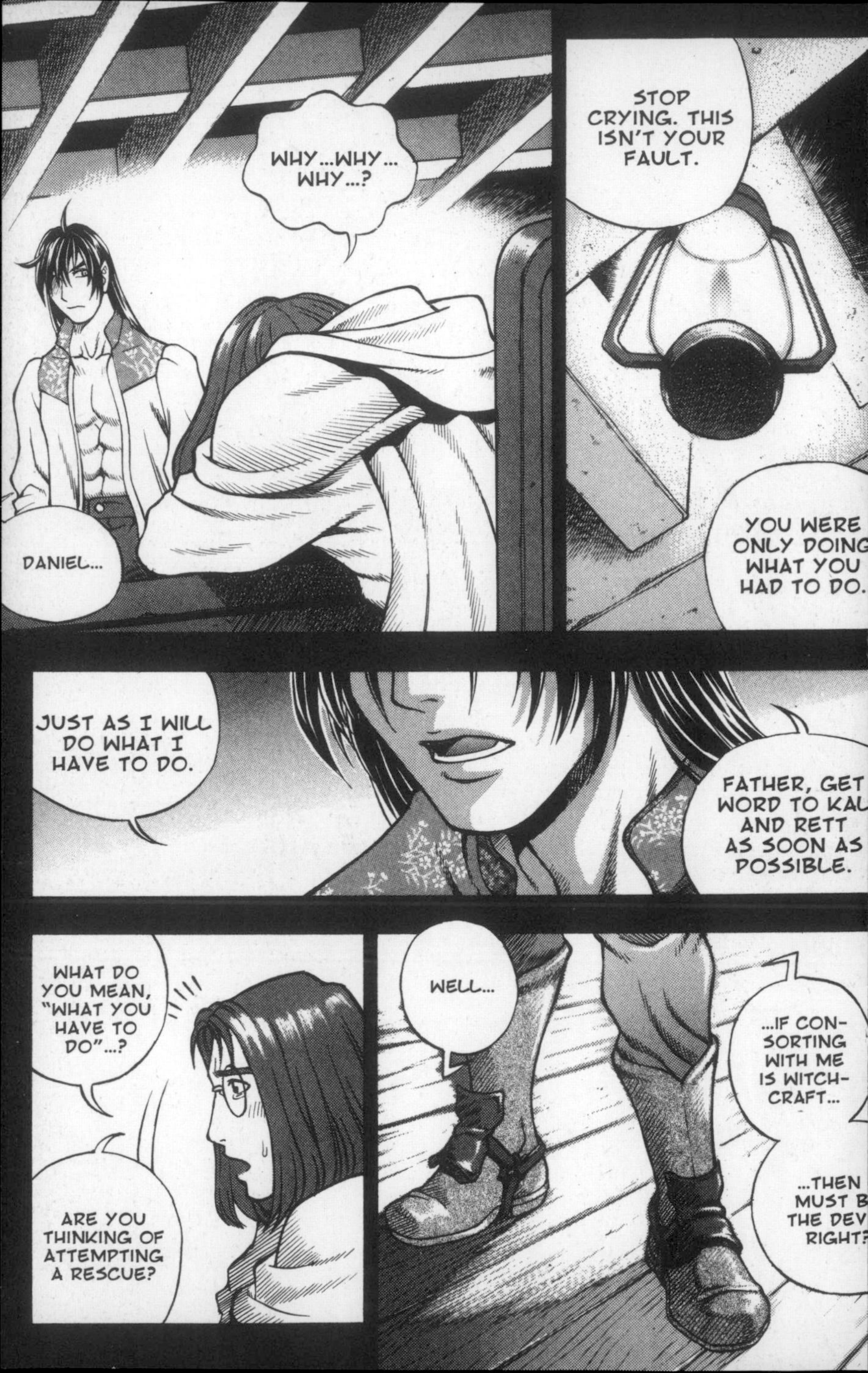
WHY...WHY... WHY...?
DANIEL...
STOP CRYING. THIS ISN'T YOUR FAULT.
YOU WERE ONLY DOING WHAT YOU HAD TO DO.
JUST AS I WILL DO WHAT I HAVE TO DO.
FATHER, GET WORD TO KA AND RETT AS SOON AS POSSIBLE.
WHAT DO YOU MEAN, "WHAT YOU HAVE TO DO"...?
ARE YOU THINKING OF ATTEMPTING A RESCUE?
WELL...
...IF CON-SORTING WITH ME IS WITCH-CRAFT...
...THEN MUST B THE DEV RIGHT?

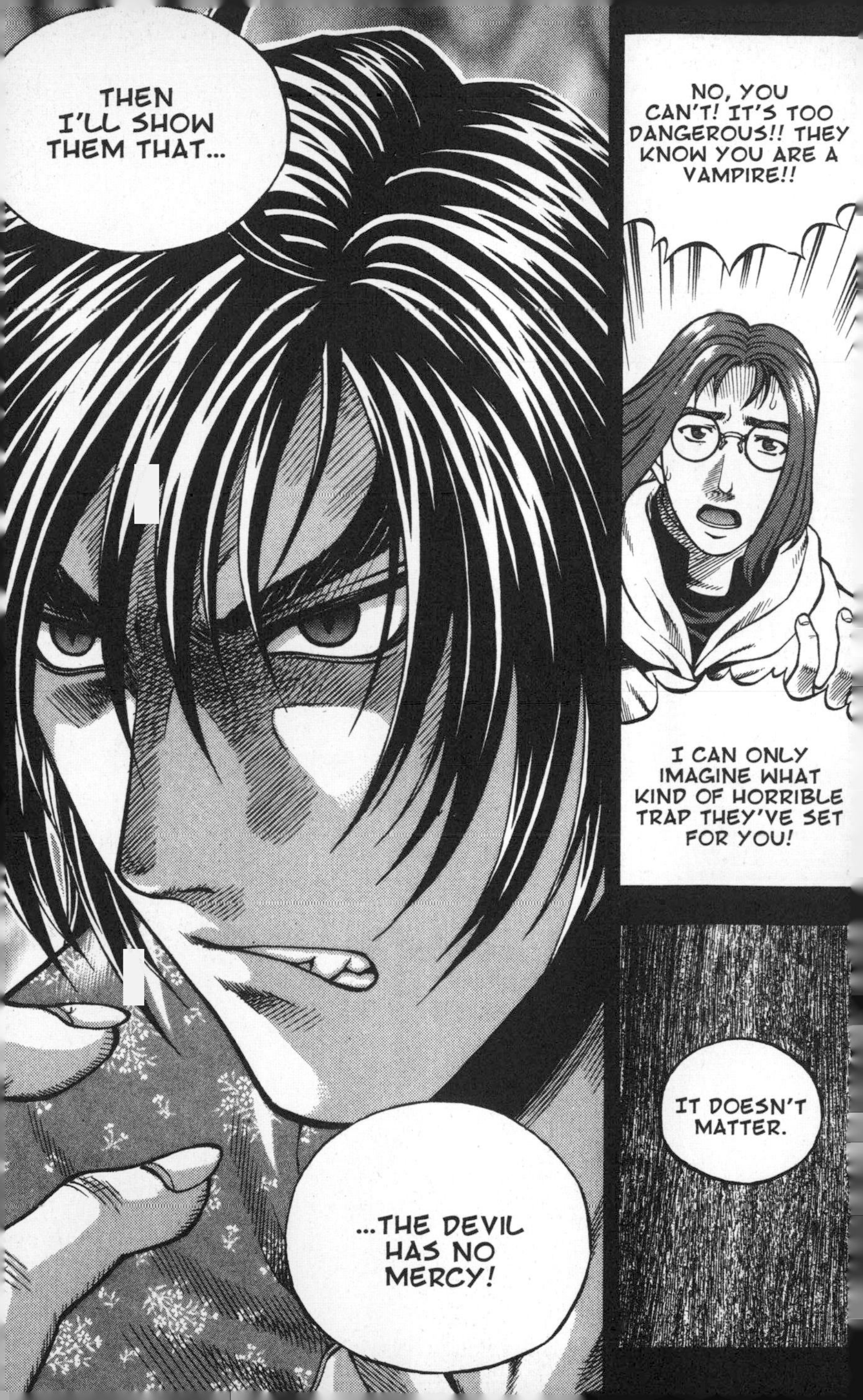
THEN I'LL SHOW THEM THAT...
...THE DEVIL HAS NO MERCY!
NO, YOU CAN'T! IT'S TOO DANGEROUS!! THEY KNOW YOU ARE A VAMPIRE!!
I CAN ONLY IMAGINE WHAT KIND OF HORRIBLE TRAP THEY'VE SET FOR YOU!
IT DOESN'T MATTER.

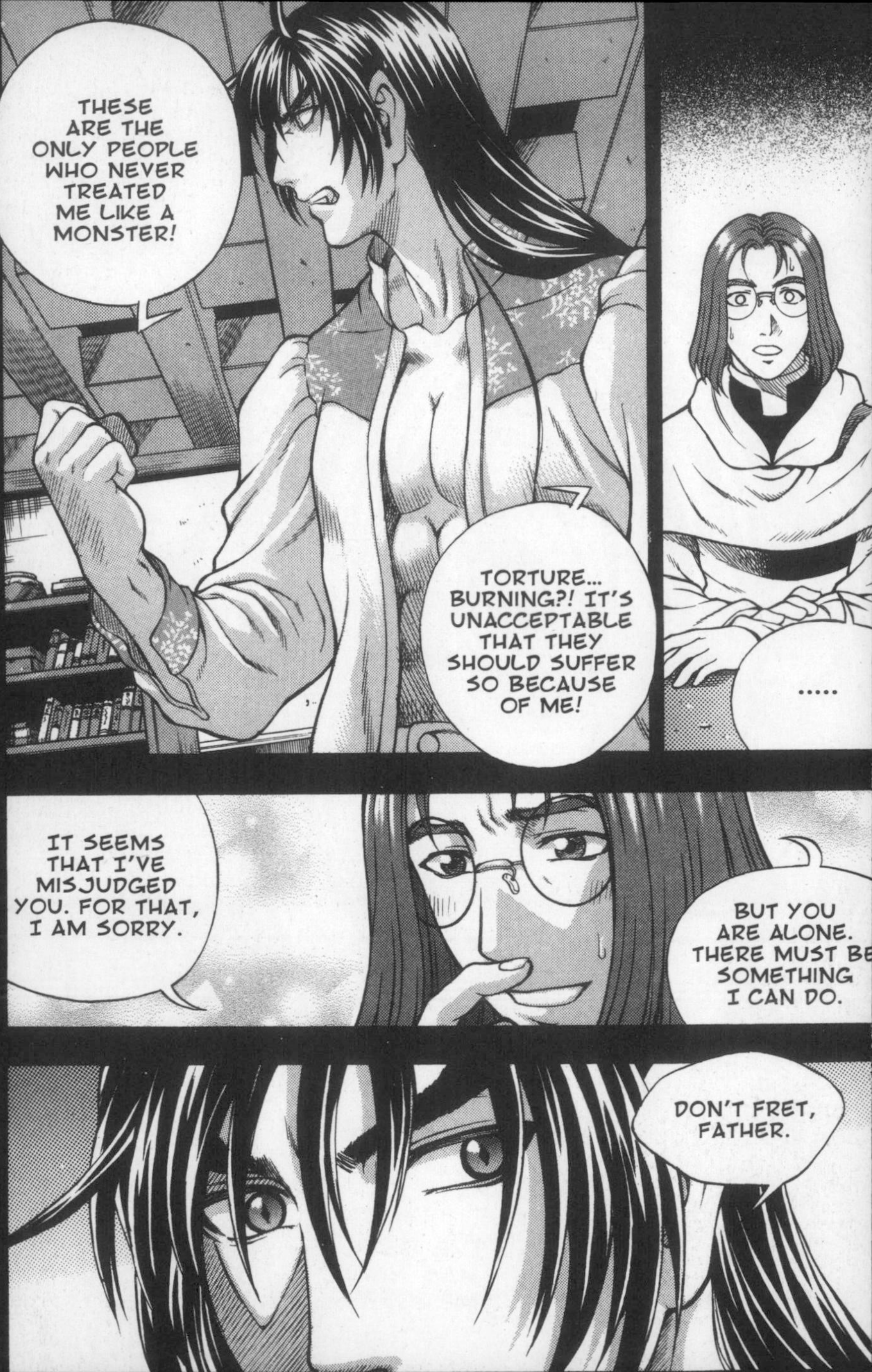
THESE ARE THE ONLY PEOPLE WHO NEVER TREATED ME LIKE A MONSTER!
TORTURE... BURNING?! IT'S UNACCEPTABLE THAT THEY SHOULD SUFFER SO BECAUSE OF ME!
.....
IT SEEMS THAT I'VE MISJUDGED YOU. FOR THAT, I AM SORRY.
BUT YOU ARE ALONE. THERE MUST BE SOMETHING I CAN DO.
DON'T FRET, FATHER.

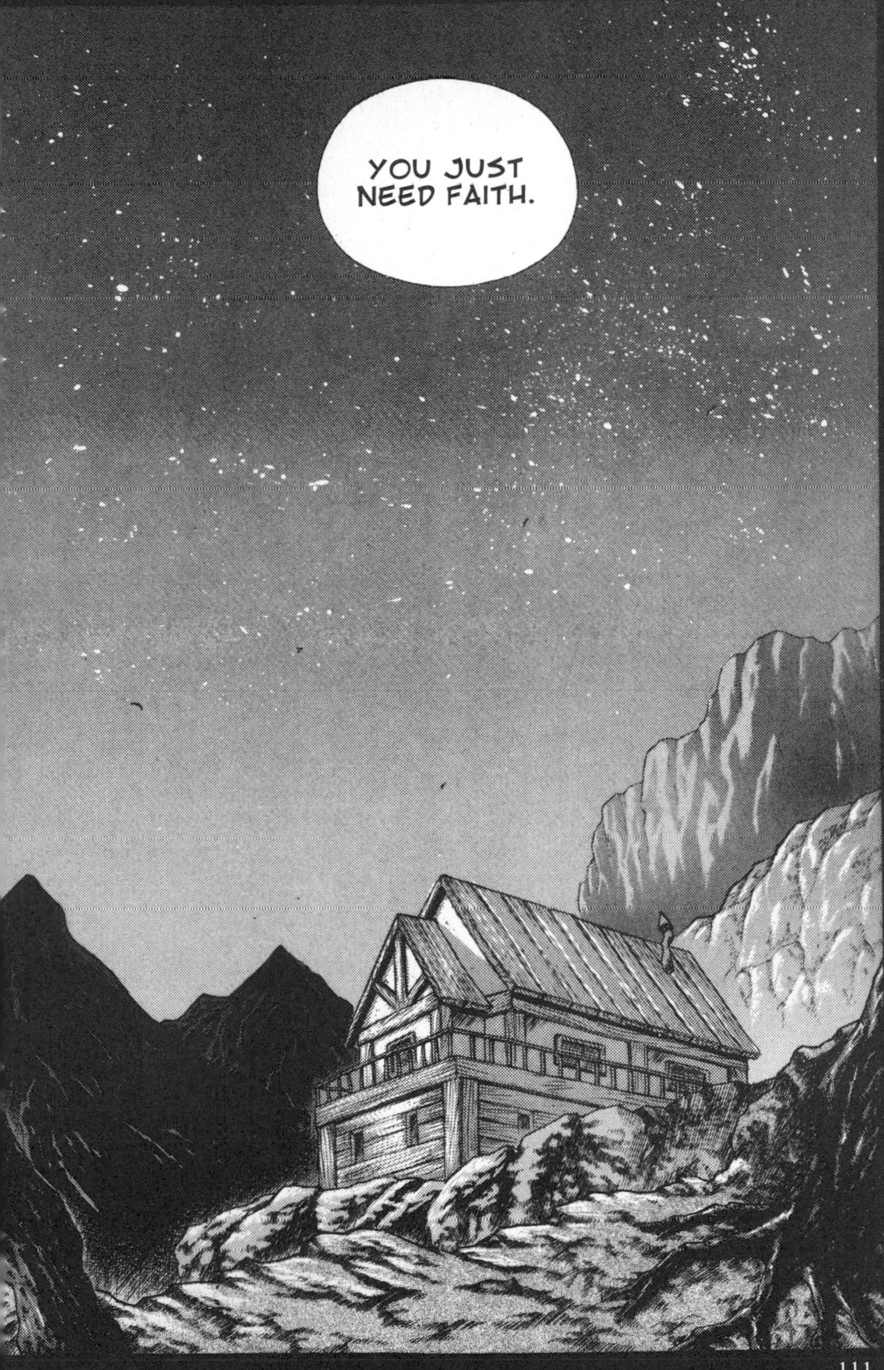
YOU JUST
NEED FAITH.

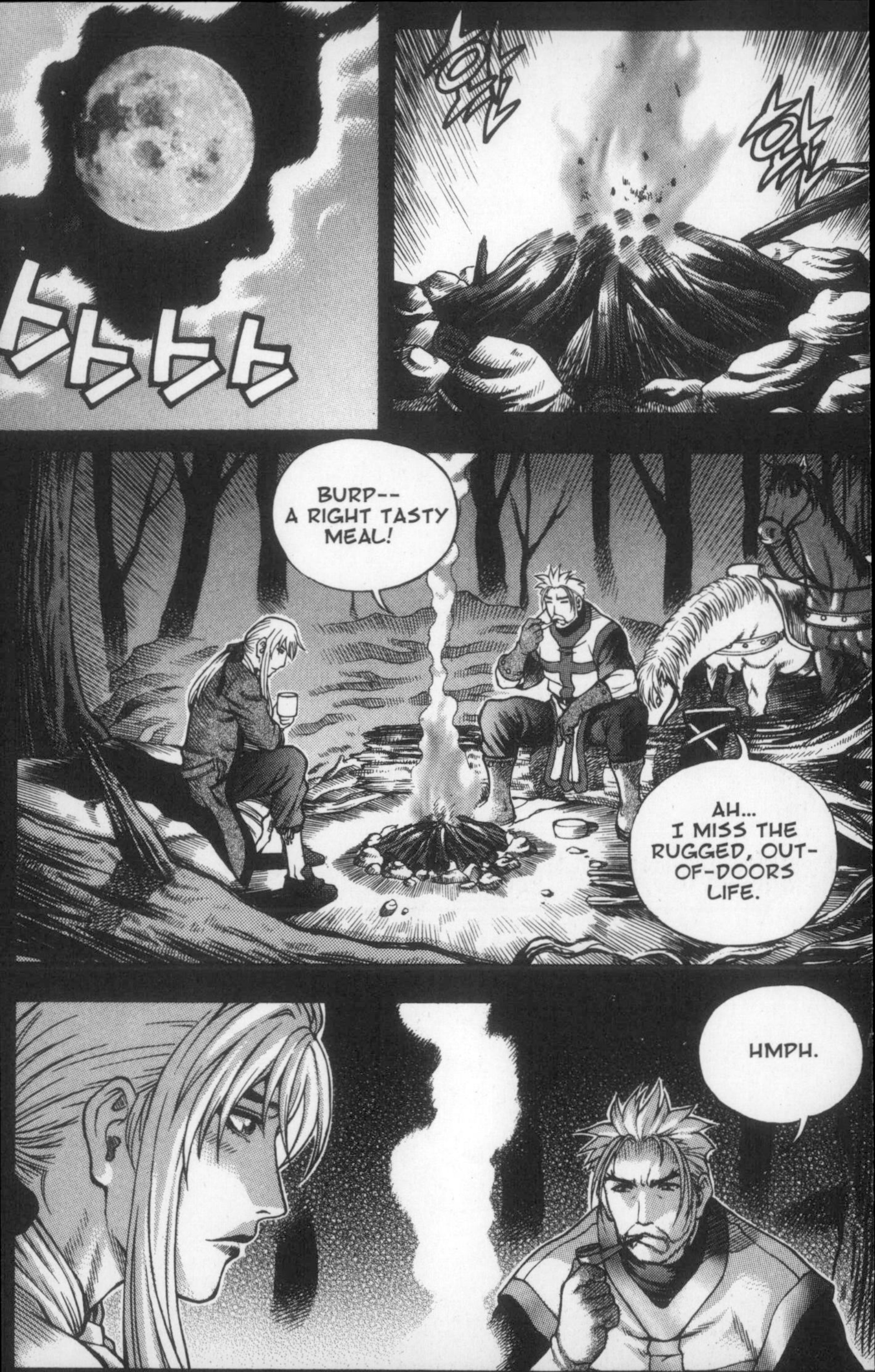
BURP-- A RIGHT TASTY MEAL!
AH... I MISS THE RUGGED, OUT-OF-DOORS LIFE.
HMPH.

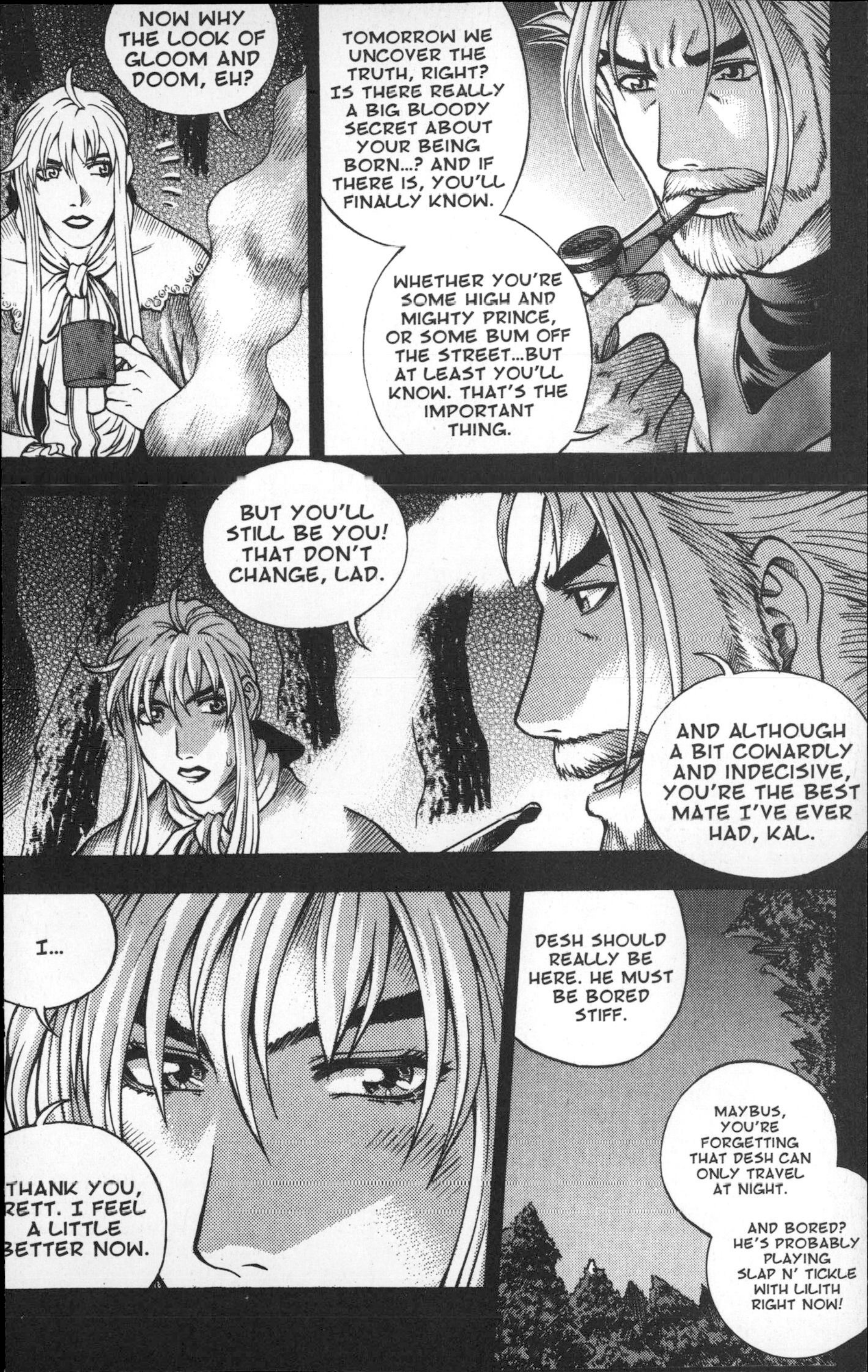
NOW WHY THE LOOK OF GLOOM AND DOOM, EH?
TOMORROW WE UNCOVER THE TRUTH, RIGHT? IS THERE REALLY A BIG BLOODY SECRET ABOUT YOUR BEING BORN...? AND IF THERE IS, YOU'LL FINALLY KNOW.
WHETHER YOU'RE SOME HIGH AND MIGHTY PRINCE, OR SOME BUM OFF THE STREET...BUT AT LEAST YOU'LL KNOW. THAT'S THE IMPORTANT THING.
BUT YOU'LL STILL BE YOU! THAT DON'T CHANGE, LAD.
AND ALTHOUGH A BIT COWARDLY AND INDECISIVE, YOU'RE THE BEST MATE I'VE EVER HAD, KAL.
I...
THANK YOU, RETT. I FEEL A LITTLE BETTER NOW.
DESH SHOULD REALLY BE HERE. HE MUST BE BORED STIFF.
MAYBUS, YOU'RE FORGETTING THAT DESH CAN ONLY TRAVEL AT NIGHT.
AND BORED? HE'S PROBABLY PLAYING SLAP N' TICKLE WITH LILITH RIGHT NOW!

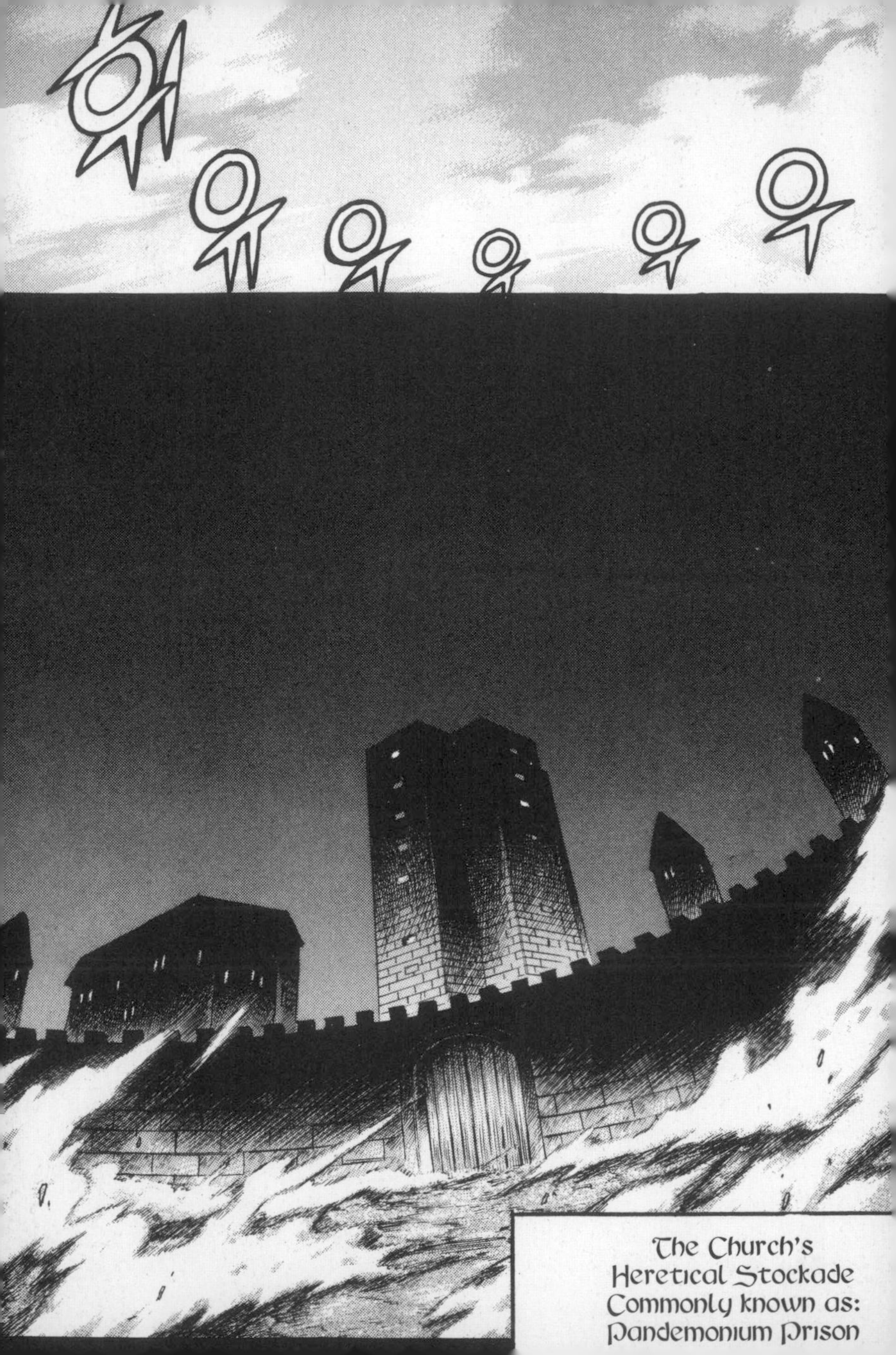
The Church's
Heretical Stockade
Commonly known as:
Pandemonium Prison

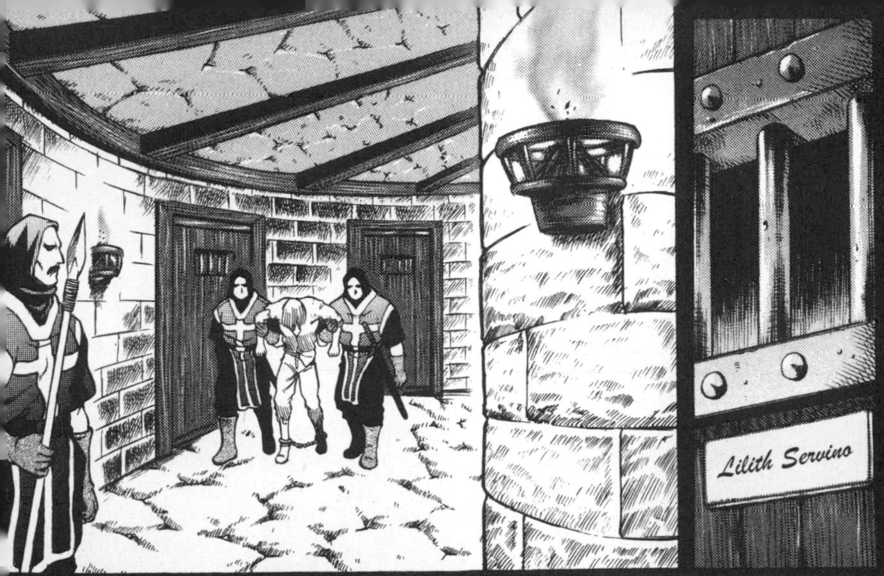
Lilith Servino
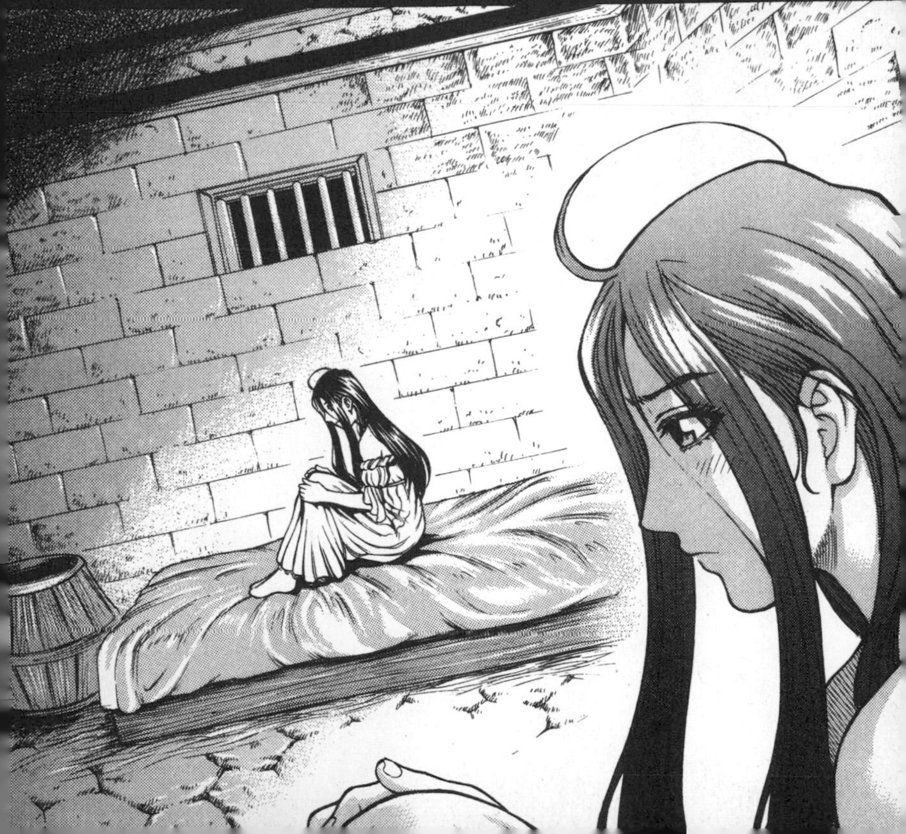

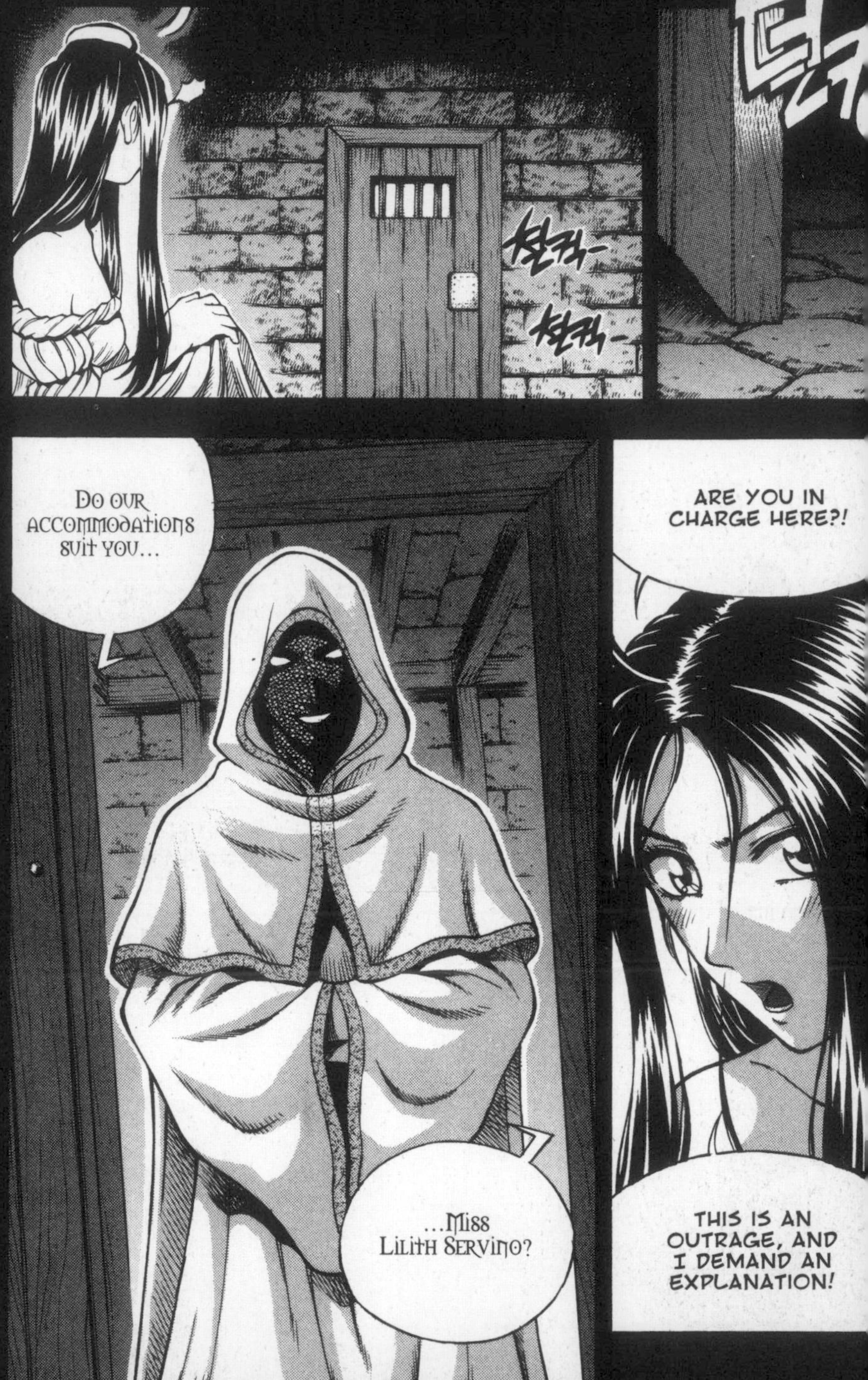
철컥—
철컥—
DO OUR ACCOMMODATIONS SUIT YOU...
...MISS LILITH SERVINO?
ARE YOU IN CHARGE HERE?!
THIS IS AN OUTRAGE, AND I DEMAND AN EXPLANATION!

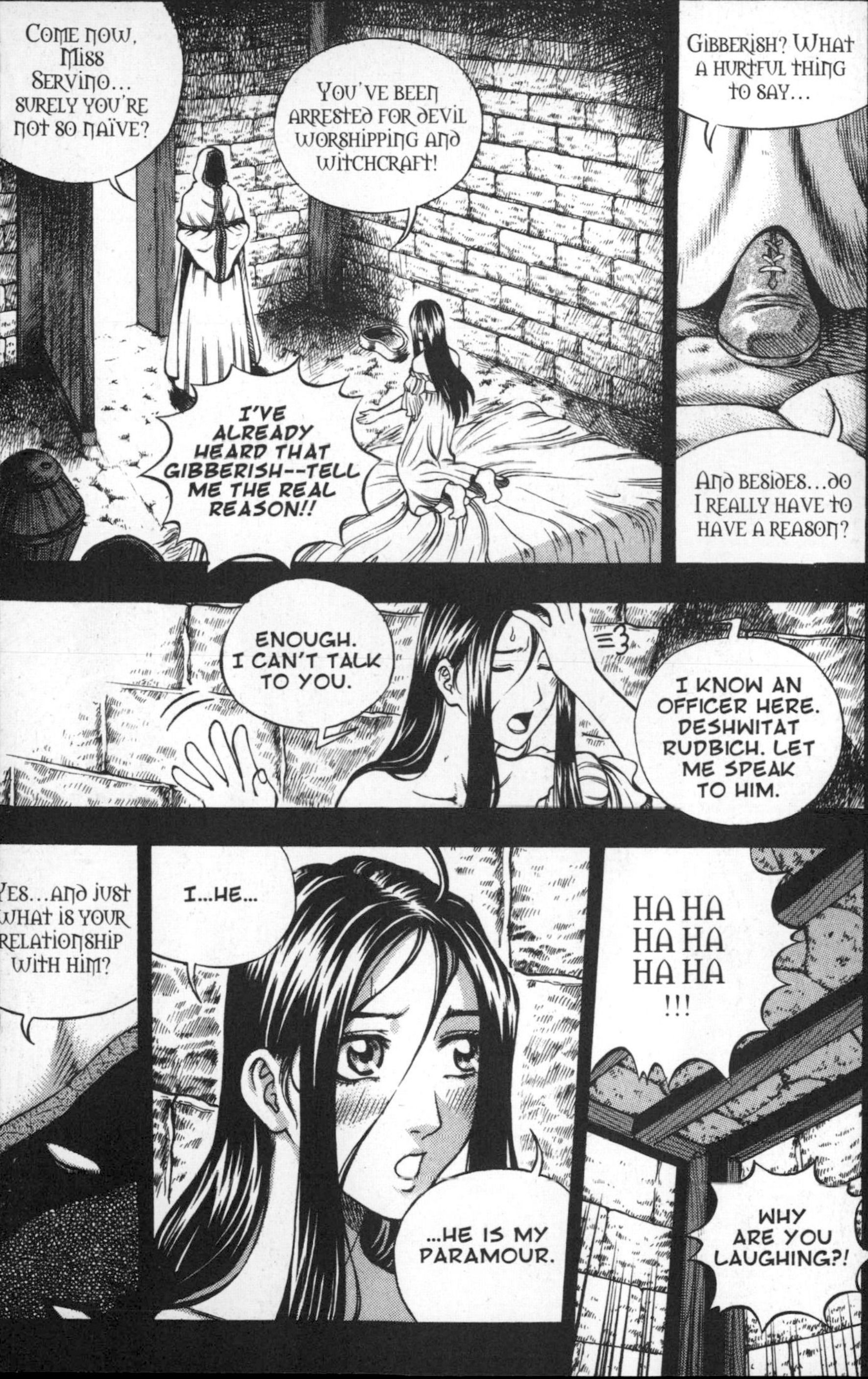
Come now, Miss Servino... surely you're not so naïve?
You've been arrested for devil worshipping and witchcraft!
I've already heard that gibberish--tell me the real reason!!
Gibberish? What a hurtful thing to say...
And besides...do I really have to have a reason?
Enough. I can't talk to you.
I know an officer here. Deshwitat Rudbich. Let me speak to him.
Yes...and just what is your relationship with him?
I...he...
...he is my paramour.
HA HA HA HA HA HA !!!
Why are you laughing?!

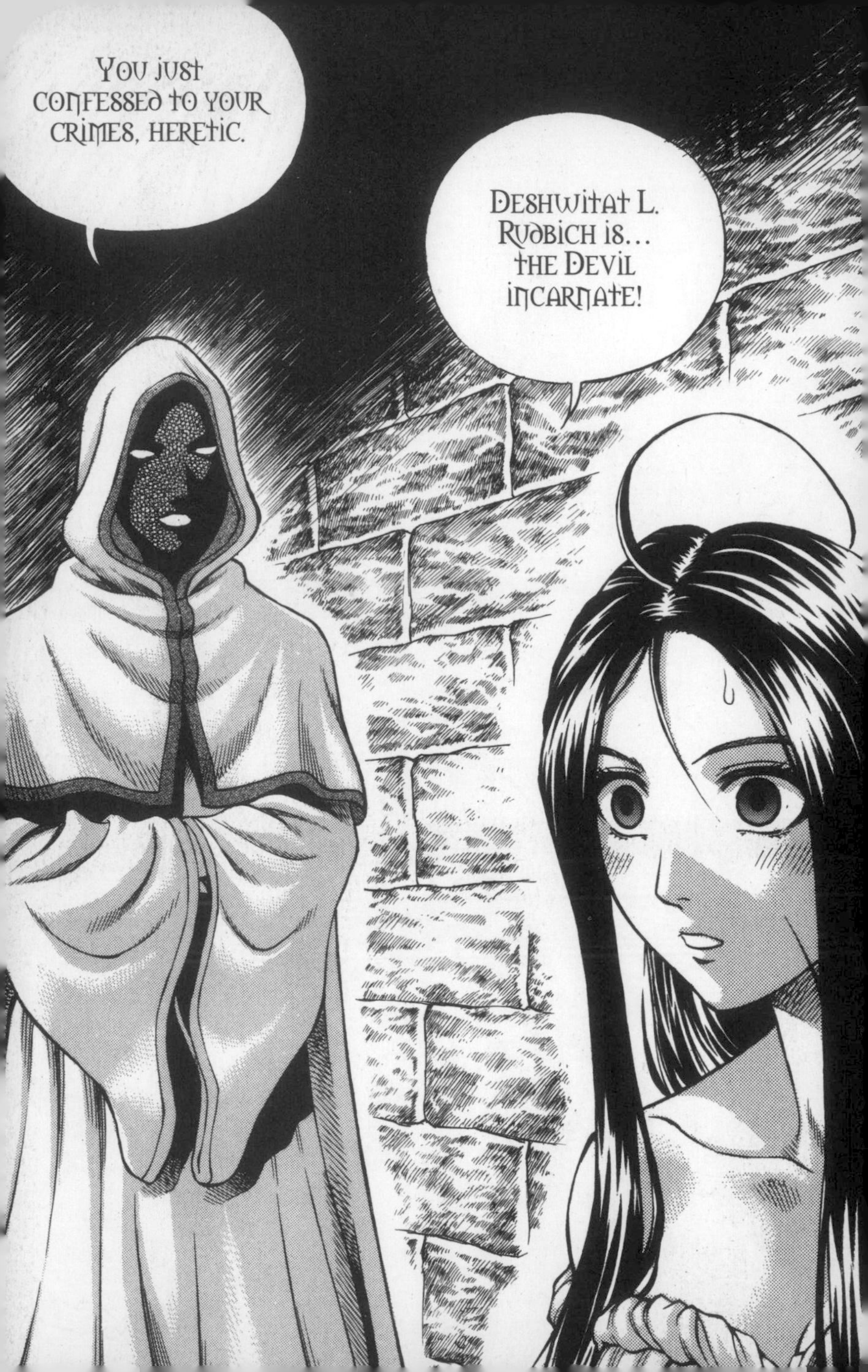
YOU JUST CONFESSED TO YOUR CRIMES, HERETIC.
DESHWITAT L. RUDBICH IS... THE DEVIL INCARNATE!

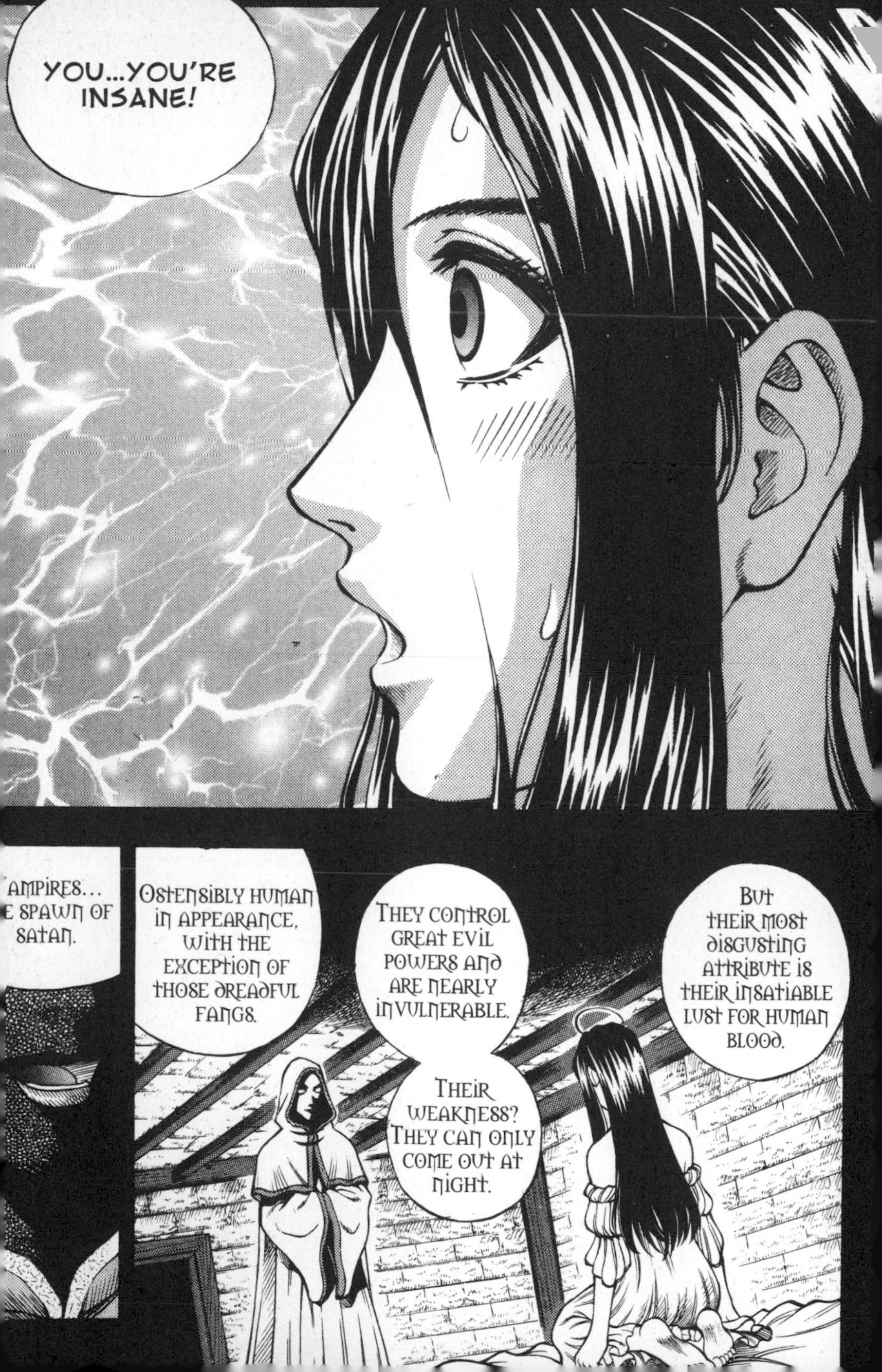
YOU...YOU'RE INSANE!
AMPIRES... E SPAWN OF SATAN.
OSTENSIBLY HUMAN IN APPEARANCE, WITH THE EXCEPTION OF THOSE DREADFUL FANGS.
THEY CONTROL GREAT EVIL POWERS AND ARE NEARLY INVULNERABLE.
THEIR WEAKNESS? THEY CAN ONLY COME OUT AT NIGHT.
BUT THEIR MOST DISGUSTING ATTRIBUTE IS THEIR INSATIABLE LUST FOR HUMAN BLOOD.

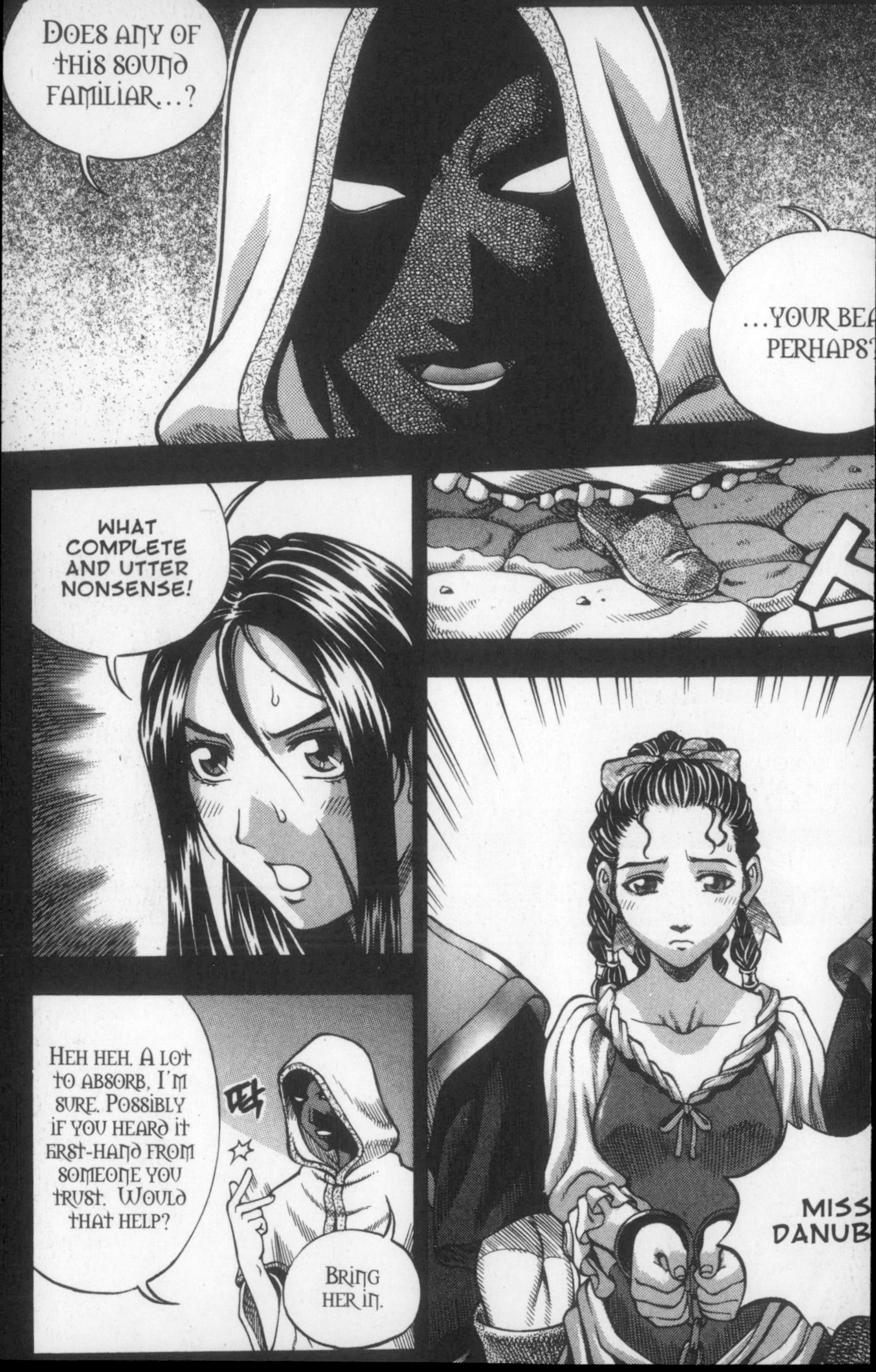
DOES ANY OF THIS SOUND FAMILIAR...?
...YOUR BEA
PERHAPS
WHAT COMPLETE AND UTTER NONSENSE!
HEH HEH. A LOT TO ABSORB, I'M SURE. POSSIBLY IF YOU HEARD IT FIRST-HAND FROM SOMEONE YOU TRUST. WOULD THAT HELP?
BRING HER IN.
MISS
DANUB

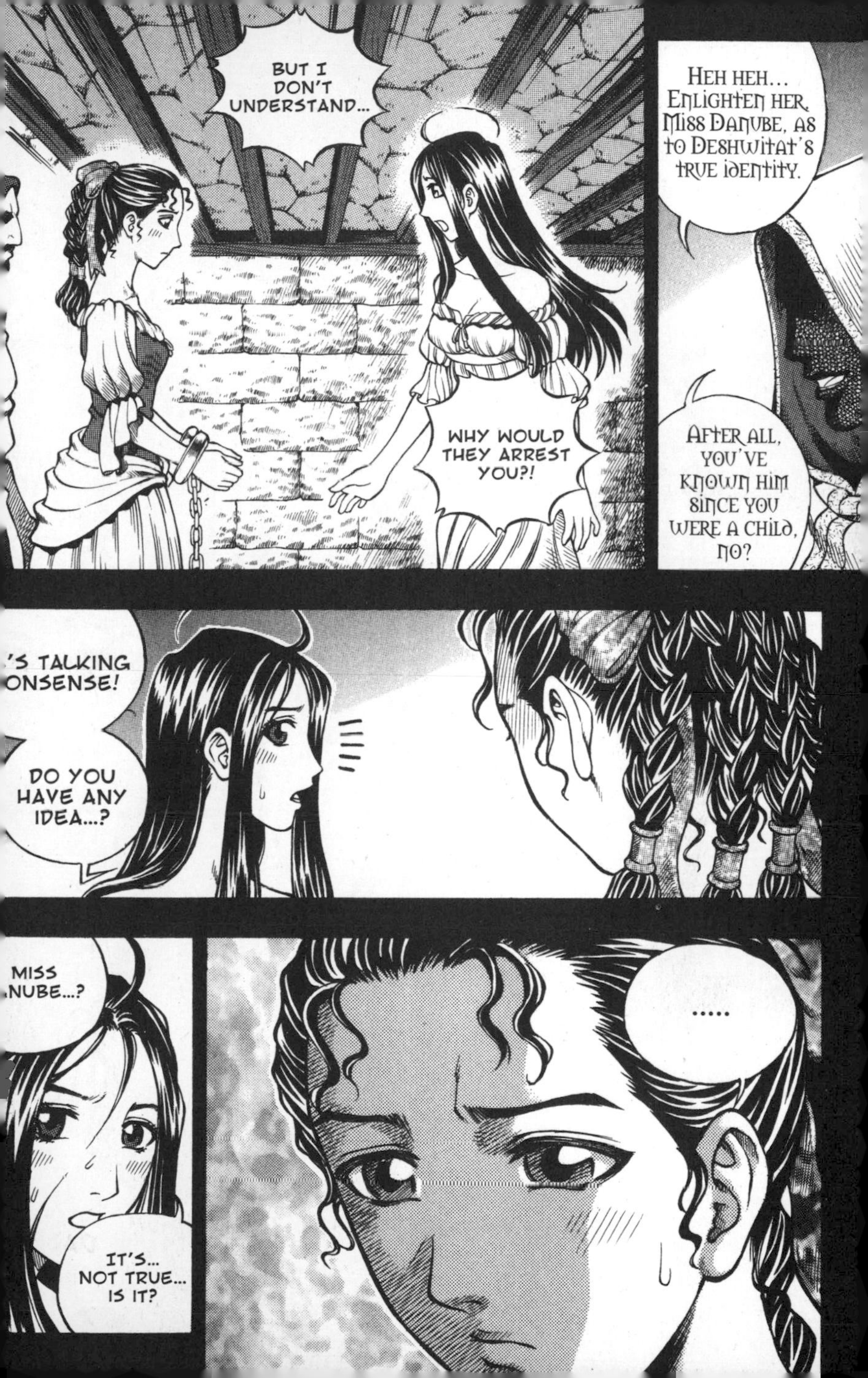
BUT I DON'T UNDERSTAND...
WHY WOULD THEY ARREST YOU?!
HEH HEH... ENLIGHTEN HER, MISS DANUBE, AS TO DESHWITAT'S TRUE IDENTITY.
AFTER ALL, YOU'VE KNOWN HIM SINCE YOU WERE A CHILD, NO?
'S TALKING ONSENSE!
DO YOU HAVE ANY IDEA...?
MISS NUBE...?
IT'S... NOT TRUE... IS IT?
.....

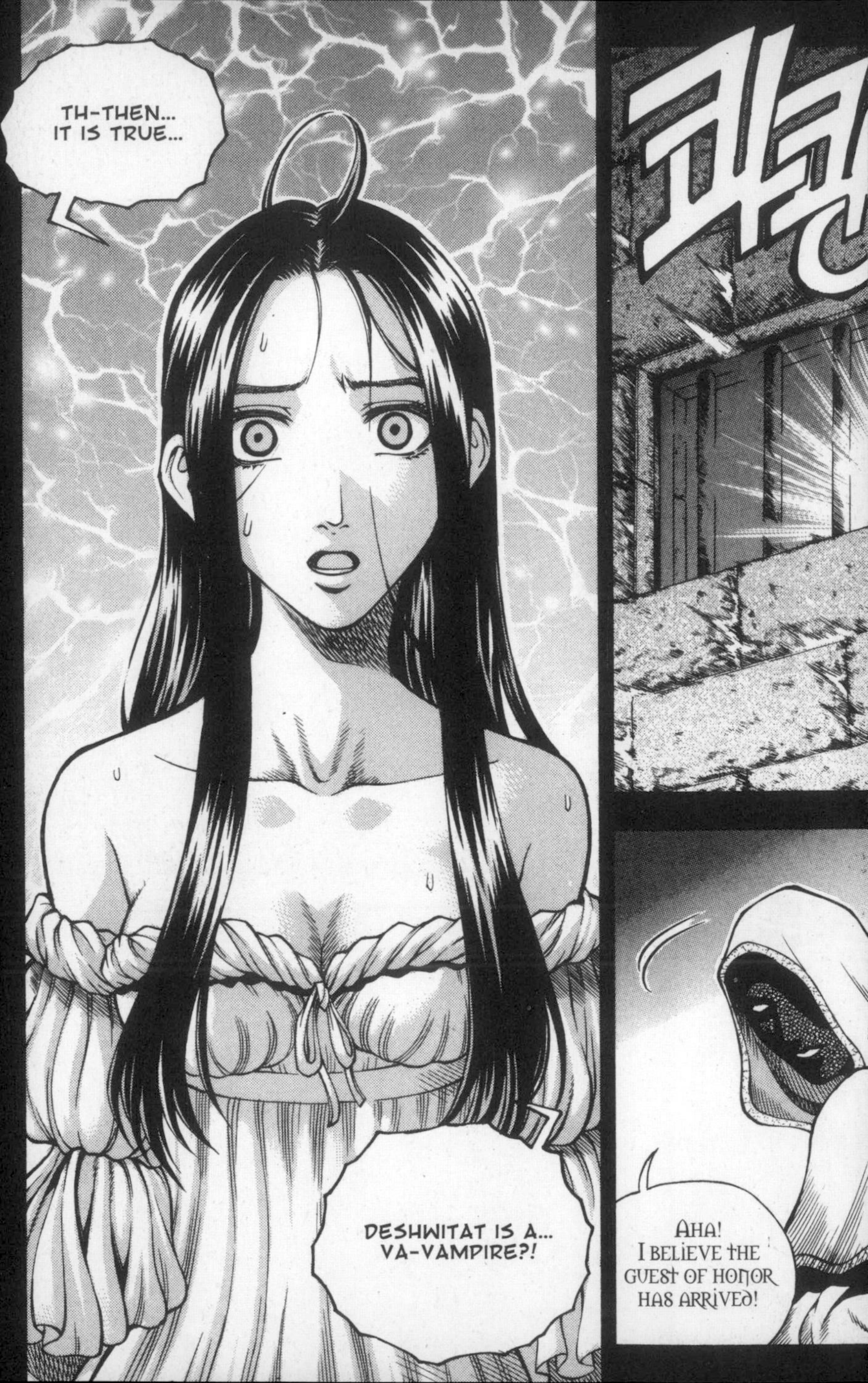
TH-THEN... IT IS TRUE...
DESHWITAT IS A... VA-VAMPIRE?!
AHA! I BELIEVE THE GUEST OF HONOR HAS ARRIVED!

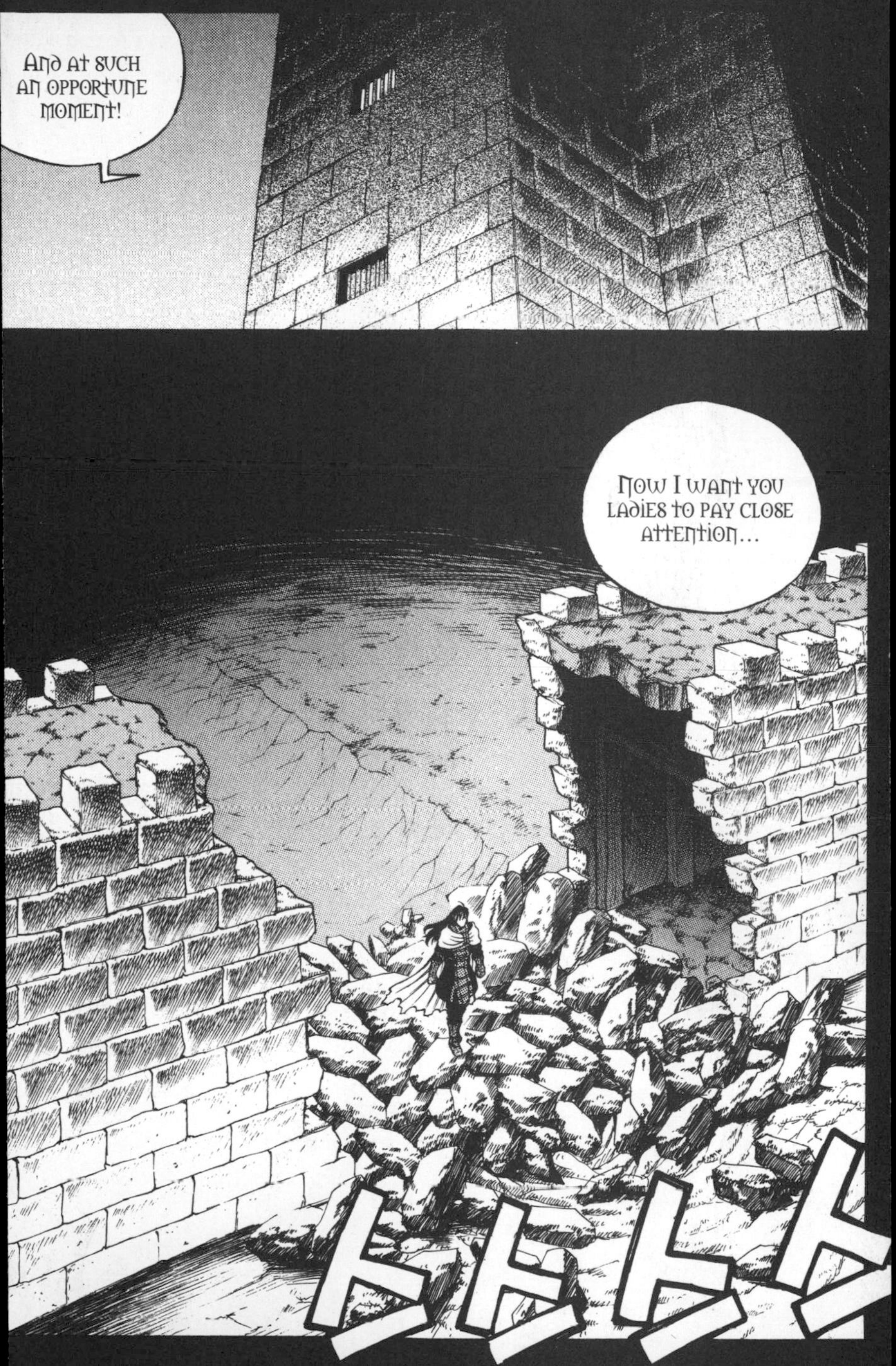
And at such an opportune moment!
Now I want you ladies to pay close attention...
トトトト

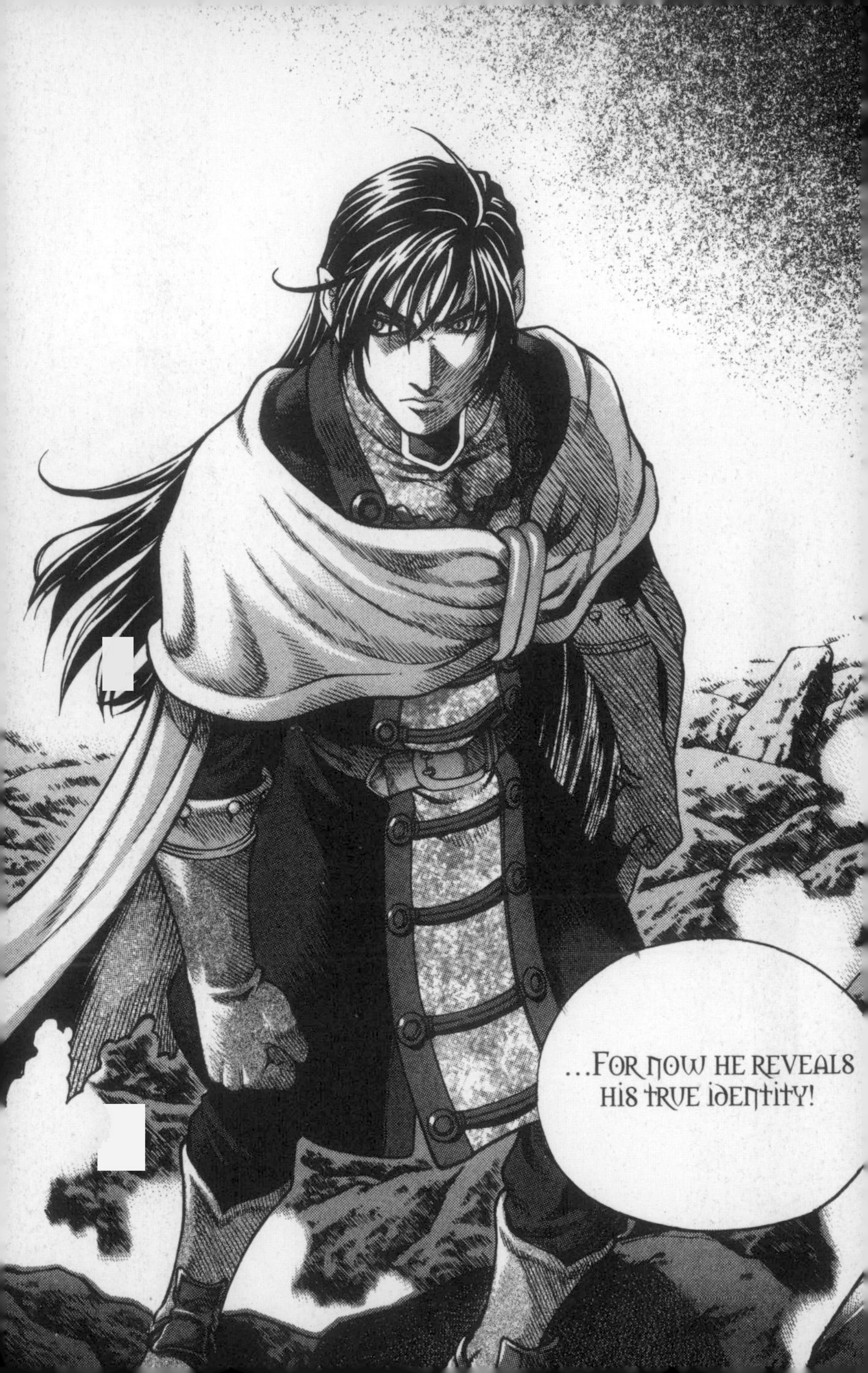
...FOR NOW HE REVEALS HIS TRUE IDENTITY!

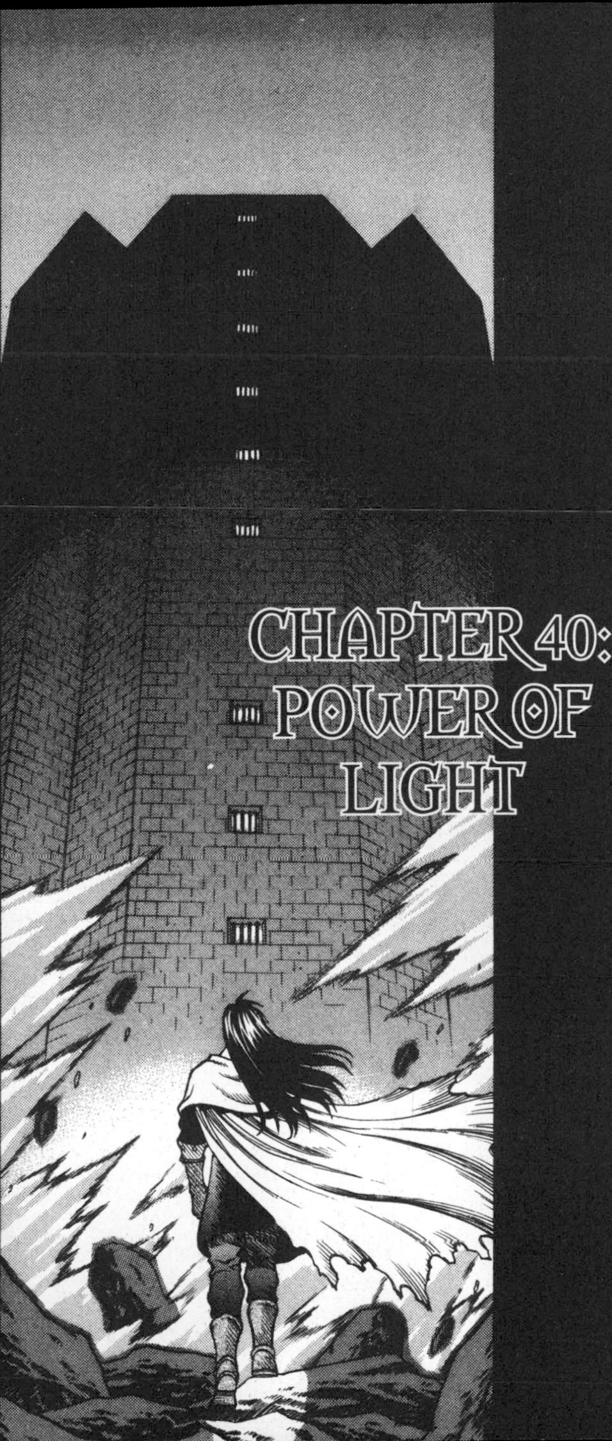
CHAPTER 40:
POWER OF LIGHT

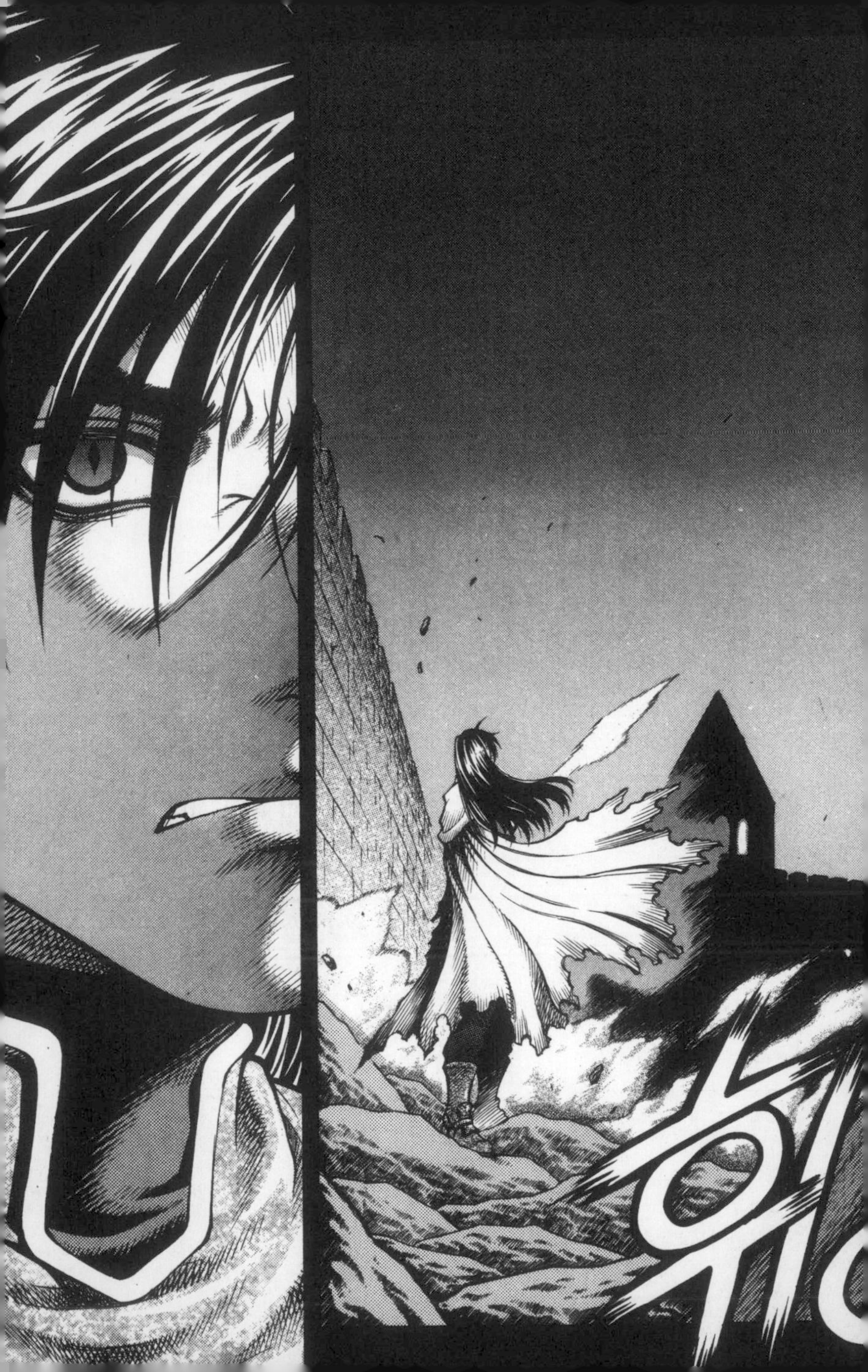

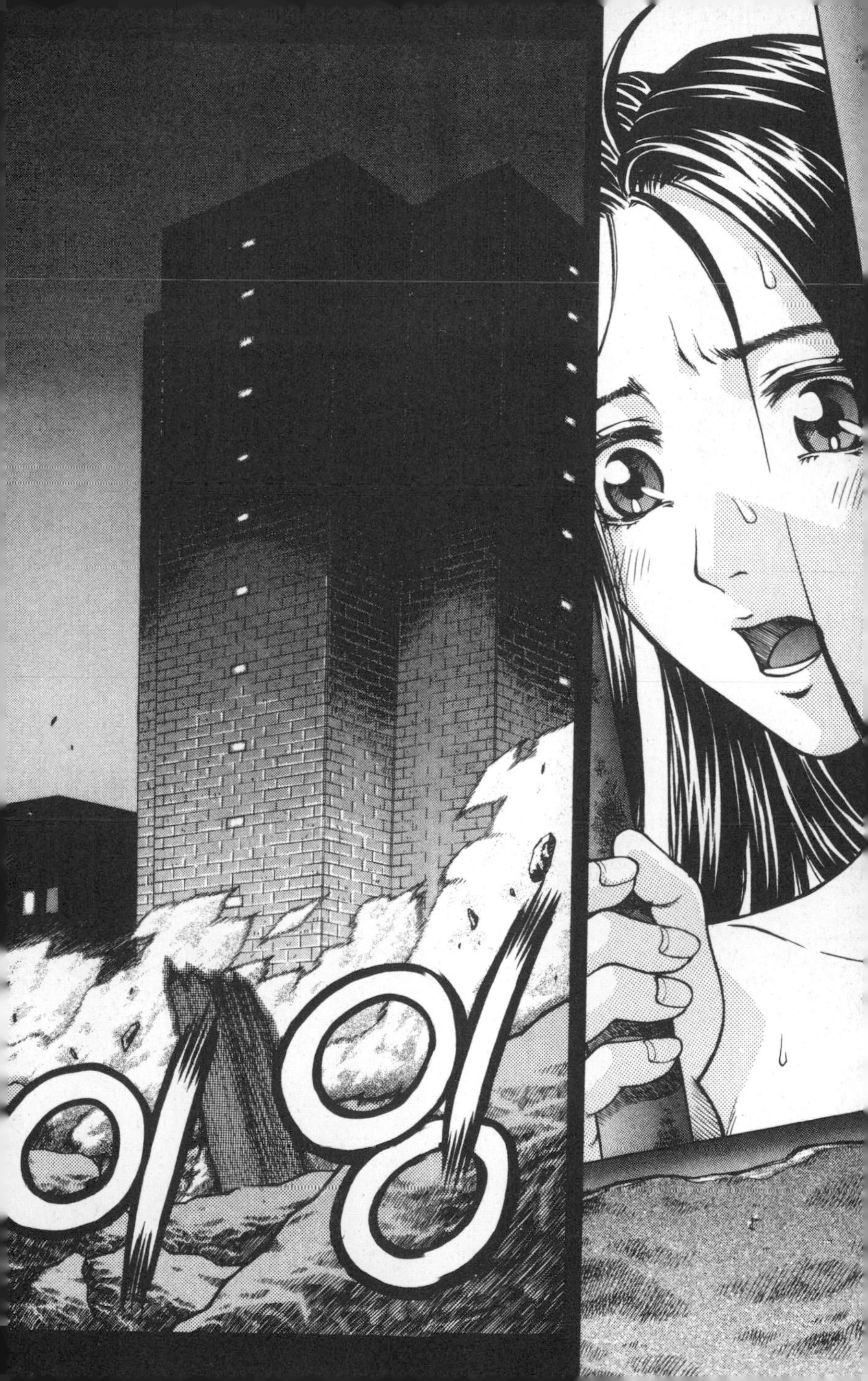

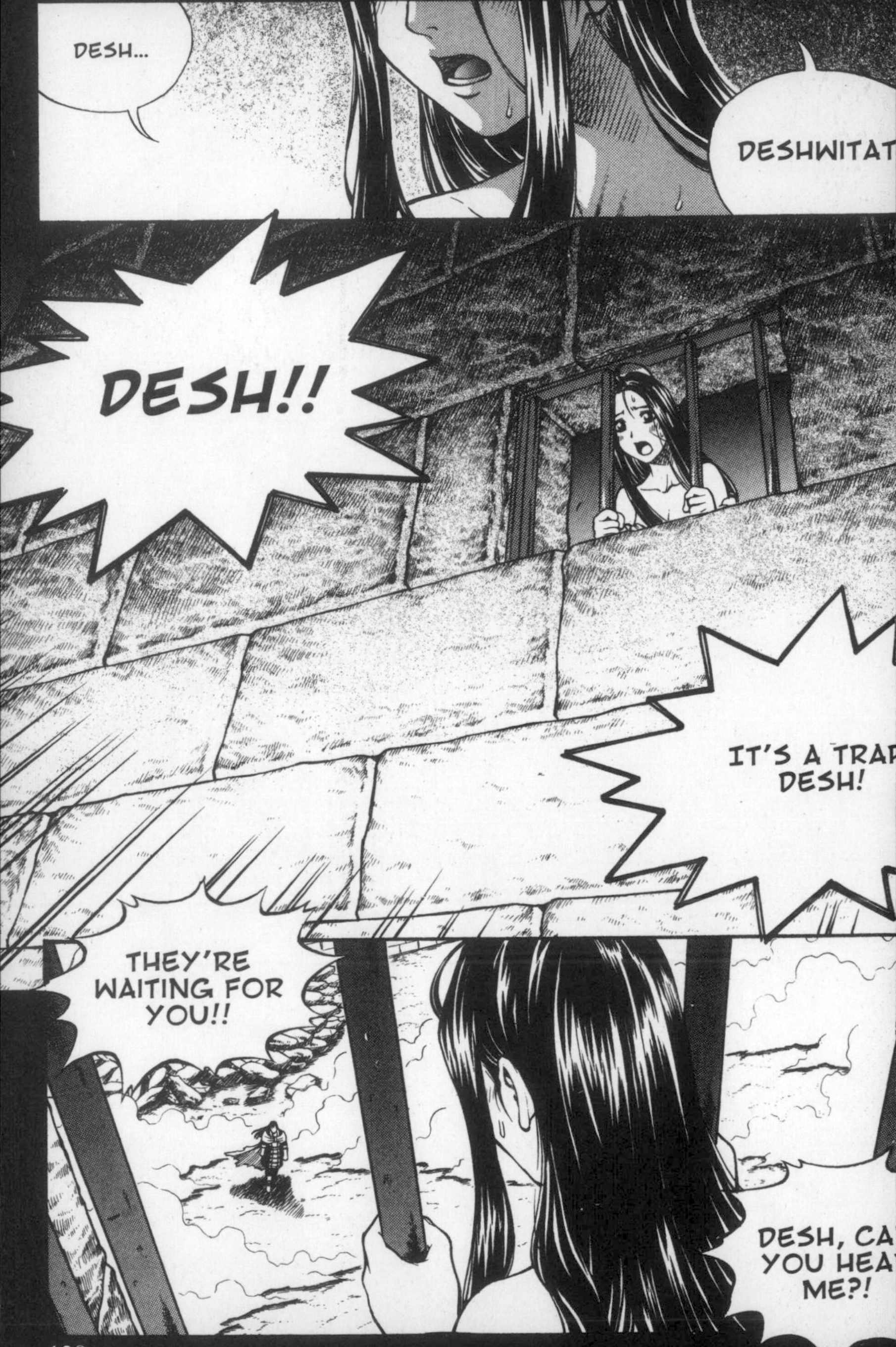
DESH...
DESHWITAT
DESH!!
IT'S A TRAP DESH!
THEY'RE WAITING FOR YOU!!
DESH, CA YOU HEA ME?!

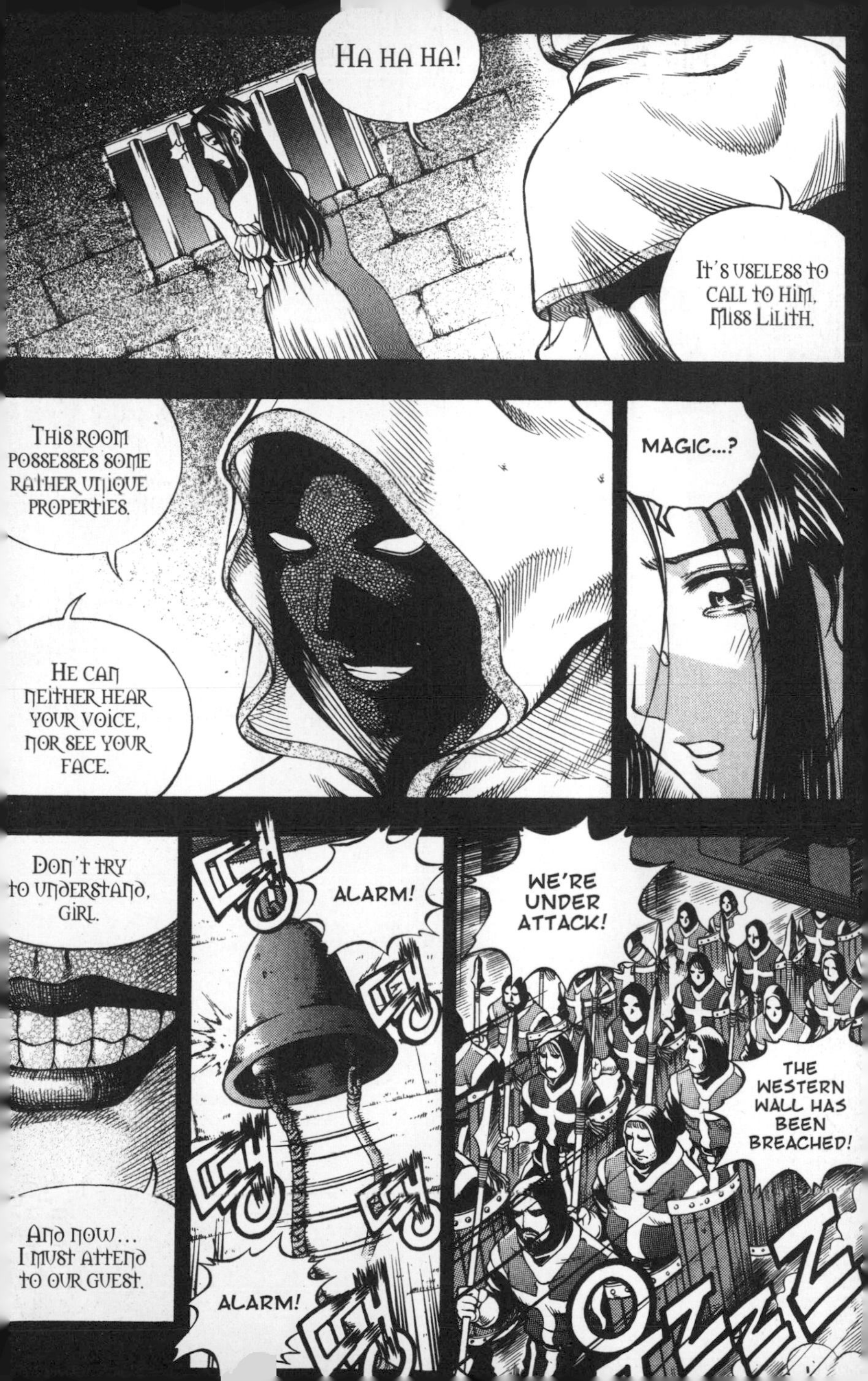
HA HA HA!
It's useless to call to him, Miss Lilith.
This room possesses some rather unique properties.
He can neither hear your voice, nor see your face.
MAGIC...?
Don't try to understand, girl.
And now... I must attend to our guest.
ALARM!
ALARM!
WE'RE UNDER ATTACK!
THE WESTERN WALL HAS BEEN BREACHED!

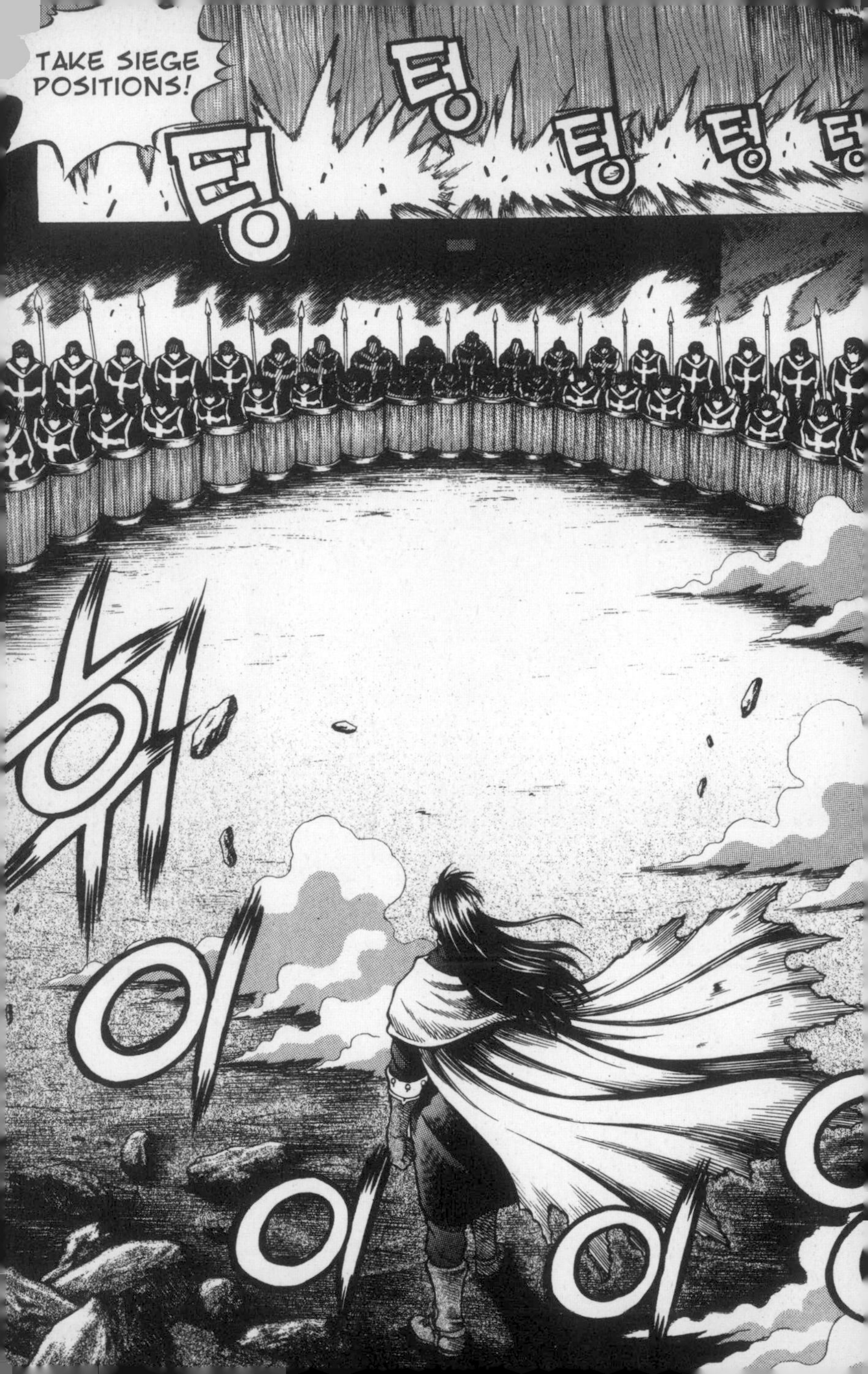
TAKE SIEGE POSITIONS!
텅 텅 텅 텅
와아아아

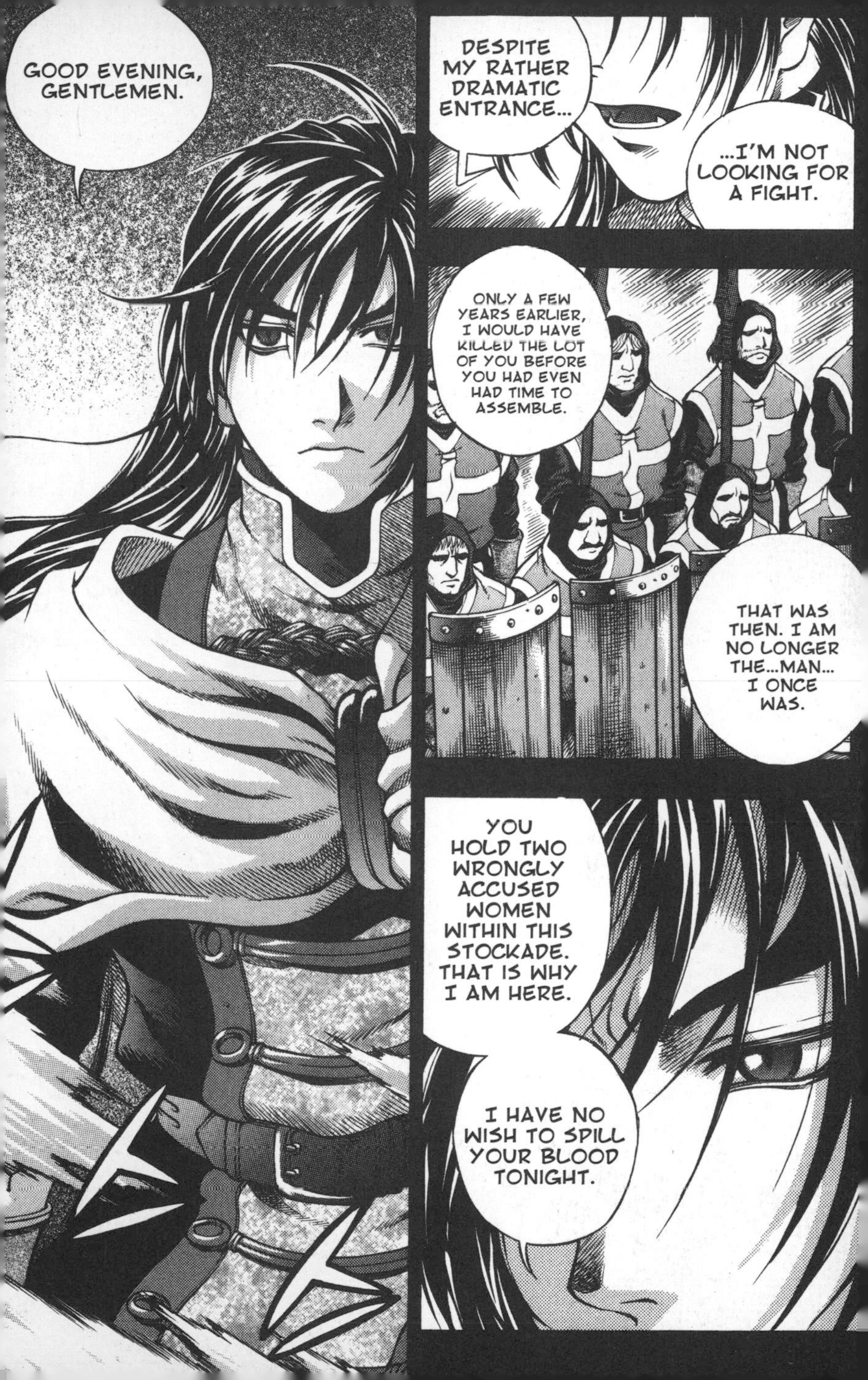
GOOD EVENING, GENTLEMEN.
DESPITE MY RATHER DRAMATIC ENTRANCE...
...I'M NOT LOOKING FOR A FIGHT.
ONLY A FEW YEARS EARLIER, I WOULD HAVE KILLED THE LOT OF YOU BEFORE YOU HAD EVEN HAD TIME TO ASSEMBLE.
THAT WAS THEN. I AM NO LONGER THE...MAN... I ONCE WAS.
YOU HOLD TWO WRONGLY ACCUSED WOMEN WITHIN THIS STOCKADE. THAT IS WHY I AM HERE.
I HAVE NO WISH TO SPILL YOUR BLOOD TONIGHT.

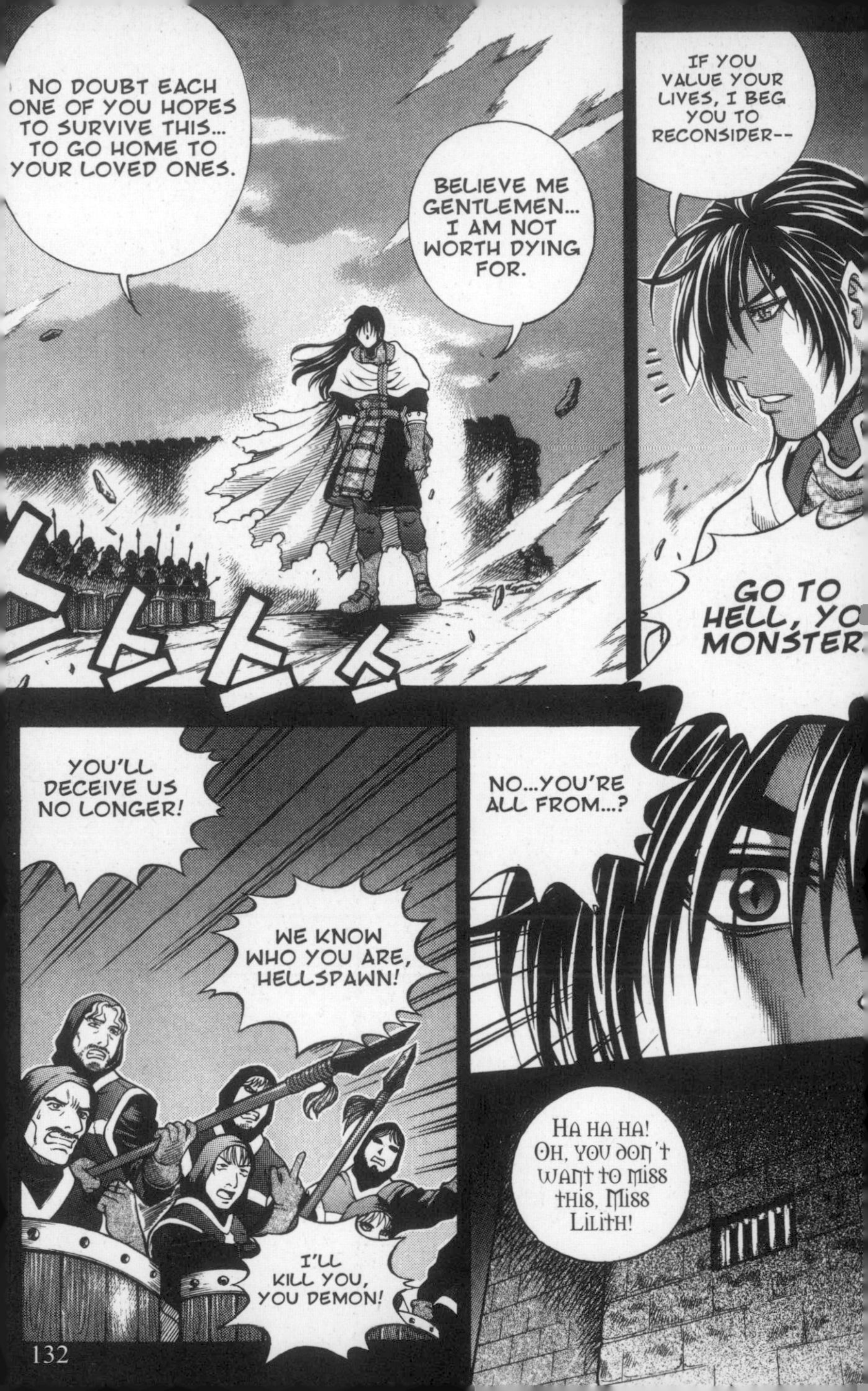
NO DOUBT EACH ONE OF YOU HOPES TO SURVIVE THIS... TO GO HOME TO YOUR LOVED ONES.
BELIEVE ME GENTLEMEN... I AM NOT WORTH DYING FOR.
IF YOU VALUE YOUR LIVES, I BEG YOU TO RECONSIDER--
GO TO HELL, YO MONSTER
YOU'LL DECEIVE US NO LONGER!
WE KNOW WHO YOU ARE, HELLSPAWN!
I'LL KILL YOU, YOU DEMON!
NO...YOU'RE ALL FROM...?
HA HA HA! OH, YOU DON'T WANT TO MISS THIS, MISS LILITH!

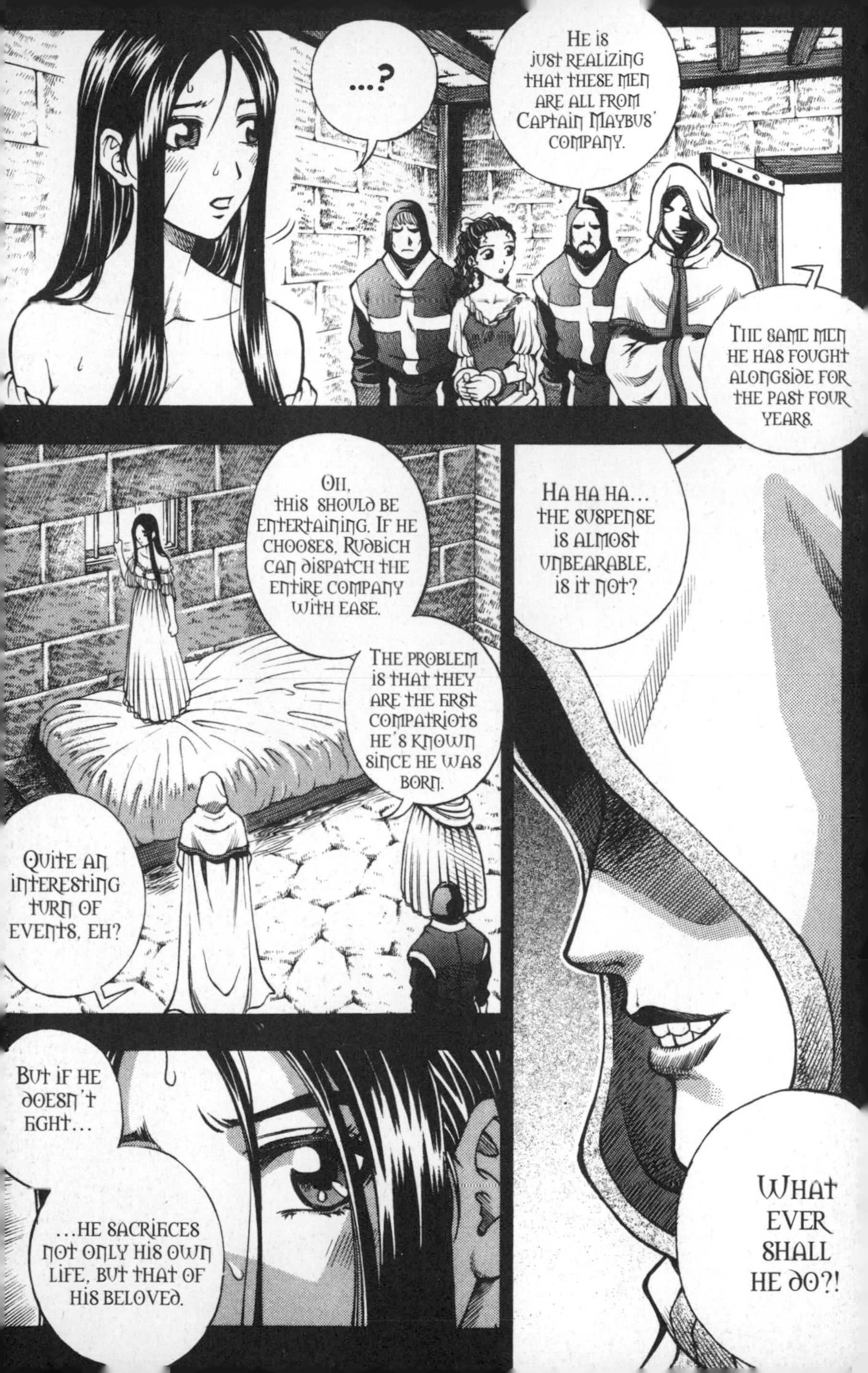
...?
He is just realizing that these men are all from Captain Maybus' company.
The same men he has fought alongside for the past four years.
Oh, this should be entertaining. If he chooses, Rudbich can dispatch the entire company with ease.
The problem is that they are the first compatriots he's known since he was born.
Quite an interesting turn of events, eh?
But if he doesn't fight...
...he sacrifices not only his own life, but that of his beloved.
Ha ha ha... the suspense is almost unbearable, is it not?
What ever shall he do?!

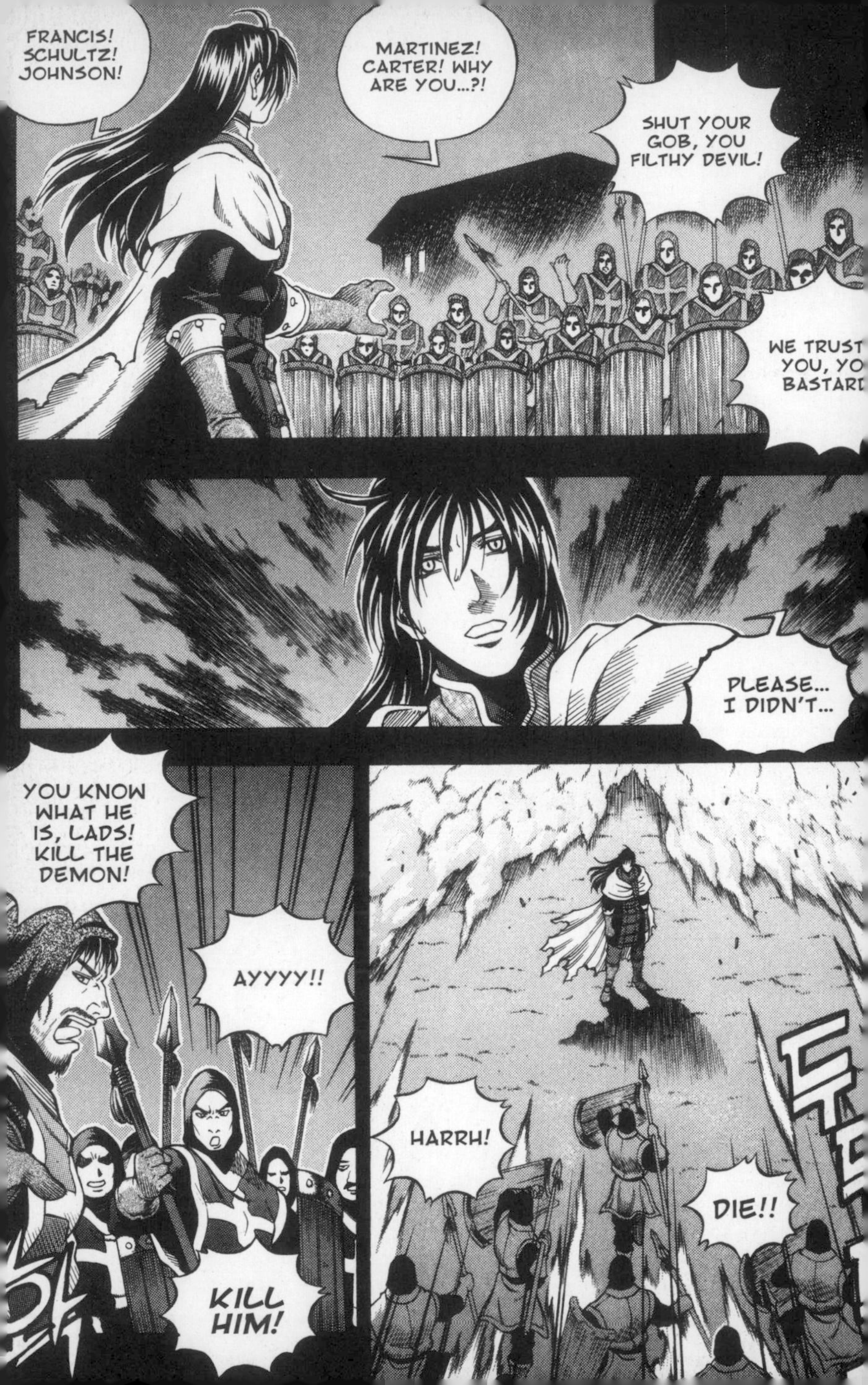
FRANCIS! SCHULTZ! JOHNSON!
MARTINEZ! CARTER! WHY ARE YOU...?!
SHUT YOUR GOB, YOU FILTHY DEVIL!
WE TRUST YOU, YO BASTARD
PLEASE... I DIDN'T...
YOU KNOW WHAT HE IS, LADS! KILL THE DEMON!
AYYYY!!
KILL HIM!
HARRH!
DIE!!

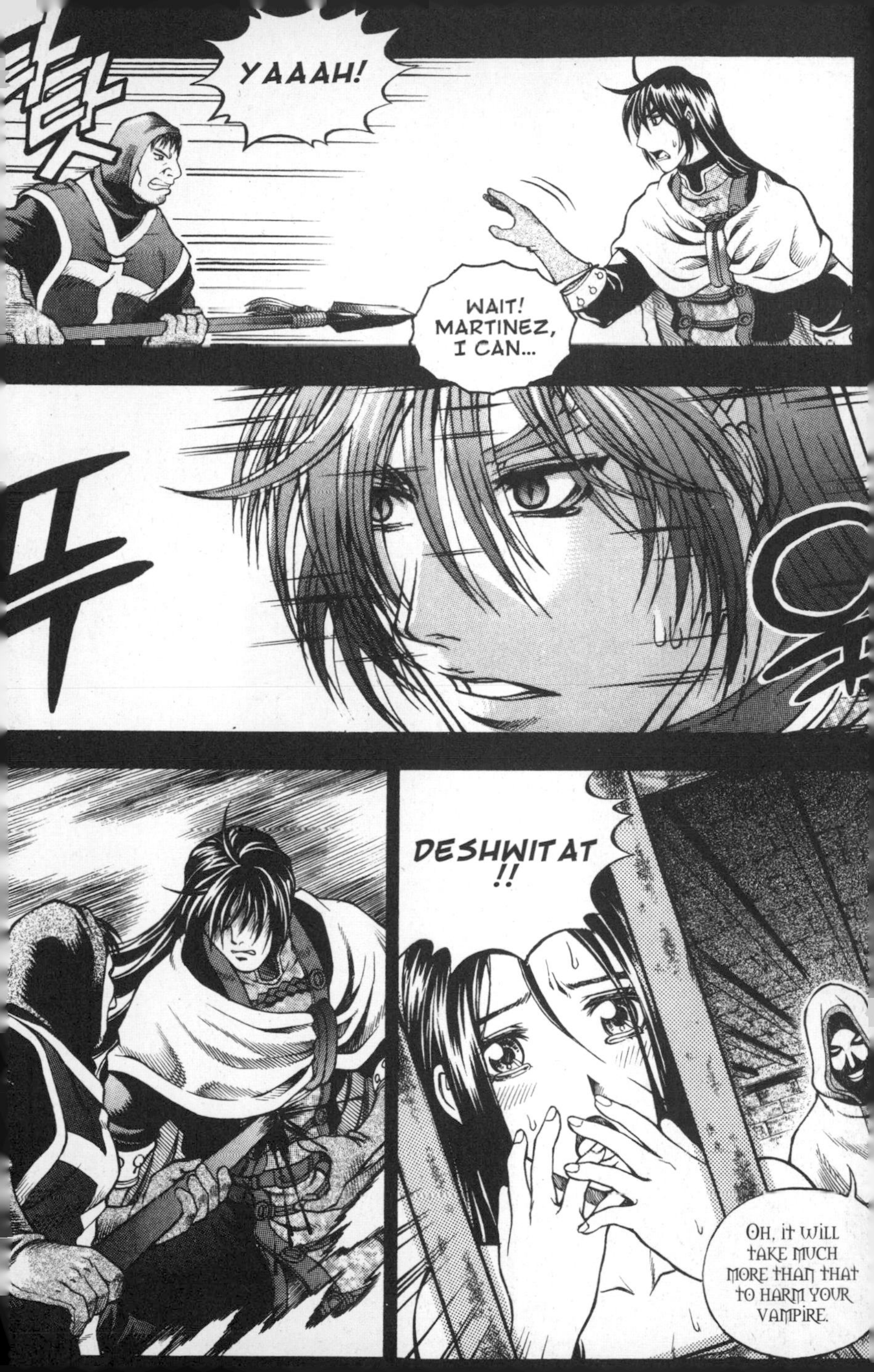
YAAAH!
WAIT! MARTINEZ, I CAN...
DESHWITAT !!
OH, IT WILL TAKE MUCH MORE THAN THAT TO HARM YOUR VAMPIRE.

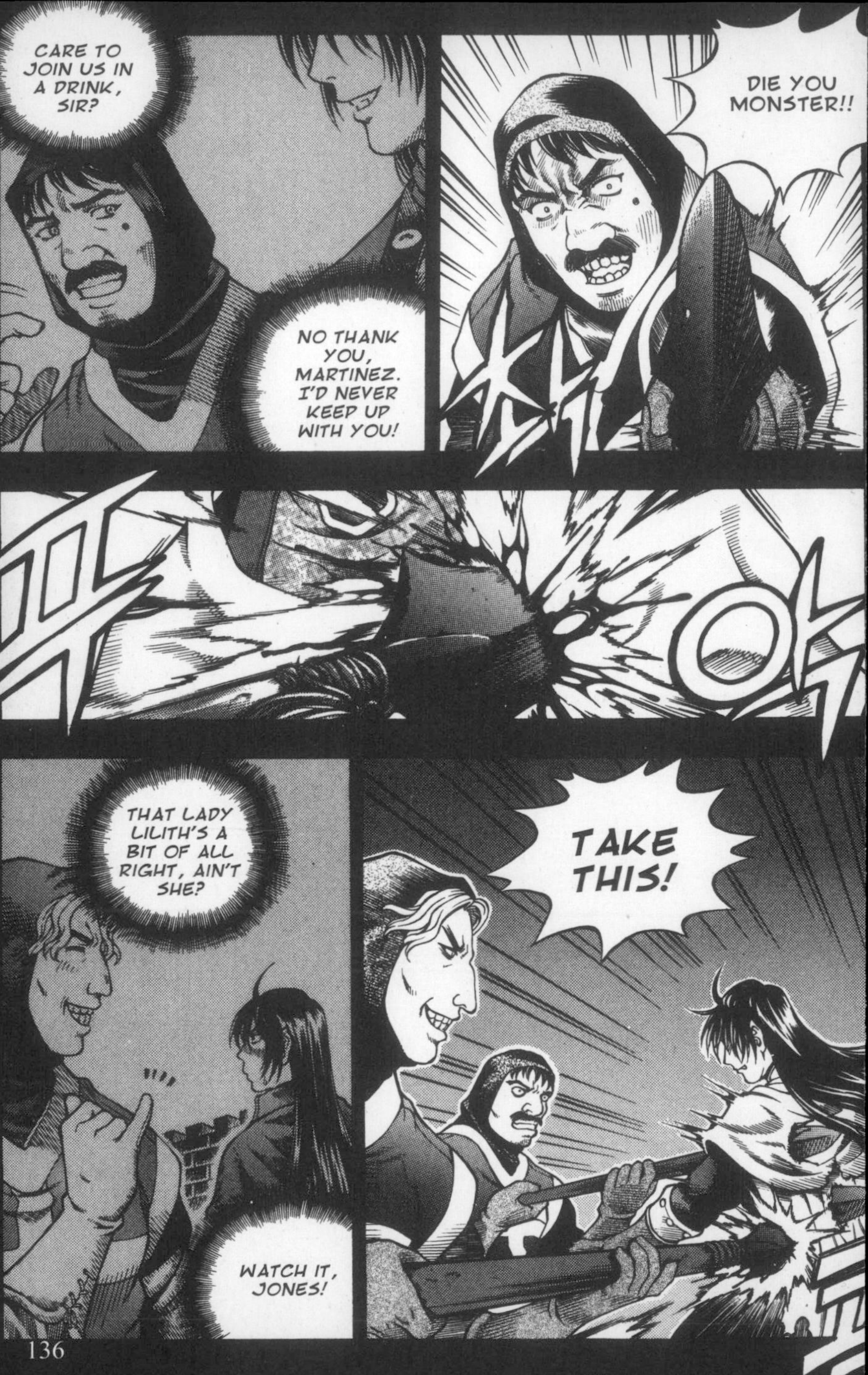
CARE TO JOIN US IN A DRINK, SIR?
NO THANK YOU, MARTINEZ. I'D NEVER KEEP UP WITH YOU!
DIE YOU MONSTER!!
THAT LADY LILITH'S A BIT OF ALL RIGHT, AIN'T SHE?
WATCH IT, JONES!
TAKE THIS!

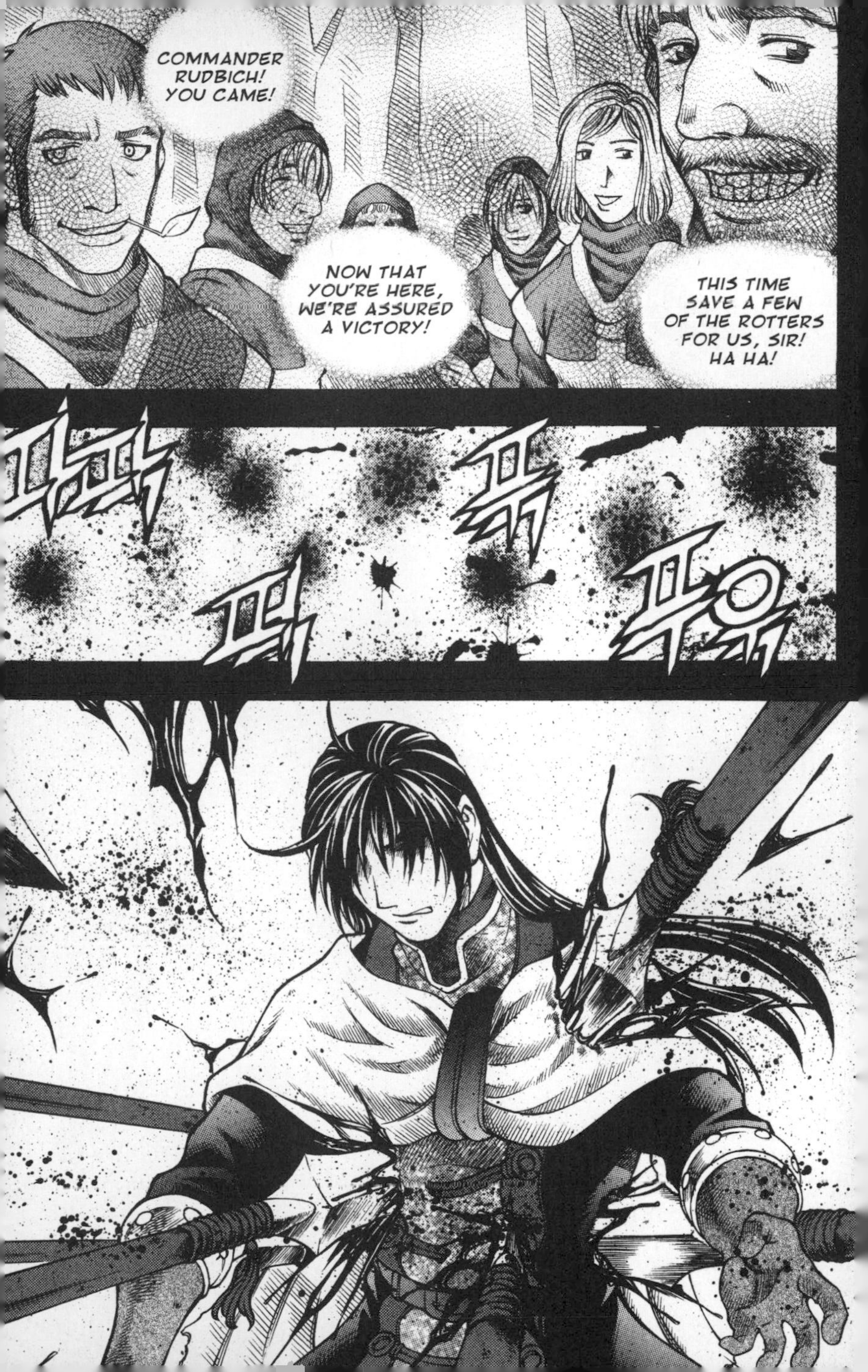
COMMANDER RUDBICH! YOU CAME!
NOW THAT YOU'RE HERE, WE'RE ASSURED A VICTORY!
THIS TIME SAVE A FEW OF THE ROTTERS FOR US, SIR! HA HA!

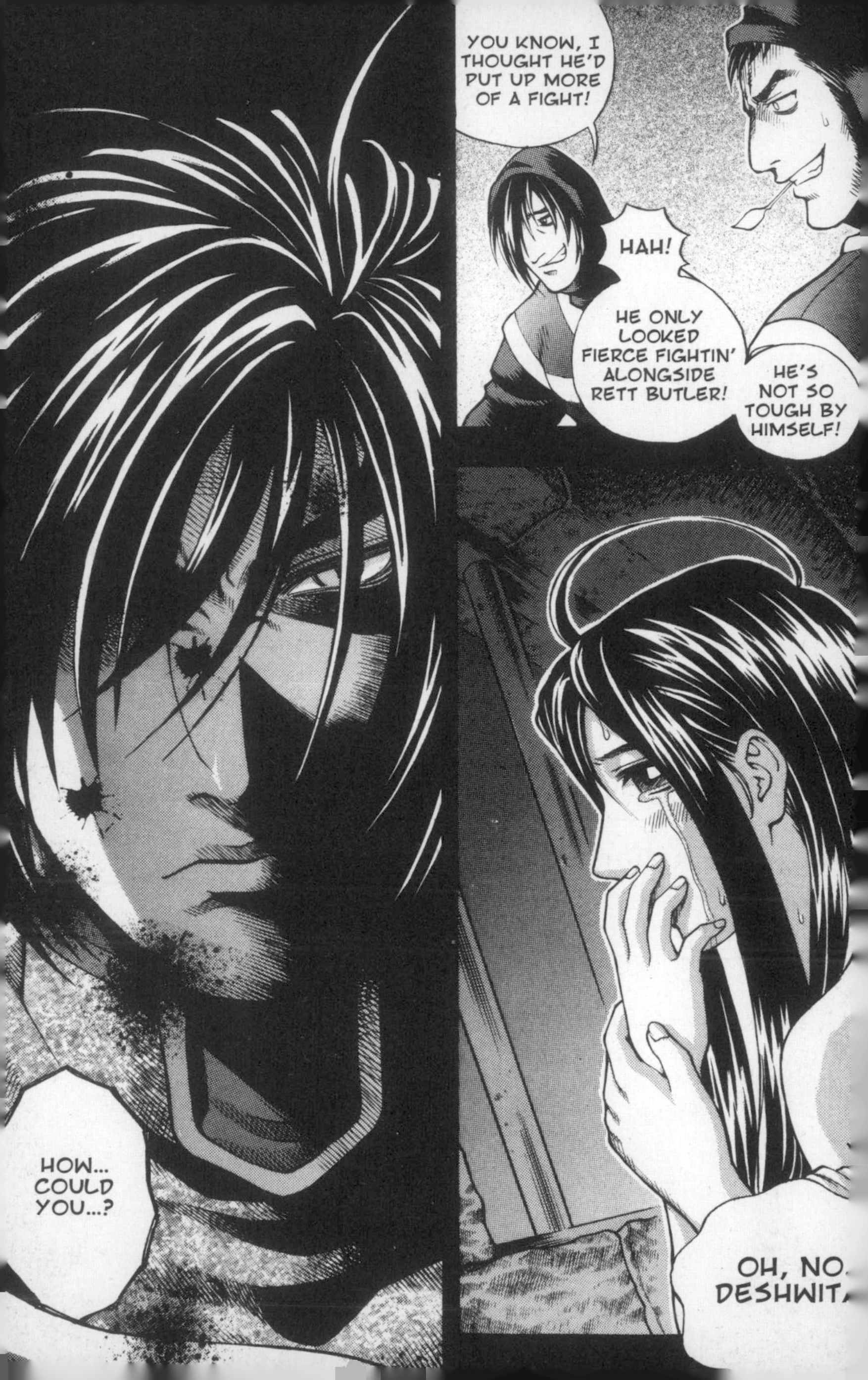
HOW... COULD YOU...?
YOU KNOW, I THOUGHT HE'D PUT UP MORE OF A FIGHT!
HAH!
HE ONLY LOOKED FIERCE FIGHTIN' ALONGSIDE RETT BUTLER!
HE'S NOT SO TOUGH BY HIMSELF!
OH, NO. DESHWIT

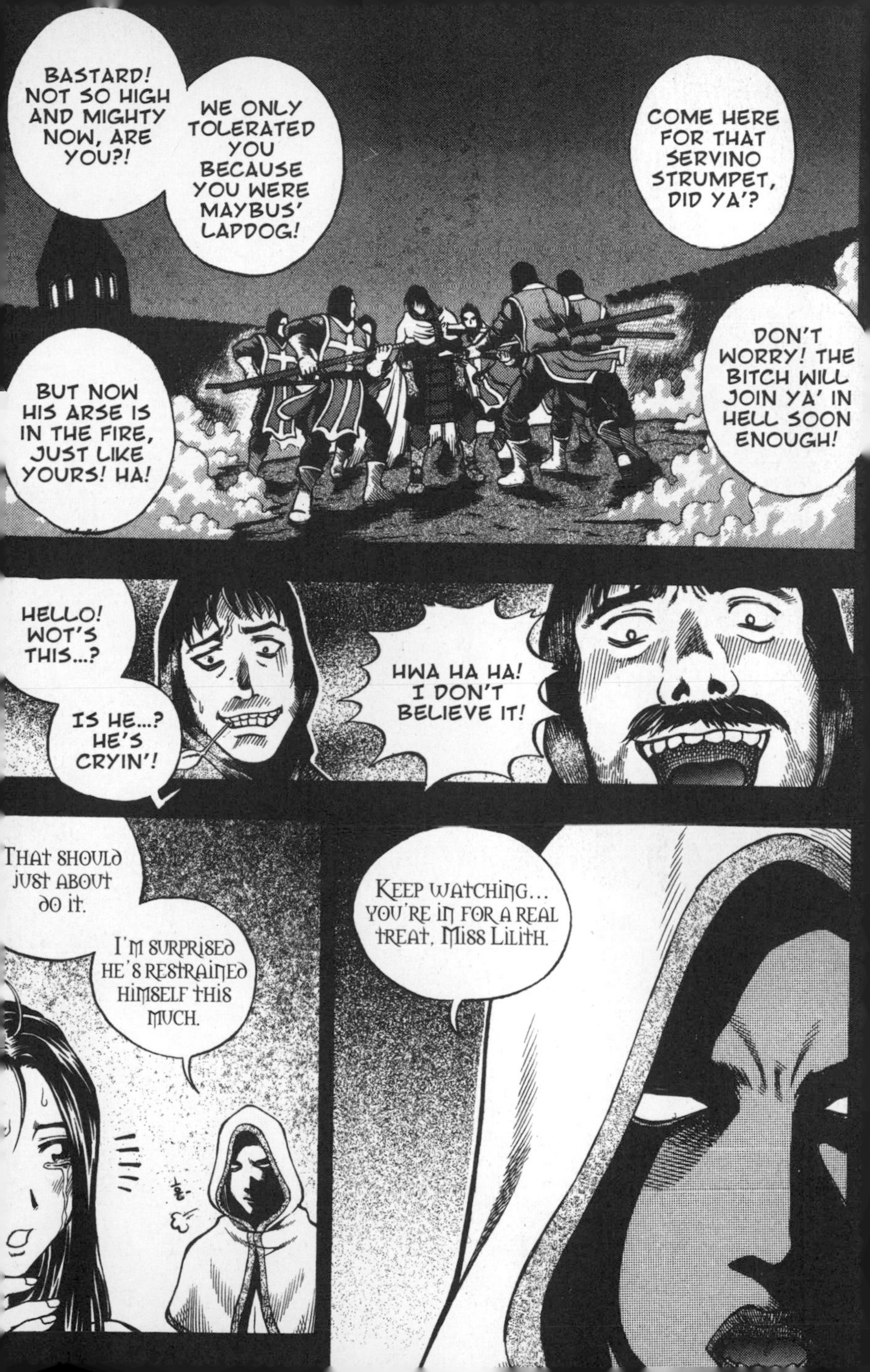
BASTARD! NOT SO HIGH AND MIGHTY NOW, ARE YOU?!
WE ONLY TOLERATED YOU BECAUSE YOU WERE MAYBUS' LAPDOG!
COME HERE FOR THAT SERVINO STRUMPET, DID YA'?
BUT NOW HIS ARSE IS IN THE FIRE, JUST LIKE YOURS! HA!
DON'T WORRY! THE BITCH WILL JOIN YA' IN HELL SOON ENOUGH!
HELLO! WOT'S THIS...?
IS HE...? HE'S CRYIN'!
HWA HA HA! I DON'T BELIEVE IT!
THAT SHOULD JUST ABOUT DO IT.
I'M SURPRISED HE'S RESTRAINED HIMSELF THIS MUCH.
KEEP WATCHING... YOU'RE IN FOR A REAL TREAT, MISS LILITH.

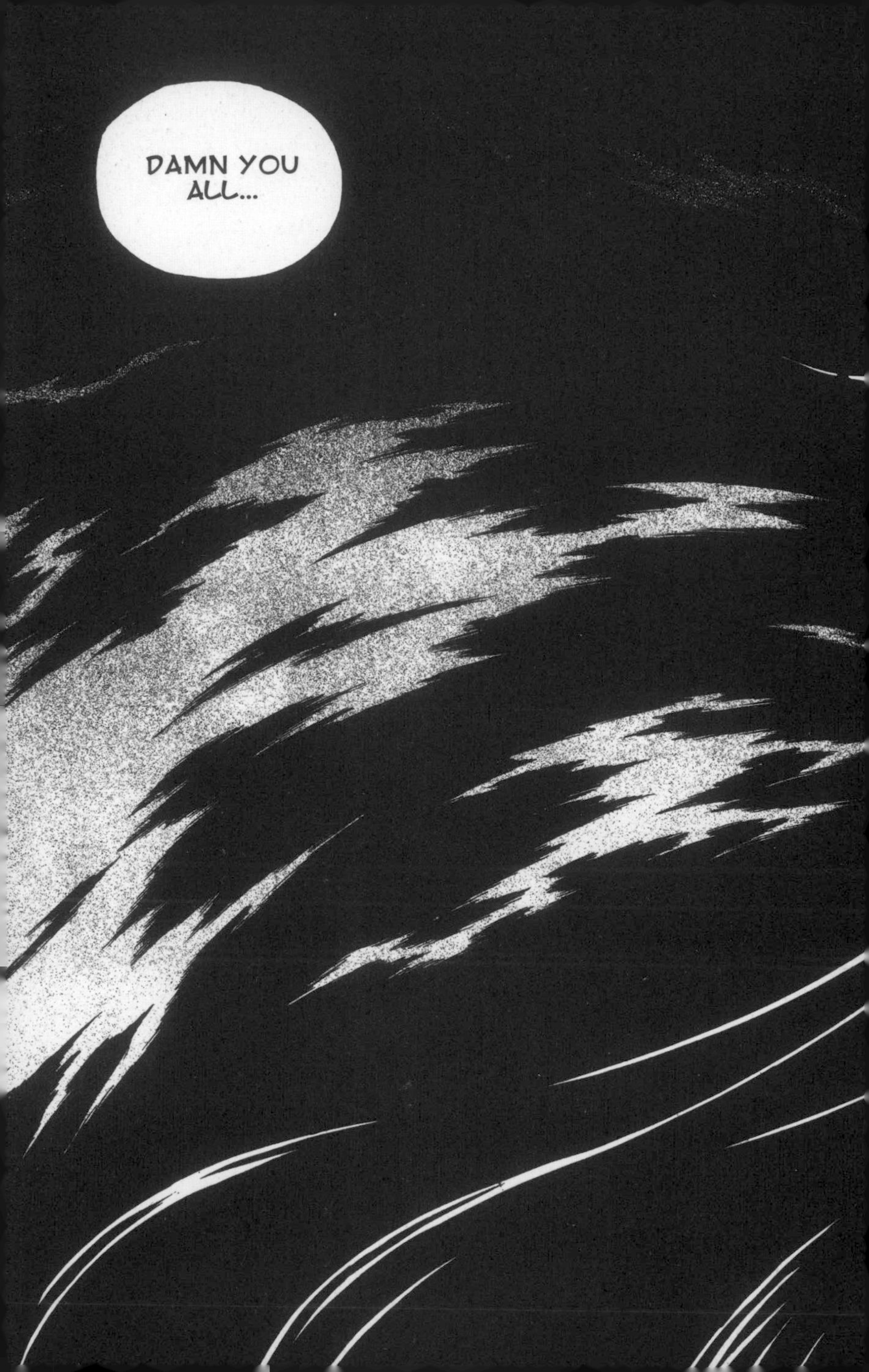
DAMN YOU ALL...

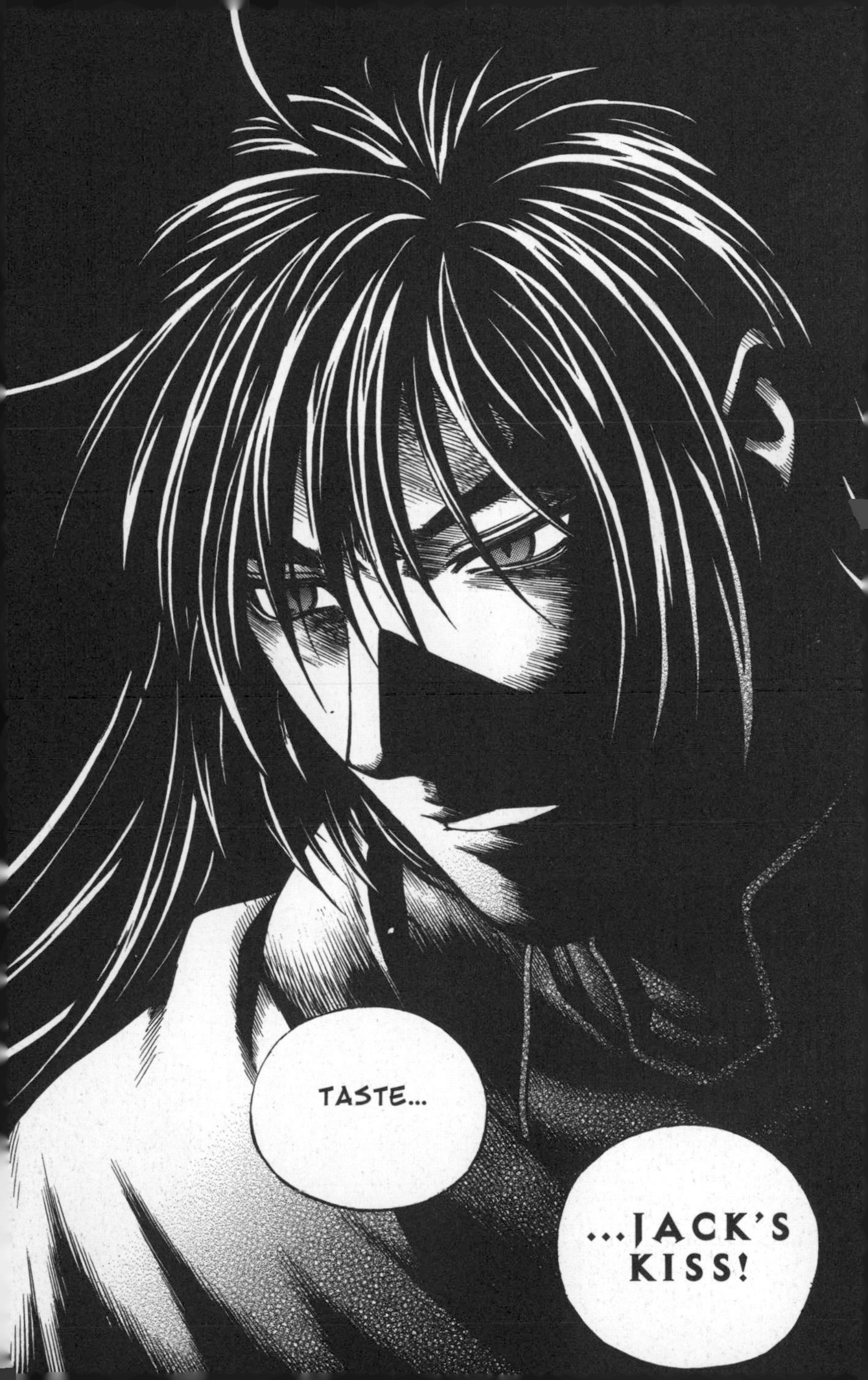
TASTE...
...JACK'S KISS!

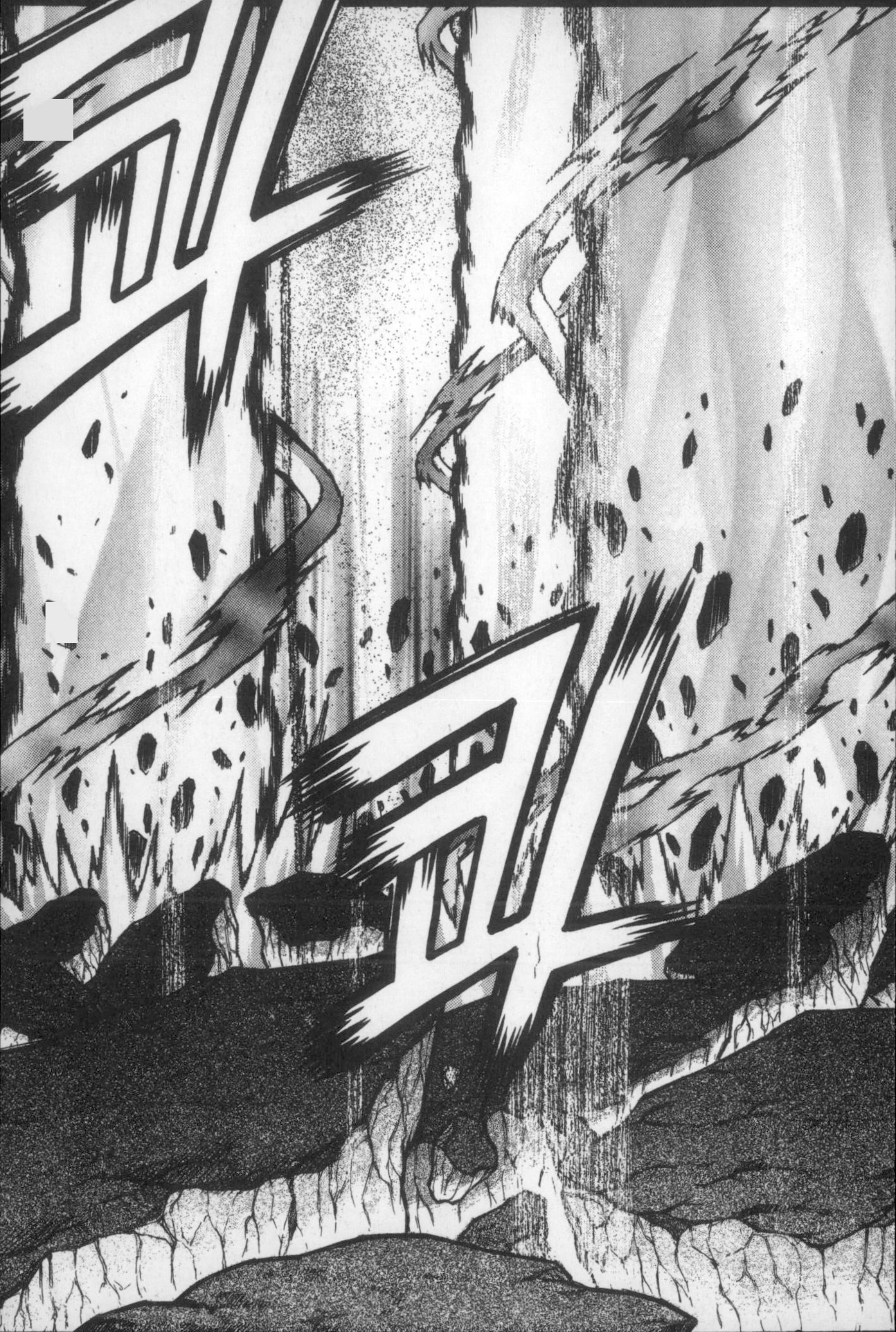

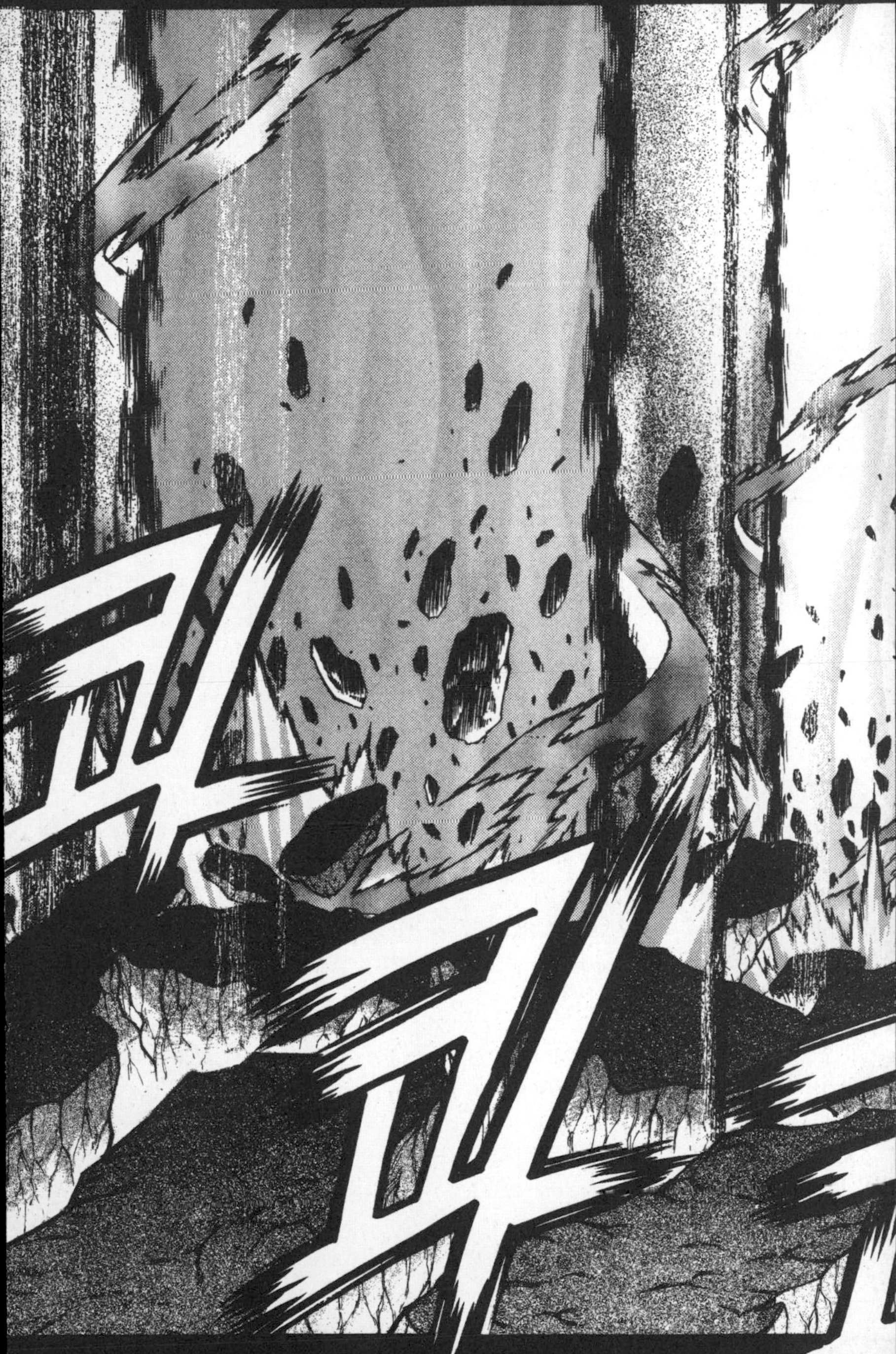

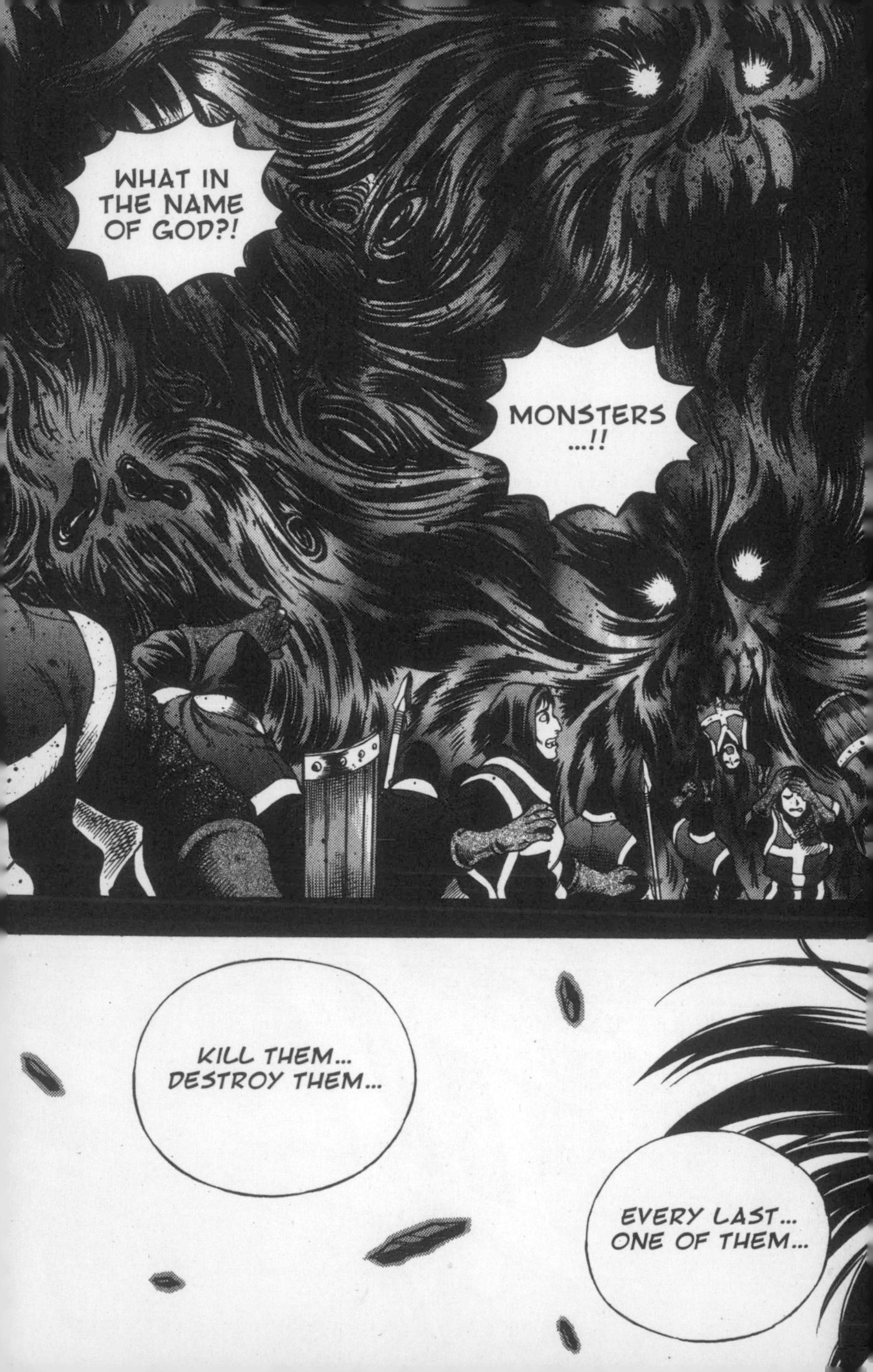
WHAT IN THE NAME OF GOD?!
MONSTERS ...!!
KILL THEM... DESTROY THEM...
EVERY LAST... ONE OF THEM...

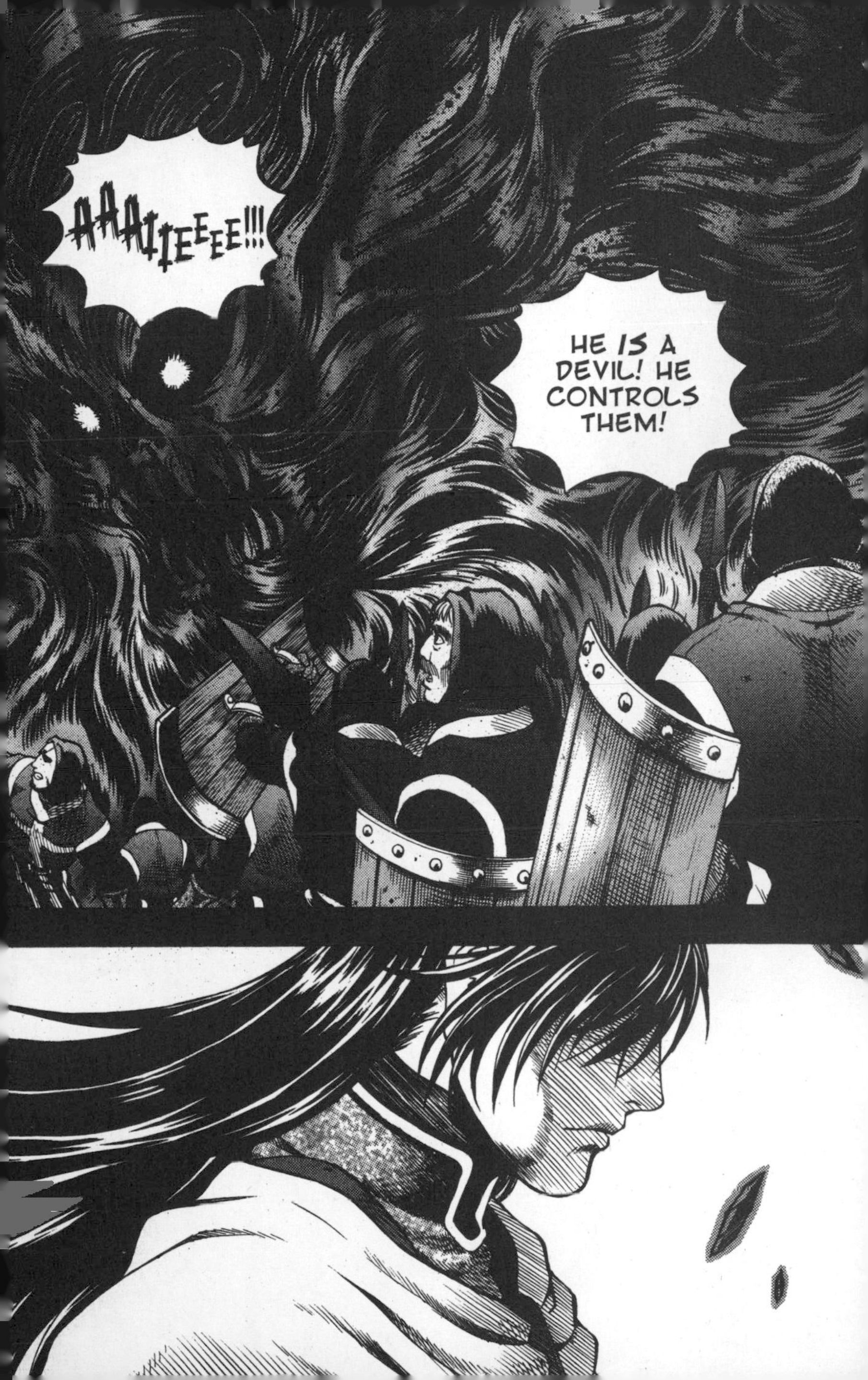
AAAIIEEEEE!!!
HE IS A DEVIL! HE CONTROLS THEM!

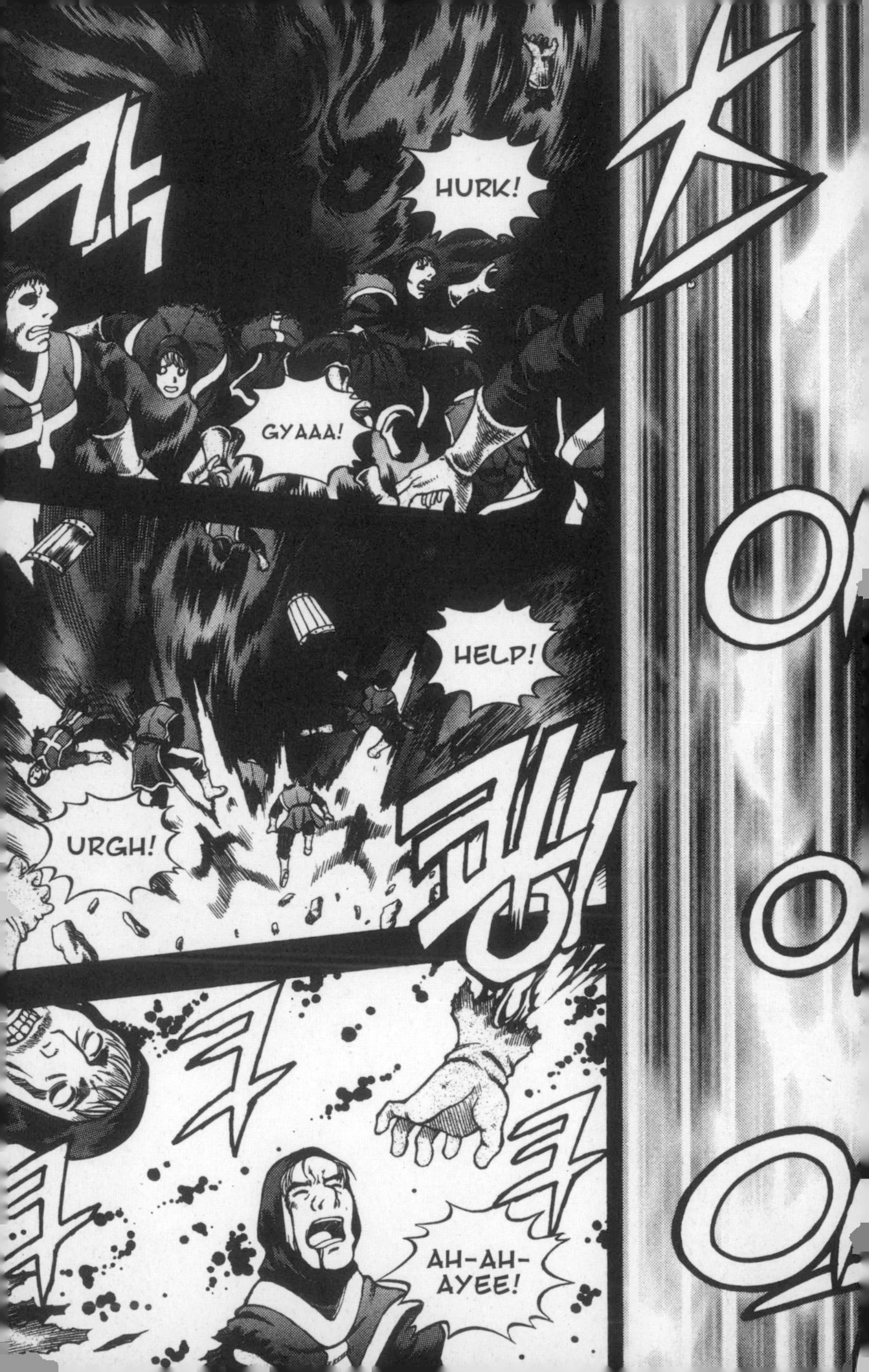
HURK!
GYAAA!
HELP!
URGH!
AH-AH-AYEE!

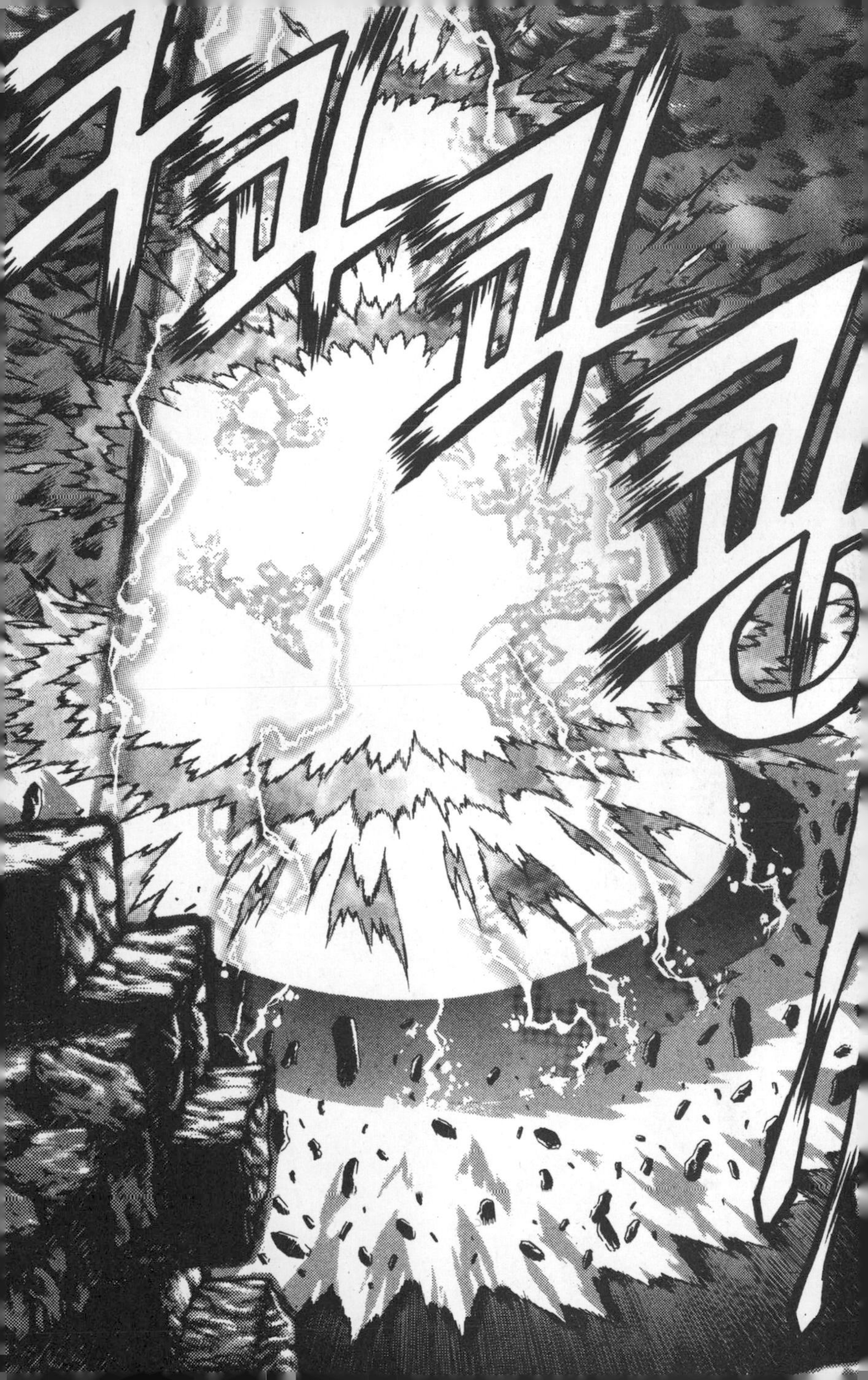

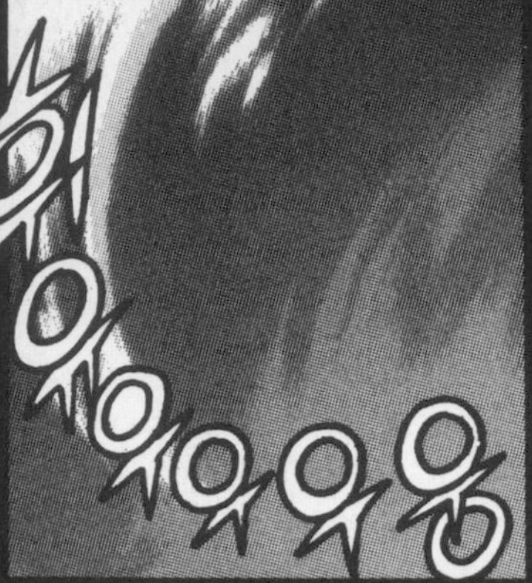
오오오오오옹
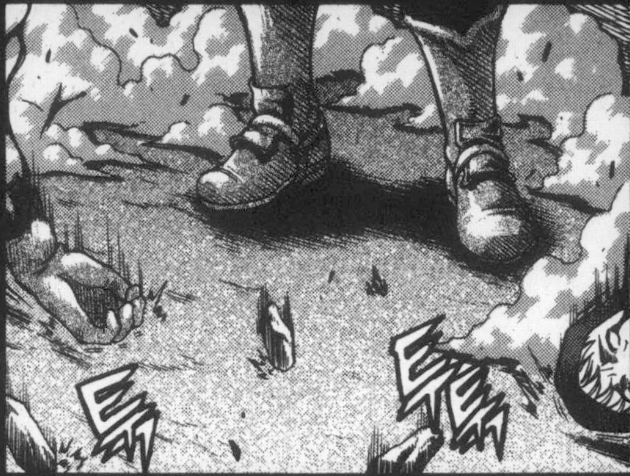
투
투
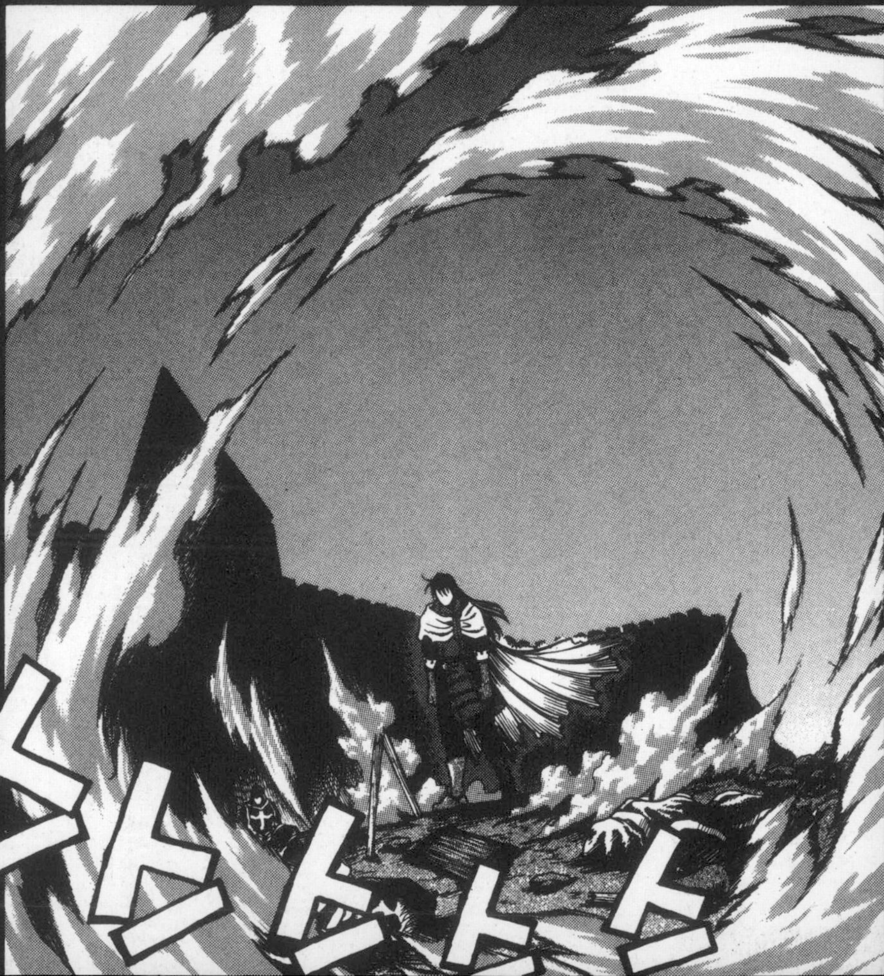

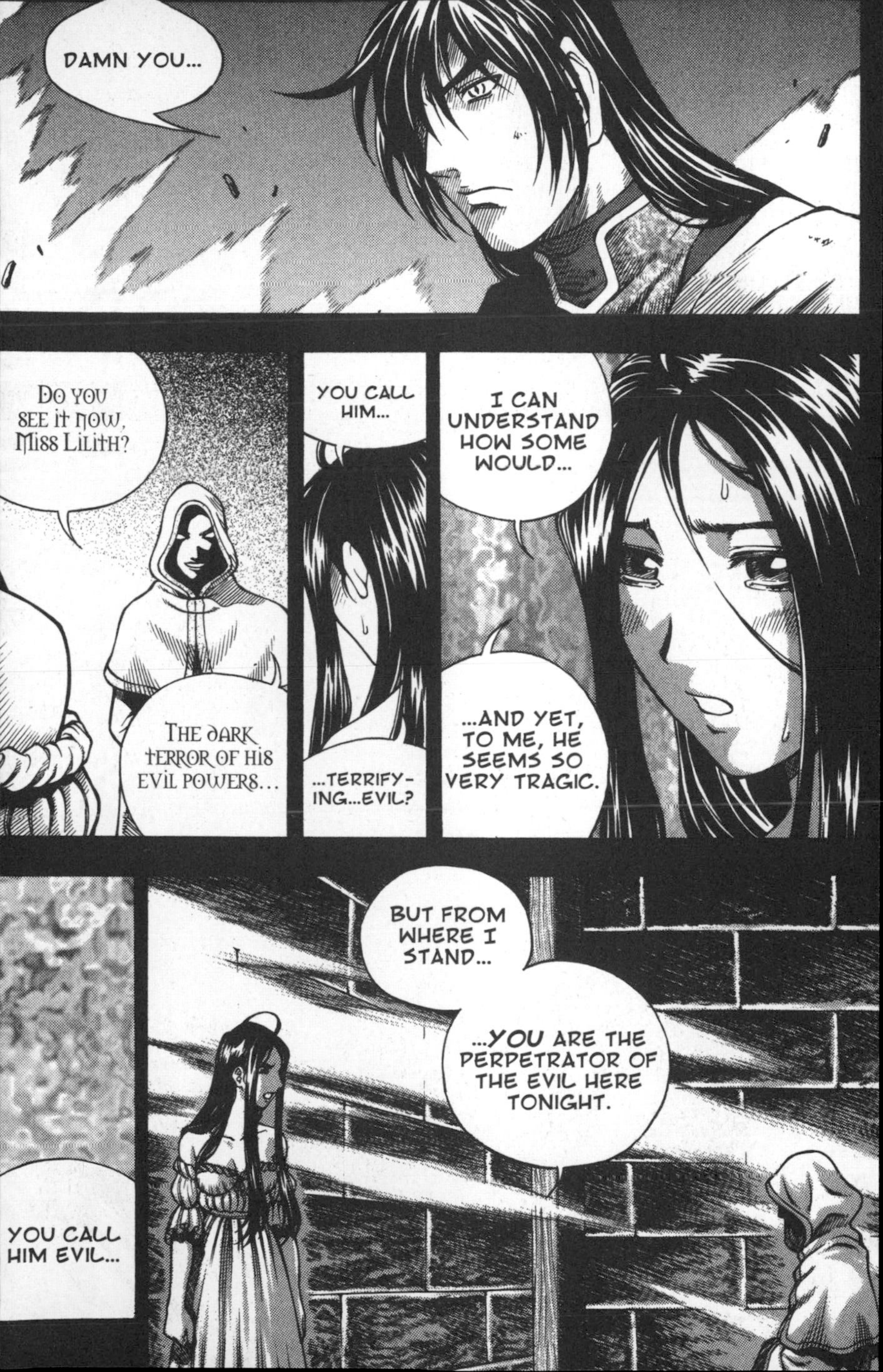
DAMN YOU...
DO YOU SEE IT NOW, MISS LILITH?
THE DARK TERROR OF HIS EVIL POWERS...
YOU CALL HIM...
...TERRIFY-ING...EVIL?
I CAN UNDERSTAND HOW SOME WOULD...
...AND YET, TO ME, HE SEEMS SO VERY TRAGIC.
YOU CALL HIM EVIL...
BUT FROM WHERE I STAND...
...*YOU* ARE THE PERPETRATOR OF THE EVIL HERE TONIGHT.

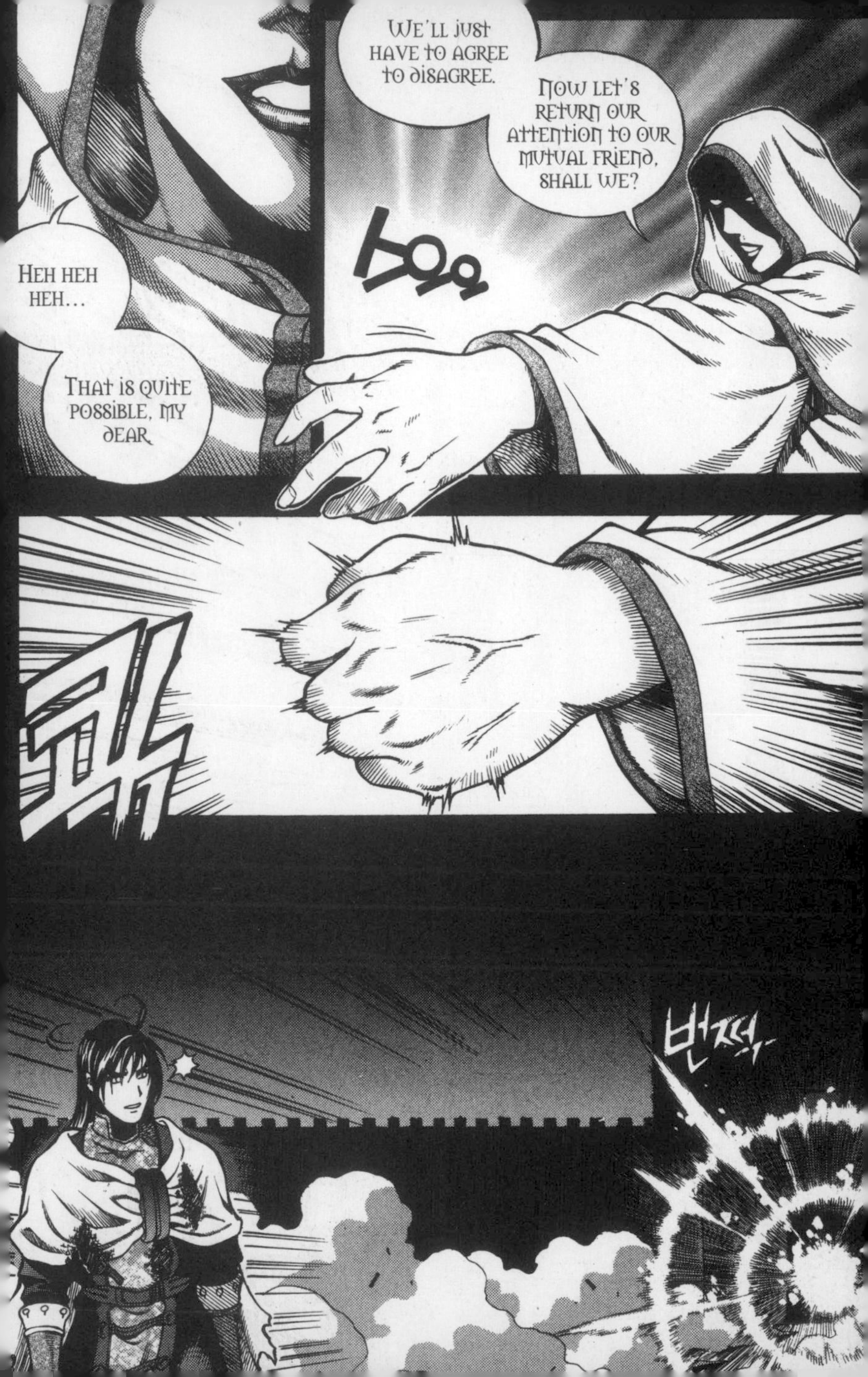
HEH HEH HEH…
THAT IS QUITE POSSIBLE, MY DEAR.
WE'LL JUST HAVE TO AGREE TO DISAGREE.
NOW LET'S RETURN OUR ATTENTION TO OUR MUTUAL FRIEND, SHALL WE?
번쩍

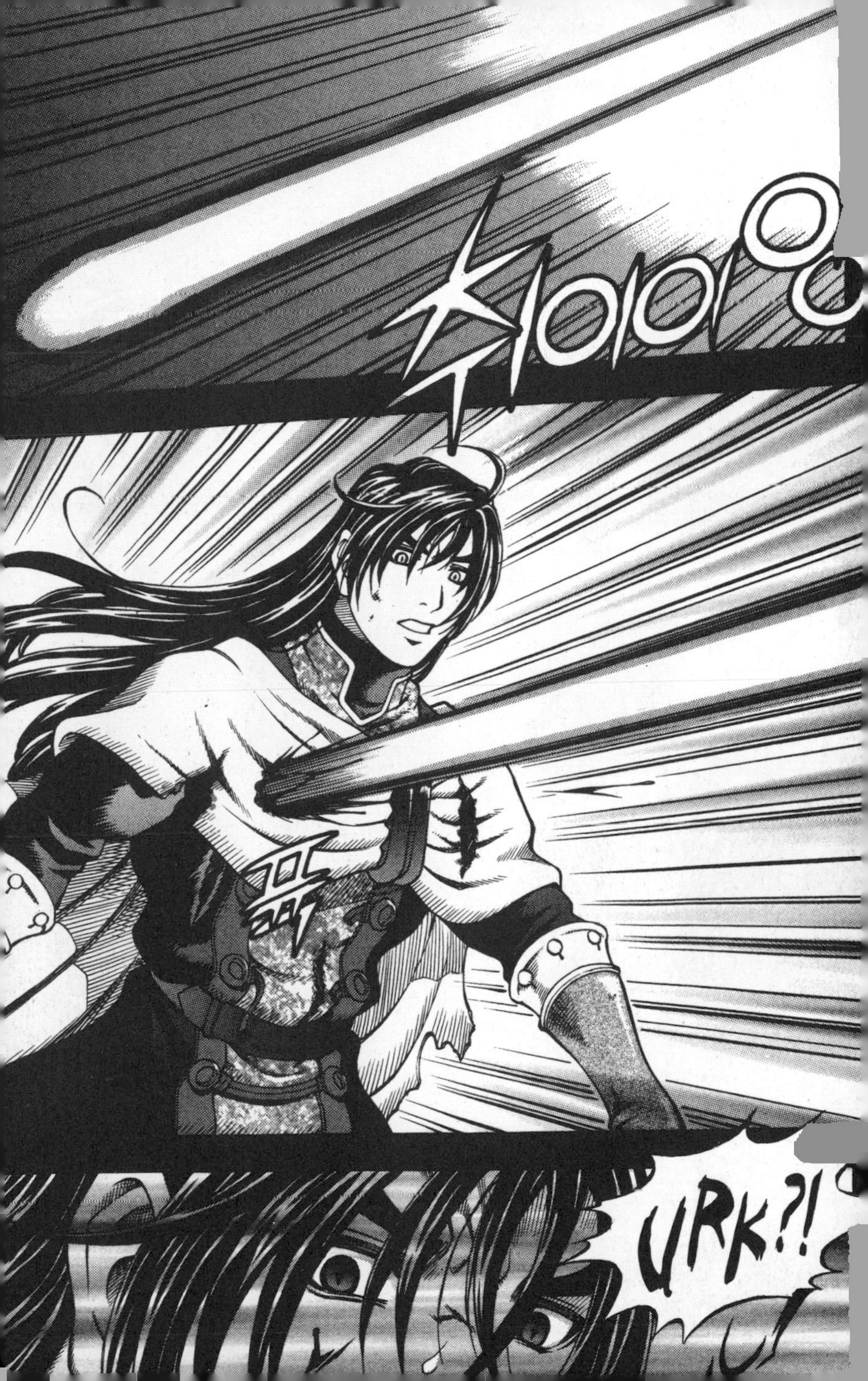
URK?!

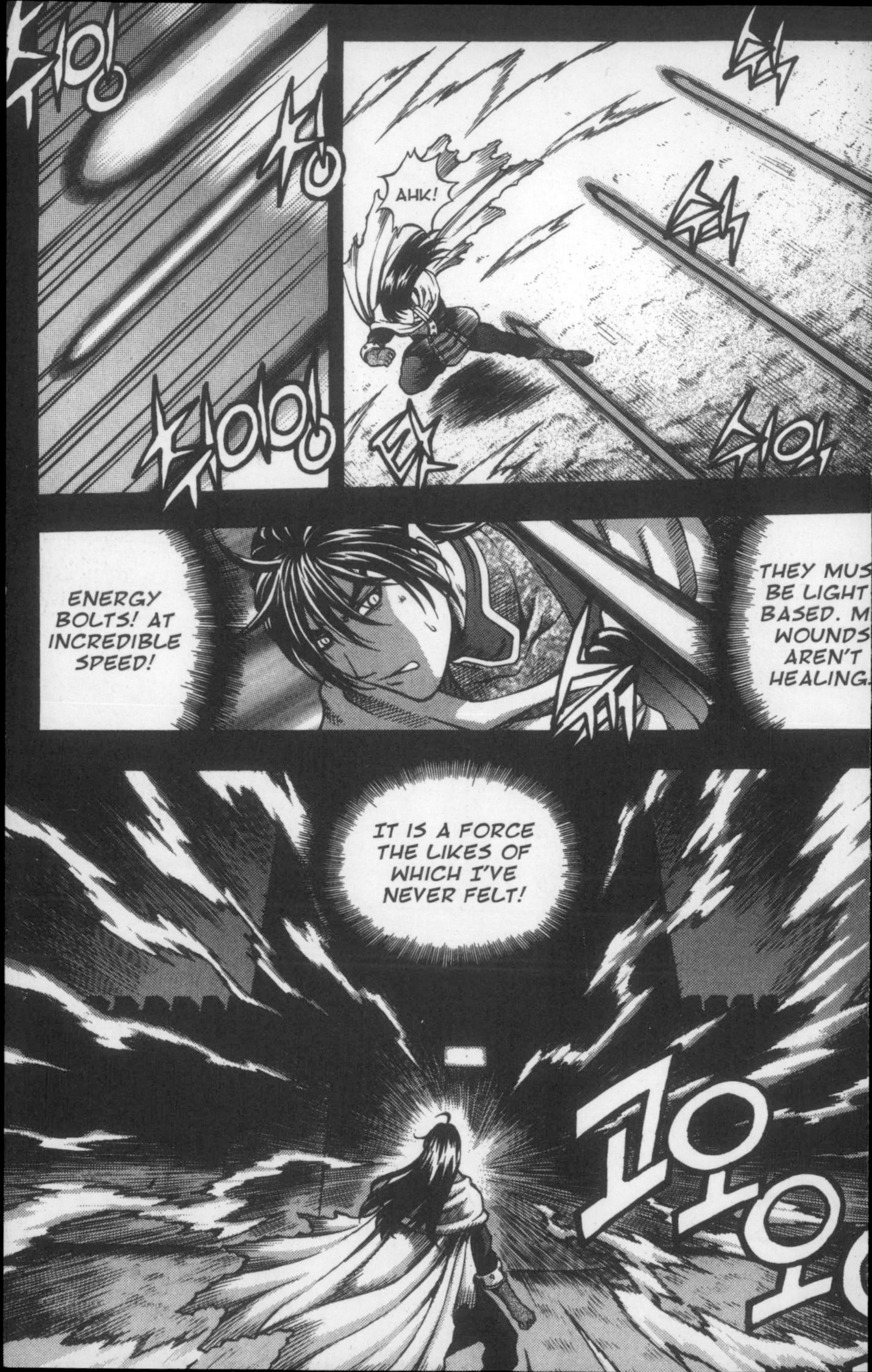

AHK!
ENERGY BOLTS! AT INCREDIBLE SPEED!
THEY MUS BE LIGHT BASED. M WOUNDS AREN'T HEALING.
IT IS A FORCE THE LIKES OF WHICH I'VE NEVER FELT!

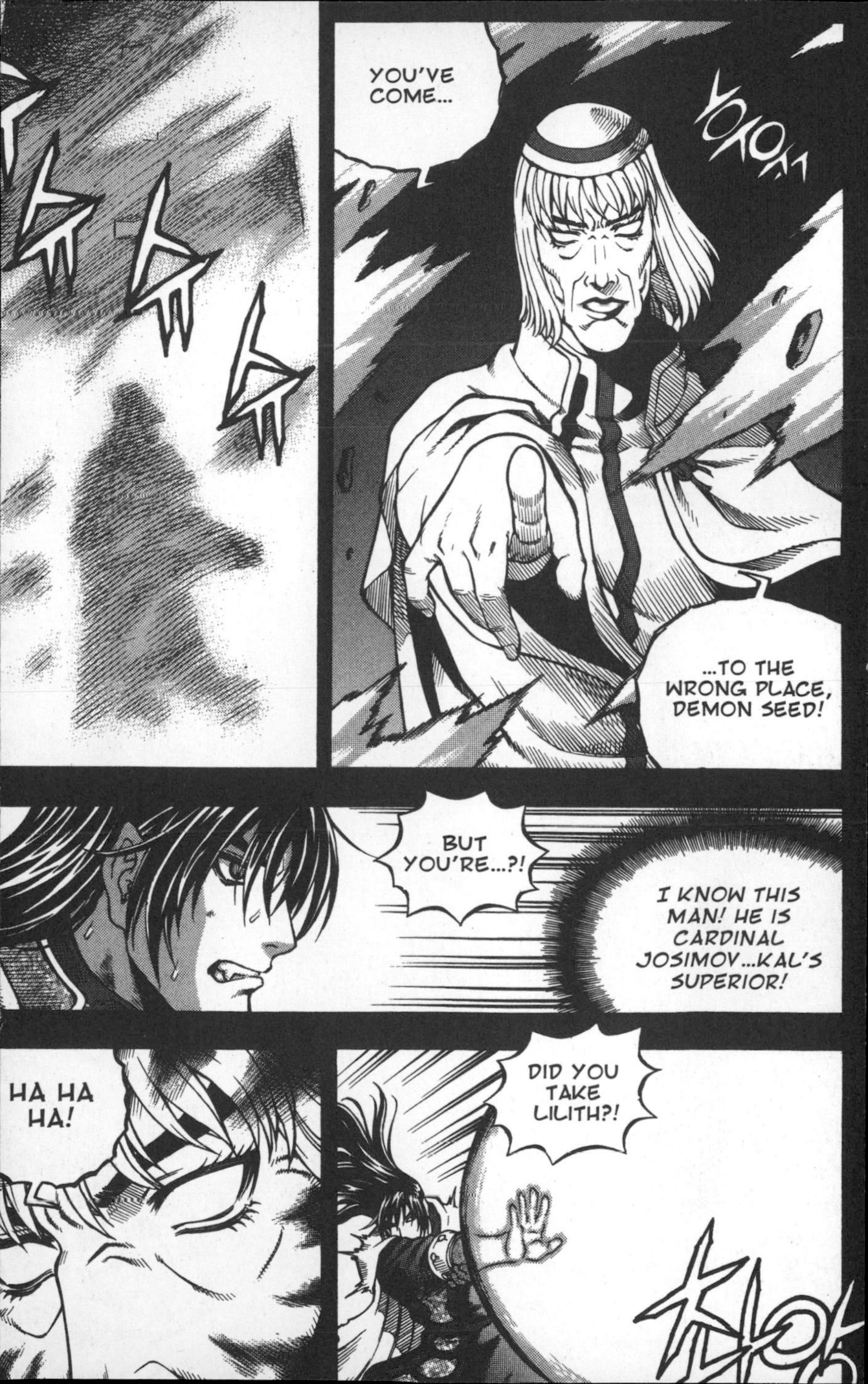
YOU'VE COME...
YOKOM
...TO THE WRONG PLACE, DEMON SEED!
BUT YOU'RE...?!
I KNOW THIS MAN! HE IS CARDINAL JOSIMOV...KAL'S SUPERIOR!
HA HA HA!
DID YOU TAKE LILITH?!

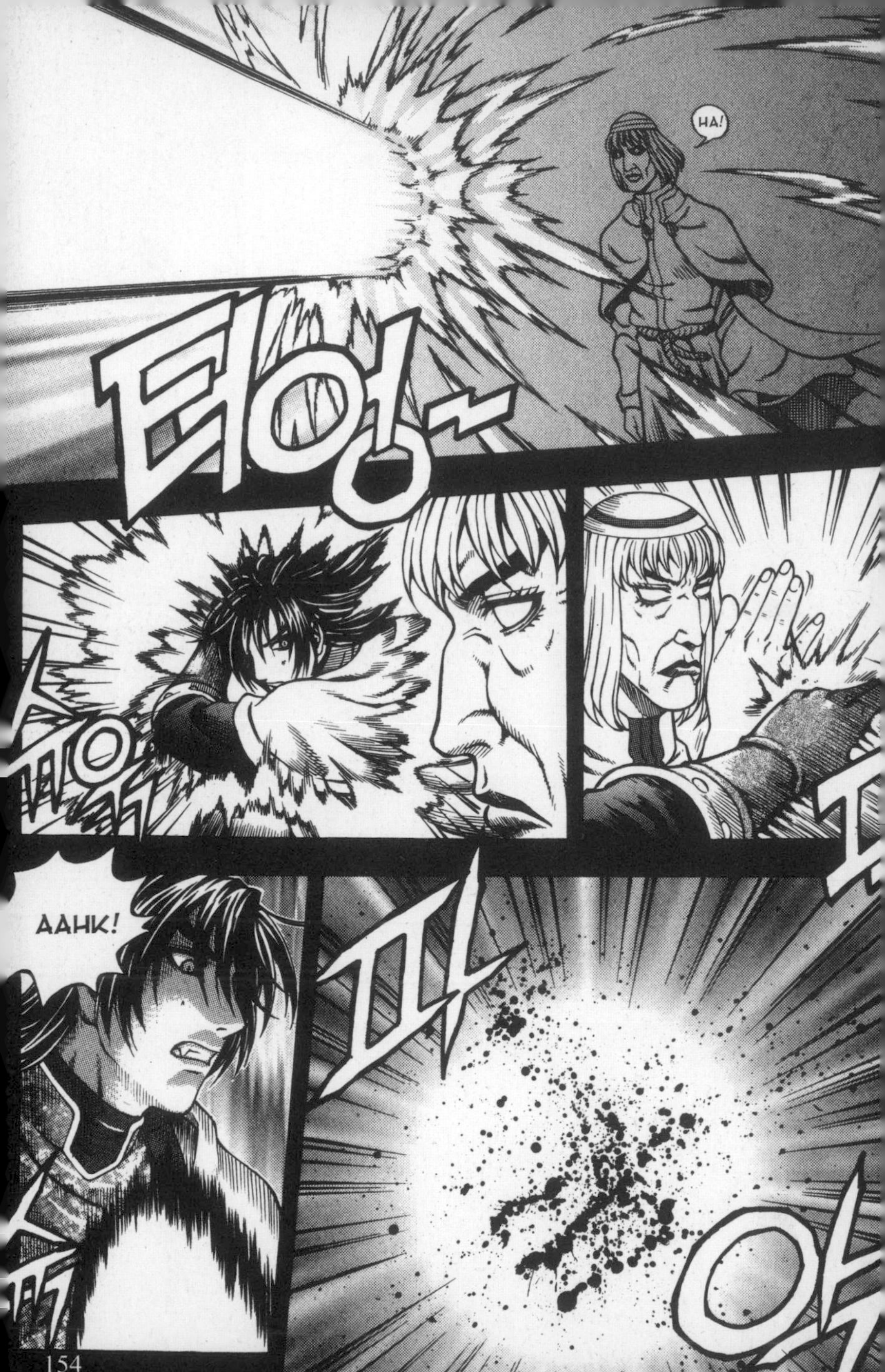
HA!
AAHK!

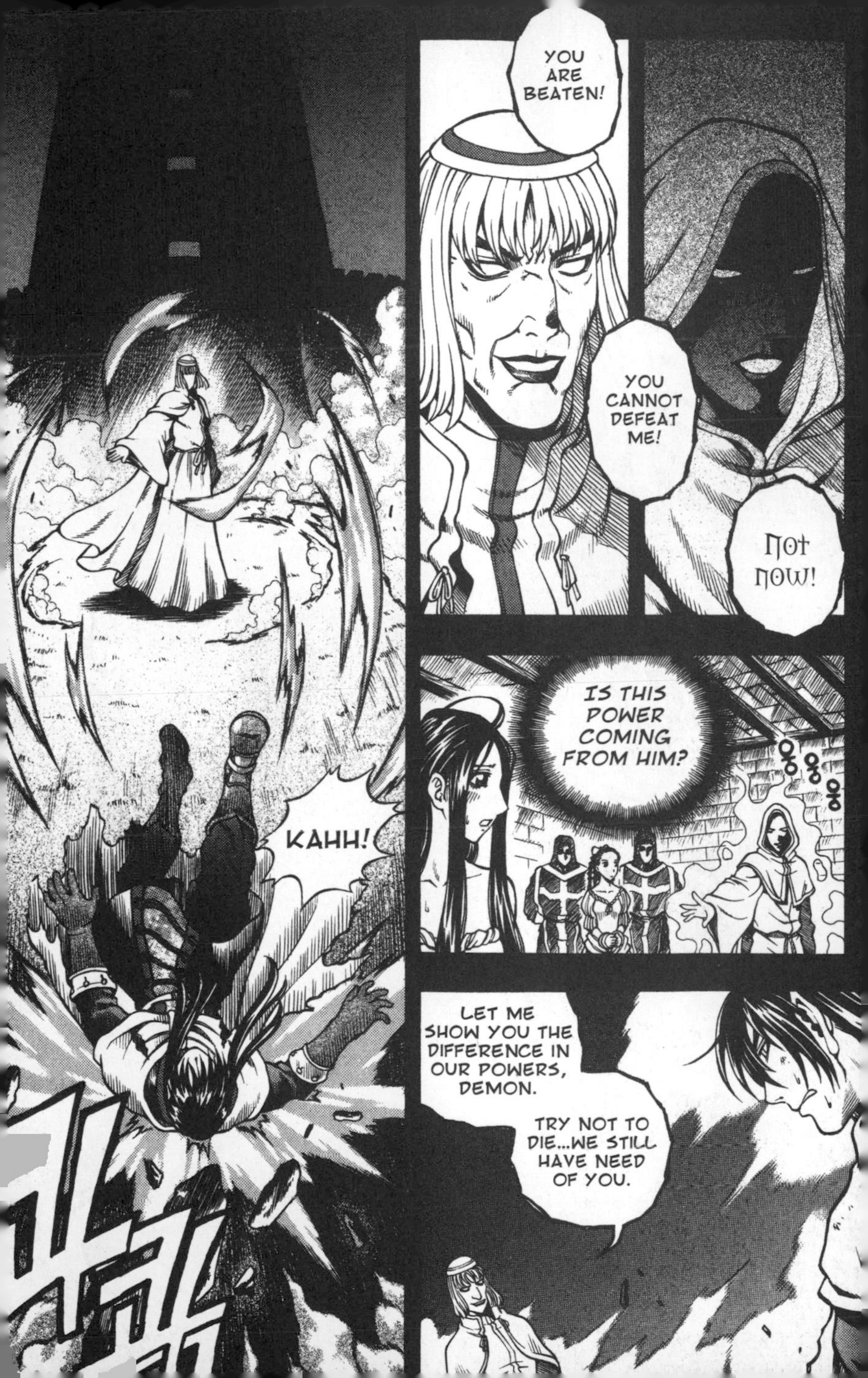
KAHH!
YOU ARE BEATEN!
YOU CANNOT DEFEAT ME!
NOT NOW!
IS THIS POWER COMING FROM HIM?
LET ME SHOW YOU THE DIFFERENCE IN OUR POWERS, DEMON.
TRY NOT TO DIE...WE STILL HAVE NEED OF YOU.

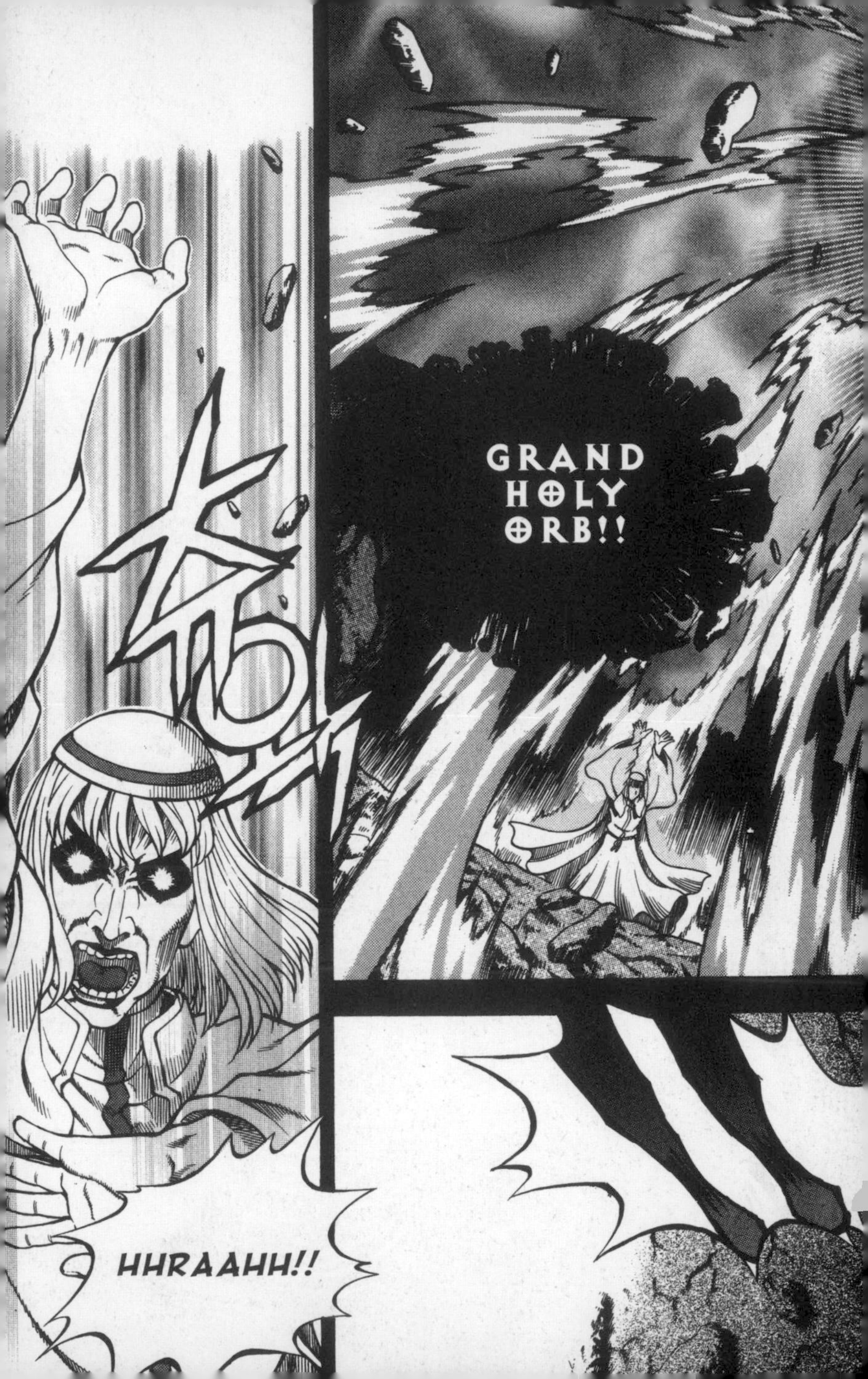
HHRAAHH!!
GRAND HOLY ORB!!

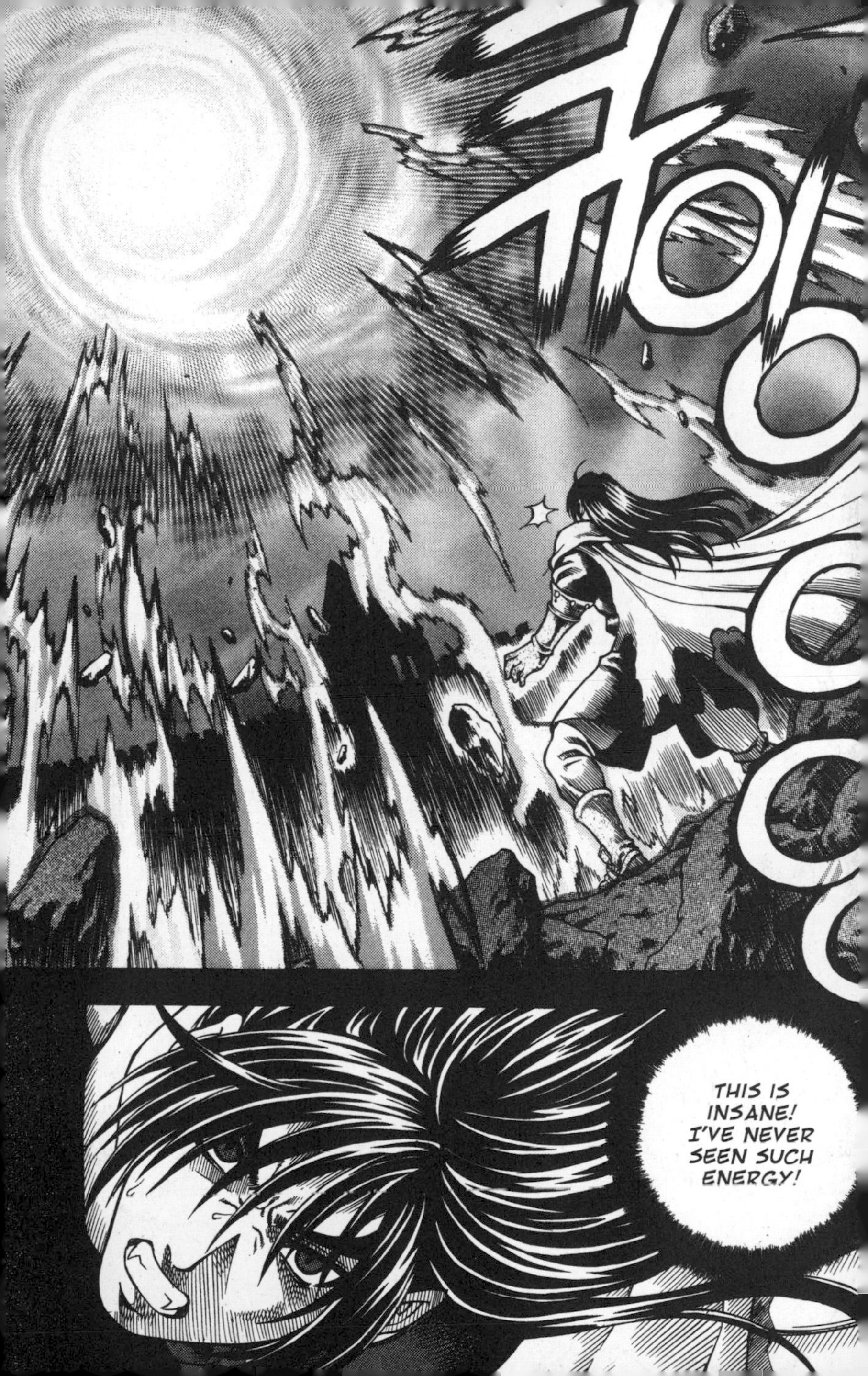
THIS IS INSANE! I'VE NEVER SEEN SUCH ENERGY!

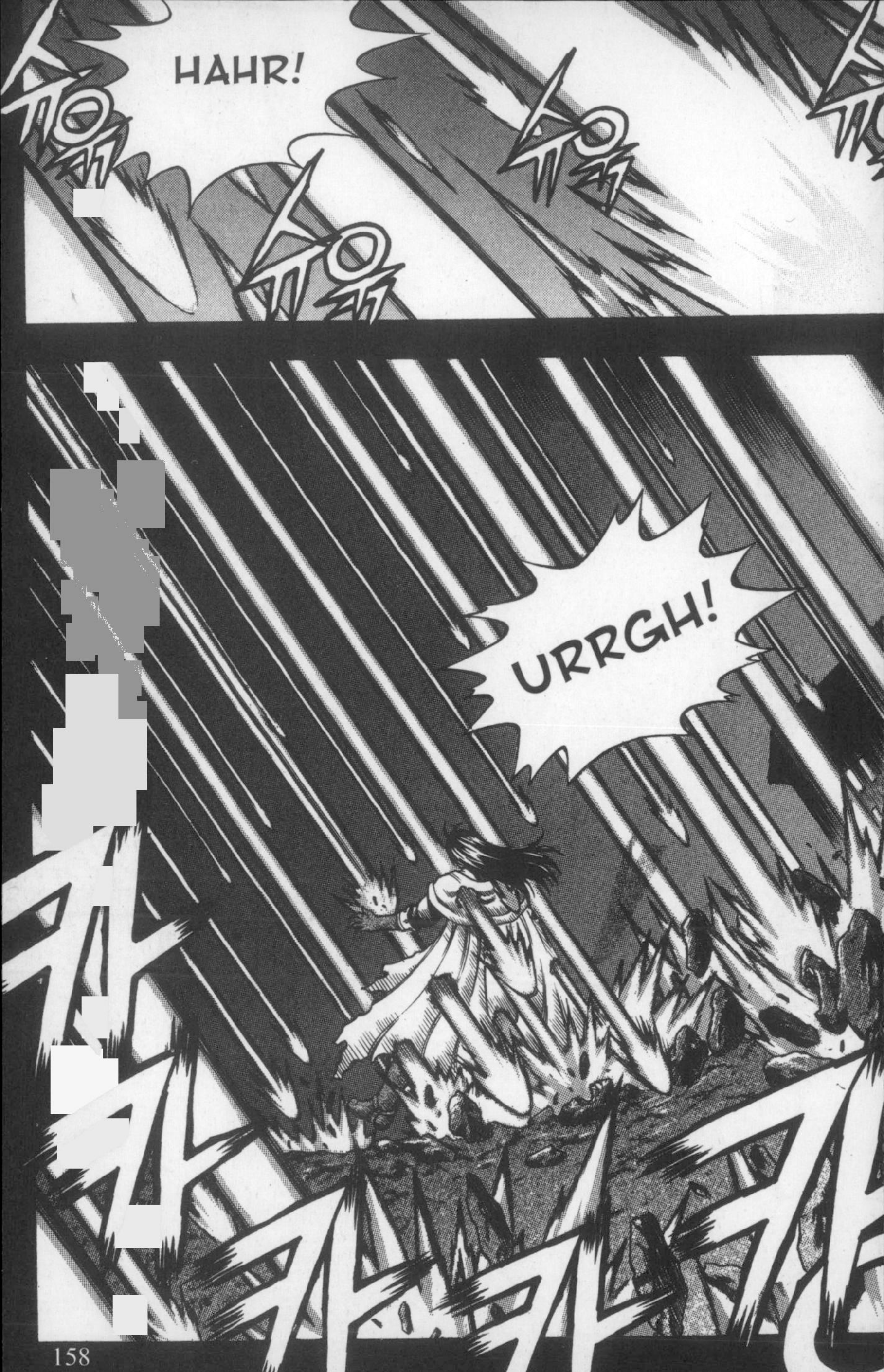
HAHR!
URRGH!

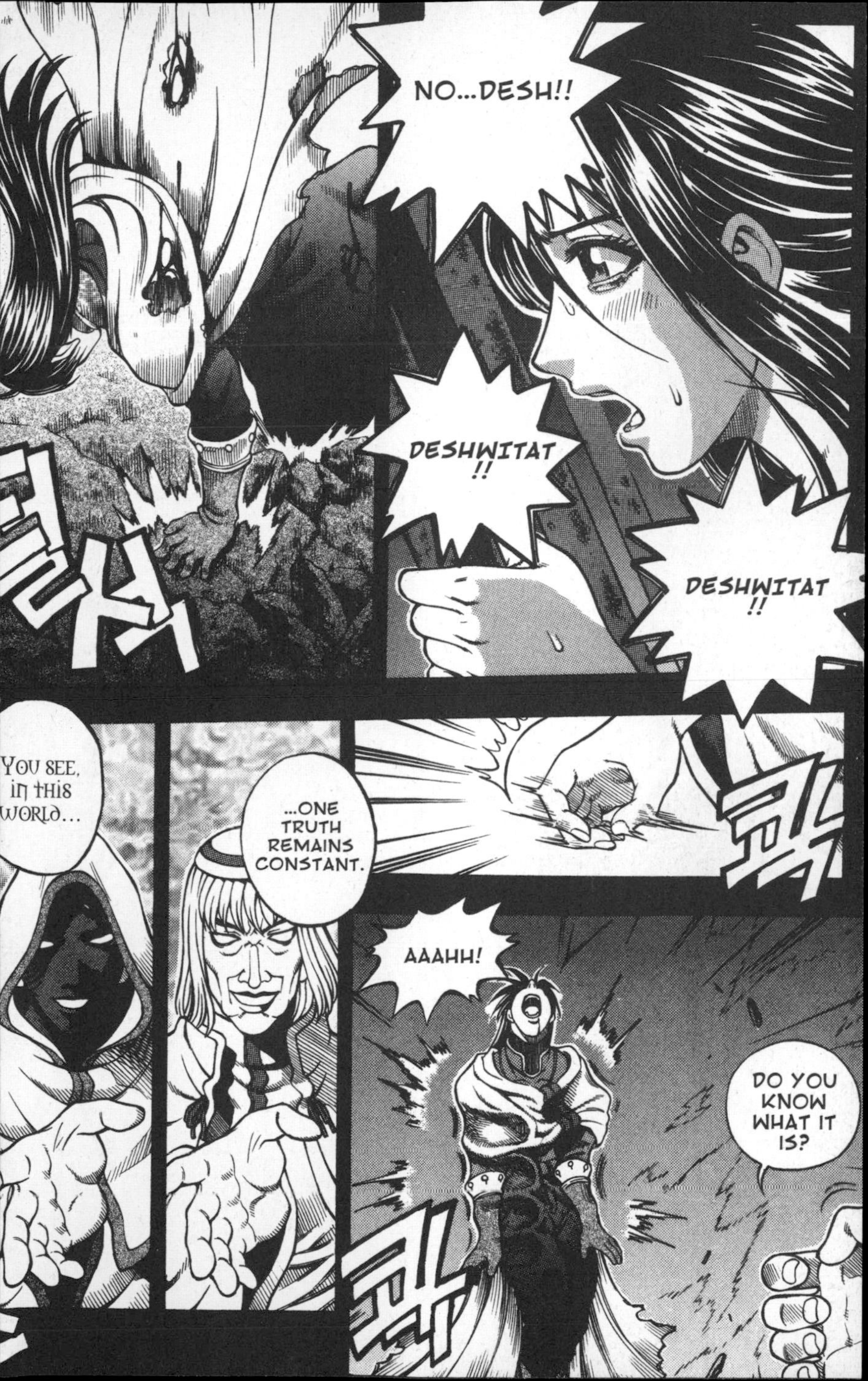
NO...DESH!!
DESHWITAT!!
DESHWITAT!!
YOU SEE, in this WORLD...
...ONE TRUTH REMAINS CONSTANT.
AAAHH!
DO YOU KNOW WHAT IT IS?

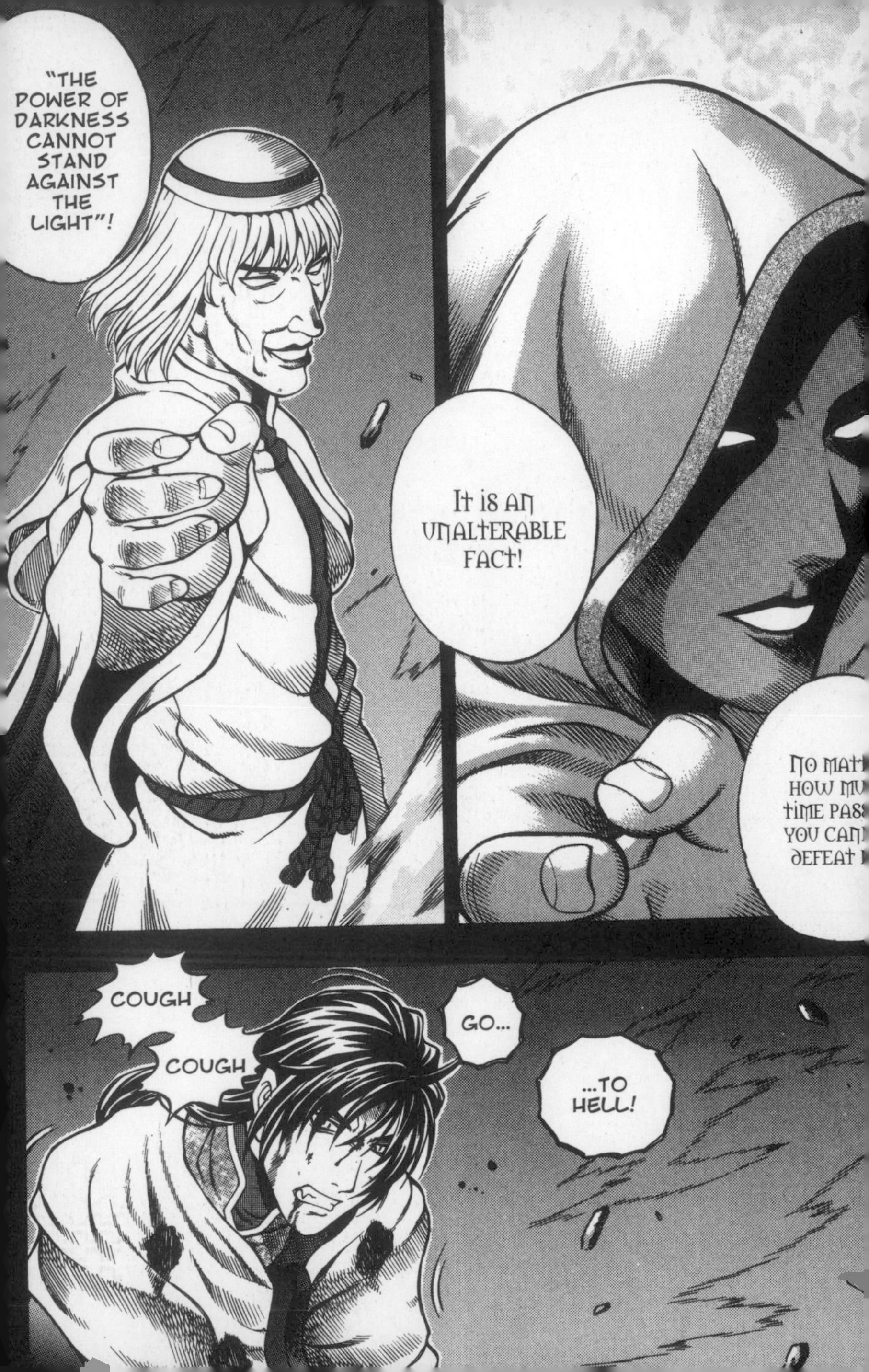
"THE POWER OF DARKNESS CANNOT STAND AGAINST THE LIGHT"!
It is AN UNALTERABLE FACT!
NO MAT HOW MU TIME PAS YOU CAN DEFEAT
COUGH
COUGH
GO...
...TO HELL!

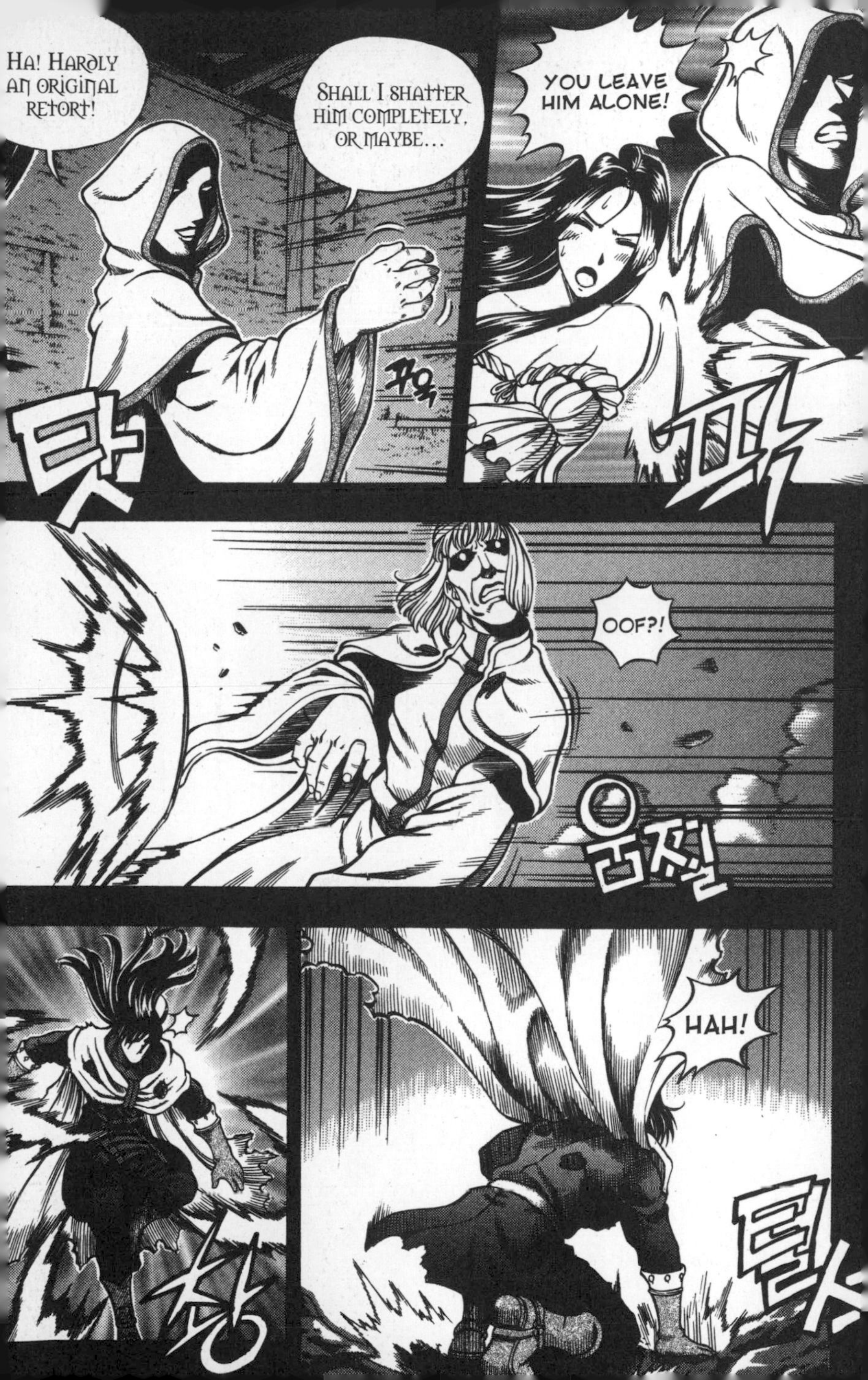
HA! HARDLY AN ORIGINAL RETORT!
SHALL I SHATTER HIM COMPLETELY, OR MAYBE...
YOU LEAVE HIM ALONE!
OOF?!
HAH!

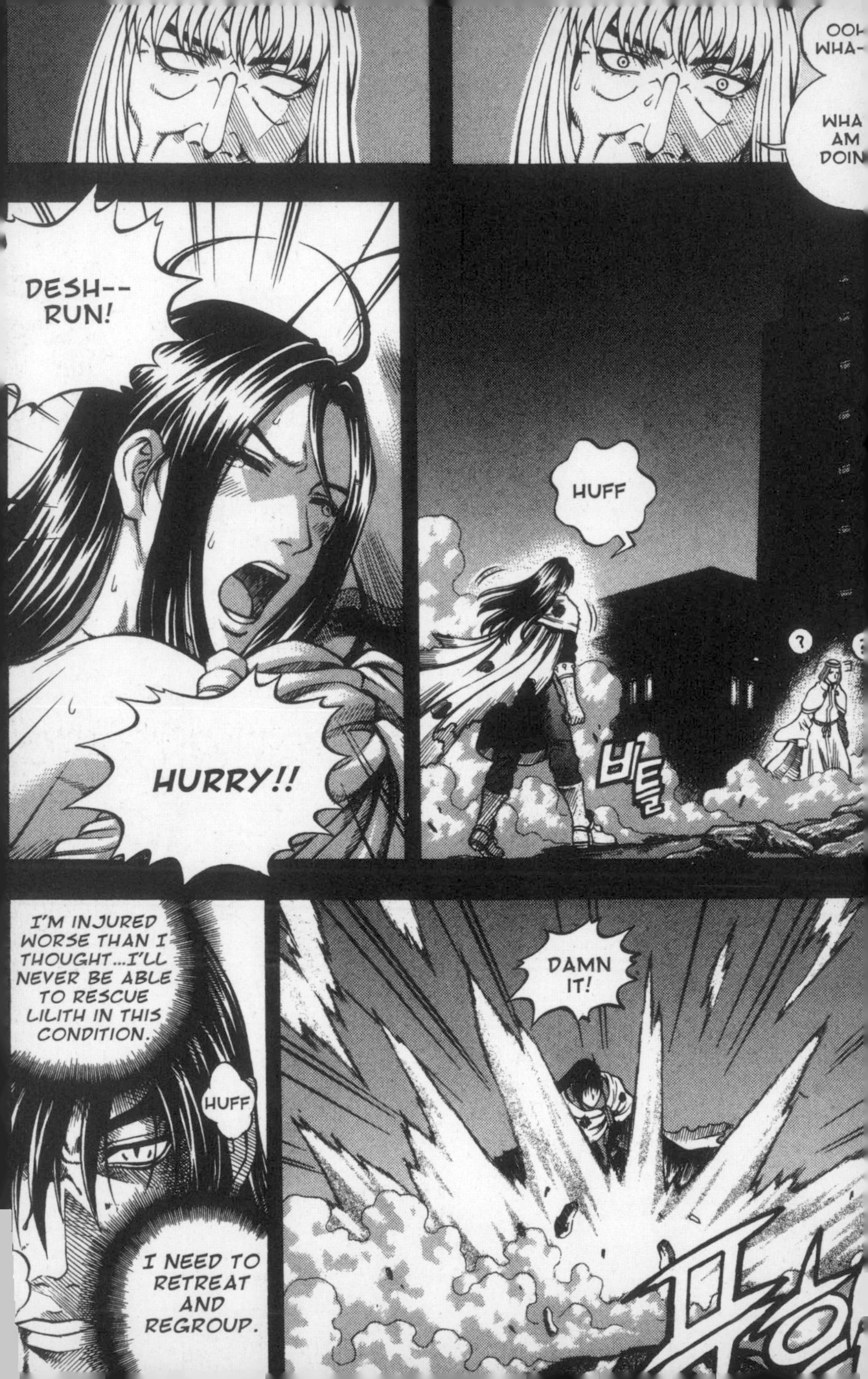
OOH WHA-
WHA AM DOIN
DESH-- RUN!
HURRY!!
HUFF
?
I'M INJURED WORSE THAN I THOUGHT...I'LL NEVER BE ABLE TO RESCUE LILITH IN THIS CONDITION.
HUFF
I NEED TO RETREAT AND REGROUP.
DAMN IT!

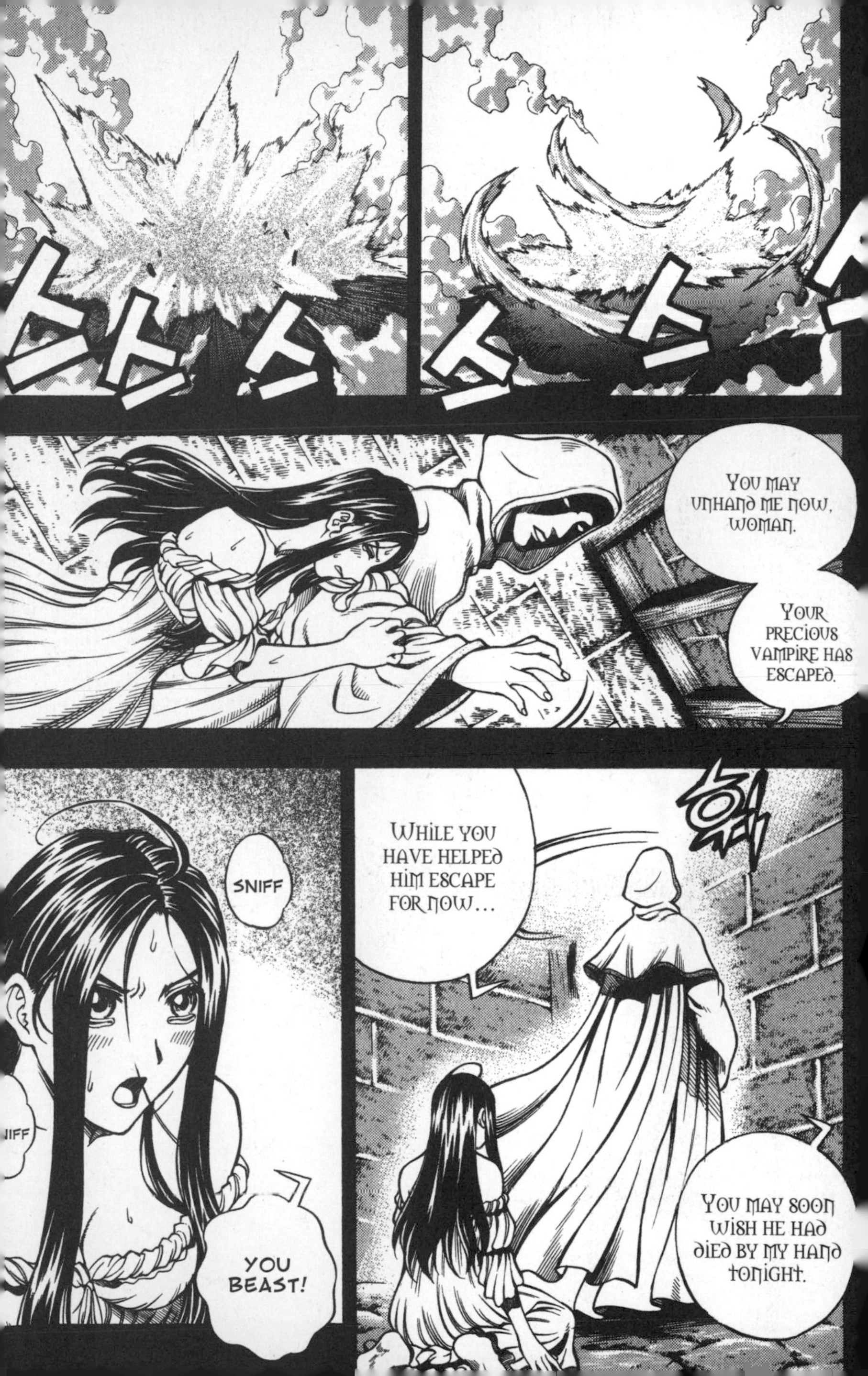
YOU MAY UNHAND ME NOW, WOMAN.
YOUR PRECIOUS VAMPIRE HAS ESCAPED.
SNIFF
YOU BEAST!
WHILE YOU HAVE HELPED HIM ESCAPE FOR NOW...
YOU MAY SOON WISH HE HAD DIED BY MY HAND TONIGHT.

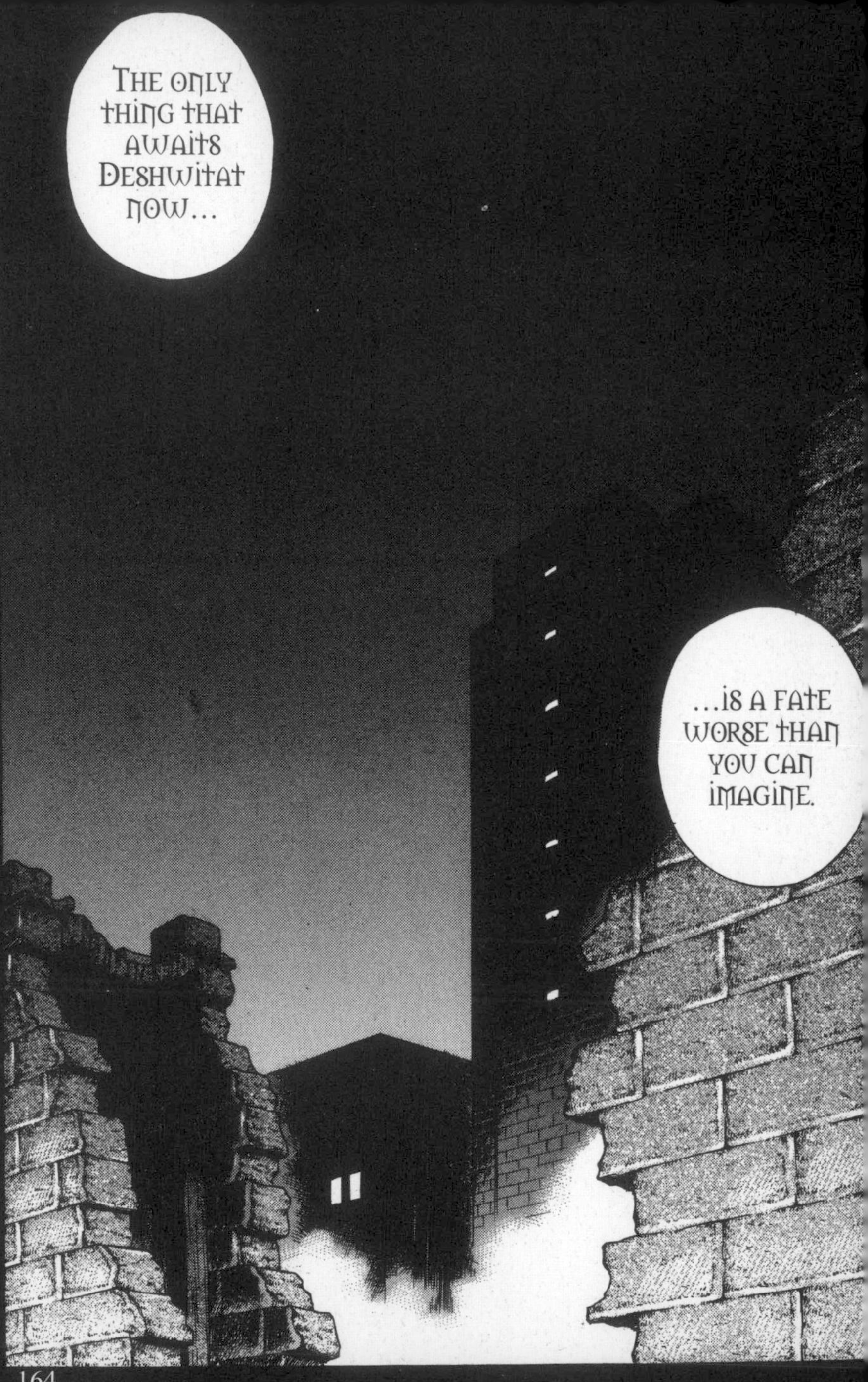
THE ONLY THING THAT AWAITS DESHWITAT NOW...
...IS A FATE WORSE THAN YOU CAN IMAGINE.

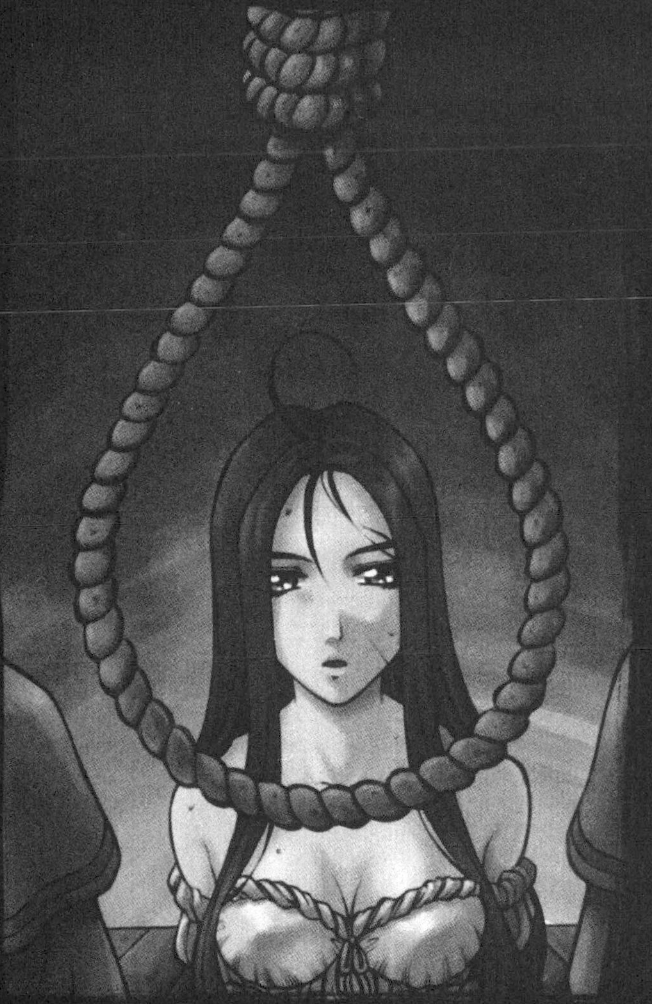

CHAPTER 41 - A: PRELUDE TO TRAGEDY

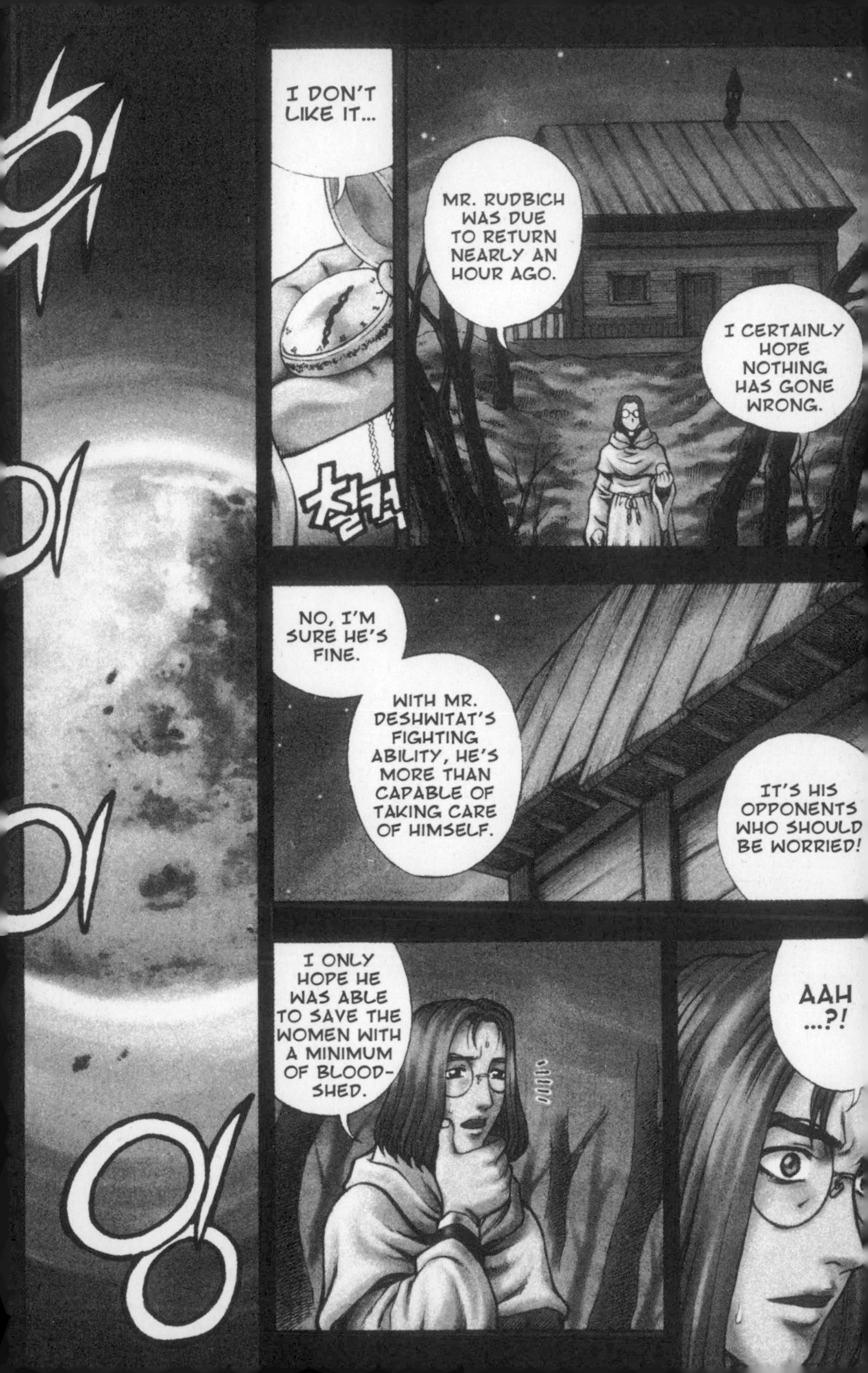
I DON'T LIKE IT...
MR. RUDBICH WAS DUE TO RETURN NEARLY AN HOUR AGO.
I CERTAINLY HOPE NOTHING HAS GONE WRONG.
NO, I'M SURE HE'S FINE.
WITH MR. DESHWITAT'S FIGHTING ABILITY, HE'S MORE THAN CAPABLE OF TAKING CARE OF HIMSELF.
IT'S HIS OPPONENTS WHO SHOULD BE WORRIED!
I ONLY HOPE HE WAS ABLE TO SAVE THE WOMEN WITH A MINIMUM OF BLOOD-SHED.
AAH ...?!

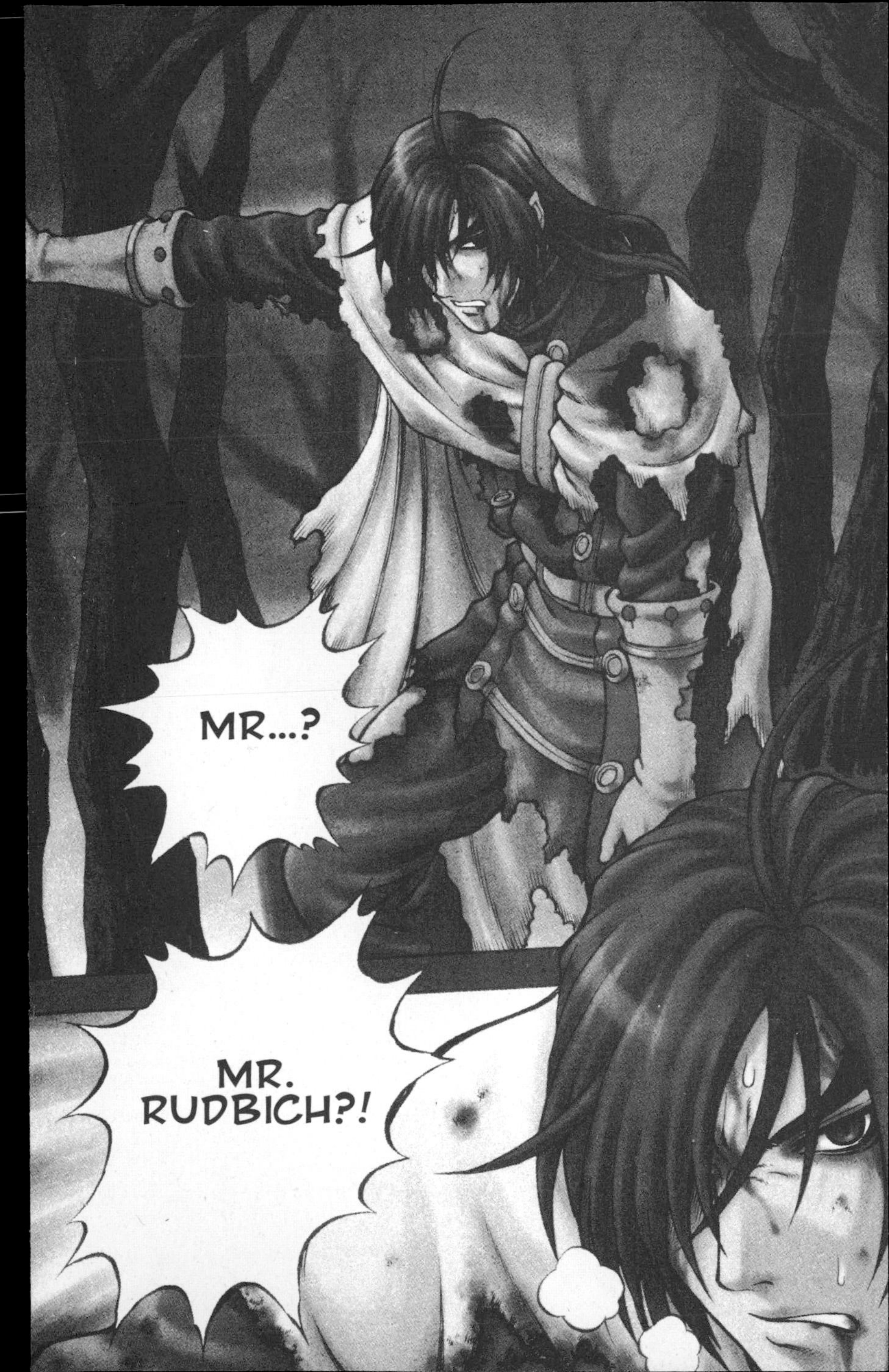
MR...?
MR. RUDBICH?!

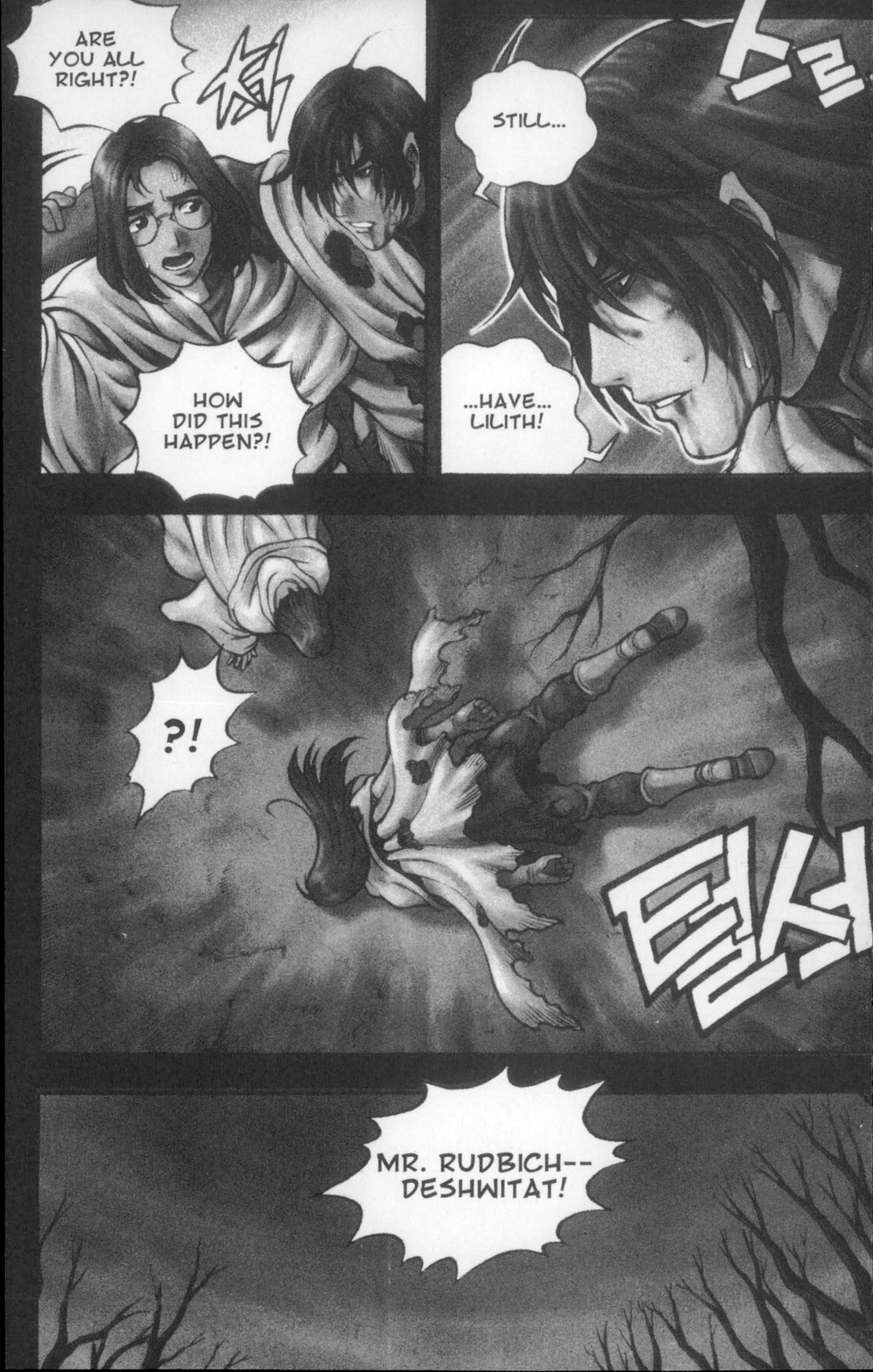
ARE YOU ALL RIGHT?!
HOW DID THIS HAPPEN?!
STILL...
...HAVE... LILITH!
?!
MR. RUDBICH--DESHWITAT!

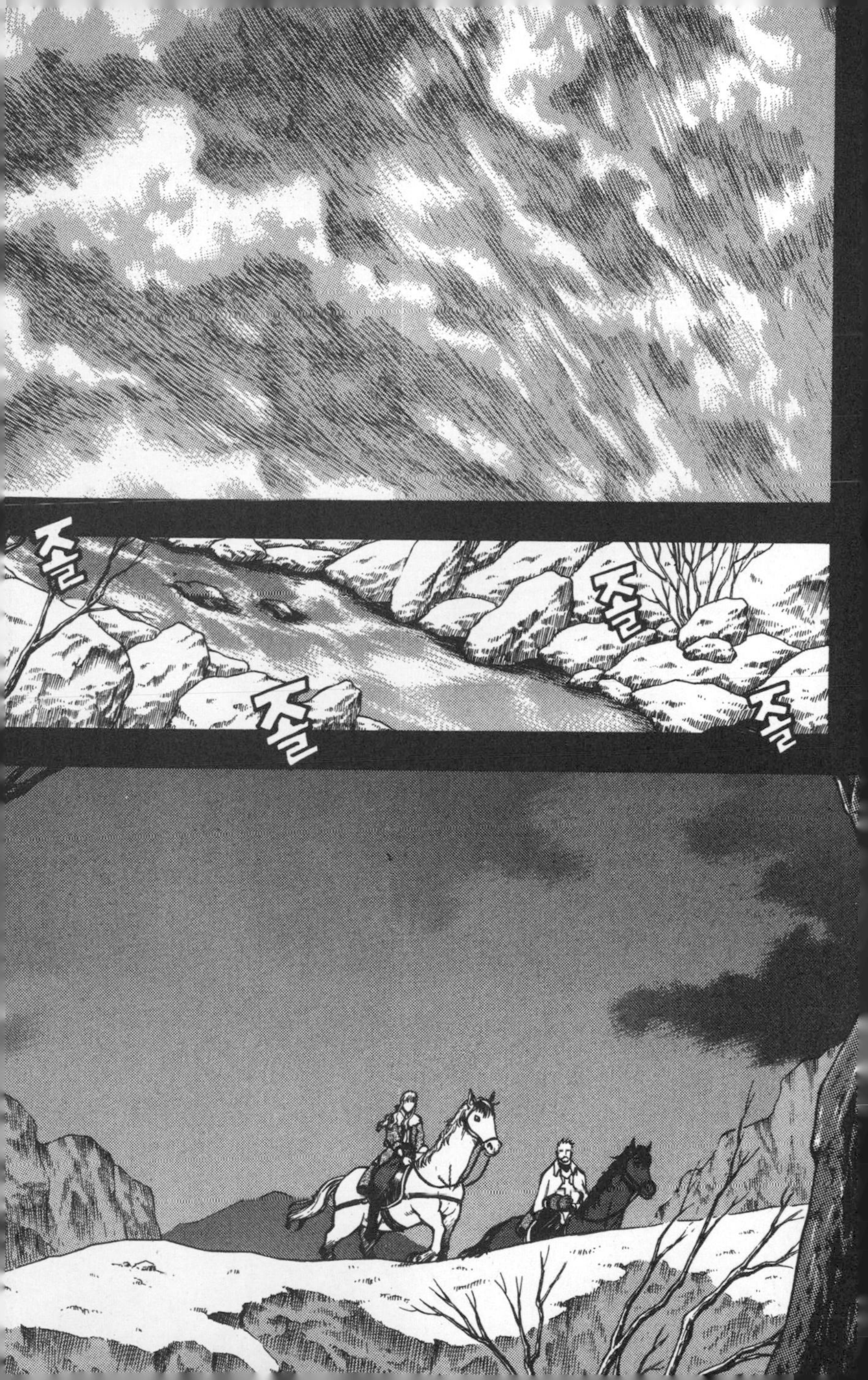
졸
졸
졸
졸

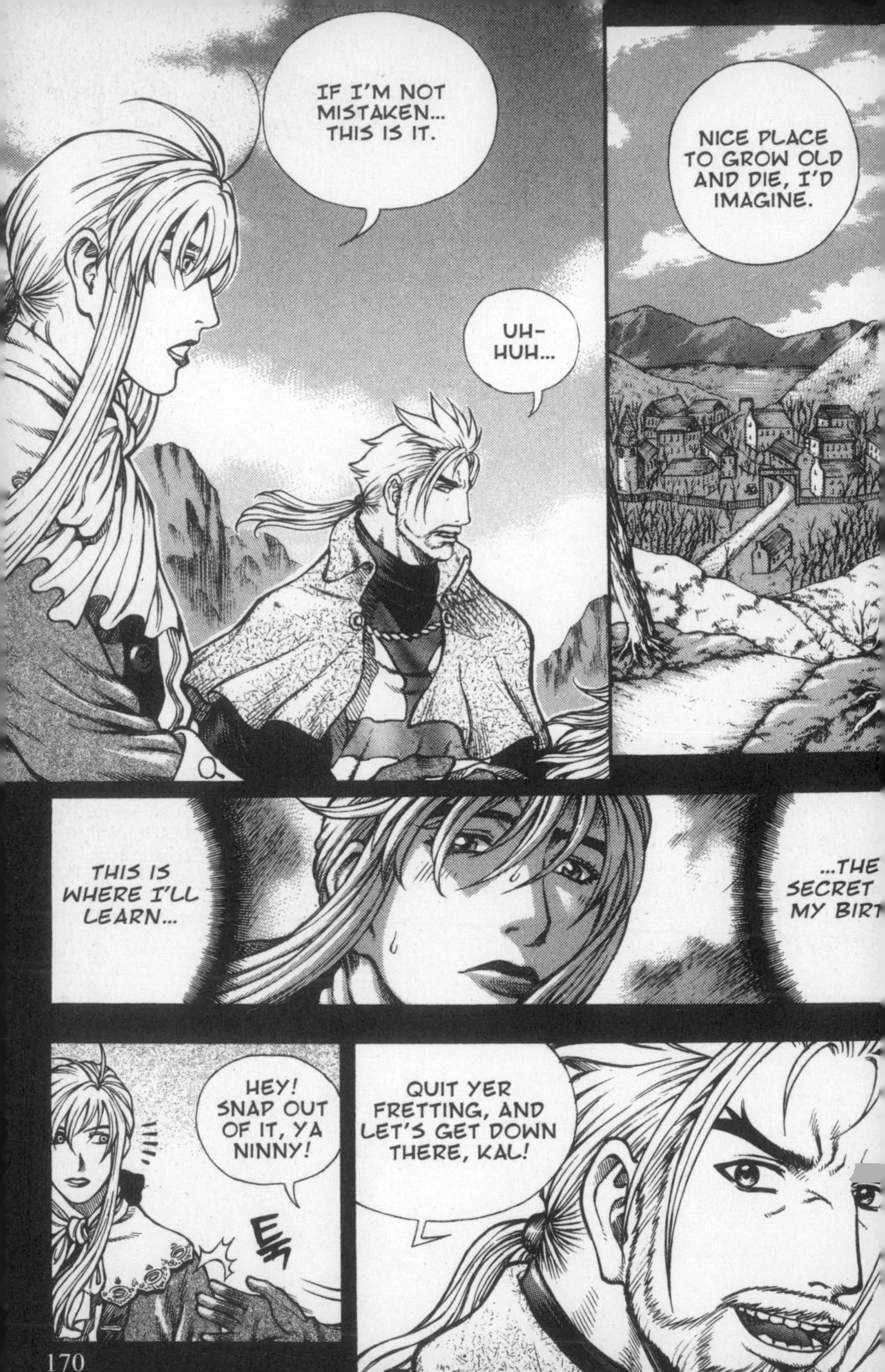
IF I'M NOT MISTAKEN... THIS IS IT.
UH-HUH...
NICE PLACE TO GROW OLD AND DIE, I'D IMAGINE.
THIS IS WHERE I'LL LEARN...
...THE SECRET MY BIRT
HEY! SNAP OUT OF IT, YA NINNY!
QUIT YER FRETTING, AND LET'S GET DOWN THERE, KAL!

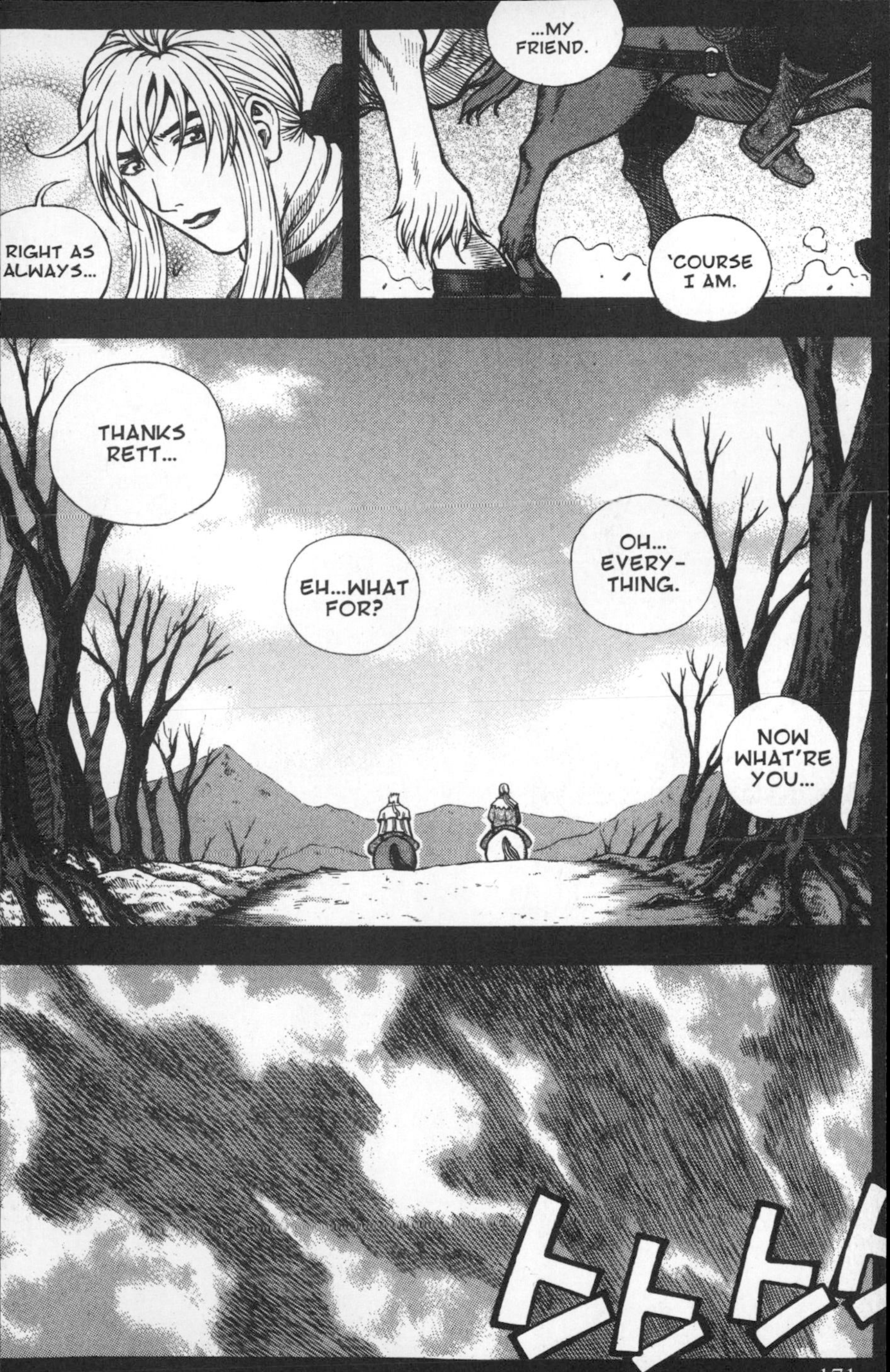
RIGHT AS ALWAYS...
...MY FRIEND.
'COURSE I AM.
THANKS RETT...
EH...WHAT FOR?
OH... EVERY-THING.
NOW WHAT'RE YOU...
トトト

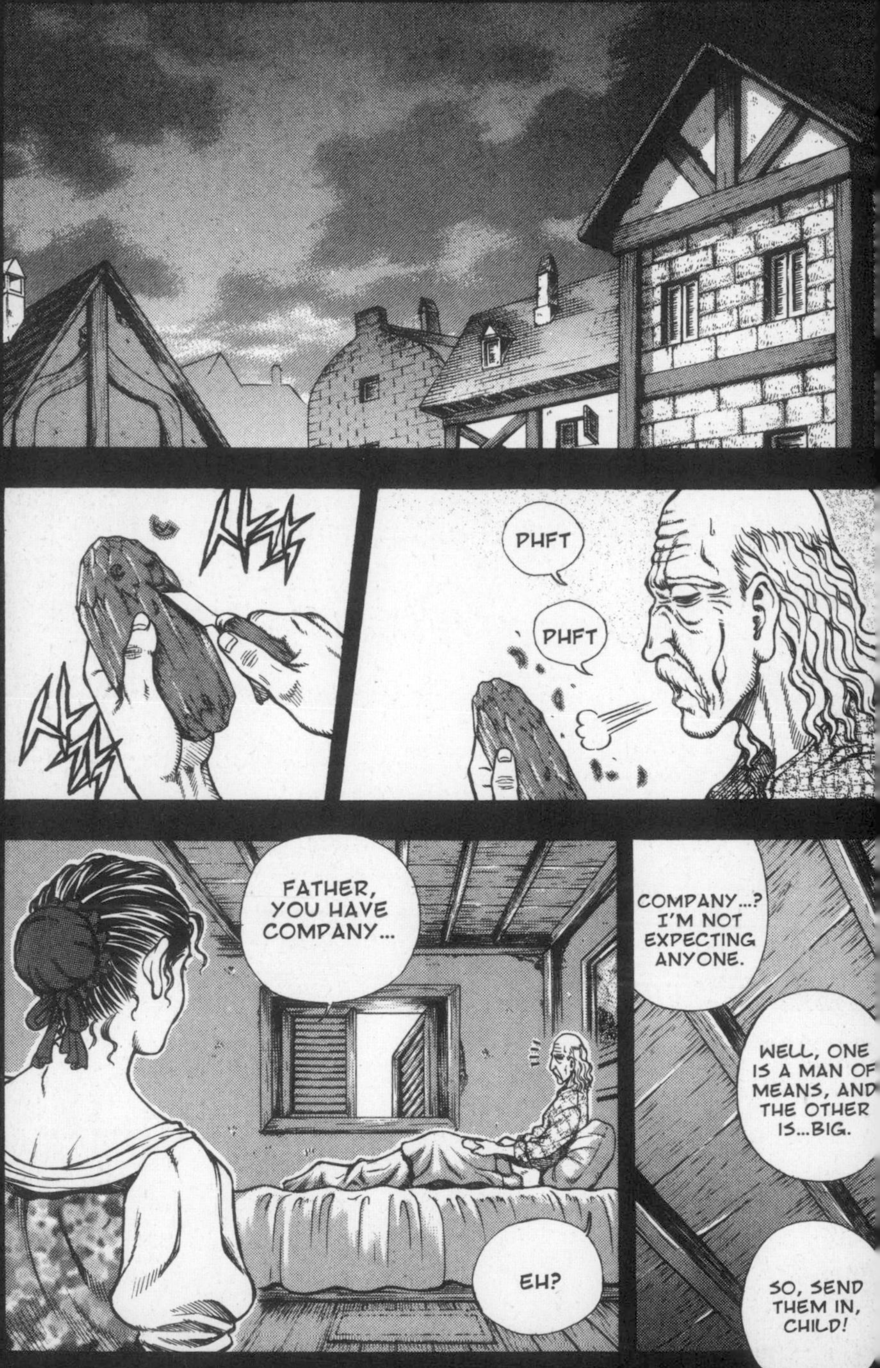
PHFT
PHFT
FATHER, YOU HAVE COMPANY...
EH?
COMPANY...? I'M NOT EXPECTING ANYONE.
WELL, ONE IS A MAN OF MEANS, AND THE OTHER IS...BIG.
SO, SEND THEM IN, CHILD!

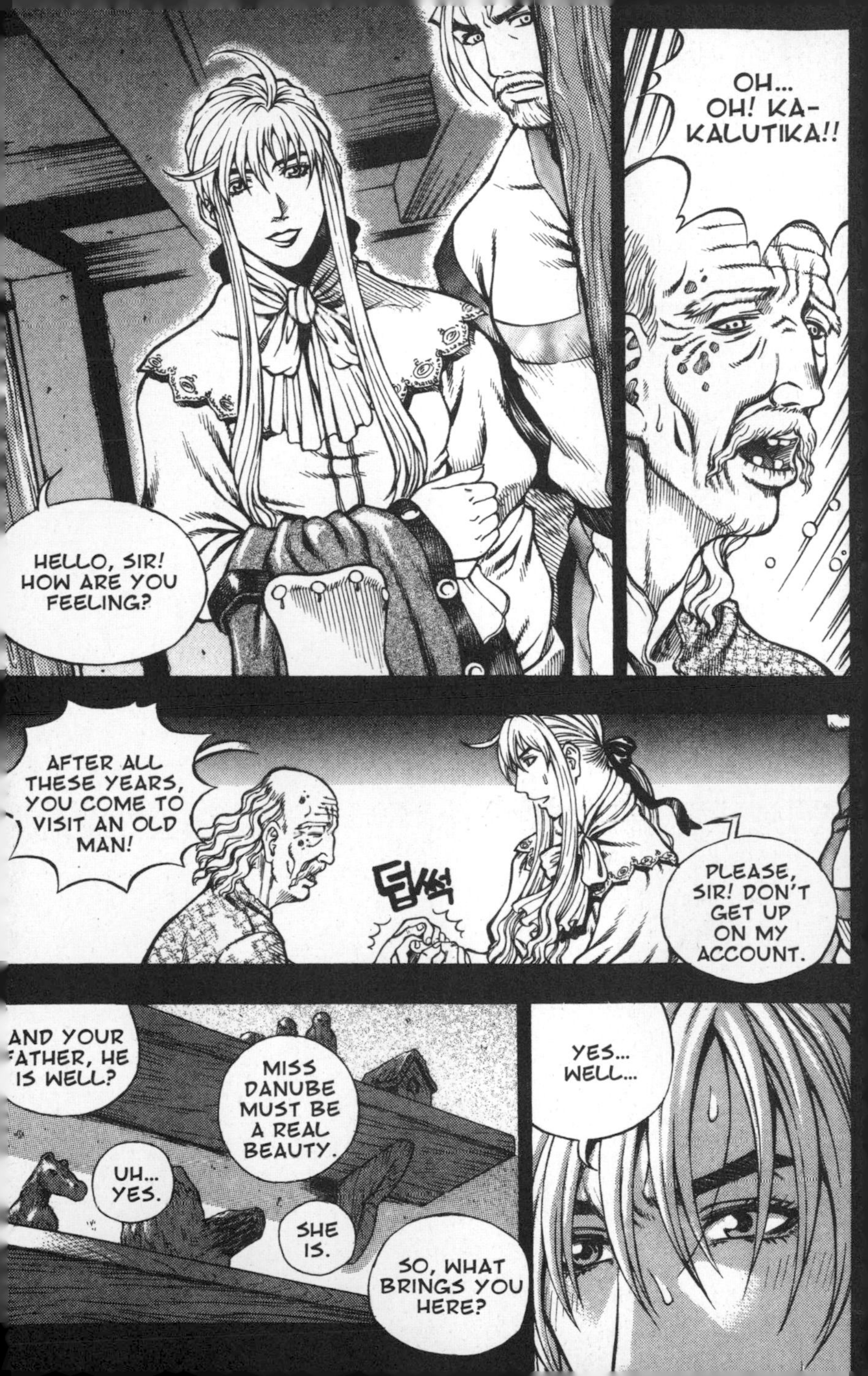
HELLO, SIR! HOW ARE YOU FEELING?
OH... OH! KA-KALUTIKA!!
AFTER ALL THESE YEARS, YOU COME TO VISIT AN OLD MAN!
덥석
PLEASE, SIR! DON'T GET UP ON MY ACCOUNT.
AND YOUR FATHER, HE IS WELL?
UH... YES.
MISS DANUBE MUST BE A REAL BEAUTY.
SHE IS.
SO, WHAT BRINGS YOU HERE?
YES... WELL...

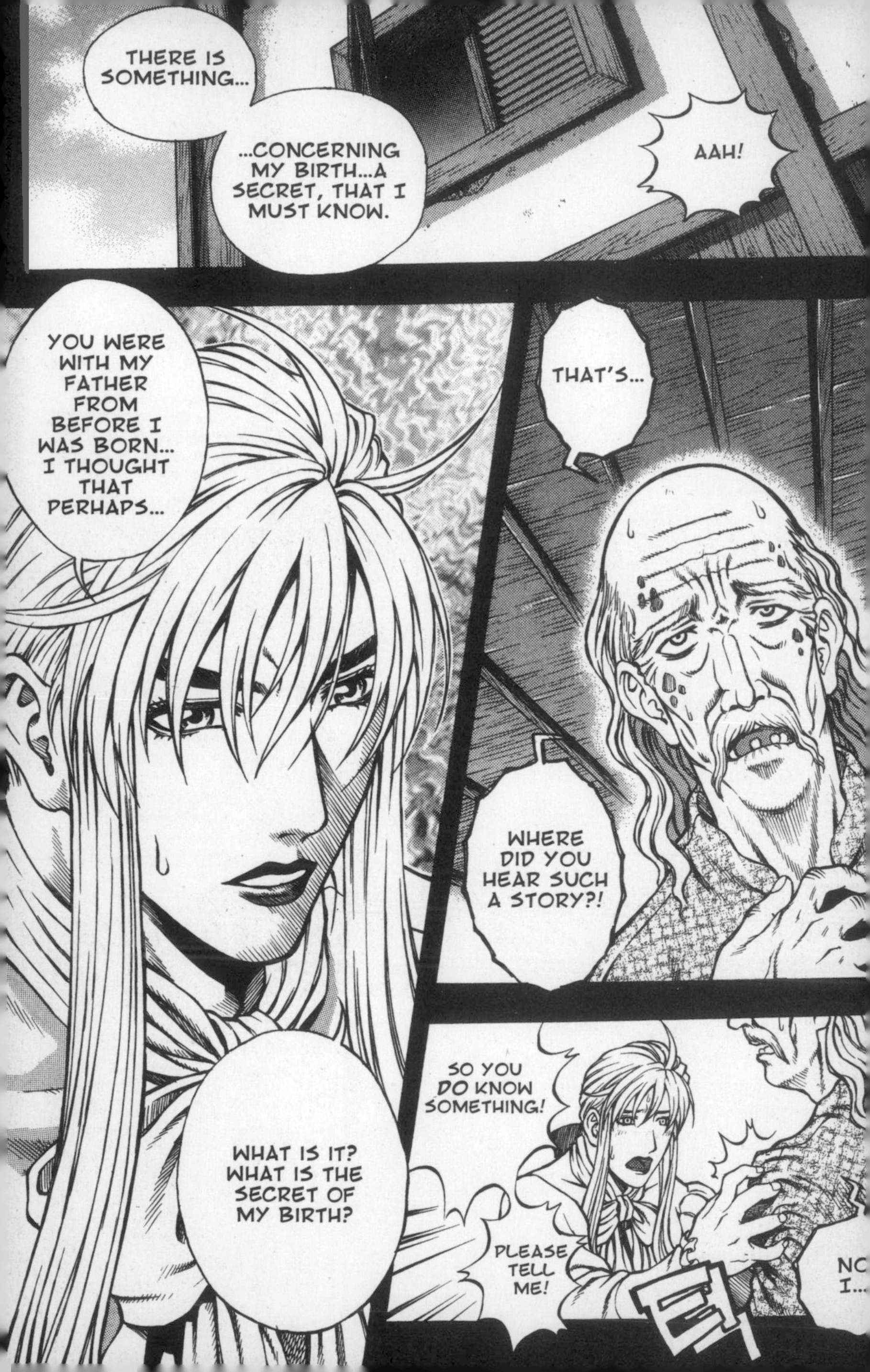
THERE IS SOMETHING...
...CONCERNING MY BIRTH...A SECRET, THAT I MUST KNOW.
AAH!
YOU WERE WITH MY FATHER FROM BEFORE I WAS BORN... I THOUGHT THAT PERHAPS...
WHAT IS IT? WHAT IS THE SECRET OF MY BIRTH?
THAT'S...
WHERE DID YOU HEAR SUCH A STORY?!
SO YOU DO KNOW SOMETHING!
PLEASE TELL ME!
NO I...

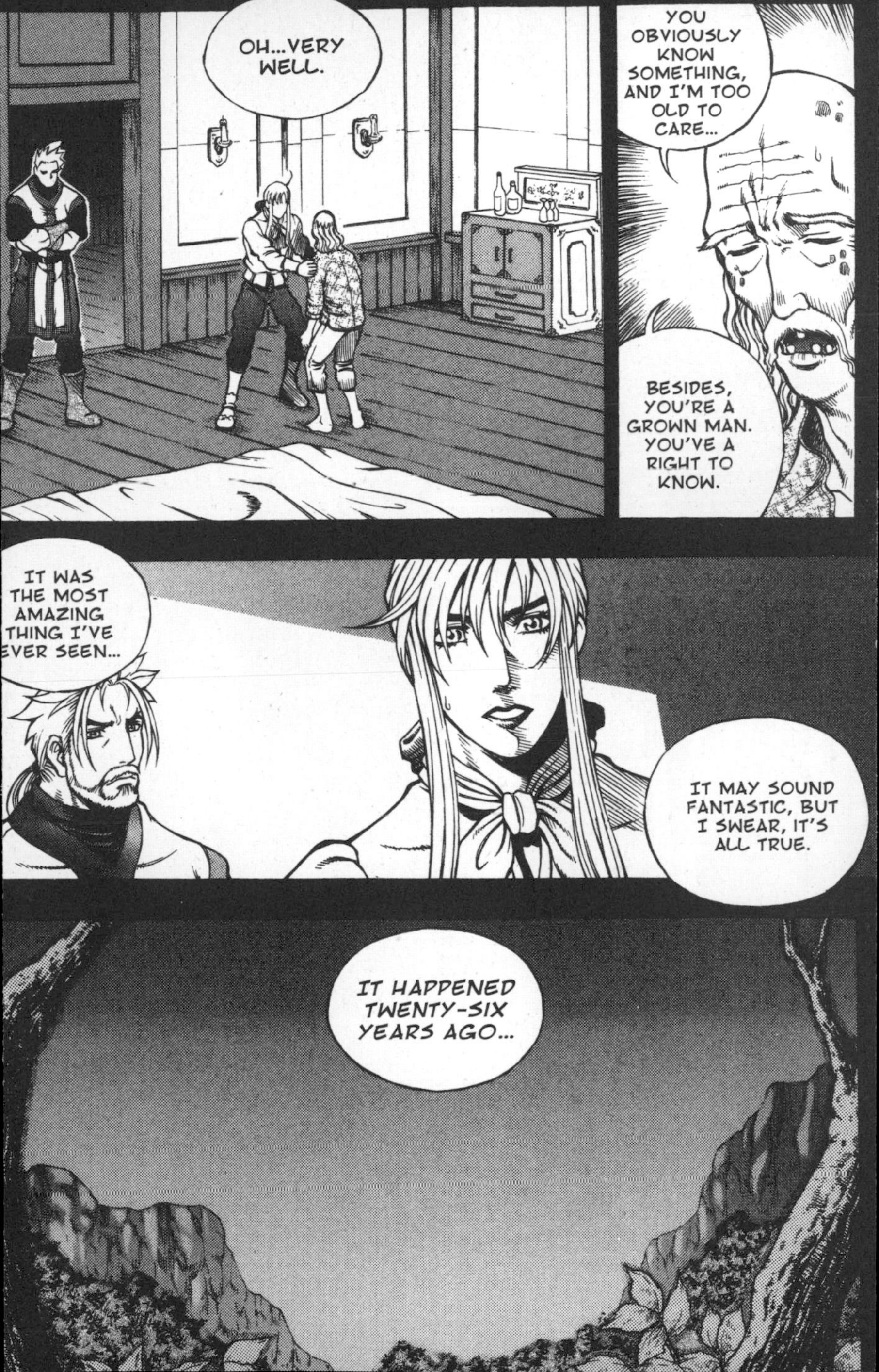
OH...VERY WELL.
YOU OBVIOUSLY KNOW SOMETHING, AND I'M TOO OLD TO CARE...
BESIDES, YOU'RE A GROWN MAN. YOU'VE A RIGHT TO KNOW.
IT WAS THE MOST AMAZING THING I'VE EVER SEEN...
IT MAY SOUND FANTASTIC, BUT I SWEAR, IT'S ALL TRUE.
IT HAPPENED TWENTY-SIX YEARS AGO...

YOUR MOTHER HAD PASSED AWAY AFTER YOUR SISTER'S BIRTH, AND YOUR FATHER WAS A VERY UNHAPPY MAN.

ARGH!

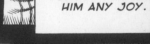

EVEN HUNTING NO LONGER BROUGHT HIM ANY JOY.

MY LIFE IS SHIT! MY WIFE DIES AFTER ONLY LEAVING ME A DAUGHTER!

I NEEDED A SON! SOMEONE TO TEACH HOW TO HUNT...TO CARRY ON MY NAME!

HIS FAVORITE HUNTING GROUNDS WERE A PLACE OF BEAUTY.

I REMEMBER THE LADY MAYBUS USED TO CALL IT "ENCHANTED."

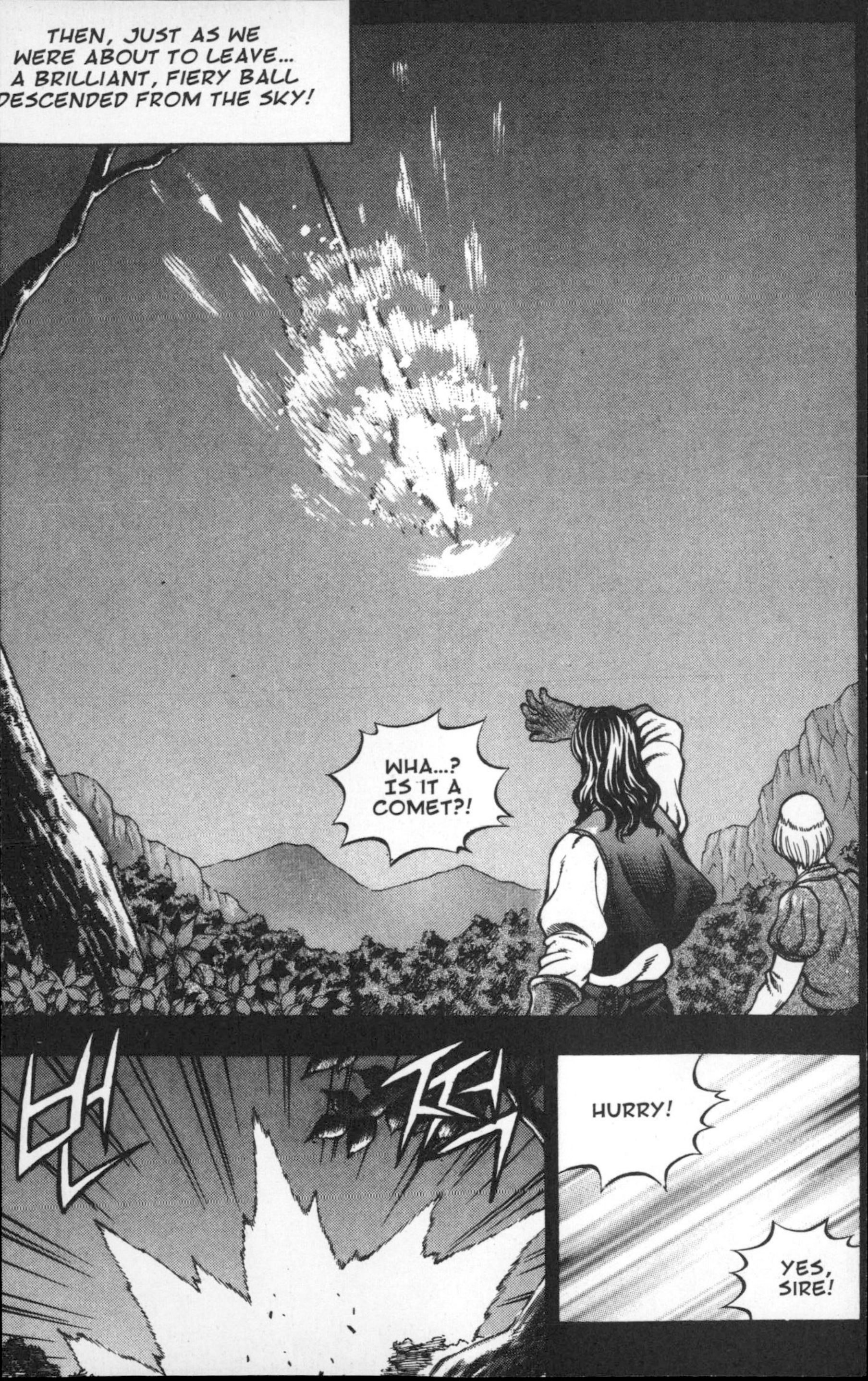
THEN, JUST AS WE WERE ABOUT TO LEAVE... A BRILLIANT, FIERY BALL DESCENDED FROM THE SKY!
WHA...? IS IT A COMET?!
HURRY!
YES, SIRE!

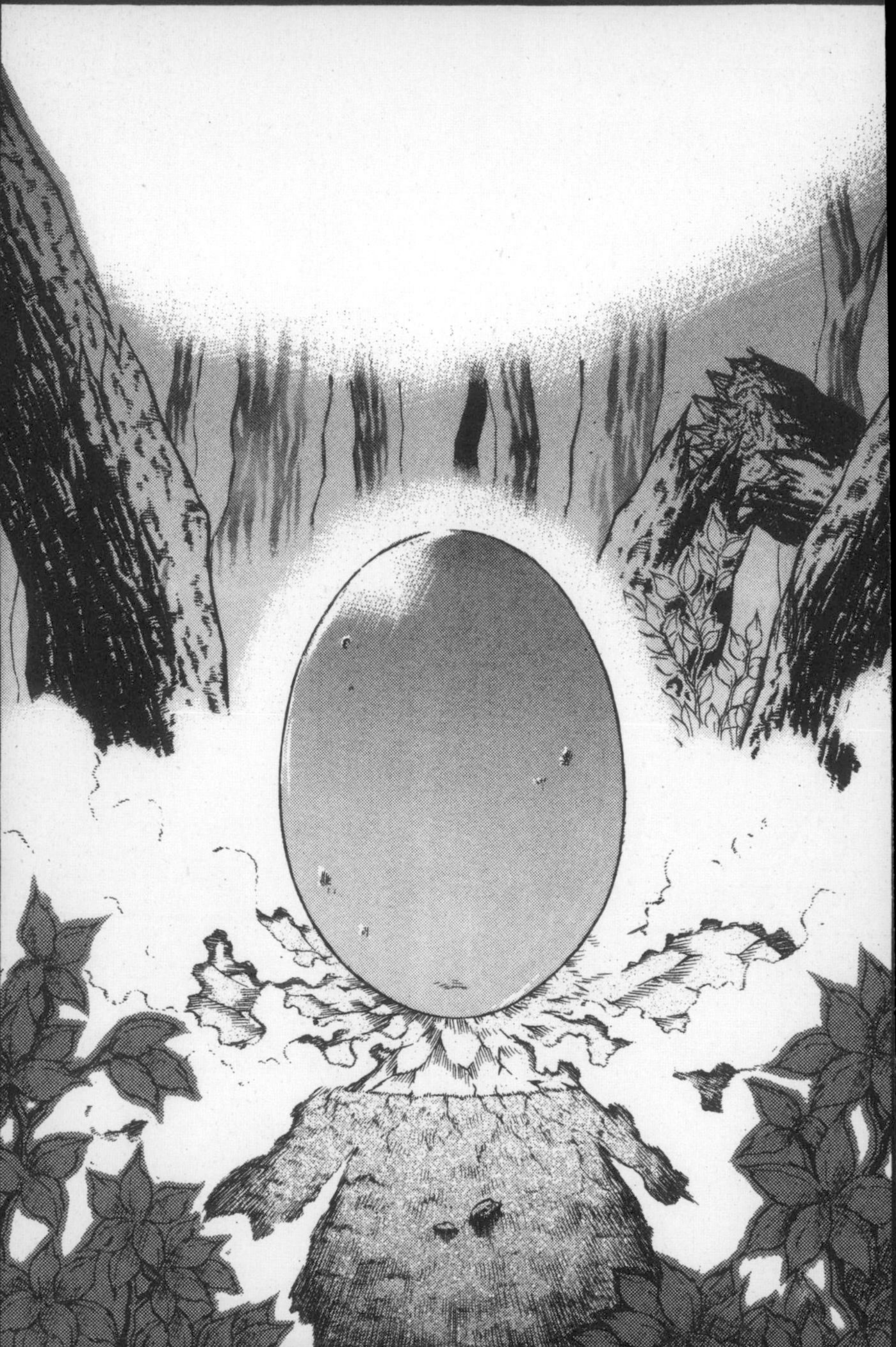

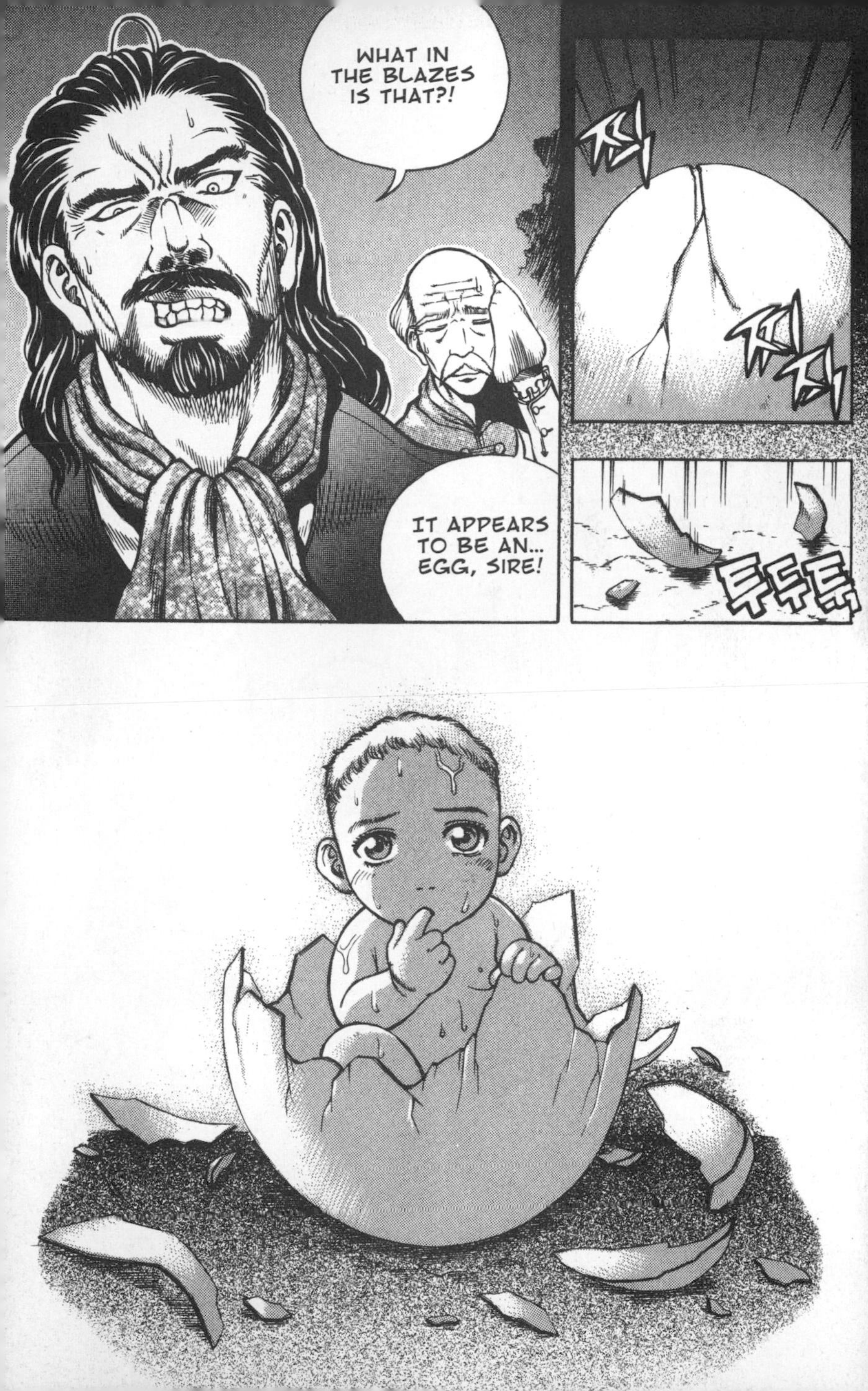
WHAT IN THE BLAZES IS THAT?!
IT APPEARS TO BE AN... EGG, SIRE!

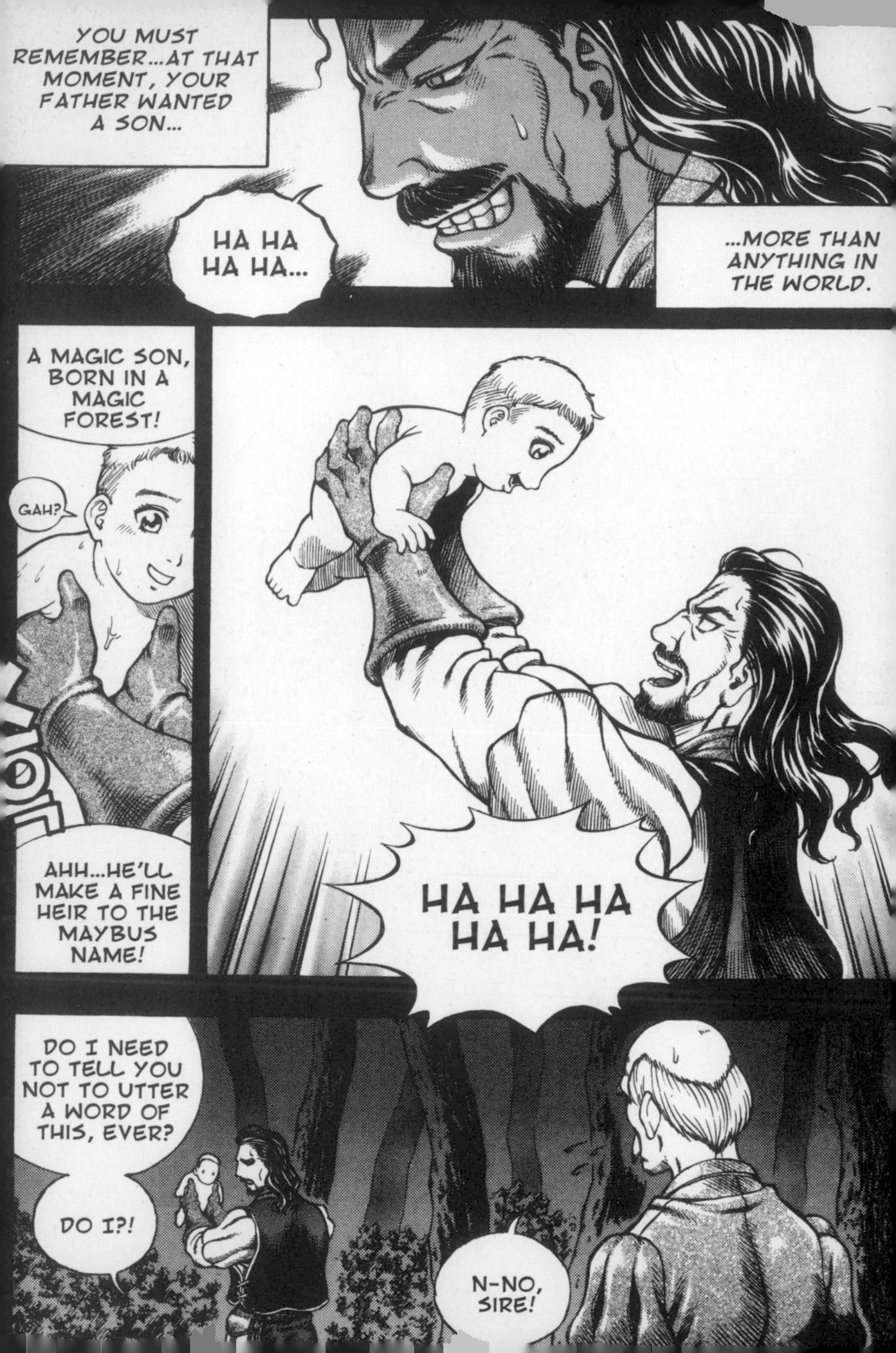
YOU MUST REMEMBER...AT THAT MOMENT, YOUR FATHER WANTED A SON...
HA HA HA HA...
...MORE THAN ANYTHING IN THE WORLD.
A MAGIC SON, BORN IN A MAGIC FOREST!
GAH?
AHH...HE'LL MAKE A FINE HEIR TO THE MAYBUS NAME!
HA HA HA HA HA!
DO I NEED TO TELL YOU NOT TO UTTER A WORD OF THIS, EVER?
DO I?!
N-NO, SIRE!

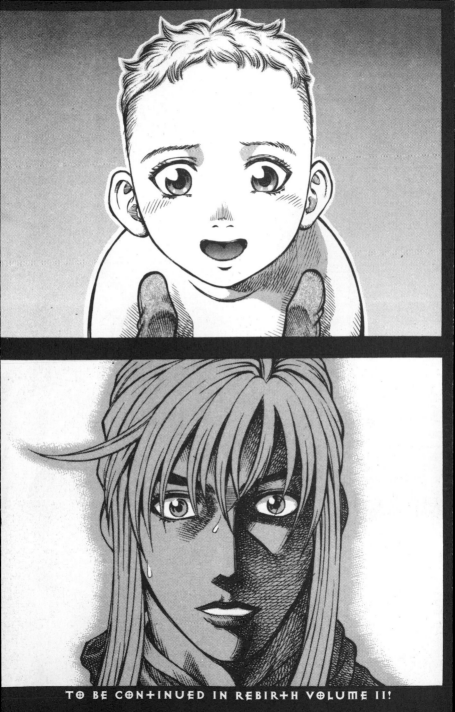

TO BE CONTINUED IN REBIRTH VOLUME II!

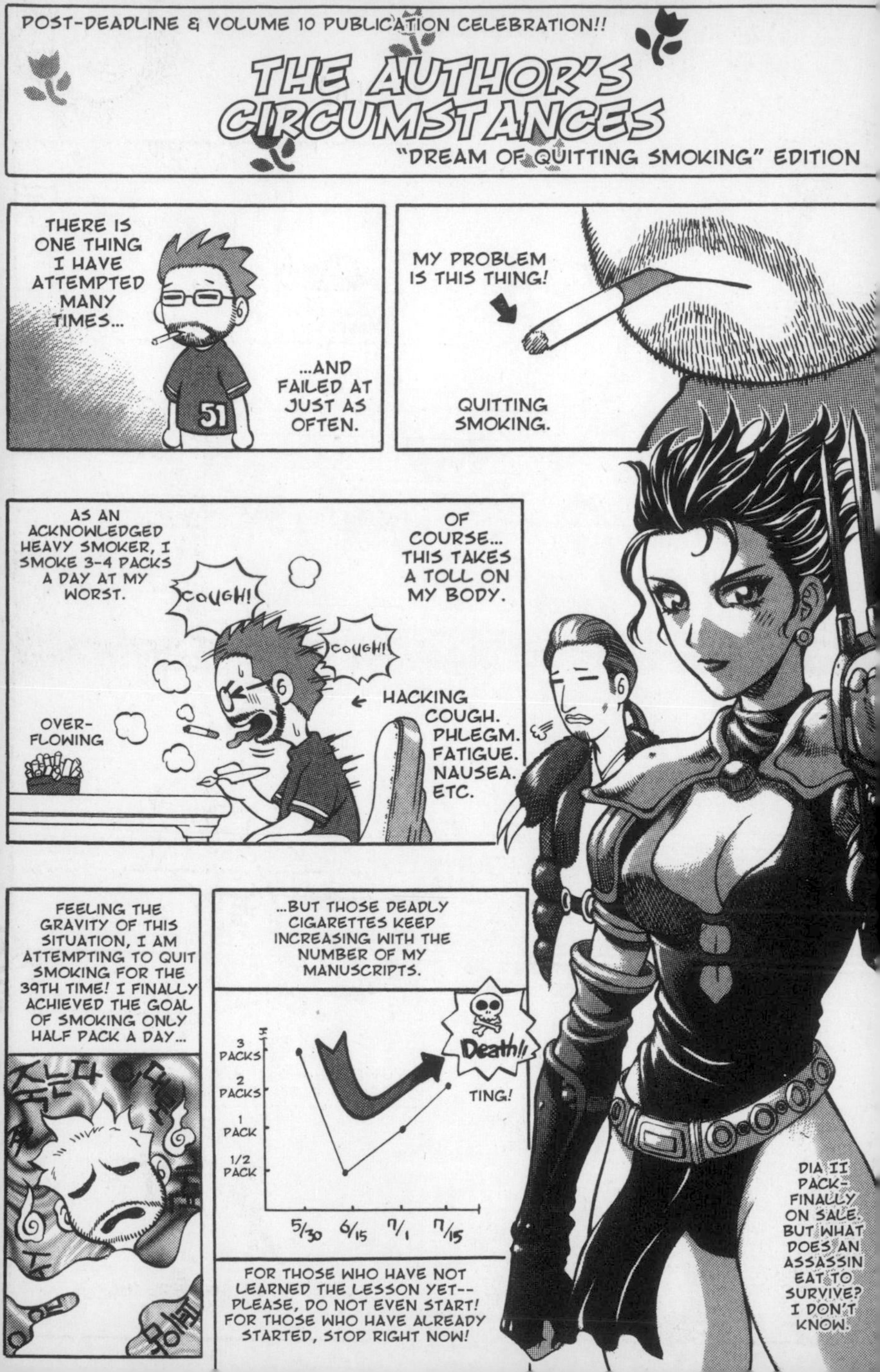
POST-DEADLINE & VOLUME 10 PUBLICATION CELEBRATION!!
THE AUTHOR'S CIRCUMSTANCES
"DREAM OF QUITTING SMOKING" EDITION
THERE IS ONE THING I HAVE ATTEMPTED MANY TIMES...
51
...AND FAILED AT JUST AS OFTEN.
MY PROBLEM IS THIS THING!
QUITTING SMOKING.
AS AN ACKNOWLEDGED HEAVY SMOKER, I SMOKE 3-4 PACKS A DAY AT MY WORST.
COUGH!
COUGH!
OF COURSE... THIS TAKES A TOLL ON MY BODY.
OVER-FLOWING
HACKING COUGH. PHLEGM. FATIGUE. NAUSEA. ETC.
FEELING THE GRAVITY OF THIS SITUATION, I AM ATTEMPTING TO QUIT SMOKING FOR THE 39TH TIME! I FINALLY ACHIEVED THE GOAL OF SMOKING ONLY HALF PACK A DAY...
...BUT THOSE DEADLY CIGARETTES KEEP INCREASING WITH THE NUMBER OF MY MANUSCRIPTS.
3 PACKS
2 PACKS
1 PACK
1/2 PACK
5/30
6/15
7/1
7/15
Death!!
TING!
FOR THOSE WHO HAVE NOT LEARNED THE LESSON YET-- PLEASE, DO NOT EVEN START! FOR THOSE WHO HAVE ALREADY STARTED, STOP RIGHT NOW!
DIA II PACK-FINALLY ON SALE. BUT WHAT DOES AN ASSASSIN EAT TO SURVIVE? I DON'T KNOW.

INTRODUCTION TO ASSISTANTS OF "REBIRTH"
Bizarre Legend

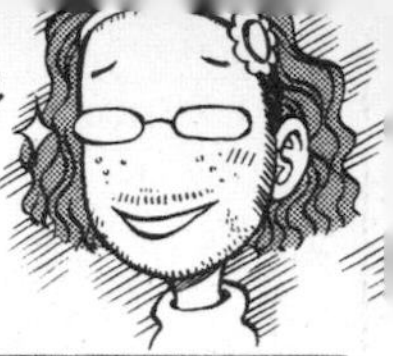
SMILE

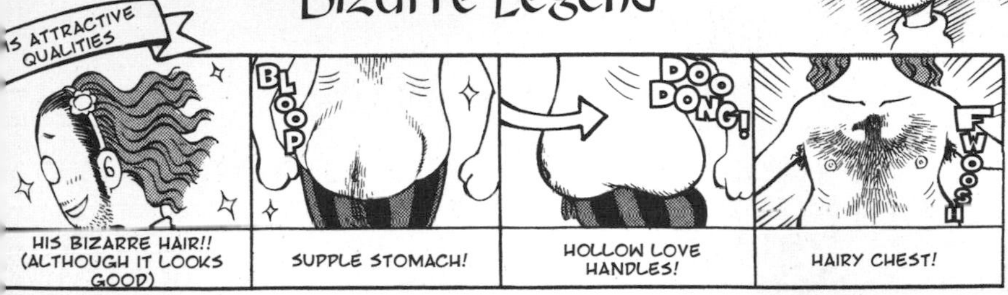
IS ATTRACTIVE QUALITIES
BLOOP
DOO DONG!
FWOOSH
HIS BIZARRE HAIR!! (ALTHOUGH IT LOOKS GOOD)
SUPPLE STOMACH!
HOLLOW LOVE HANDLES!
HAIRY CHEST!

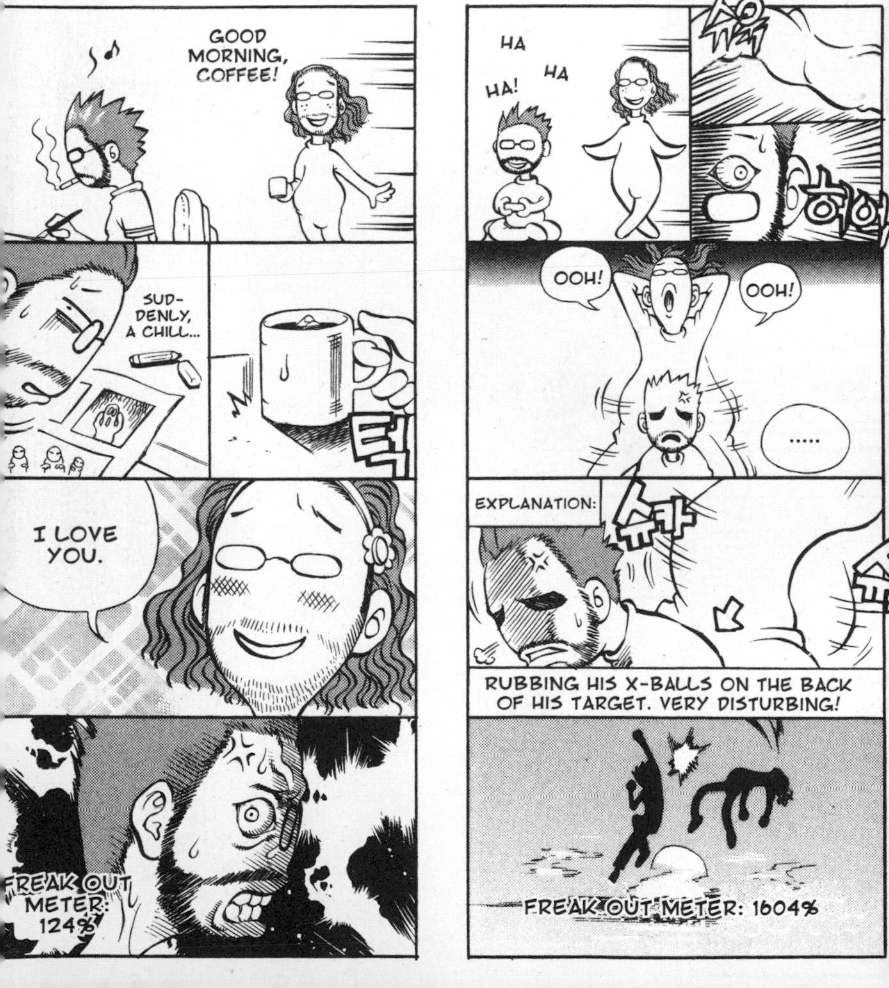
GOOD MORNING, COFFEE!
SUD-DENLY, A CHILL...
I LOVE YOU.
FREAK OUT METER: 124%
HA
HA
HA!
OOH!
OOH!
.....
EXPLANATION:
RUBBING HIS X-BALLS ON THE BACK OF HIS TARGET. VERY DISTURBING!
FREAK OUT METER: 1604%

Preview: Vol. 11

As Deshwitat recovers from his nearly fatal wounds, Kalutika and Rett—still reeling from the discovery of Kal's secret origins—return to even more shocking news. Josimov has scheduled the execution of both Lilith and Danube within two days! Now, in a race against time and in the face of nearly insurmountable odds, this mismatched band of brothers must find a way to save the lives of two innocent women.

Little do they realize that this is exactly what the malevolent Man in the Robe is expecting them to do.

The "Day of Promise" is nearly at hand...

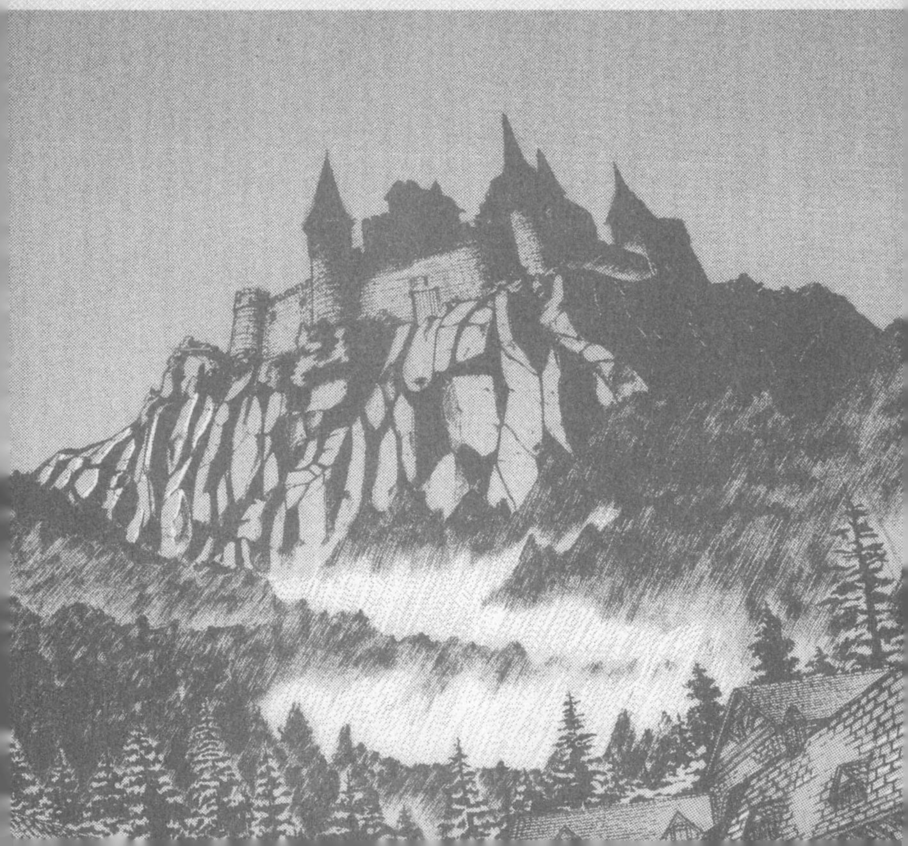

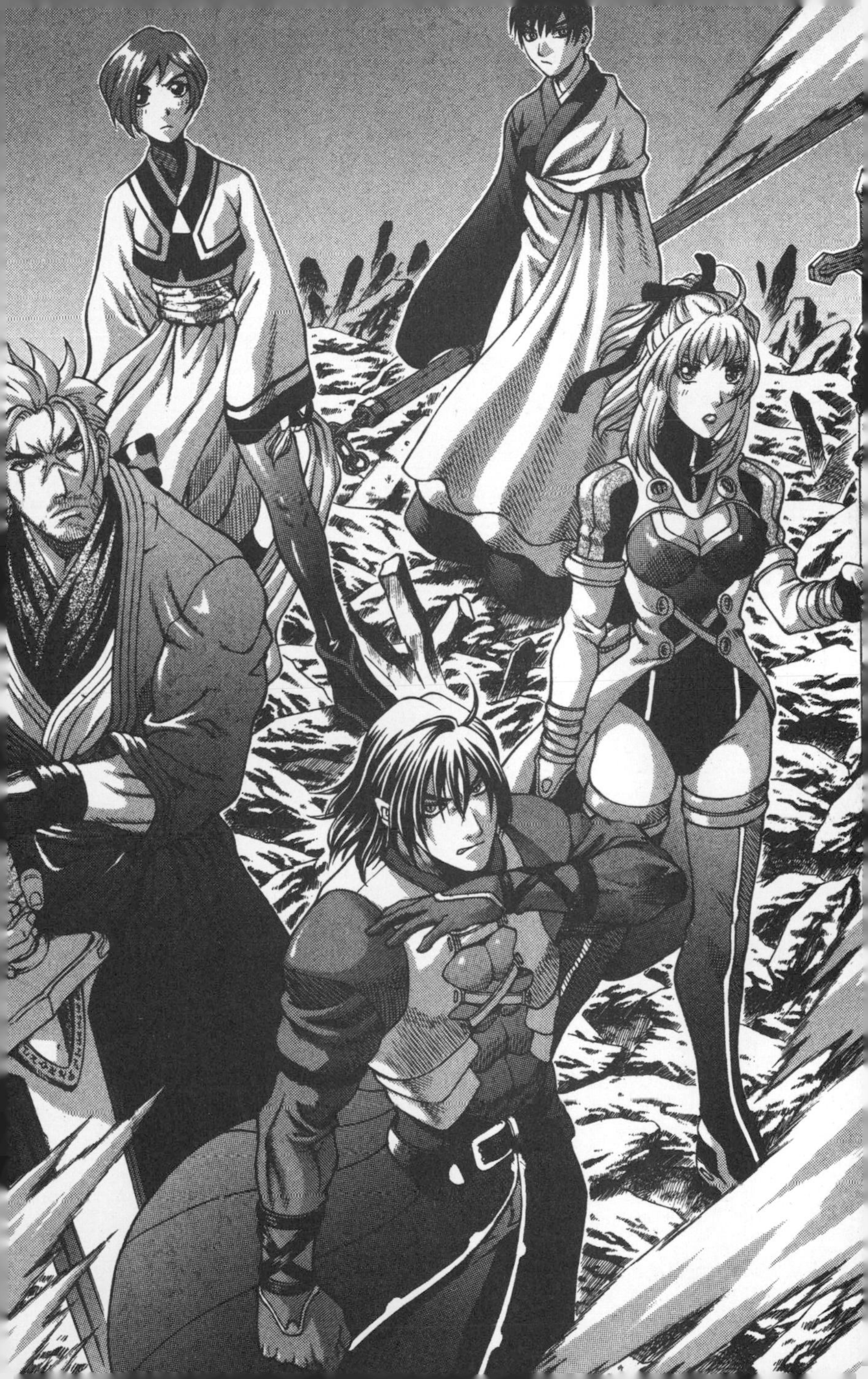

ALSO AVAILABLE FROM TOKYOPOP®

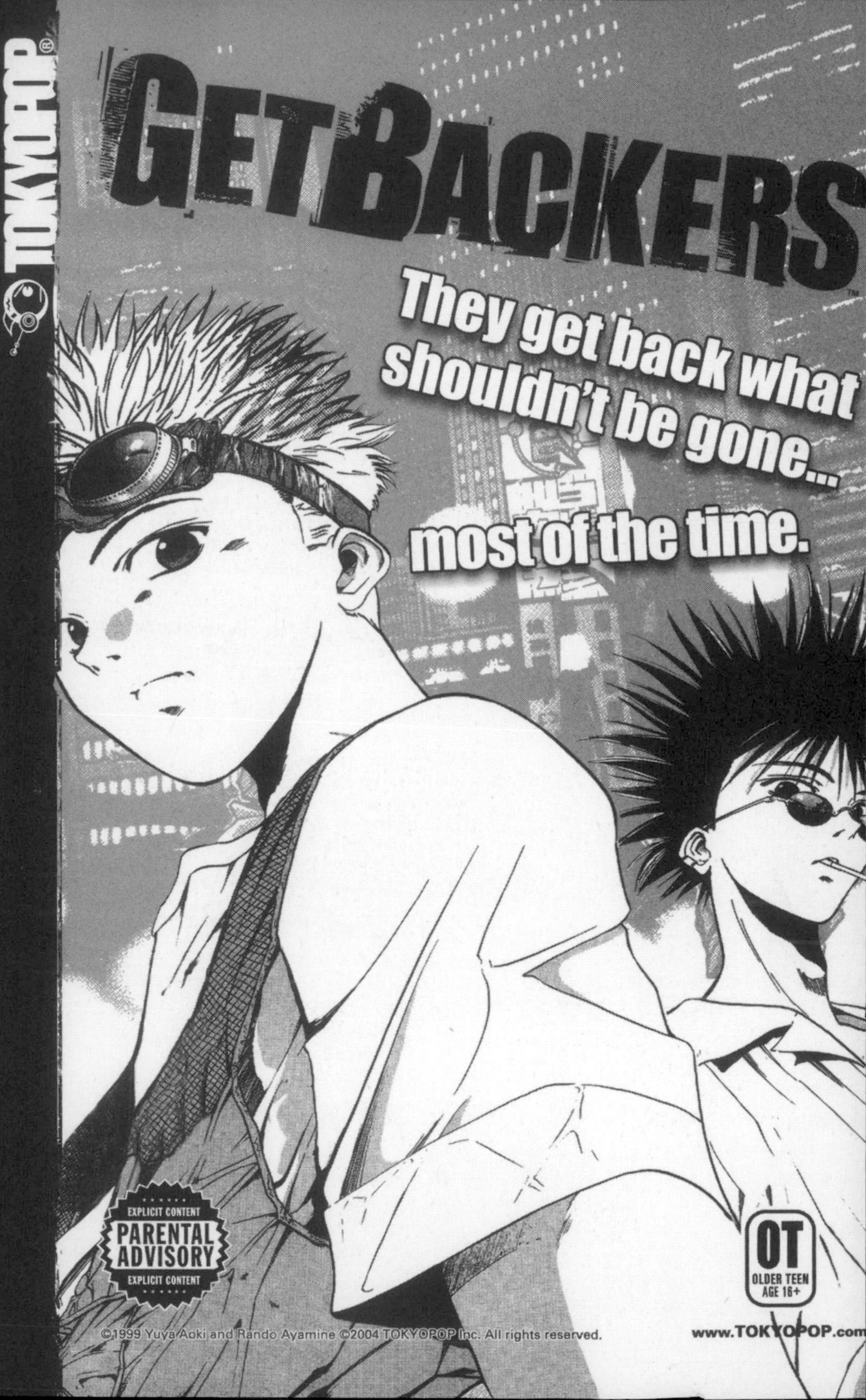

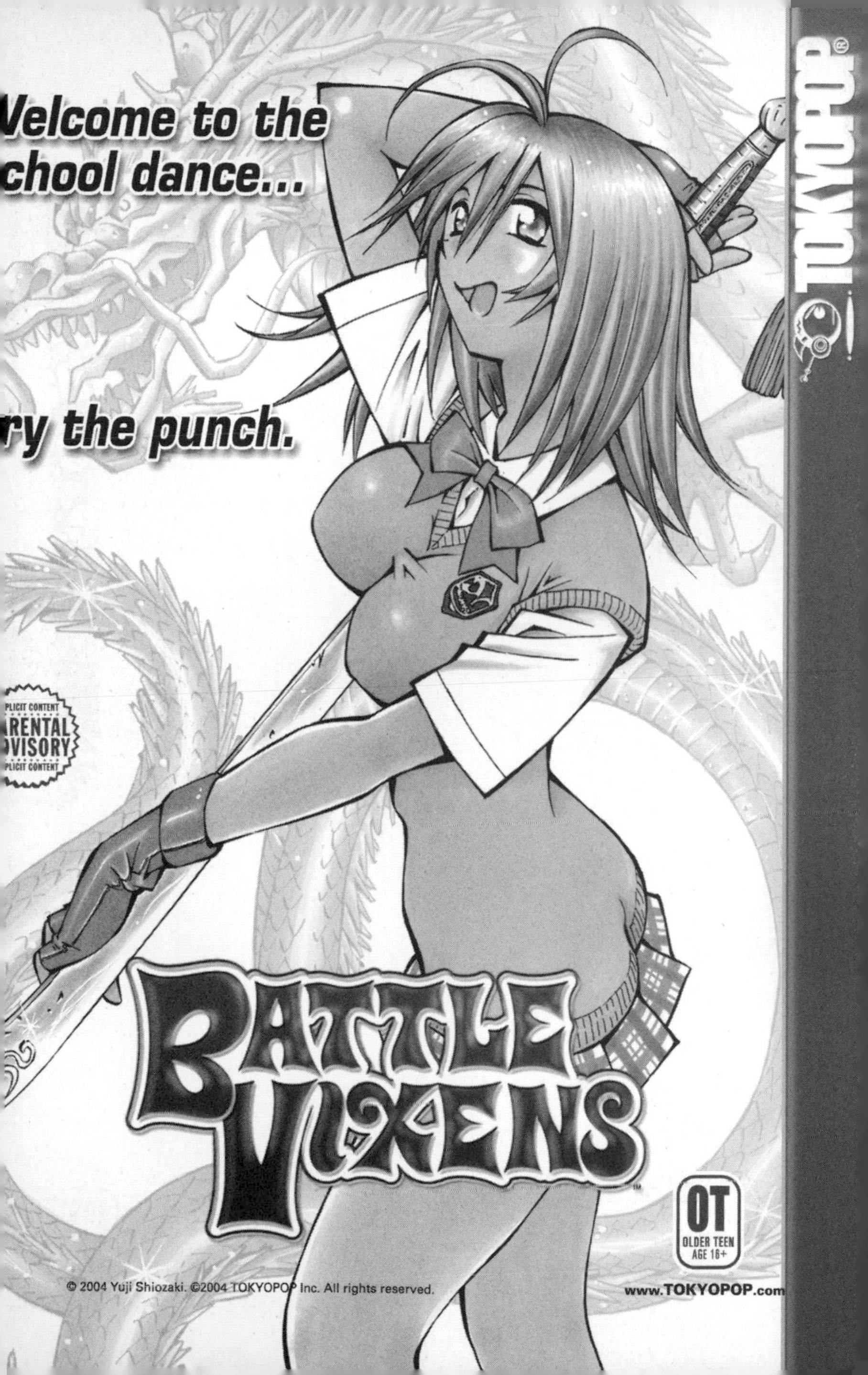
Velcome to the
chool dance...
ry the punch.
TOKYOPOP
PLICIT CONTENT
ARENTAL
DVISORY
PLICIT CONTENT
BATTLE VIXENS
OT
OLDER TEEN
AGE 16+
© 2004 Yuji Shiozaki. ©2004 TOKYOPOP Inc. All rights reserved.
www.TOKYOPOP.com

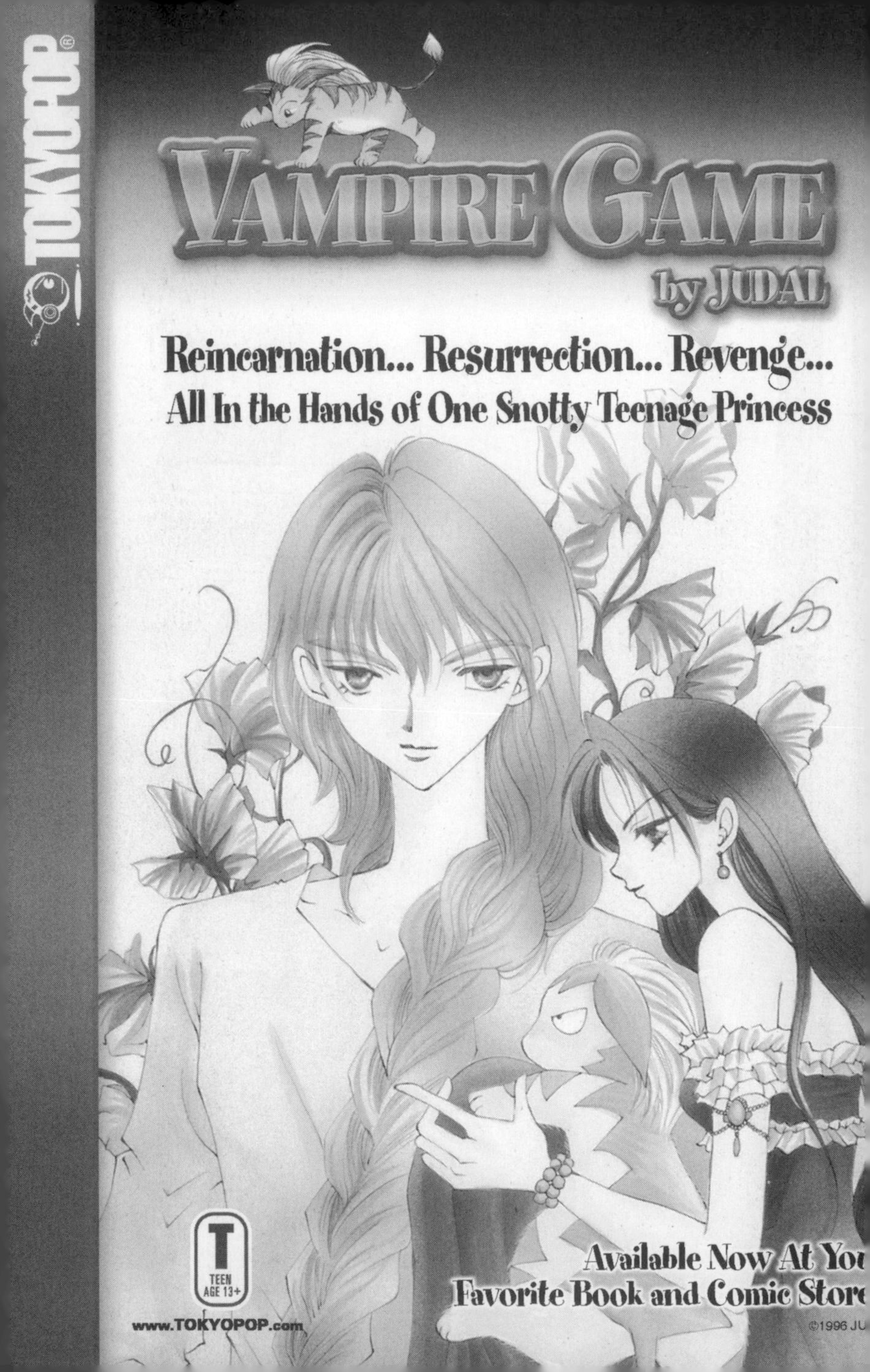
TOKYOPOP
VAMPIRE GAME
by JUDAL
Reincarnation... Resurrection... Revenge...
All In the Hands of One Snotty Teenage Princess
T
TEEN
AGE 13+
Available Now At You
Favorite Book and Comic Stor
www.TOKYOPOP.com
©1996 JU

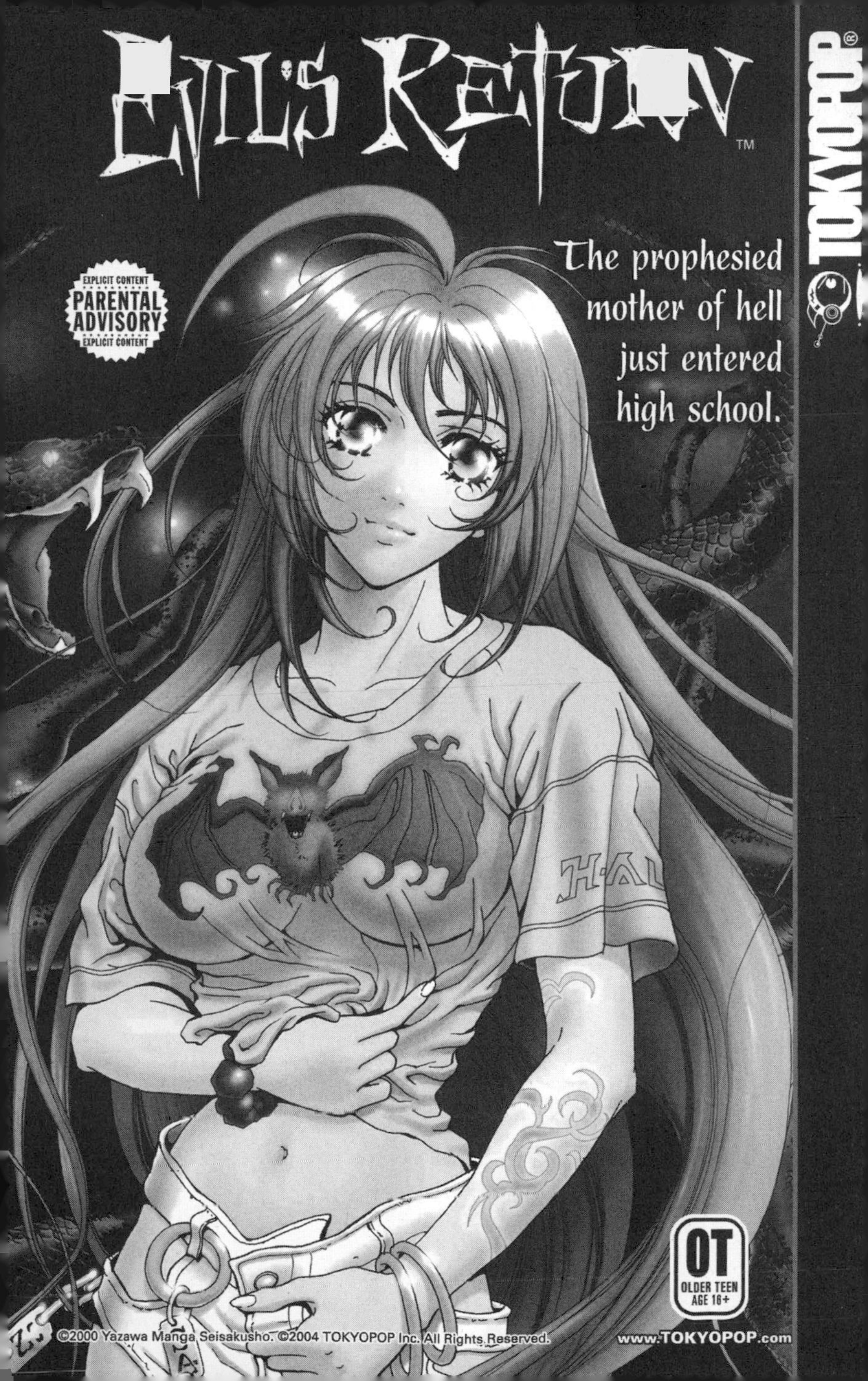
EVIL'S RETURN™
The prophesied mother of hell just entered high school.
EXPLICIT CONTENT
PARENTAL ADVISORY
EXPLICIT CONTENT
TOKYOPOP®
OT
OLDER TEEN
AGE 16+
©2000 Yazawa Manga Seisakusho. ©2004 TOKYOPOP Inc. All Rights Reserved.
www.TOKYOPOP.com

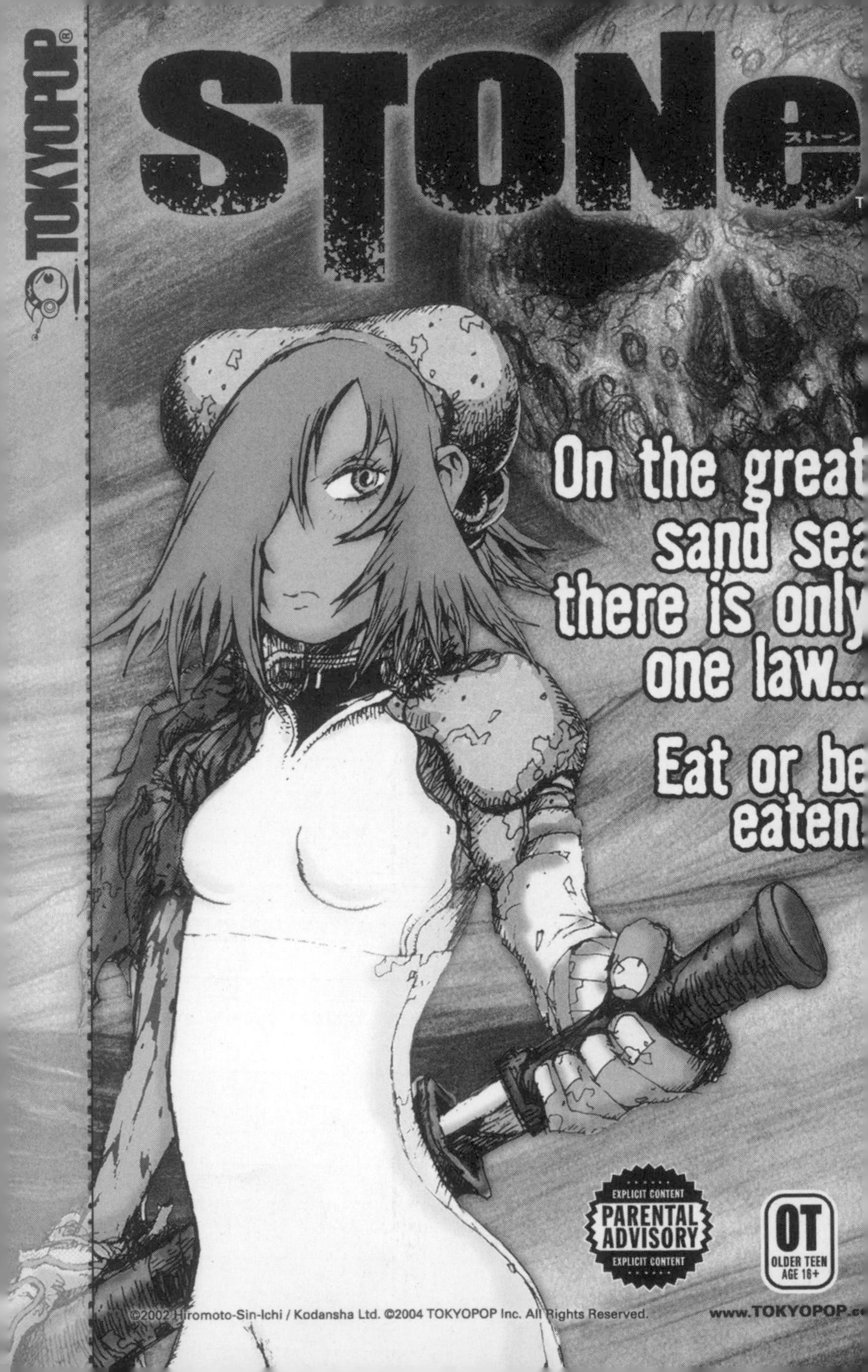
TOKYOPOP
STONe
ストーン
On the great
sand sea
there is only
one law...
Eat or be
eaten.
EXPLICIT CONTENT
PARENTAL ADVISORY
EXPLICIT CONTENT
OT
OLDER TEEN AGE 16+
©2002 Hiromoto-Sin-Ichi / Kodansha Ltd. ©2004 TOKYOPOP Inc. All Rights Reserved.
www.TOKYOPOP.c